THE UPANISHADS – II

KENA AND OTHER UPANISHADS

Sri Aurobindo

THE UPANISHADS-II

Kena and Other Upanishads

Sri Aurobindo Ashram
Pondicherry

First edition 2001
Second impression 2004

Rs. 140.00
ISBN 81-7058-748-4

Published by Sri Aurobindo Ashram Publication Department
Pondicherry - 605 002
Website: http://sabda.sriaurobindoashram.org

Printed at Sri Aurobindo Ashram Press
Pondicherry - 605 002
PRINTED IN INDIA

Publisher's Note

This volume comprises Sri Aurobindo's translations of and commentaries on Upanishads other than the Isha Upanishad. (His writings on that Upanishad appear in *Isha Upanishad*, volume 17 of THE COMPLETE WORKS OF SRI AUROBINDO.) It also includes his translations of later Vedantic texts and writings on the Upanishads and Vedanta philosophy in general.

The volume is divided into three parts. The first consists of translations and commentaries that were published during Sri Aurobindo's lifetime. The pieces in this part, along with his final translation of and commentary on the Isha Upanishad, are his most mature works of Upanishadic interpretation. The second and third parts consist of material from Sri Aurobindo's manuscripts. The second includes early translations of the Prashna, Mandukya, Aitareya and Taittiriya Upanishads, and incomplete translations of and commentaries on some other Upanishads and Vedantic texts. The third part comprises incomplete and fragmentary writings on the Upanishads and Vedanta in general.

All the texts have been checked against the relevant manuscript and printed versions.

Guide to Editorial Notation

The contents of Parts Two and Three of this volume were never prepared by Sri Aurobindo for publication. They have been transcribed from manuscripts that sometimes present textual difficulties. In this edition these problems have been indicated as far as possible by means of the notation shown below.

Notation	Textual Problem
[.......]	Word(s) lost through damage to the manuscript (at the beginning of a piece, sometimes indicates that a page or pages of the manuscript have been lost)
[word]	Word(s) omitted by the author or lost through damage to the manuscript that are required by grammar or sense, and that could be supplied by the editors
[ ]	Blank left by the author to be filled in later but left unfilled, which the editors were not able to fill
[*note*]	Situations requiring textual explication; all such information is printed in italics

CONTENTS

CONTENTS

Part One

Translations and Commentaries
Published by Sri Aurobindo

These texts were first published between 1909 and 1920. Sri Aurobindo later revised most of them. The revised versions are printed here.

Kena Upanishad

The Kena Upanishad

FIRST PART

केनेषितं पतति प्रेषितं मनः केन प्राणः प्रथमः प्रैति युक्तः।
केनेषितां वाचमिमां वदन्ति चक्षुः श्रोत्रं क उ देवो युनक्ति ॥ १ ॥

1. By whom missioned falls the mind shot to its mark? By
   whom yoked moves the first life-breath forward on its
   paths? By whom impelled is this word that men speak?
   What god set eye and ear to their workings?

श्रोत्रस्य श्रोत्रं मनसो मनो यद् वाचो ह वाचं स उ प्राणस्य प्राणः।
चक्षुषश्चक्षुरतिमुच्य धीराः प्रेत्यास्माल्लोकादमृता भवन्ति ॥ २ ॥

2. That which is hearing of our hearing, mind of our mind,
   speech of our speech, that too is life of our life-breath and
   sight of our sight. The wise are released beyond and they
   pass from this world and become immortal.

न तत्र चक्षुर्गच्छति न वाग् गच्छति नो मनः।
न विद्मो न विजानीमो यथैतदनुशिष्यात्।
अन्यदेव तद्विदितादथो अविदितादधि।
इति शुश्रुम पूर्वेषां ये नस्तद् व्याचचक्षिरे ॥ ३ ॥

3. There sight travels not, nor speech, nor the mind. We know
   It not nor can distinguish how one should teach of It: for It
   is other than the known; It is there above the unknown. It
   is so we have heard from men of old who declared That to
   our understanding.

यद्वाचानभ्युदितं येन वागभ्युद्यते।
तदेव ब्रह्म त्वं विद्धि नेदं यदिदमुपासते ॥ ४ ॥

4. That which is unexpressed by the word, that by which the

word is expressed, know That to be the Brahman and not
this which men follow after here.

यन्मनसा न मनुते येनाहुर्मनो मतम् ।
तदेव ब्रह्म त्वं विद्धि नेदं यदिदमुपासते ॥ ५ ॥

5. That which thinks not by the mind,[1] that by which the mind
is thought, know That to be the Brahman and not this which
men follow after here.

यच्चक्षुषा न पश्यति येन चक्षूंषि पश्यति ।
तदेव ब्रह्म त्वं विद्धि नेदं यदिदमुपासते ॥ ६ ॥

6. That which sees not with the eye,[2] that by which one sees
the eye's seeings, know That to be the Brahman and not this
which men follow after here.

यच्छ्रोत्रेण न शृणोति येन श्रोत्रमिदं श्रुतम् ।
तदेव ब्रह्म त्वं विद्धि नेदं यदिदमुपासते ॥ ७ ॥

7. That which hears not with the ear,[3] that by which the ear's
hearing is heard, know That to be the Brahman and not this
which men follow after here.

यत्प्राणेन न प्राणिति येन प्राणः प्रणीयते ।
तदेव ब्रह्म त्वं विद्धि नेदं यदिदमुपासते ॥ ८ ॥

8. That which breathes not with the breath,[4] that by which the
life-breath is led forward in its paths, know That to be the
Brahman and not this which men follow after here.

---

[1] Or, "that which one thinks not with the mind".
[2] Or, "that which one sees not with the eye".
[3] Or, "that which one hears not with the ear".
[4] Or, "that which one breathes not (i.e. smells not) with the breath".

SECOND PART

यदि मन्यसे सुवेदेति दभ्रमेवापि नूनं त्वं वेत्थ ब्रह्मणो रूपम् ।
यदस्य त्वं यदस्य देवेष्वथ नु मीमांस्यमेव ते मन्ये विदितम् ॥ १ ॥

1. If thou thinkest that thou knowest It well, little indeed dost thou know the form of the Brahman. That of It which is thou, that of It which is in the gods, this thou hast to think out. I think It known.

नाहं मन्ये सुवेदेति नो न वेदेति वेद च ।
यो नस्तद्वेद तद्वेद नो न वेदेति वेद च ॥ २ ॥

2. I think not that I know It well and yet I know that It is not unknown to me. He of us who knows It, knows That; he knows that It is not unknown to him.

यस्यामतं तस्य मतं मतं यस्य न वेद सः ।
अविज्ञातं विजानतां विज्ञातमविजानताम् ॥ ३ ॥

3. He by whom It is not thought out, has the thought of It; he by whom It is thought out, knows It not. It is unknown to the discernment of those who discern of It, by those who seek not to discern of It, It is discerned.

प्रतिबोधविदितं मतममृतत्वं हि विन्दते ।
आत्मना विन्दते वीर्यं विद्यया विन्दतेऽमृतम् ॥ ४ ॥

4. When It is known by perception that reflects It, then one has the thought of It, for one finds immortality; by the self one finds the force to attain and by the knowledge one finds immortality.

इह चेदवेदीदथ सत्यमस्ति न चेदिहावेदीन्महती विनष्टिः ।
भूतेषु भूतेषु विचित्य धीराः प्रेत्यास्माल्लोकादमृता भवन्ति ॥ ५ ॥

5. If here one comes to that knowledge, then one truly is; if here one comes not to the knowledge, then great is the perdition.

The wise distinguish That in all kinds of becomings and they pass forward from this world and become immortal.

THIRD PART

ब्रह्म ह देवेभ्यो विजिग्ये तस्य ह ब्रह्मणो विजये देवा अमहीयन्त। त ऐक्षन्तास्माकमेवायं विजयोऽस्माकमेवायं महिमेति ॥ १ ॥

1. The Eternal conquered for the gods and in the victory of the Eternal the gods grew to greatness. They saw, "Ours the victory, ours the greatness."

तद्धैषां विजज्ञौ तेभ्यो ह प्रादुर्बभूव तन्न व्यजानत किमिदं यक्ष-मिति ॥ २ ॥

2. The Eternal knew their thought and appeared before them; and they knew not what was this mighty Daemon.

तेऽग्निमब्रुवञ्जातवेद एतद्विजानीहि किमेतद्यक्षमिति तथेति ॥ ३ ॥

3. They said to Agni, "O thou that knowest all things born, learn of this thing, what may be this mighty Daemon," and he said, "So be it."

तदभ्यद्रवत् तमभ्यवदत् कोऽसीत्यग्निर्वा अहमस्मीत्यब्रवीज्जातवेदा वा अहमस्मीति ॥ ४ ॥

4. He rushed towards the Eternal and It said to him, "Who art thou?" "I am Agni," he said, "I am he that knows all things born."

तास्मिस्त्वयि किं वीर्यमित्यपीद सर्वं दहेयं यदिदं पृथिव्यामिति ॥ ५ ॥

5. "Since such thou art, what is the force in thee?" "Even all this I could burn, all that is upon the earth."

तस्मै तृणं निदधावेतद्दहेति तदुपप्रेयाय सर्वजवेन तन्न शशाक दग्धुं स तत एव निववृते नैतदशकं विज्ञातुं यदेतद्यक्षमिति ॥ ६ ॥

6. The Eternal set before him a blade of grass; "This burn;" and he made towards it with all his speed, but could not burn it. There he ceased, and turned back; "I could not know of It, what might be this mighty Daemon."

अथ वायुमब्रुवन् वायवेतद्द्विजानीहि किमेतद्यक्षमिति तथेति ॥ ७ ॥

7. Then they said to Vayu, "O Vayu, this discern, what is this mighty Daemon." He said, "So be it."

तदभ्यद्रवत् तमभ्यवदत् कोऽसीति वायुर्वा अहमस्मीत्यब्रवीन्मातरिश्वा वा अहमस्मीति ॥ ८ ॥

8. He rushed upon That; It said to him, "Who art thou?" "I am Vayu," he said, "and I am he that expands in the Mother of things."

तस्मिंस्त्वयि किं वीर्यमित्यपीदं सर्वमाददीय यदिदं पृथिव्यामिति ॥ ९ ॥

9. "Since such thou art, what is the force in thee?" "Even all this I can take for myself, all this that is upon the earth."

तस्मै तृणं निदधावेतदादत्स्वेति तदुपप्रेयाय सर्वजवेन तन्न शशाकादातुं स तत एव निववृते नैतदशकं विज्ञातुं यदेतद्यक्षमिति ॥ १० ॥

10. That set before him a blade of grass; "This take." He went towards it with all his speed and he could not take it. Even there he ceased, even thence he returned; "I could not discern of That, what is this mighty Daemon."

अथेन्द्रमब्रुवन् मघवन्नेतद्द्विजानीहि किमेतद्यक्षमिति तथेति तदभ्यद्रवत् तस्मात्तिरोदधे ॥ ११ ॥

11. Then they said to Indra, "Master of plenitudes, get thou the knowledge, what is this mighty Daemon." He said, "So be it." He rushed upon That. That vanished from before him.

स तस्मिन्नेवाकाशे स्त्रियमाजगाम बहुशोभमानामुमां हैमवतीं तां होवाच किमेतद्यक्षमिति ॥ १२ ॥

12. He in the same ether came upon the Woman, even upon Her who shines out in many forms, Uma daughter of the snowy summits. To her he said, "What was this mighty Daemon?"

FOURTH PART

सा ब्रह्मेति होवाच ब्रह्मणो वा एतद्विजये महीयध्वमिति ततो हैव विदांचकार ब्रह्मेति ॥ १ ॥

1. She said to him, "It is the Eternal. Of the Eternal is this victory in which ye shall grow to greatness." Then alone he came to know that this was the Brahman.

तस्माद्वा एते देवा अतितरामिवान्यान् देवान् यदग्निर्वायुरिन्द्रस्ते ह्येनन्नेदिष्ठं पस्पर्शुस्ते ह्येनत्प्रथमो विदांचकार ब्रह्मेति ॥ २ ॥

2. Therefore are these gods as it were beyond all the other gods, even Agni and Vayu and Indra, because they came nearest to the touch of That... [5]

तस्माद्वा इन्द्रोऽतितरामिवान्यान्देवान् स ह्येनन्नेदिष्ठं पस्पर्श स ह्येनत् प्रथमो विदांचकार ब्रह्मेति ॥ ३ ॥

3. Therefore is Indra as it were beyond all the other gods because he came nearest to the touch of That, because he first knew that it was the Brahman.

तस्यैष आदेशो यदेतद्विद्युतो व्यद्युतदा३ इतीन्न्यमीमिषदा३ इत्यधि- दैवतम् ॥ ४ ॥

4. Now this is the indication of That, — as is this flash of the lightning upon us or as is this falling of the eyelid, so in that which is of the gods.

---

[5] By some mistake of early memorisers or later copyists the rest of the verse has become hopelessly corrupted. It runs, "They he first came to know that it was the Brahman," which is neither fact nor sense nor grammar. The close of the third verse has crept into and replaced the original close of the second.

अथाध्यात्मं यदेतद्गच्छतीव च मनोऽनेन चैतदुपस्मरत्यभीक्ष्णं सं-
कल्पः ॥ ५ ॥

5. Then in that which is of the Self, — as the motion of this
mind seems to attain to That and by it afterwards the will
in the thought continually remembers It.

तद्ध तद्वनं नाम तद्वनमित्युपासितव्यं स य एतदेवं वेदाभि हैनं सर्वाणि
भूतानि संवाञ्छन्ति ॥ ६ ॥

6. The name of That is "That Delight"; as That Delight one
should follow after It. He who so knows That, towards him
verily all existences yearn.

उपनिषदं भो ब्रूहीत्युक्ता त उपनिषद् ब्राह्मीं वाव त उपनिषदमब्रू-
मेति ॥ ७ ॥

7. Thou hast said "Speak to me Upanishad";[6] spoken to thee
is Upanishad. Of the Eternal verily is the Upanishad that we
have spoken.

तस्यै तपो दमः कर्मेति प्रतिष्ठा वेदाः सर्वाङ्गानि सत्यमायतनम् ॥ ८ ॥

8. Of this knowledge austerity and self-conquest and works
are the foundation, the Vedas are all its limbs, truth is its
dwelling place.

यो वा एतामेवं वेदापहत्य पाप्मानमनन्ते स्वर्गे लोके ज्येये प्रतितिष्ठति
प्रतितिष्ठति ॥ ९ ॥

9. He who knows this knowledge, smites evil away from him
and in that vaster world and infinite heaven finds his foundation, yea, he finds his foundation.

---

[6] Upanishad means inner knowledge, that which enters into the final Truth and settles
in it.

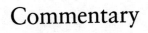

Commentary

I

The Subject of the Upanishad

THE TWELVE great Upanishads are written round one body of ancient knowledge; but they approach it from different sides. Into the great kingdom of the Brahmavidya each enters by its own gates, follows its own path or detour, aims at its own point of arrival. The Isha Upanishad and the Kena are both concerned with the same grand problem, the winning of the state of Immortality, the relations of the divine, all-ruling, all-possessing Brahman to the world and to the human consciousness, the means of passing out of our present state of divided self, ignorance and suffering into the unity, the truth, the divine beatitude. As the Isha closes with the aspiration towards the supreme felicity, so the Kena closes with the definition of Brahman as the Delight and the injunction to worship and seek after That as the Delight. Nevertheless there is a variation in the starting-point, even in the standpoint, a certain sensible divergence in the attitude.

For the precise subject of the two Upanishads is not identical. The Isha is concerned with the whole problem of the world and life and works and human destiny in their relation to the supreme truth of the Brahman. It embraces in its brief eighteen verses most of the fundamental problems of Life and scans them swiftly with the idea of the supreme Self and its becomings, the supreme Lord and His workings as the key that shall unlock all gates. The oneness of all existences is its dominating note.

The Kena Upanishad approaches a more restricted problem, starts with a more precise and narrow inquiry. It concerns itself only with the relation of mind-consciousness to Brahman-consciousness and does not stray outside the strict boundaries of its subject. The material world and the physical life are taken for granted, they are hardly mentioned. But the material world and the physical life exist for us only by virtue of our internal self and our internal life. According as our mental instruments represent to us the external world, according as our vital force in obedience to the mind deals with its impacts and objects, so will be our outward life and existence. The world is for us, not fundamentally but practically at any rate, what our mind and senses declare it to be; life is what our mentality or at least our half-mentalised vital being determines that it shall become. The question is asked by the Upanishad, what then are these mental instruments? what is this mental life which uses the external? Are they the last witnesses, the supreme and final power? Are mind and life and body all or is this human existence only a veil of something greater, mightier, more remote and profound than itself?

The Upanishad replies that there is such a greater existence behind, which is to the mind and its instruments, to the life-force and its workings what they are to the material world. Matter does not know Mind, Mind knows Matter; it is only when the creature embodied in Matter develops mind, becomes the mental being that he can know his mental self and know by that self Matter also in its reality to Mind. So also Mind does not know That which is behind it, That knows Mind; and it is only when the being involved in Mind can deliver out of its appearances his true Self that he can become That, know it as himself and by it know also Mind in its reality to that which is more real than Mind. How to rise beyond the mind and its instruments, enter into himself, attain to the Brahman becomes then the supreme aim for the mental being, the all-important problem of his existence.

For given that there is a more real existence than the mental existence, a greater life than the physical life, it follows that the lower life with its forms and enjoyments which are all that men here ordinarily worship and pursue, can no longer be an object of desire for the awakened spirit. He must aspire beyond; he must free himself from this world of death and mere phenomena to become himself in his true state of immortality beyond them. Then alone he really exists when here in this mortal life itself he can free himself from the mortal consciousness and know and be the Immortal and Eternal. Otherwise he feels that he has lost himself, has fallen from his true salvation.

But this Brahman-consciousness is not represented by the Upanishad as something quite alien to the mental and physical world, aloof from it and in no way active upon it or concerned with its activities. On the contrary, it is the Lord and ruler of all the world; the energies of the gods in the mortal consciousness are its energies; when they conquer and grow great, it is because Brahman has fought and won. This world therefore is an inferior action, a superficial representation of something infinitely greater, more perfect, more real than itself.

What is that something? It is the All-Bliss which is infinite being and immortal force. It is that pure and utter bliss and not the desires and enjoyments of this world which men ought to worship and to seek. How to seek it is the one question that matters; to follow after it with all one's being is the only truth and the only wisdom.

II
The Question. *What Godhead?*

MIND IS the principal agent of the lower or phenomenal consciousness; vital force or the life-breath, speech and the five senses of knowledge are the instruments of the mind. Prana, the life-force in the nervous system, is indeed the one main instrument of our mental consciousness; for it is that by which the mind receives the contacts of the physical world through the organs of knowledge, sight, hearing, smell, touch and taste, and reacts upon its object by speech and the other four organs of action; all these senses are dependent upon the nervous Life-force for their functioning. The Upanishad therefore begins by a query as to the final source or control of the activities of the Mind, Life-Force, Speech, Senses.

The question is, *kena*, by whom or what? In the ancient conception of the universe our material existence is formed from the five elemental states of Matter, the ethereal, aerial, fiery, liquid and solid; everything that has to do with our material existence is called the elemental, *adhibhūta*. In this material there move non-material powers manifesting through the Mind-Force and Life-Force that work upon Matter, and these are called Gods or devas; everything that has to do with the working of the non-material in us is called *adhidaiva*, that which pertains to the Gods. But above the non-material powers, containing them, greater than they is the Self or Spirit, *ātman*, and everything that has to do with this highest existence in us is called the spiritual, *adhyātma*. For the purpose of the Upanishads the *adhidaiva* is the subtle in us; it is that which is represented by Mind and Life as opposed to gross Matter; for in Mind and Life we have the characteristic action of the Gods.

The Upanishad is not concerned with the elemental, the *adhibhūta*; it is concerned with the relation between the subtle existence and the spiritual, the *adhidaiva* and *adhyātma*. But the

Mind, the Life, the speech, the senses are governed by cosmic powers, by Gods, by Indra, Vayu, Agni. Are these subtle cosmic powers the beginning of existence, the true movers of mind and life, or is there some superior unifying force, one in itself behind them all?

By whom or what is the mind missioned and sent on its errand so that it falls on its object like an arrow shot by a skilful archer at its predetermined mark, like a messenger, an envoy sent by his master to a fixed place for a fixed object? What is it within us or without us that sends forth the mind on its errand? What guides it to its object?

Then there is the Life-force, the Prana, that works in our vital being and nervous system. The Upanishad speaks of it as the first or supreme Breath; elsewhere in the sacred writings it is spoken of as the chief Breath or the Breath of the mouth, *mukhya*, *āsanya*; it is that which carries in it the Word, the creative expression. In the body of man there are said to be five workings of the life-force called the five Pranas. One specially termed Prana moves in the upper part of the body and is preeminently the breath of life, because it brings the universal Life-force into the physical system and gives it there to be distributed. A second in the lower part of the trunk, termed Apana, is the breath of death; for it gives away the vital force out of the body. A third, the Samana, regulates the interchange of these two forces at their meeting-place, equalises them and is the most important agent in maintaining the equilibrium of the vital forces and their functions. A fourth, the Vyana, pervasive, distributes the vital energies throughout the body. A fifth, the Udana, moves upward from the body to the crown of the head and is a regular channel of communication between the physical life and the greater life of the spirit. None of these are the first or supreme Breath, although the Prana most nearly represents it; the Breath to which so much importance is given in the Upanishads, is the pure life-force itself, — first, because all the others are secondary to it, born from it and only exist as its special functions. It is imaged in the Veda as the Horse; its various energies are the forces that draw the chariots of the Gods. The Vedic image is recalled by the choice of the terms employed in the Upanishad, *yukta*, yoked, *praiti*, goes forward, as a horse driven by the charioteer advances in its path.

Who then has yoked this Life-force to the many workings of existence or by what power superior to itself does it move forward in its paths? For it is not primal, self-existent or its own agent. We are conscious of a power behind which guides, drives, controls, uses it.

The force of the vital breath enables us to bring up and speed outward from the body this speech that we use to express, to throw out into a world of action and new-creation the willings and thought-formations of the mind. It is propelled by Vayu, the life-breath; it is formed by Agni, the secret will-force and fiery shaping energy in the mind and body. But these are the agents. Who or what is the secret Power that is behind them, the master of the word that men speak, its real former and the origin of that which expresses itself?

The ear hears the sound, the eye sees the form; but hearing and vision are particular operations of the life-force in us used by the mind in order to put itself into communication with the world in which the mental being dwells and to interpret it in the forms of sense. The life-force shapes them, the mind uses them, but something other than the life-force and the mind enables them to shape and to use their objects and their instruments. What God sets eye and ear to their workings? Not Surya, the God of light, not Ether and his regions; for these are only conditions of vision and hearing.

The Gods combine, each bringing his contribution, the operations of the physical world that we observe as of the mental world that is our means of observation; but the whole universal action is one, not a sum of fortuitous atoms; it is one, arranged in its parts, combined in its multiple functionings by virtue of a single conscient existence which can never be constructed or put together (*akṛta*) but is for ever, anterior to all these workings. The Gods work only by this Power anterior to themselves, live only by its life, think only by its thought, act only for its purposes. We look into ourselves and all things and become aware of it there, an "I", an "Is", a Self, which is other, firmer, vaster than any separate or individual being.

But since it is not anything that the mind can make its object or the senses throw into form for the mind, what then is it — or who? What absolute Spirit? What one, supreme and eternal Godhead? *Ko devaḥ.*

The Supramental Godhead

THE ETERNAL question has been put which turns man's eyes away from the visible and the outward to that which is utterly within, away from the little known that he has become to the vast unknown he is behind these surfaces and must yet grow into and be because that is his Reality and out of all masquerade of phenomenon and becoming the Real Being must eventually deliver itself. The human soul once seized by this compelling direction can no longer be satisfied with looking forth at mortalities and seemings through those doors of the mind and sense which the Self-existent has made to open outward upon a world of forms; it is driven to gaze inward into a new world of realities.

Here in the world that man knows, he possesses something which, however imperfect and insecure, he yet values. For he aims at and to some extent he procures enlarged being, increasing knowledge, more and more joy and satisfaction and these things are so precious to him that for what he can get of them he is ready to pay the price of continual suffering from the shock of their opposites. If then he has to abandon what he here pursues and clasps, there must be a far more powerful attraction drawing him to the Beyond, a secret offer of something so great as to be a full reward for all possible renunciation that can be demanded of him here. This is offered, — not an enlarged becoming, but infinite being; not always relative piecings of knowledge mistaken in their hour for the whole of knowledge, but the possession of our essential consciousness and the flood of its luminous realities; not partial satisfactions, but *the* delight. In a word, Immortality.

The language of the Upanishad makes it strikingly clear that it is no metaphysical abstraction, no void Silence, no indeterminate Absolute which is offered to the soul that aspires, but rather the absolute of all that is possessed by it here in the relative world of its sojourning. All here in the mental is a growing light, consciousness and life; all there in the supramental is an infinite life, light and consciousness. That which is here shadowed, is there found; the incomplete here is there the fulfilled. The Beyond is not an annullation, but a transfiguration of all that we are here in our world of forms; it is sovran Mind of this mind, secret Life of this life, the absolute Sense which supports and justifies our limited senses.

We renounce ourselves in order to find ourselves; for in the mental life there is only a seeking, but never an ultimate finding till mind is overpassed. Therefore there is behind all our mentality a perfection of ourselves which appears to us as an antinomy and contrast to what we are. For here we are a constant becoming; there we possess our eternal being. Here we conceive of ourselves as a changeful consciousness developed and always developing by a hampered effort in the drive of Time; there we are an immutable consciousness of which Time is not the master but the instrument as well as the field of all that it creates and watches. Here we live in an organisation of mortal consciousness which takes the form of a transient world; there we are liberated into the harmonies of an infinite self-seeing which knows all world in the light of the eternal and immortal. The Beyond is our reality; that is our plenitude; that is the absolute satisfaction of our self-existence. It is immortality and it is "That Delight".

Here in our imprisoned mentality the ego strives to be master and possessor of its inner field and its outer environment, yet cannot hold anything to enjoy it, because it is not possible really to possess what is not-self to us. But there in the freedom of the eternal our self-existence possesses without strife by the sufficient fact that all things are itself. Here is the apparent man, there the real man, the Purusha: here are gods, there is the Divine: here is the attempt to exist, Life flowering out of an all-devouring death, there Existence itself and a dateless immortality.

The answer that is thus given is involved in the very form of the original question. The Truth behind Mind, Life, Sense must be that which controls by exceeding it; it is the Lord, the all-possessing Deva. This was the conclusion at which the Isha Upanishad arrived by the synthesis of all existences; the Kena arrives at it by the antithesis of one governing self-existence to all this that exists variously by another power of being than its own. Each follows its own method for the resolution of all things into the one Reality, but the conclusion is identical. It is the All-possessing and All-enjoying, who is reached by the renunciation of separate being, separate possession and separate delight.

But the Isha addresses itself to the awakened seeker; it begins therefore with the all-inhabiting Lord, proceeds to the all-becoming Self and returns to the Lord as the Self of the cosmic movement, because it has to justify works to the seeker of the Uncreated and to institute a divine life founded on the joy of immortality and on the unified consciousness of the individual made one with the universal. The Kena addresses itself to the soul still attracted by the external life, not yet wholly awakened nor wholly a seeker; it begins therefore with the Brahman as the Self beyond Mind and proceeds to the Brahman as the hidden Lord of all our mental and vital activities, because it has to point this soul upward beyond its apparent and outward existence. But the two opening chapters of the Kena only state less widely from this other view-point the Isha's doctrine of the Self and its becomings; the last two repeat in other terms of thought the Isha's doctrine of the Lord and His movement.

IV

The Eternal Beyond the Mind

THE UPANISHAD first affirms the existence of this profounder, vaster, more puissant consciousness behind our mental being. That, it affirms, is Brahman. Mind, Life, Sense, Speech are not the utter Brahman; they are only inferior modes and external instruments. Brahman-consciousness is our real self and our true existence.

Mind and body are not our real self; they are mutable formations or images which we go on constructing in the drive of Time as a result of the mass of our past energies. For although those energies seem to us to lie dead in the past because their history is behind us, yet are they still existent in their mass and always active in the present and the future.

Neither is the ego-function our real self. Ego is only a faculty put forward by the discriminative mind to centralise round itself the experiences of the sense-mind and to serve as a sort of lynchpin in the wheel which keeps together the movement. It is no more than an instrument, although it is true that so long as we are limited by our normal mentality, we are compelled by the nature of that mentality and the purpose of the instrument to mistake our ego-function for our very self.

Neither is it the memory that constitutes our real self. Memory is another instrument, a selective instrument for the practical management of our conscious activities. The ego-function uses it as a rest and support so as to preserve the sense of continuity without which our mental and vital activities could not be organised for a spacious enjoyment by the individual. But even our mental self comprises and is influenced in its being by a host of things which are not present to our memory, are subconscious and hardly grasped at all by our surface existence. Memory is essential to the continuity of the ego-sense, but it is not the constituent of the ego-sense, still less of the being.

Neither is moral personality our real self. It is only a changing formation, a pliable mould framed and used by our subjective life in order to give some appearance of fixity to the constantly mutable becoming which our mental limitations successfully tempt us to call ourselves.

Neither is the totality of that mutable conscious becoming, although enriched by all that subconsciously underlies it, our real self. What we become is a fluent mass of life, a stream of experience pouring through time, a flux of Nature upon the crest of which our mentality rides. What we are is the eternal essence of that life, the immutable consciousness that bears the experience, the immortal substance of Nature and mentality.

For behind all and dominating all that we become and experience, there is something that originates, uses, determines, enjoys, yet is not changed by its origination, not affected by its instruments, not determined by its determinations, not worked upon by its enjoyings. What that is, we cannot know unless we go behind the veil of our mental being which knows only what is affected, what is determined, what is worked upon, what is changed. The mind can only be aware of that as something which we indefinably are, not as something which it definably knows. For the moment our mentality tries to fix this something, it loses itself in the flux and the movement, grasps at parts, functions, fictions, appearances which it uses as planks of safety in the welter or tries to cut out a form from the infinite and say "This is I." In the words of the Veda, "when the mind approaches That and studies it, That vanishes."

But behind the Mind is this other or Brahman-consciousness, Mind of our mind, Sense of our senses, Speech of our speech, Life of our life. Arriving at that, we arrive at Self; we can draw back from mind the image into Brahman the Reality.

But what differentiates that real from this apparent self? Or — since we can say no more than we have said already in the way of definition, since we can only indicate that "That" is not what "this" is, but is the mentally inexpressible absolute of all that is here, — what is the relation of this phenomenon to that reality? For it is the question of the relation that the Upanishad makes its starting-point; its opening question assumes that there is a relation and that the reality originates and governs the phenomenon.

Obviously, Brahman is not a thing subject to our mind, senses, speech or life-force; it is no object seen, heard, expressed, sensed, formed by thought, nor any state of body or mind that we become in the changing movement of the life. But the thought of the Upanishad attempts to awaken deeper echoes from our gulfs than this obvious denial of the mental and sensuous objectivity of the Brahman. It affirms that not only is it not an object of mind or a formation of life, but it is not even dependent on our mind, life and senses for the exercise of its lordship and activity. It is that which does not think by the mind, does not live by the life, does not sense by the senses, does not find expression in the speech, but rather makes these things themselves the object of its superior, all-comprehending, all-knowing consciousness.

Brahman thinks out the mind by that which is beyond mind; it sees the sight and hears the hearing by that absolute vision and audition which are not phenomenal and instrumental but direct and inherent; it forms our expressive speech out of its creative word; it speeds out this life we cling to from that eternal movement of its energy which is not parcelled out into forms but has always the freedom of its own inexhaustible infinity.

Thus the Upanishad begins its reply to its own question. It first describes Brahman as Mind of the mind, Sight of the sight, Hearing of the hearing, Speech of the speech, Life of the life. It then takes up each of these expressions and throws them successively into a more expanded form so as to suggest a more definite and ample idea of their meaning, so far as that can be done by words. To the expression "Mind of the mind" corresponds the expanded phrase "That which thinks not with the mind, that by which mind is thought" and so on with each of the original descriptive expressions to the closing definition of the Life behind this life as "That which breathes not with the life-breath, that by which the life-power is brought forward into its movement."

And each of these exegetic lines is emphasised by the reiterated admonition, "That Brahman seek to know and not this which men follow after here." Neither Mind, Life, Sense and Speech nor their objects and expressions are the Reality which we have to know and pursue. True knowledge is of That which forms these instruments for us but is itself independent of their utilities. True possession and enjoyment is of that which, while it creates these objects of our pursuit, itself makes nothing the object of its pursuit and passion, but is eternally satisfied with all things in the joy of its immortal being.

V
The Supreme Word

THE UPANISHAD, reversing the usual order of our logical thought which would put Mind and Sense first or Life first and Speech last as a subordinate function, begins its negative description of Brahman with an explanation of the very striking phrase, Speech of our speech. And we can see that it means a Speech beyond ours, an absolute expression of which human language is only a shadow and as if an artificial counterfeit. What idea underlies this phrase of the Upanishad and this precedence given to the faculty of speech?

Continually, in studying the Upanishads, we have to divest ourselves of modern notions and to realise as closely as possible the associations that lay behind the early Vedantic use of words. We must recollect that in the Vedic system the Word was the creatrix; by the Word Brahma creates the forms of the universe. Moreover, human speech at its highest merely attempts to recover by revelation and inspiration an absolute expression of Truth which already exists in the Infinite above our mental comprehension. Equally, then, must that Word be above our power of mental construction.

All creation is expression by the Word; but the form which is expressed is only a symbol or representation of the thing which is. We see this in human speech which only presents to the mind a mental form of the object; but the object it seeks to express is itself only a form or presentation of another Reality. That reality is Brahman. Brahman expresses by the Word a form or presentation of himself in the objects of sense and consciousness which constitute the universe, just as the human word expresses a mental image of those objects. That Word is creative in a deeper and more original sense than human speech and with a power of which the utmost creativeness of human speech can be only a far-off and feeble analogy.

The word used here for utterance means literally a raising up to confront the mind. Brahman, says the Upanishad, is that which cannot be so raised up before the mind by speech.

Human speech, as we see, raises up only the presentation of a presentation, the mental figure of an object which is itself only a figure of the sole Reality, Brahman. It has indeed a power of new creation, but even that power only extends to the creation of new mental images, that is to say of adaptive formations based upon previous mental images. Such a limited power gives no idea of the original creative puissance which the old thinkers attributed to the divine Word.

If, however, we go a little deeper below the surface, we shall arrive at a power in human speech which does give us a remote image of the original creative Word. We know that vibration of sound has the power to create — and to destroy — forms; this is a commonplace of modern Science. Let us suppose that behind all forms there has been a creative vibration of sound.

Next, let us examine the relation of human speech to sound in general. We see at once that speech is only a particular application of the principle of sound, a vibration made by pressure of the breath in its passage through the throat and mouth. At first, beyond doubt, it must have been formed naturally and spontaneously to express the sensations and emotions created by an object or occurrence and only afterwards seized upon by the mind to express first the idea of the object and then ideas about the object. The value of speech would therefore seem to be only representative and not creative.

But, in fact, speech is creative. It creates forms of emotion, mental images and impulses of action. The ancient Vedic theory and practice extended this creative action of speech by the use of the Mantra. The theory of the Mantra is that it is a word of power born out of the secret depths of our being where it has been brooded upon by a deeper consciousness than the mental, framed in the heart and not originally constructed by the intellect, held in the mind, again concentrated on by the waking mental consciousness and then thrown out silently or vocally — the silent word is perhaps held to be more potent than the spoken — precisely for the work of creation. The Mantra can not only create new subjective states in ourselves, alter our psychical being, reveal knowledge and faculties we did not before possess, can not only produce similar results in other minds than that of the user, but can produce vibrations in the mental and vital atmosphere which result in effects, in actions and even in the production of material forms on the physical plane.

As a matter of fact, even ordinarily, even daily and hourly we do produce by the word within us thought-vibrations, thought-forms which result in corresponding vital and physical vibrations, act upon ourselves, act upon others, and end in the indirect creation of actions and of forms in the physical world. Man is constantly acting upon man both by the silent and the spoken word and he so acts and creates though less directly and powerfully even in the rest of Nature. But because we are stupidly engrossed with the external forms and phenomena of the world and do not trouble to examine its subtle and non-physical processes, we remain ignorant of all this field of science behind.

The Vedic use of the Mantra is only a conscious utilisation of this secret power of the word. And if we take the theory that underlies it together with our previous hypothesis of a creative vibration of sound behind every formation, we shall begin to understand the idea of the original creative Word. Let us suppose a conscious use of the vibrations of sound which will produce corresponding forms or changes of form. But Matter is only, in the ancient view, the lowest of the planes of existence. Let us realise then that a vibration of sound on the material plane presupposes a corresponding vibration on the vital without which it could not have come into play; that again presupposes a corresponding originative vibration on the mental; the mental presupposes a corresponding originative vibration on the supramental at the very root of things. But a mental vibration implies thought and perception and a supramental vibration implies a supreme vision and discernment. All vibration of sound on that higher plane is, then, instinct with and expressive of this supreme discernment of a truth in things and is at the same time creative, instinct with a supreme power which casts into forms the truth discerned and eventually, descending from plane to plane, reproduces it in the physical form or object created in Matter by etheric sound. Thus we see that the theory of creation by the Word which is the absolute expression of the Truth, and the theory of the material creation by sound-vibration in the ether correspond and are two logical poles of the same idea. They both belong to the same ancient Vedic system.

This, then, is the supreme Word, Speech of our speech. It is vibration of pure Existence, instinct with the perceptive and originative power of infinite and omnipotent consciousness, shaped by the Mind behind mind into the inevitable word of the Truth of things; out of whatever substance on whatever plane, the form or physical expression emerges by its creative agency. The Supermind using the Word is the creative Logos.

The Word has its seed-sounds — suggesting the eternal syllable of the Veda, A U M, and the seed-sounds of the Tantriks — which carry in them the principles of things; it has its forms which stand behind the revelatory and inspired speech that comes to man's supreme faculties, and these compel the forms of things in the universe; it has its rhythms, — for it is no disordered vibration, but moves out into great cosmic measures, — and according to the rhythm is the law, arrangement, harmony, processes of the world it builds. Life itself is a rhythm of God.

But what is it that is expressed or raised up before the mental consciousness by the Word in the phenomenal world? Not Brahman, but truths, forms and phenomena of Brahman. Brahman is not, cannot be expressed by the Word; he does not use the word here to express his very self, but is known only to his own self-awareness. And even the truths of himself that stand behind the forms of cosmic things are in their true reality always self-expressed to his eternal vision in a higher than the mental vibration, a rhythm and voice of themselves that is their own very soul of movement. Speech, a lesser thing, creates, expresses, but is itself only a creation and expression. Brahman is not expressed by speech, but speech is itself expressed by Brahman. And that which expresses speech in us, brings it up out of our consciousness with its strivings to raise up the truth of things to our mind, is Brahman himself as the Word, a Thing that is in the supreme superconscience. That Word, Speech of our speech, is in its essence of Power the Eternal himself and in its supreme movements a part of his very form and everlasting spiritual body, *brahmaṇo rūpam.*

Therefore it is not the happenings and phenomena of the world that we have to accept finally as our object of pursuit, but That which brings out from itself the Word by which they were thrown into form for our observation by the consciousness and for our pursuit by the will. In other words, the supreme Existence that has originated all.

Human speech is only a secondary expression and at its highest a shadow of the divine Word, of the seed-sounds, the satisfying rhythms, the revealing forms of sound that are the omniscient and omnipotent speech of the eternal Thinker, Harmonist, Creator. The highest inspired speech to which the human mind can attain, the word most unanalysably expressive of supreme truth, the most puissant syllable or mantra can only be its far-off representation.

The Necessity of Supermind

AS THE Upanishad asserts a speech behind this speech, which is the expressive aspect of the Brahman-consciousness, so it asserts a Mind behind this mind which is its cognitive aspect. And as we asked ourselves what could be the rational basis for the theory of the divine Word superior to our speech, so we have now to ask ourselves what can be the rational basis for this theory of a cognitive faculty or principle superior to Mind. We may say indeed that if we grant a divine Word creative of all things, we must also grant a divine Mind cognitive of the Word and of all that it expresses. But this is not a sufficient foundation; for the theory of the divine Word presents itself only as a rational possibility. A cognition higher than Mind presents itself on the other hand as a necessity which arises from the very nature of Mind itself, a necessity from which we cannot logically escape.

In the ancient system which admitted the soul's survival of the body, Mind was the man, in a very profound and radical sense of the phrase. It is not only that the human being is the one reasoning animal upon earth, the thinking race; he is essentially the mental being in a terrestrial body, the *manu*. Quite apart from the existence of a soul or self one in all creatures, the body is not even the phenomenal self of man; the physical life also is not himself; both may be dissolved, man will persist. But if the mental being also is dissolved, man as man ceases to be; for this is his centre and the nodus of his organism.

On the contrary, according to the theory of a material evolution upheld by modern Science, man is only matter that has developed mind by an increasing sensibility to the shocks of its environment; and matter being the basis of existence there is nothing, except the physical elements, that can survive the dissolution of the body. But this formula is at most the obverse and inferior side of a much larger truth. Matter could not develop Mind if in or behind the force that constitutes physical forms there were not already a principle of Mind striving towards self-manifestation. The will to enlighten and consciously govern the life and the form must have been already existent in that which appears to us inconscient; it must have been there before mind was evolved. For, if there were no such necessity of Mind in Matter, if the stuff of mentality were not there already and the will to mentalise, Mind could not possibly have come into being out of inconscient substance.

But in the mere chemical elements which go to constitute material forms or in electricity or in any other purely physical factor, whatever unconscious will or sensation they may be possessed by or possess, we can discover nothing which could explain the emergence of conscious sensation, which could constitute a will towards the evolution of thought or which could impose the necessity of such an evolution on inconscient physical substance. It is not then in the form of Matter itself, but in the Force which is at work in Matter, that we must seek the origin of Mind. That Force must either be itself conscious or contain the grain of mental consciousness inherent in its being and therefore the potentiality and indeed the necessity of its emergence. This imprisoned consciousness, though originally absorbed in the creation first of forms and then of physical relations and reactions between physical forms, must still have held in itself from the beginning, however long kept back and suppressed, a will to the ultimate enlightenment of these relations by the creation of corresponding conscious or mental values. Mind is then a concealed necessity which the subconscient holds in itself from the commencement of things; it is the thing that must emerge once the attractions and repulsions of Matter begin to be established; it is the suppressed secret and cause of the reactions of life in the metal, plant and animal.

If on the other hand we say that Mind in some such secret and suppressed form is not already existent in Matter, we must then suppose that it exists outside Matter and embraces it or enters into it. We must suppose a mental plane of existence which presses upon the physical and tends to possess it. In that case the mental being would be in its origin an entity which is formed outside the material world; but it prepares in that world bodies which become progressively more and more able to house and express Mind. We may image it forming, entering into and possessing the body, breaking into it, as it were, — as the Purusha in the Aitareya Upanishad is said to form the body and then to enter in by breaking open a door in Matter. Man would in this view be a mental being incarnate in the living body who at its dissolution leaves it with full possession of his mentality.

The two theories are far from being incompatible with each other; they can be viewed as complements forming a single truth. For the involution of Mind, its latency in the material Force of the physical universe and in all its movements does not preclude the existence of a mental world beyond and above the reign of the physical principle. In fact, the emergence of such a latent Mind might well depend upon and would certainly profit by the aid and pressure of forces from a supra-physical kingdom, a mental plane of existence.

There are always two possible views of the universe. The one supposes, with modern Science, Matter to be the beginning of things and studies everything as an evolution from Matter; or, if not Matter, then, with the Sankhya philosophy, an indeterminate inconscient active Force or Prakriti of which even mind and reason are mechanical operations, — the Conscious Soul, if any exists, being a quite different and, although conscient, yet inactive entity. The other supposes the conscious soul, the Purusha, to be the material as well as the cause of the universe and Prakriti to be only its Shakti or the Force of its conscious being which operates upon itself as the material of forms.[1] The latter is the view of the Upanishads. Certainly if we study the material world only, excluding all evidence of other planes as a dream or a hallucination, if we equally exclude all evidence of operations

---

[1] Cf. for example, the Aitareya Upanishad which shows us the Atman or Self using the Purusha as that in which all the operations of Nature are formed.

in mind which exceed the material limitation and study only its ordinary equation with Matter, we must necessarily accept the theory of Matter as the origin and as the indispensable basis and continent. Otherwise, we shall be irresistibly led towards the early Vedantic conclusions.

However this may be, even from the standpoint of the sole material world Man in the substance of his manhood is a mind occupying and using the life of the body — a mind that is greater than the Matter in which it has emerged. He is the highest present expression of the will in the material universe; the Force that has built up the worlds, so far as we are able to judge of its intention from its actual operations as we see them in their present formula upon earth, arrives in him at the thing it was seeking to express. It has brought out the hidden principle of Mind that now operates consciously and intelligently on the life and the body. Man is the satisfaction of the necessity which Nature bore secretly in her from the very commencement of her works; he is the highest possible Name or Numen on this planet; he is the realised terrestrial godhead.

But all this is true only if we assume that for Nature's terrestrial activities Mind is the ultimate formula. In reality and when we study more deeply the phenomena of consciousness, the facts of mentality, the secret tendency, aspiration and necessity of man's own nature, we see that he cannot be the highest term. He is the highest realised here and now; he is not the highest realisable. As there is something below him, so there is something, if even only a possibility, above. As physical Nature concealed a secret beyond herself which in him she has released into creation, so he too conceals a secret beyond himself which he in turn must deliver to the light. That is his destiny.

This must necessarily be so because Mind too is not the first principle of things and therefore cannot be their last possibility. As Matter contained Life in itself, contained it as its own secret necessity and had to be delivered of that birth, and as Life contained Mind in itself, contained it as its own secret necessity and had to be delivered of the birth it held, so Mind too contains in itself that which is beyond itself, contains it as its own secret necessity and presses to be delivered, it also, of this supreme birth.

What is the rational necessity which forbids us to suppose Mind to be Nature's last birth and compels us to posit something beyond it of which itself is the indication? A consideration of the nature and working of mentality supplies us with the answer. For mentality is composed of three principal elements, thought, will and sensation. Sensation may be described as an attempt of divided consciousness to seize upon its object and enjoy it, thought as its attempt to seize upon the truth of the object and possess it, will as its attempt to seize upon the potentiality of the object and use it. At least these three things are such an attempt in their essentiality, in their instinct, in their subconscious purpose. But obviously the attempt is imperfect in its conditions and its success; its very terms indicate a barrier, a gulf, an incapacity. As Life is limited and hampered by the conditions of its synthesis with Matter, so Mind is limited and hampered by the conditions of its synthesis with Life in Matter. Neither Matter nor Life has found anything proper to their own formula which could help to conquer or sufficiently expand its limitations; they have been compelled each to call in a new principle, Matter to call into itself Life, Life to call into itself Mind. Mind also is not able to find anything proper to its own formula which can conquer or sufficiently expand the limitations imposed upon its workings; Mind also has to call in a new principle beyond itself, freer than itself and more powerful.

In other words, Mind does not exhaust the possibilities of consciousness and therefore cannot be its last and highest expression. Mind tries to arrive at Truth and succeeds only in touching it imperfectly with a veil between; there must be in the nature of things a faculty or principle which sees the Truth unveiled, an eternal faculty of knowledge which corresponds to the eternal fact of the Truth. There is, says the Veda, such a principle; it is the Truth-Consciousness which sees the truth directly and is in possession of it spontaneously. Mind labours to effect the will in it and succeeds only in accomplishing partially, with difficulty and insecurely the potentiality at which it works; there must be a faculty or principle of conscious effective force which corresponds to the unconscious automatic principle of self-fulfilment in Nature, and this principle must be sought for in the form of consciousness that exceeds Mind. Mind, finally, aspires to seize and enjoy the essential delight-giving quality, the *rasa* of things, but it succeeds only in attaining to it indirectly, holding it in an imperfect grasp and enjoying it externally and fragmentarily; there must be a principle which can attain directly, hold rightly, enjoy intimately and securely. There is, says the Veda, an eternal Bliss-consciousness which corresponds to the eternal *rasa* or essential delight-giving quality of all experience and is not limited by the insecure approximations of the sense in Mind.

If, then, such a deeper principle of consciousness exists, it must be that and not mind which is the original and fundamental intention concealed in Nature and which eventually and somewhere must emerge. But is there any reason for supposing that it must emerge here and in Mind, as Mind has emerged in Life and Life in Matter? We answer in the affirmative because Mind has in itself, however obscurely, that tendency, that aspiration and, at bottom, that necessity. There is one law from the lowest to the highest. Matter, when we examine it closely, proves to be instinct with the stuff of Life — the vibrations, actions and reactions, attractions and repulsions, contractions and expansions, the tendencies of combination, formation and growth, the seekings and responses which are the very substance of life; but the visible principle of life can only emerge when the necessary material conditions have been prepared which will permit it to organise itself in Matter. So also Life is instinct with the stuff of Mind, abounds with an unconscious[2] sensation, will, intelligence, but the visible principle of Mind can only emerge when the necessary vital conditions have been prepared which will permit it to organise itself in living Matter. Mind too is instinct with the stuff of supermind — sympathies, unities, intuitions, emergences of preexistent knowledge, instincts, imperative lights and movements, inherent self-effectivities of will which disguise

---

[2] I use the language of the materialist Haeckel in spite of its paradoxical form.

themselves in a mental form; but the visible principle of super-mind can only emerge when the necessary mental conditions are prepared which will permit it to organise itself in man, the mental living creature.

This necessary preparation is proceeding in human development as the corresponding preparations were developed in the lower stages of the evolution, — with the same gradations, retardations, inequalities; but still it is more enlightened, increasingly self-conscious, nearer to a conscious sureness. And the very fact that this progress is attended by less absorption in the detail, less timidity of error, a less conservative attachment to the step gained suggests as much as it contradicts the hope and almost the assurance that when the new principle emerges it will not be by the creation of a new and quite different type which, separated after its creation, will leave the rest of mankind in the same position to it as are the animals to man, but, if not by the elevation of humanity as a whole to a higher level, yet by an opening of the greater possibility to all of the race who have the will to rise. For Man, first among Nature's children, has shown the capacity to change himself by his own effort and the conscious aspiration to transcend.

These considerations justify to the reason the idea of a Mind beyond our mind, but only as a final evolution out of Matter. The Upanishad, however, enthrones it as the already existing creator and ruler of Mind; it is a secret principle already conscient and not merely contained inconsciently in the very stuff of things. But this is the natural conclusion — even apart from spiritual experience — from the nature of the supramental principle. For it is at its highest an eternal knowledge, will, bliss and conscious being and it is more reasonable to conclude that it is eternally conscious, though we are not conscious of it, and the source of the universe, than that it is eternally inconscient and only becomes conscient in Time as a result of the universe. Our inconscience of it is no proof that it is inconscient of us: and yet our own incapacity is the only real basis left for the denial of an eternal Mind beyond mind superior to its creations and originative of the cosmos.

All other foundations for the rejection of this ancient wisdom have disappeared or are disappearing before the increasing light of modern knowledge.

Mind and Supermind

W E ARRIVE then at this affirmation of an all-cognitive Principle superior to Mind and exceeding it in nature, scope and capacity. For the Upanishad affirms a Mind beyond mind as the result of intuition and spiritual experience and its existence is equally a necessary conclusion from the facts of the cosmic evolution. What then is this Mind beyond mind? how does it function? or by what means shall we arrive at the knowledge of it or possess it?

The Upanishad asserts about this supreme cognitive principle, first, that it is beyond the reach of mind and the senses; secondly, that it does not itself think with the mind; thirdly, that it is that by which mind itself is thought or mentalised; fourthly, that it is the very nature or description of the Brahman-consciousness.

When we say, however, that "Mind of mind" is the nature or description of the Brahman-consciousness, we must not forget that the absolute Brahman in itself is held to be unknowable and therefore beyond description. It is unknowable, not because it is a void and capable of no description except that of nothingness, nor because, although positive in existence, it has no content or quality, but because it is beyond all things that our present instruments of knowledge can conceive and because the methods of ideation and expression proper to our mentality do not apply to it. It is the absolute of all things that we know and of each thing that we know and yet nothing nor any sum of things can exhaust or characterise its essential being. For its manner of being is other than that which we call existence; its unity resists all analysis, its multiple infinities exceed every synthesis. Therefore it is not in its absolute essentiality that it can be described as Mind of the mind, but in its fundamental nature in regard to our mental existence.

Brahman-consciousness is the eternal outlook of the Absolute upon the relative.

But even of this outlook we may say that it is beyond the reach of mind and speech and senses. Yet mind, speech and senses seem to be our only available means for acquiring and expressing knowledge. Must we not say then that this Brahman-consciousness also is unknowable and that we can never hope to know it or possess it while in this body? Yet the Upanishad commands us to *know* this Brahman and by knowledge to possess it — for the knowledge intended by the words *viddhi, avedīt,* is a knowledge that discovers and takes possession, — and it declares later on that it is here, in this body and on this earth that we must thus possess Brahman in knowledge, otherwise great is the perdition. A good deal of confusion has been brought into the interpretation of this Upanishad by a too trenchant dealing with the subtlety of its distinctions between the knowability and the unknowability of the Brahman. We must therefore try to observe exactly what the Upanishad says and especially to seize the whole of its drift by synthetic intuition rather than cut up its meaning so as to make it subject to our logical mentality.

The Upanishad sets out by saying that this Ruler of the mind, senses, speech and life is Mind of our mind, Life of our life, Sense of our senses, Speech of our speech; and it then proceeds to explain what it intends by these challenging phrases. But it introduces between the description and the explanation a warning that neither the description nor the explanation must be pushed beyond their proper limits or understood as more than guide-posts pointing us towards our goal. For neither Mind, Speech nor Sense can travel to the Brahman; therefore Brahman must be beyond all these things in its very nature, otherwise it would be attainable by them in their function. The Upanishad, although it is about to teach of the Brahman, yet affirms, "we know It not, we cannot distinguish how one should teach of It." The two Sanskrit words that are here used, *vidmah* and *vijānīmah,* seem to indicate the one a general grasp and possession in knowledge, the other a total and exact comprehension in whole and detail, by synthesis and analysis. The reason of this entire inability

is next given, "because Brahman is other than the known and
It is there over the unknown," possessing it and, as it were,
presiding over it. The known is all that we grasp and possess by
our present mentality; it is all that is not the supreme Brahman
but only form and phenomenon of it to our sense and mental
cognition. The unknown is that which is beyond the known
and though unknown is not unknowable if we can enlarge our
faculties or attain to others that we do not yet possess.

Yet the Upanishad next proceeds to maintain and explain
its first description and to enjoin on us the knowledge of the
Brahman which it so describes. This contradiction is not at once
reconciled; it is only in the second chapter that the difficulty
is solved and only in the fourth that the means of knowledge
are indicated. The contradiction arises from the nature of our
knowledge itself which is a relation between the consciousness
that seeks and the consciousness that is sought; where that relation disappears, knowledge is replaced by sheer identity. In what
we call existence, the highest knowledge can be no more than
the highest relation between that which seeks and that which
is sought, and it consists in a modified identity through which
we may pass beyond knowledge to the absolute identity. This
metaphysical distinction is of importance because it prevents
us from mistaking any relation in knowledge for the absolute
and from becoming so bound by our experience as to lose or
miss the fundamental awareness of the absolute which is beyond
all possible description and behind all formulated experience.
But it does not render the highest relation in our knowledge,
the modified identity in experience worthless or otiose. On the
contrary, it is that we must aim at as the consummation of our
existence in the world. For if we possess it without being limited
by it, — and if we are limited by it we have not true possession
of it, — then in and through it we shall, even while in this body,
remain in touch with the Absolute.

The means for the attainment of this highest knowledge
is the constant preparation of the mind by the admission into
it of a working higher than itself until the mind is capable of
giving itself up to the supramental action which exceeds it and

which will finally replace it. In fact, Mind also has to follow the law of natural progression which has governed our evolution in this world from matter into life and life into mind. For just as life-consciousness is beyond the imprisoned material being and unattainable by it through its own instruments, just as mind-consciousness is beyond the first inconscient movements of life, so too this supramental consciousness is beyond the divided and dividing nature of Mind and unattainable by it through its own instruments. But as Matter is constantly prepared for the manifestation of Life until Life is able to move in it, possess it, manage in it its own action and reaction, and as Life is constantly prepared for the manifestation of Mind until Mind is able to use it, enlighten its actions and reactions by higher and higher mental values, so must it be with Mind and that which is beyond Mind.

And all this progression is possible because these things are only different formations of one being and one consciousness. Life only reveals in Matter that which is involved in Matter, that which is the secret meaning and essence of Matter. It reveals, as it were, to material existence its own soul, its own end. So too Mind reveals in Life all that Life means, all that it obscurely is in essence but cannot realise because it is absorbed in its own practical motion and its own characteristic form. So also Supermind must intervene to reveal Mind to itself, to liberate it from its absorption in its own practical motion and characteristic form and enable the mental being to realise that which is the hidden secret of all its formal practice and action. Thus shall man come to the knowledge of that which rules within him and missions his mind to its mark, sends forth his speech, impels the life-force in its paths and sets his senses to their workings.

This supreme cognitive Principle does not think by the mind. Mind is to it an inferior and secondary action, not its own proper mode. For Mind, based on limitation and division, can act only from a given centre in the lower and obscured existence; but Supermind is founded on unity and it comprehends and pervades; its action is in the universal and is in conscious communion with a transcendent source eternal and beyond the formations of the universe. Supermind regards the individual in the universal and does not begin with him or make of him a separate being. It starts from the Transcendent and sees the universal and individual as they are in relation to it, as its terms, as its formulas; it does not start from the individual and universal to arrive at the Transcendent. Mind acquires knowledge and mastery; it reaches it by a constant mentalising and willing: Supermind possesses knowledge and mastery; possessing, it throws itself out freely in various willing and knowing. Mind gropes by divided sensation; it arrives at a sort of oneness through sympathy: Supermind possesses by a free and all-embracing sense; it lives in the unity of which various love and sympathy are only a secondary play of manifestation. Supermind starts from the whole and sees in it its parts and properties, it does not build up the knowledge of the whole by an increasing knowledge of the parts and properties; and even the whole is to it only a unity of sum, only a partial and inferior term of the higher unity of infinite essence.

We see, then, that these two cognitive Principles start from two opposite poles and act in opposite directions by opposite methods. Yet it is by the higher cognitive that the lower is formed and governed. Mind is thought by that which is beyond Mind; the mentalising consciousness shapes and directs its movement according to the knowledge and impulse it receives from this higher Supermind and even the stuff of which it is formed belongs to that Principle. Mentality exists because that which is beyond Mind has conceived an inverse action of itself working in a thinner, poorer, darker, less powerful substance of conscious being and founded upon its self-concentration on different points in its own being and in different forms of its own being. Supermind fixes these points, sees how consciousness must act from them on other forms of itself and in obedience to the pressure of those other forms, once a particular rhythm or law of universal action is given; it governs the whole action of mentality according to what it thus fixes and sees. Even our ignorance is only the distorted action of a truth projected from the Supermind and could not exist except as such a distortion; and so likewise all our dualities of knowledge, sensation, emotion, force proceed from that higher vision, obey it and are a secondary and, as one might say, perverse action of the concealed Supermind itself which governs always this lower action in harmony with its first conception of a located consciousness, divided indeed and therefore not in possession of its world or itself, but feeling out towards that possession and towards the unity which, because of the Supermind in us, it instinctively, if obscurely, knows to be its true nature and right.

But, for this very reason, the feeling out, the attempt at acquisition can only succeed in proportion as the mental being abandons his characteristic mentality and its limitations in order to rise beyond to that Mind of the mind which is his origin and his secret governing principle. His mentality must admit Supramentality as Life has admitted Mind. So long as he worships, follows after, adheres to all this that he now accepts as the object of his pursuit, to the mind and its aims, to its broken methods, its constructions of will and opinion and emotion dependent on egoism, division and ignorance, he cannot rise beyond this death to that immortality which the Upanishad promises to the seeker. That Brahman we have to know and seek after and not this which men here adore and pursue.

The Supreme Sense

THE UPANISHAD is not satisfied with the definition of the Brahman-consciousness as Mind of the mind. Just as it has described it as Speech of the speech, so also it describes it as Eye of the eye, Ear of the ear. Not only is it an absolute cognition behind the play of expression, but also an absolute Sense behind the action of the senses. Every part of our being finds its fulfilment in that which is beyond its present forms of functioning and not in those forms themselves.

This conception of the all-governing supreme consciousness does not fall in with our ordinary theories about sense and mind and the Brahman. We know of sense only as an action of the organs through which embodied mind communicates with external Matter, and these sense-organs have been separately developed in the course of evolution; the senses therefore are not fundamental things, but only subordinate conveniences and temporary physical functionings of the embodied Mind. Brahman, on the other hand, we conceive of by the elimination of all that is not fundamental, by the elimination even of the Mind itself. It is a sort of positive zero, an x or unknowable which corresponds to no possible equation of physical or psychological quantities. In essence this may or may not be true; but we have now to think not of the Unknowable but of its highest manifestation in consciousness; and this we have described as the outlook of the Absolute on the relative and as that which is the cause and governing power of all that we and the universe are. There in that governing cause there must be something essential and supreme of which all our fundamental functionings here are a rendering in the terms of embodied consciousness.

Sense, however, is not or does not appear to be fundamental; it is only an instrumentation of Mind using the nervous system. It is not even a pure mental functioning, but depends so much upon the currents of the Life-force, upon its electric energy vibrating up and down the nerves, that in the Upanishads the senses are called Pranas, powers or functionings of the Life-force. It is true that Mind turns these nervous impressions when communicated to it into mental values, but the sense-action itself seems to be rather nervous than mental. In any case there would, at first sight, appear to be no warrant in reason for attributing a Sense of the sense to that which is not embodied, to a supramental consciousness which has no need of any such instrumentation.

But this is not the last word about sense; this is only its outward appearance behind which we must penetrate. What, not in its functioning, but in its essence, is the thing we call sense? In its functioning, if we analyse that thoroughly, we see that it is the contact of the mind with an eidolon of Matter, — whether that eidolon be of a vibration of sound, a light-image of form, a volley of earth-particles giving the sense of odour, an impression of *rasa* or sap that gives the sense of taste, or that direct sense of disturbance of our nervous being which we call touch. No doubt, the contact of Matter with Matter is the original cause of these sensations; but it is only the eidolon of Matter, as for instance the image of the form cast upon the eye, with which the mind is directly concerned. For the mind operates upon Matter not directly, but through the Life-force; that is its instrument of communication and the Life-force, being in us a nervous energy and not anything material, can seize on Matter only through nervous impressions of form, through contactual images, as it were, which create corresponding values in the energy-consciousness called in the Upanishads the Prana. Mind takes these up and replies to them with corresponding mental values, mental impressions of form, so that the thing sensed comes to us after a triple process of translation, first the material eidolon, secondly the nervous or energy-image, third the image reproduced in stuff of mind.

This elaborate process is concealed from us by the lightning-like rapidity with which it is managed, — rapidity in our impressions of Time; for in another notation of Time by a creature differently constituted each part of the operation might be distinctly sensible. But the triple translation is always there, because there are really three sheaths of consciousness in us, the material, *annakoṣa*, in which the physical contact and image are received and formed, the vital and nervous, *prāṇakoṣa*, in which there is a nervous contact and formation, the mental, *manaḥkoṣa*, in which there is mental contact and imaging. We dwell centred in the mental sheath and therefore the experience of the material world has to come through the other two sheaths before it can reach us.

The foundation of sense, therefore, is contact, and the essential contact is the mental without which there would not be sense at all. The plant, for instance, feels nervously, feels in terms of life-energy, precisely as the human nervous system does, and it has precisely the same reactions; but it is only if the plant has rudimentary mind that we can suppose it to be, as we understand the word, sensible of these nervous or vital impressions and reactions. For then it would feel not only nervously, but in terms of mind. Sense, then, may be described as in its essence mental contact with an object and the mental reproduction of its image.

All these things we observe and reason of in terms of this embodiment of mind in Matter; for these sheaths or *koṣas* are formations in a more and more subtle substance reposing on gross Matter as their base. Let us imagine that there is a mental world in which Mind and not Matter is the base. There sense would be quite a different thing in its operation. It would feel mentally an image in Mind and throw it out into form in more and more gross substance; and whatever physical formations there might already be in that world would respond rapidly to the Mind and obey its modifying suggestions. Mind would be masterful, creative, originative, not as with us either obedient to Matter and merely reproductive or else in struggle with it and only with difficulty able to modify a material predetermined and dully reluctant to its touch. It would be, subject to whatever supramental power might be above it, master of a ductile and easily responsive material. But still Sense would be there, because contact in mental consciousness and formation of images would still be part of the law of being.

Mind, in fact, or active consciousness generally has four necessary functions which are indispensable to it wherever and however it may act and of which the Upanishads speak in the four terms, *vijñāna*, *prajñāna*, *saṁjñāna* and *ājñāna*. *Vijñāna* is the original comprehensive consciousness which holds an image of things at once in its essence, its totality and its parts and properties; it is the original, spontaneous, true and complete view of it which belongs properly to the supermind and of which mind has only a shadow in the highest operations of the comprehensive intellect. *Prajñāna* is the consciousness which holds an image of things before it as an object with which it has to enter into relations and to possess by apprehension and a combined analytic and synthetic cognition. *Saṁjñāna* is the contact of consciousness with an image of things by which there is a sensible possession of it in its substance; if *prajñāna* can be described as the outgoing of apprehensive consciousness to possess its object in conscious energy, to know it, *saṁjñāna* can be described as the inbringing movement of apprehensive consciousness which draws the object placed before it back to itself so as to possess it in conscious substance, to feel it. *Ājñāna* is the operation by which consciousness dwells on an image of things so as to hold, govern and possess it in power. These four, therefore, are the basis of all conscious action.

As our human psychology is constituted, we begin with *saṁjñāna*, the sense of an object in its image; the apprehension of it in knowledge follows. Afterwards we try to arrive at the comprehension of it in knowledge and the possession of it in power. There are secret operations in us, in our subconscient and superconscient selves, which precede this action, but of these we are not aware in our surface being and therefore for us they do not exist. If we knew of them, our whole conscious functioning would be changed. As it is what happens is a rapid process by which we sense an image and have of it an apprehensive percept and concept, and a slower process of the intellect by which we try to comprehend and possess it. The former process is the natural action of the mind which has entirely developed in us; the latter is an acquired action, an action of the intellect and the intelligent will which represent in Mind an attempt of the mental being to do what can only be done with perfect spontaneity and mastery by something higher than Mind. The intellect and intelligent will form a bridge by which the mental being is trying to establish a conscious connection with the supramental and to prepare the embodied soul for the descent into it of a supramental action. Therefore the first process is comparatively easy, spontaneous, rapid, perfect; the second slow, laboured, imperfect. In proportion as the intellectual action becomes associated with and dominated by a rudimentary supramental action, — and it is this which constitutes the phenomenon of genius, — the second process also becomes more and more easy, spontaneous, rapid and perfect.

If we suppose a supreme consciousness, master of the world, which really conducts behind the veil all the operations the mental gods attribute to themselves, it will be obvious that that consciousness will be the entire Knower and Lord. The basis of its action or government of the world will be the perfect, original and all-possessing *vijñāna* and *ājñāna*. It will comprehend all things in its energy of conscious knowledge, control all things in its energy of conscious power. These energies will be the spontaneous inherent action of its conscious being creative and possessive of the forms of the universe. What part then will be left for the apprehensive consciousness and the sense? They will be not independent functions, but subordinate operations involved in the action of the comprehensive consciousness itself. In fact, all four there will be one rapid movement. If we had all these four acting in us with the unified rapidity with which the *prajñāna* and *saṁjñāna* act, we should then have in our notation of Time some inadequate image of the unity of the supreme action of the supreme energy.

If we consider, we shall see that this must be so. The supreme consciousness must not only comprehend and possess in its conscious being the images of things which it creates as its self-expression, but it must place them before it — always in its own being, not externally — and have a certain relation with them by the two terms of apprehensive consciousness. Otherwise the universe would not take the form that it has for us; for we only reflect in the terms of our organisation the movements of the supreme Energy. But by the very fact that the images of things are there held in front of an apprehending consciousness within the comprehending conscious being and not externalised as our individual mind externalises them, the supreme Mind and supreme Sense will be something quite different from our mentality and our forms of sensation. They will be terms of an entire knowledge and self-possession and not terms of an ignorance and limitation which strives to know and possess.

In its essential and general term our sense must reflect and be the creation of this supreme Sense. But the Upanishad speaks of a Sight behind our sight and a Hearing behind our hearing, not in general terms of a Sense behind our sense. Certainly eye and ear are only taken as typical of the senses, and are chosen because they are the highest and subtlest of them all. But still the differentiation of sense which forms part of our mentality is evidently held to correspond with a differentiation of some kind in the supreme Sense. How is this possible? It is what we have next to unravel by examining the nature and source of the functioning of the separate senses in ourselves, — their source in our mentality and not merely their functioning in the actual terms of our life-energy and our body. What is it in Mind that is fundamental to sight and hearing? Why do we see and hear and not simply sense with the mind?

Sense of Our Senses

MIND WAS called by Indian psychologists the eleventh and ranks as the supreme sense. In the ancient arrangement of the senses, five of knowledge and five of action, it was the sixth of the organs of knowledge and at the same time the sixth of the organs of action. It is a commonplace of psychology that the effective functioning of the senses of knowledge is inoperative without the assistance of the mind; the eye may see, the ear may hear, all the senses may act, but if the mind pays no attention, the man has not heard, seen, felt, touched or tasted. Similarly, according to psychology, the organs of action act only by the force of the mind operating as will or, physiologically, by the reactive nervous force from the brain which must be according to materialistic notions the true self and essence of all will. In any case, the senses or all senses, if there are other than the ten, — according to a text in the Upanishad there should be at least fourteen, seven and seven, — all senses appear to be only organisations, functionings, instrumentations of the mind-consciousness, devices which it has formed in the course of its evolution in living Matter.

Modern psychology has extended our knowledge and has admitted us to a truth which the ancients already knew but expressed in other language. We know now or we rediscover the truth that the conscious operation of mind is only a surface action. There is a much vaster and more potent subconscious mind which loses nothing of what the senses bring to it; it keeps all its wealth in an inexhaustible store of memory, *akṣitaṁ śravaḥ*. The surface mind may pay no attention, still the subconscious mind attends, receives, treasures up with an infallible accuracy. The illiterate servant-girl hears daily her master reciting Hebrew in his study; the surface mind pays no attention to the unintelligible gibberish, but the subconscious mind hears, remembers and, when in an abnormal condition it comes up to the surface, reproduces those learned recitations with a portentous accuracy which the most correct and retentive scholar might envy. The man or mind has not heard because he did not attend; the greater man or mind within has heard because he always attends, or rather sub-tends, with an infinite capacity. So too a man put under an anaesthetic and operated upon has felt nothing; but release his subconscious mind by hypnosis and he will relate accurately every detail of the operation and its appropriate sufferings; for the stupor of the physical sense-organ could not prevent the larger mind within from observing and feeling.

Similarly we know that a large part of our physical action is instinctive and directed not by the surface but by the subconscious mind. And we know now that it is a mind that acts and not merely an ignorant nervous reaction from the brute physical brain. The subconscious mind in the catering insect knows the anatomy of the victim it intends to immobilise and make food for its young and it directs the sting accordingly, as unerringly as the most skilful surgeon, provided the more limited surface mind with its groping and faltering nervous action does not get in the way and falsify the inner knowledge or the inner will-force.

These examples point us to truths which western psychology, hampered by past ignorance posing as scientific orthodoxy, still ignores or refuses to acknowledge. The Upanishads declare that the Mind in us is infinite; it knows not only what has been seen but what has not been seen, not only what has been heard but what has not been heard, not only what has been discriminated by the thought but what has not been discriminated by the thought. Let us say, then, in the tongue of our modern knowledge that the surface man in us is limited by his physical experiences; he knows only what his nervous life in the body brings to his embodied mind; and even of those bringings he knows, he can retain and utilise only so much as his surface mind-sense attends to and consciously remembers; but there is a larger subliminal consciousness within him which is not thus limited. That consciousness senses what has not been sensed by the surface mind and its organs and knows what the surface mind has not learned by its acquisitive thought. That in the insect knows the anatomy of its victim; that in the man outwardly insensible not only feels and remembers the action of the surgeon's knife, but knows the appropriate reactions of suffering which were in the physical body inhibited by the anaesthetic and therefore non-existent; that in the illiterate servant-girl heard and retained accurately the words of an unknown language and could, as Yogic experience knows, by a higher action of itself understand those superficially unintelligible sounds.

To return to the Vedantic words we have been using, there is a vaster action of the Sanjnana which is not limited by the action of the physical sense-organs; it was this which sensed perfectly and made its own through the ear the words of the unknown language, through the touch the movements of the unfelt surgeon's knife, through the sense-mind or sixth sense the exact location of the centres of locomotion in the victim insect. There is also associated with it a corresponding vaster action of Prajnana, Ajnana and Vijnana not limited by the smaller appre-hensive and comprehensive faculties of the external mind. It is this vaster Prajnana which perceived the proper relation of the words to each other, of the movement of the knife to the unfelt suffering of the nerves and of the successive relation in space of the articulations in the insect's body. Such perception was inherent in the right reproduction of the words, the right nar-ration of the sufferings, the right successive action of the sting. The Ajnana or Knowledge-Will originating all these actions was also vaster, not limited by the faltering force that governs the operations directed by the surface mind. And although in these examples the action of the vaster Vijnana is not so apparent, yet it was evidently there working through them and ensuring their coordination.

But at present it is with the Sanjnana that we are concerned. Here we should note, first of all, that there is an action of the sense-mind which is superior to the particular action of the senses and is aware of things even without imaging them in forms of sight, sound, contact, but which also as a sort of sub-ordinate operation, subordinate but necessary to completeness of presentation, does image in these forms. This is evident in psychical phenomena. Those who have carried the study and experimentation of them to a certain extent, have found that we can sense things known only to the minds of others, things that exist only at a great distance, things that belong to another plane than the terrestrial but have here their effects; we can both sense them in their images and also feel, as it were, all that they are without any definite image proper to the five senses.

This shows, in the first place, that sight and the other senses are not mere results of the development of our physical organs in the terrestrial evolution. Mind, subconscious in all Matter and evolving in Matter, has developed these physical organs in order to apply its inherent capacities of sight, hearing etc., on the physical plane by physical means for a physical life; but they are inherent capacities and not dependent on the circumstance of terrestrial evolution and they can be employed without the use of the physical eye, ear, skin, palate. Supposing that there are psychical senses which act through a psychical body and we thus explain these psychical phenomena, still that action also is only an organisation of the inherent functioning of the essential sense, the Sanjnana, which in itself can operate without bodily organs. This essential sense is the original capacity of consciousness to feel in itself all that consciousness has formed and to feel it in all the essential properties and operations of that which has form, whether represented materially by vibration of sound or images of light or any other physical symbol.

The trend of knowledge leads more and more to the conclusion that not only are the properties of form, even the most obvious such as colour, light etc., merely operations of Force, but form itself is only an operation of Force. This Force again proves to be self-power of conscious-being[1] in a state of energy and activity. Practically, therefore, all form is only an operation of consciousness impressing itself with presentations of its own workings. We see colour because that is the presentation which

---

[1] *Devātmaśaktiṁ svaguṇair nigūḍhām*, self-power of the divine Existent hidden by its own modes. Swetaswatara Upanishad.

consciousness makes to itself of one of its own operations; but colour is only an operation of Force working in the form of Light, and Light again is only a movement, that is to say an operation of Force. The question is what is essential to this operation of Force taking on itself the presentation of form? For it is this that must determine the working of Sanjnana or Sense on whatever plane it may operate.

Everything begins with vibration or movement, the original *kṣobha* or disturbance. If there is no movement of the conscious being, it can only know its own pure static existence. Without vibration[2] or movement of being in consciousness there can be no act of knowledge and therefore no sense; without vibration or movement of being in force there can be no object of sense. Movement of conscious being as knowledge becoming sensible of itself as movement of force, in other words the knowledge separating itself from its own working to watch that and take it into itself again by feeling, — this is the basis of universal Sanjnana. This is true both of our internal and external operations. I become anger by a vibration of conscious force acting as nervous emotion and I feel the anger that I have become by another movement of conscious force acting as light of knowledge. I am conscious of my body because I have myself become the body; that same force of conscious being which has made this form of itself, this presentation of its workings, knows it in that form, in that presentation. I can know nothing except what I myself am; if I know others, it is because they also are myself, because my self has assumed these apparently alien presentations as well as that which is nearest to my own mental centre. All sensation, all action of sense is thus the same in essence whether external or internal, physical or psychical.

But this vibration of conscious being is presented to itself by various forms of sense which answer to the successive operations of movement in its assumption of form. For first

---

[2] The term is used not because it is entirely adequate or accurate, no physical term can be, but because it is most suggestive of the original outgoing of consciousness to seek itself.

we have intensity of vibration creating regular rhythm which is the basis or constituent of all creative formation; secondly, contact or intermiscence of the movements of conscious being which constitute the rhythm; thirdly, definition of the grouping of movements which are in contact, their shape; fourthly, the constant welling up of the essential force to support in its continuity the movement that has been thus defined; fifthly, the actual enforcement and compression of the force in its own movement which maintains the form that has been assumed. In Matter these five constituent operations are said by the Sankhyas to represent themselves as five elemental conditions of substance, the etheric, atmospheric, igneous, liquid and solid; and the rhythm of vibration is seen by them as *śabda*, sound, the basis of hearing, the intermiscence as contact, the basis of touch, the definition as shape, the basis of sight, the upflow of force as *rasa*, sap, the basis of taste, and the discharge of the atomic compression as *gandha*, odour, the basis of smell. It is true that this is only predicated of pure or subtle matter; the physical matter of our world being a mixed operation of force, these five elemental states are not found there separately except in a very modified form. But all these are only the physical workings or symbols. Essentially all formation, to the most subtle and most beyond our senses such as form of mind, form of character, form of soul, amount when scrutinised to this five-fold operation of conscious-force in movement.

All these operations, then, the Sanjnana or essential sense must be able to seize, to make its own by that union in knowledge of knower and object which is peculiar to itself. Its sense of the rhythm or intensity of the vibrations which contain in themselves all the meaning of the form, will be the basis of the essential hearing of which our apprehension of physical sound or the spoken word is only the most outward result; so also its sense of the contact or intermiscence of conscious force with conscious force must be the basis of the essential touch; its sense of the definition or form of force must be the basis of the essential sight; its sense of the upflow of essential being in the form, that which is the secret of its self-delight, must be the basis of the essential taste; its sense of the compression of force and the self-discharge of its essence of being must be the basis of the essential inhalation grossly represented in physical substance by the sense of smell. On whatever plane, to whatever kind of formation these essentialities of sense will apply themselves and on each they will seek an appropriate organisation, an appropriate functioning.

This various sense will, it is obvious, be in the highest consciousness a complex unity, just as we have seen that there the various operation of knowledge is also a complex unity. Even if we examine the physical senses, say, the sense of hearing, if we observe how the underlying mind receives their action, we shall see that in their essence all the senses are in each other. That mind is not only aware of the vibration which we call sound; it is aware also of the contact and interchange between the force in the sound and the nervous force in us with which that intermixes; it is aware of the definition or form of the sound and of the complex contacts or relations which make up the form; it is aware of the essence or outwelling conscious force which constitutes and maintains the sound and prolongs its vibrations in our nervous being; it is aware of our own nervous inhalation of the vibratory discharge proceeding from the compression of force which makes, so to speak, the solidity of the sound. All these sensations enter into the sensitive reception and joy of music which is the highest physical form of this operation of force, — they constitute our physical sensitiveness to it and the joy of our nervous being in it; diminish one of them and the joy and the sensitiveness are to that extent dulled. Much more must there be this complex unity in a higher than the physical consciousness and most of all must there be unity in the highest. But the essential sense must be capable also of seizing the secret essence of all conscious being in action, in itself and not only through the results of the operation; its appreciation of these results can be nothing more than itself an outcome of this deeper sense which it has of the essence of the Thing behind its appearances.

If we consider these things thus subtly in the light of our

own deeper psychology and pursue them beyond the physical appearances by which they are covered, we shall get to some intellectual conception of the sense behind our senses or rather the Sense of our senses, the Sight of our sight and the Hearing of our hearing. The Brahman-consciousness of which the Upanishad speaks is not the Absolute withdrawn into itself, but that Absolute in its outlook on the relative; it is the Lord, the Master-Soul, the governing Transcendent and All, He who constitutes and controls the action of the gods on the different planes of our being. Since it constitutes them, all our workings can be no more than psychical and physical results and representations of something essential proper to its supreme creative outlook, our sense a shadow of the divine Sense, our sight of the divine Sight, our hearing of the divine Hearing. Nor are that divine sight and hearing limited to things physical, but extend themselves to all forms and operations of conscious being.

The supreme Consciousness does not depend on what we call sight and hearing for its own essential seeing and audition. It operates by a supreme Sense, creative and comprehensive, of which our physical and psychical sight and hearing are external results and partial operations. Neither is it ignorant of these, nor excludes them; for since it constitutes and controls, it must be aware of them but from a supreme plane, *param dhāma*, which includes all in its view; for its original action is that highest movement of Vishnu which, the Veda tells us, the seers behold like an eye extended in heaven. It is that by which the soul sees its seeings and hears its hearings; but all sense only assumes its true value and attains to its absolute, its immortal reality when we cease to pursue the satisfactions of the mere external and physical senses and go beyond even the psychical being to this spiritual or essential which is the source and fountain, the knower, constituent and true valuer of all the rest.

This spiritual sense of things, secret and superconscient in us, alone gives their being, worth and reality to the psychical and physical sense; in themselves they have none. When we attain to it, these inferior operations are as it were taken up into it and the whole world and everything in it changes to us and takes on a different and a non-material value. That Master-consciousness in us senses our sensations of objects, sees our seeings, hears our hearings no longer for the benefit of the senses and their desires, but with the embrace of the self-existent Bliss which has no cause, beginning or end, eternal in its own immortality.

The Superlife — Life of Our Life

BUT THE Brahman-consciousness is not only Mind of our mind, Speech of our speech, Sense of our sense; it is also Life of our life. In other words, it is a supreme and universal energy of existence of which our own material life and its sustaining energy are only an inferior result, a physical symbol, an external and limited functioning. That which governs our existence and its functionings, does not live and act by them, but is their superior cause and the supra-vital principle out of which they are formed and by which they are controlled.

The English word life does duty for many very different shades of meaning; but the word Prana familiar in the Upanishad and in the language of Yoga is restricted to the life-force whether viewed in itself or in its functionings. The popular significance of Prana was indeed the breath drawn into and thrown out from the lungs and so, in its most material and common sense, the life or the life-breath; but this is not the philosophic significance of the word as it is used in the Upanishads. The Prana of the Upanishads is the life-energy itself which was supposed to occupy and act in the body with a fivefold movement, each with its characteristic name and each quite as necessary to the functioning of the life of the body as the act of respiration. Respiration in fact is only one action of the chief movement of the life-energy, the first of the five, — the action which is most normally necessary and vital to the maintenance and distribution of the energy in the physical frame, but which can yet be suspended without the life being necessarily destroyed.

The existence of a vital force or life-energy has been doubted by western Science, because that Science concerns itself only with the most external operations of Nature and has as yet no true knowledge of anything except the physical and outward. This Prana, this life-force is not physical in itself; it is not material energy, but rather a different principle supporting Matter and involved in it. It supports and occupies all forms and without it no physical form could have come into being or could remain in being. It acts in all material forces such as electricity and is nearest to self-manifestation in those that are nearest to pure force; material forces could not exist or act without it, for from it they derive their energy and movement and they are its vehicles. But all material aspects are only field and form of the Prana which is in itself a pure energy, their cause and not their result. It cannot therefore be detected by any physical analysis; physical analysis can only resolve for us the combinations of those material happenings which are its results and the external signs and symbols of its presence and operation.

How then do we become aware of its existence? By that purification of our mind and body and that subtilisation of our means of sensation and knowledge which become possible through Yoga. We become capable of analysis other than the resolution of forms into their gross physical elements and are able to distinguish the operations of the pure mental principle from those of the material and both of these from the vital or dynamic which forms a link between them and supports them both. We are then able to distinguish the movements of the Pranic currents not only in the physical body which is all that we are normally aware of, but in that subtle frame of our being which Yoga detects underlying and sustaining the physical. This is ordinarily done by the process of Pranayama, the government and control of the respiration. By Pranayama the Hathayogin is able to control, suspend and transcend the ordinary fixed operation of the Pranic energy which is all that Nature needs for the normal functioning of the body and of the physical life and mind, and he becomes aware of the channels in which that energy distributes itself in all its workings and is therefore able to do things with his body which seem miraculous to the ignorant, just as the physical scientist by his knowledge of the workings of material forces is able to do things with them which would seem to us magic if their law and process were not divulged. For all the workings of life in the physical form are governed by the Prana and not only those which are normal and constant and those which, being always potential, can be easily brought forward and set in action, but those which are of a more remote potentiality and seem to our average experience difficult or impossible.

But the Pranic energy supports not only the operations of our physical life, but also those of the mind in the living body. Therefore by the control of the Pranic energy it is not only possible to control our physical and vital functionings and to transcend their ordinary operation, but to control also the workings of the mind and to transcend its ordinary operations. The human mind in fact depends always on the pranic force which links it with the body through which it manifests itself, and it is able to deploy its own force only in proportion as it can make that energy available for its own uses and subservient to its own purposes. In proportion, therefore, as the Yogin gets back to the control of the Prana, and by the direction of its batteries opens up those nervous centres (*cakras*) in which it is now sluggish or only partially operative, he is able to manifest powers of mind, sense and consciousness which transcend our ordinary experience. The so-called occult powers of Yoga are such faculties which thus open up of themselves as the Yogin advances in the control of the Pranic force and, purifying the channels of its movement, establishes an increasing communication between the consciousness of his subtle subliminal being and the consciousness of his gross physical and superficial existence.

Thus the Prana is vital or nervous force which bears the operations of mind and body, is yoked by them as it were like a horse to a chariot and driven by the mind along the paths on which it wishes to travel to the goal of its desire. Therefore it is described in this Upanishad as yoked and moving forward and again as being led forward, the images recalling the Vedic symbol of the Horse by which the pranic force is constantly designated in the Rig Veda. It is in fact that which does all the action of the world in obedience to conscious or subconscious mind and in the conditions of material force and material form. While the mind is that movement of Nature in us which represents in the mould of our material and phenomenal existence and within the triple term of the Ignorance the knowledge aspect of the Brahman, the consciousness of the knower, and body is that which similarly represents the being of the existent in the mask of phenomenally divisible substance, so Prana or life-energy represents in the flux of phenomenal things the force, the active dynamis of the Lord who controls and enjoys the manifestation of His own being.[1] It is a universal energy present in every atom and particle of the universe and active in every stirring and current of the constant flux and interchange which constitutes the world.

But just as mind is only an inferior movement of the supreme Conscious-Being and above mind there is a divine and infinite principle of consciousness, will and knowledge which controls the ignorant action of mind, and it is by this superior principle and not by mind that Brahman cognises His own being whether in itself or in its manifestation, so also it must be with this Life-force. The characteristics of the life-force as it manifests itself in us are desire, hunger, an enjoyment which devours the object enjoyed and a sensational movement and activity of response which gropes after possession and seeks to pervade, embrace, take into itself the object of its desire.[2] It is not in this breath of desire and mortal enjoyment that the true life can consist or the highest, divine energy act, any more than the supreme knowledge can think in the terms of ignorant, groping, limited and divided mind. As the movements of mind are merely representations in the terms of the duality and the ignorance, reflections of a supreme consciousness and knowledge, so the movements of this life-force can only be similar representations of a supreme energy expressing a higher and truer existence possessed of that consciousness and knowledge and therefore free from desire, hunger, transient enjoyment and hampered activity. What is desire here must there be self-existent Will or Love; what is hunger

---

[1] The three are the reverse aspects of Chit, Sat and Chit-Tapas.

[2] All these significances are intended by the Vedic Rishis in their use of the word Ashwa, Horse, for the Prana, the root being capable of all of them as we see from the words *āśā*, hope; *aśanā*, hunger; *aś*, to eat; *aś*, to enjoy; *āśu*, swift; *aś*, to move, attain, pervade, etc.

here must there be desireless satisfaction; what is here enjoyment must there be self-existent delight; what is here a groping action and response, must be there self-possessing and all-possessing energy, — such must be the Life of our life by which this inferior action is sustained and led to its goal. Brahman does not breathe with the breath, does not live by this Life-force and its dual terms of birth and death.

What then is this Life of our life? It is the supreme Energy[3] which is nothing but the infinite force in action of the supreme conscious Being in His own illumined self. The Self-existent is luminously aware of Himself and full of His own delight; and that self-awareness is a timeless self-possession which in action reveals itself as a force of infinite consciousness omnipotent as well as omniscient; for it exists between two poles, one of eternal stillness and pure identity, the other of eternal energy and identity of All with itself, the stillness eternally supporting the energy. That is the true existence, the Life from which our life proceeds; that is the immortality, while what we cling to as life is "hunger that is death". Therefore the object of the wise must be to pass in their illumined consciousness beyond the false and phenomenal terms of life and death to this immortality.

Yet is this Life-force, however inferior its workings, instinct with the being, will, light of that which it represents, of that which transcends it; by That it is "led forward" on its paths to a goal which its own existence implies by the very imperfection of its movements and renderings. This death called life is not only a dark figure of that light, but it is the passage by which we pass through transmutation of our being from the death-sleep of Matter into the spirit's infinite immortality.

---

[3] Tapas or Chit-Shakti.

The Great Transition

THE THOUGHT of the Upanishad, as expressed in its first chapter in the brief and pregnant sentences of the Upanishadic style, amounts then to this result that the life of the mind, senses, vital activities in which we dwell is not the whole or the chief part of our existence, not the highest, not self-existent, not master of itself. It is an outer fringe, a lower result, an inferior working of something beyond; a superconscient Existence has developed, supports and governs this partial and fragmentary, this incomplete and unsatisfying consciousness and activity of the mind, life and senses. To rise out of this external and surface consciousness towards and into that superconscient is our progress, our goal, our destiny of completeness and satisfaction.

The Upanishad does not assert the unreality, but only the incompleteness and inferiority of our present existence. All that we follow after here is an imperfect representation, a broken and divided functioning of what is eternally in an absolute perfection on that higher plane of existence. This mind of ours unpossessed of its object, groping, purblind, besieged by error and incapacity, its action founded on an external vision of things, is only the shadow thrown by a superconscient Knowledge which possesses, creates and securely uses the truth of things because nothing is external to it, nothing is other than itself, nothing is divided or at war within its all-comprehensive self-awareness. That is the Mind of our mind. Our speech, limited, mechanical, imperfectly interpretative of the outsides of things, restricted by the narrow circle of the mind, based on the appearances of sense is only the far-off and feeble response, the ignorant vibration returned to a creative and revelatory Word which has built up all the forms which our mind and speech seek to comprehend and express. Our sense, a movement in stuff of consciousness vibratory to outward impacts, attempting imperfectly to grasp them by laboured and separately converging reactions, is only the faulty image of a supreme Sense which at once, fully, harmoniously unites itself with and enjoys all that the supreme Mind and Speech create in the self-joyous activity of the divine and infinite existence. Our life, a breath of force and movement and possession attached to a form of mind and body and restricted by the form, limited in its force, hampered in its movement, besieged in its possession and therefore a thing of discords at war with itself and its environment, hungering and unsatisfied, moving inconstantly from object to object and unable to embrace and retain their multiplicity, devouring its objects of enjoyment and therefore transient in its enjoyments, is only a broken movement of the one, undivided, infinite Life which is all-possessing and ever satisfied because in all it enjoys its eternal self unimprisoned by the divisions of space, unoccupied by the moments of Time, undeluded by the successions of Cause and Circumstance.

This superconscient Existence, one, conscious of itself, conscious both of its eternal peace and its omniscient and omnipotent force, is also conscious of our cosmic existence which it holds in itself, inspires secretly and omnipotently governs. It is the Lord of the Isha Upanishad who inhabits all the creations of His Force, all form of movement in the ever mobile principle of cosmos. It is our self and that of which and by which we are constituted in all our being and activities, the Brahman. The mortal life is a dual representation of That with two conflicting elements in it, negative and positive. Its negative elements of death, suffering, incapacity, strife, division, limitation are a dark figure which conceal and serve the development of that which its positive elements cannot yet achieve, — immortality hiding itself from life in the figure of death, delight hiding itself from pleasure in the figure of suffering, infinite force hiding itself from finite effort in the figure of incapacity, fusion of love hiding itself from desire in the figure of strife, unity hiding itself from acquisition in the figure of division, infinity hiding itself from growth in the figure of limitation. The positive elements suggest what the Brahman is, but never are what the Brahman is, although their victory, the victory of the gods, is always the victory of the Brahman over its own self-negations, always the self-affirmation of His vastness against the denials of the dark and limiting figure of things. Still, it is not this vastness merely, but the absolute infinity which is Brahman itself. And therefore within this dual figure of things we cannot attain to our self, our Highest; we have to transcend in order to attain. Our pursuit of the positive elements of this existence, our worship of the gods of the mind, life, sense is only a preparatory to the real travail of the soul, and we must leave this lower Brahman and know that Higher if we are to fulfil ourselves. We pursue, for instance, our mental growth, we become mental beings full of an accomplished thought-power and thought-acquisition, *dhīrāḥ*, in order that we may by thought of mind go beyond mind itself to the Eternal. For always the life of mind and senses is the jurisdiction of death and limitation; beyond is the immortality.

The wise, therefore, the souls seated and accomplished in luminous thought-power put away from them the dualities of our mind, life and senses and go forward from this world; they go beyond to the unity and the immortality. The word used for going forward is that which expresses the passage of death; it is also that which the Upanishad uses for the forward movement of the Life-force yoked to the car of embodied mind and sense on the paths of life. And in this coincidence we can find a double and most pregnant suggestion.

It is not by abandoning life on earth in order to pursue immortality on other more favourable planes of existence that the great achievement becomes possible. It is here, *ihaiva*, in this mortal life and body that immortality must be won, here in this lower Brahman and by this embodied soul that the Higher must be known and possessed. "If here one find it not, great is the perdition." This life-force in us is led forward by the attraction of the supreme Life on its path of constant acquisition through types of the Brahman until it reaches a point where it has to go entirely forward, to go across out of the mortal life, the mortal vision of things to some Beyond. So long as death is not entirely conquered, this going beyond is represented in the terms of death and by a passing into other worlds where death is not present, where a type of immortality is tasted corresponding to that which we have found here in our soul-experience; but the attraction of death and limitation is not overpassed because they still conceal something of immortality and infinity which we have not yet achieved; therefore there is a necessity of return, an insistent utility of farther life in the mortal body which we do not overcome until we have passed beyond all types to the very being of the Infinite, One and Immortal.

The worlds of which the Upanishad speaks are essentially soul-conditions and not geographical divisions of the cosmos. This material universe is itself only existence as we see it when the soul dwells on the plane of material movement and experience in which the spirit involves itself in form, and therefore all the framework of things in which it moves by the life and which it embraces by the consciousness is determined by the principle of infinite division and aggregation proper to Matter, to substance of form. This becomes then its world or vision of things. And to whatever soul-condition it climbs, its vision of things will change from the material vision and correspond to that other condition, and in that other framework it will move in its living and embrace it in its consciousness. These are the worlds of the ancient tradition.

But the soul that has entirely realised immortality passes beyond all worlds and is free from frameworks. It enters into the being of the Lord; like this supreme superconscient Self and Brahman, it is not subdued to life and death. It is no longer subject to the necessity of entering into the cycle of rebirth, of travelling continually between the imprisoning dualities of death and birth, affirmation and negation; for it has transcended name and form. This victory, this supreme immortality it must achieve here as an embodied soul in the mortal framework of things. Afterwards, like the Brahman, it transcends and yet embraces the cosmic existence without being subject to it. Personal freedom, personal fulfilment is then achieved by the liberation of the soul from imprisonment in the form of this changing personality and by its ascent to the One that is the All. If afterwards there is any assumption of the figure of mortality, it is an assumption and

not a subjection, a help brought to the world and not a help
to be derived from it, a descent of the ensouled superconscient
existence not from any personal necessity, but from the universal
need in the cosmic labour for those yet unfree and unfulfilled
to be helped and strengthened by the force that has already
described the path up to the goal in its experience and achieved
under the same conditions the Work and the Sacrifice.

Mind and the Brahman

BEFORE we can proceed to the problem how, being what we are and the Brahman being what it is, we can effect the transition from the status of mind, life and senses proper to man over to the status proper to the supreme Consciousness which is master of mind, life and senses, another and prior question arises. The Upanishad does not state it explicitly, but implies and answers it with the strongest emphasis on the solution and the subtlest variety in its repetition of the apparent paradox that is presented.

The Master-Consciousness of the Brahman is that for which we have to abandon this lesser status of the mere creature subject to the movement of Nature in the cosmos; but after all this Master-Consciousness, however high and great a thing it may be, has a relation to the universe and the cosmic movement; it cannot be the utter Absolute, Brahman superior to all relativities. This Conscious-Being who originates, supports and governs our mind, life, senses is the Lord; but where there is no universe of relativities, there can be no Lord, for there is no movement to transcend and govern. Is not then this Lord, as one might say in a later language, not so much the creator of Maya as himself a creation of Maya? Do not both Lord and cosmos disappear when we go beyond all cosmos? And is it not beyond all cosmos that the only true reality exists? Is it not this only true reality and not the Mind of our mind, the Sense of our sense, the Life of our life, the Word behind our speech, which we have to know and possess? As we must go behind all effects to the Cause, must we not equally go beyond the Cause to that in which neither cause nor effects exist? Is not even the immortality spoken of in the Veda and Upanishads a petty thing to be overpassed and abandoned? and should we not reach towards the utter Ineffable where mortality and immortality cease to have any meaning?

The Upanishad does not put to itself the question in this form and language which only became possible when Nihilistic Buddhism and Vedantic Illusionism had passed over the face of our thought and modified philosophical speech and concepts. But it knows of the ineffable Absolute which is the utter reality and absoluteness of the Lord even as the Lord is the absolute of all that is in the cosmos. Of That it proceeds to speak in the only way in which it can be spoken of by the human mind.

Its answer to the problem is that That is precisely the Unknowable[1] of which no relations can be affirmed[2] and about which therefore our intellect must for ever be silent. The injunction to know the utterly Unknowable would be without any sense or practical meaning. Not that That is a Nihil, a pure Negative, but it cannot either be described by any of the positives of which our mind, speech or perception is capable, nor even can it be indicated by any of them. It is only a little that we know; it is only in the terms of the little that we can put the mental forms of our knowledge. Even when we go beyond to the real form of the Brahman which is not this universe, we can only indicate, we cannot really describe. If then we think we have known it perfectly, we betray our ignorance; we show that we know very little indeed, not even the little that we can put into the forms of our knowledge. For the universe seen as our mind sees it is the little, the divided, the parcelling out of existence and consciousness in which we know and express things by fragments, and we can never really cage in our intellectual and verbal fictions that infinite totality. Yet it is through the principles manifested in the universe that we have to arrive at That, through the life, through the mind and through that highest mental knowledge which grasps at the fundamental Ideas that are like doors concealing behind them the Brahman and yet seeming to reveal Him.

Much less, then, if we can only thus know the Master-Consciousness which is the form of the Brahman, can we pretend to know its utter ineffable reality which is beyond all knowledge.

---

[1] *Ajñeyam atarkyam.*
[2] *Avyavahāryam.*

But if this were all, there would be no hope for the soul and a resigned Agnosticism would be the last word of wisdom. The truth is that though thus beyond our mentality and our highest ideative knowledge, the Supreme does give Himself both to this knowledge and to our mentality in the way proper to each and by following that way we can arrive at Him, but only on condition that we do not take our mentalising by the mind and our knowing by the higher thought for the full knowledge and rest in that with a satisfied possession.

The way is to use our mind rightly for such knowledge as is open to its highest, purified capacity. We have to know the form of the Brahman, the Master-Consciousness of the Lord through and yet beyond the universe in which we live. But first we must put aside what is mere form and phenomenon in the universe; for that has nothing to do with the form of the Brahman, the body of the Self, since it is not His form, but only His most external mask. Our first step therefore must be to get behind the forms of Matter, the forms of Life, the forms of Mind and go back to that which is essential, most real, nearest to actual entity. And when we have gone on thus eliminating, thus analysing all forms into the fundamental entities of the cosmos, we shall find that these fundamental entities are really only two, ourselves and the gods.

The gods of the Upanishad have been supposed to be a figure for the senses, but although they act in the senses, they are yet much more than that. They represent the divine power in its great and fundamental cosmic functionings whether in man or in mind and life and matter in general; they are not the functionings themselves but something of the Divine which is essential to their operation and its immediate possessor and cause. They are, as we see from other Upanishads, positive self-representations of the Brahman leading to good, joy, light, love, immortality as against all that is a dark negation of these things. And it is necessarily in the mind, life, senses, and speech of man that the battle here reaches its height and approaches to its full meaning. The gods seek to lead these to good and light; the Titans, sons of darkness, seek to pierce them with ignorance and evil.[3] Behind the gods is the Master-Consciousness of which they are the positive cosmic self-representations.

The other entity which represents the Brahman in the cosmos is the self of the living and thinking creature, man. This self also is not an external mask; it is not form of the mind or form of the life or form of the body. It is something that supports these and makes them possible, something that can say positively like the gods, "I am" and not only "I seem". We have then to scrutinise these two entities and see what they are in relation to each other and to the Brahman; or, as the Upanishad puts it, "That of it which is thou, that of it which is in the gods, *this* is what thy mind has to resolve." Well, but what then of the Brahman is myself? and what of the Brahman is in the Gods? The answer is evident. I am a representation in the cosmos, but for all purposes of the cosmos a real representation of the Self; and the gods are a representation in the cosmos — a real representation since without them the cosmos could not continue — of the Lord. The one supreme Self is the essentiality of all these individual existences; the one supreme Lord is the Godhead in the gods.

The Self and the Lord are one Brahman, whom we can realise through our self and realise through that which is essential in the cosmic movement. Just as our self constitutes our mind, body, life, senses, so that Self constitutes all mind, body, life, senses; it is the origin and essentiality of things. Just as the gods govern, supported by our self, the cosmos of our individual being, the action of our mind, senses and life, so the Lord governs as Mind of the mind, Sense of the sense, Life of the life, supporting His active divinity by His silent essential self-being, all cosmos and all form of being. As we have gone behind the forms of the cosmos to that which is essential in their being and movement and found our self and the gods, so we have to go behind our self and the gods and find the one supreme Self and the one supreme Godhead. Then we can say, "I think that I know."

---

[3] Chhandogya and Brihadaranyaka Upanishads.

But at once we have to qualify our assertion. I think not that I know perfectly, for that is impossible in the terms of our instruments of knowledge. I do not think for a moment that I know the Unknowable, that that can be put into the forms through which I must arrive at the Self and Lord; but at the same time I am no longer in ignorance, I know the Brahman in the only way in which I can know Him, in His self-revelation to me in terms not beyond the grasp of my psychology, manifest as the Self and the Lord. The mystery of existence is revealed in a way that utterly satisfies my being because it enables me first to comprehend it through these figures as far as it can be comprehended by me and, secondly, to enter into, to live in, to be one in law and being with and even to merge myself in the Brahman.

If we fancy that we have grasped the Brahman by the mind and in that delusion fix down our knowledge of Him to the terms our mentality has found, then our knowledge is no knowledge; it is the little knowledge that turns to falsehood. So too those who try to fix Him into our notion of the fundamental ideas in which we discern Him by the thought that rises above ordinary mental perception, have no real discernment of the Brahman, since they take certain idea-symbols for the Reality. On the other hand if we recognise that our mental perceptions are simply so many clues by which we can rise beyond mental perception and if we use these fundamental idea-symbols and the arrangement of them which our uttermost thought makes in order to go beyond the symbol to that reality, then we have rightly used mind and the higher discernment for their supreme purpose. Mind and the higher discernment are satisfied of the Brahman even in being exceeded by Him.

The mind can only reflect in a sort of supreme understanding and experience the form, the image of the supreme as He shows Himself to our mentality. Through this reflection we find, we know; the purpose of knowledge is accomplished, for we find immortality, we enter into the law, the being, the beatitude of the Brahman-consciousness. By self-realisation of Brahman as our self we find the force, the divine energy which lifts us beyond the limitation, weakness, darkness, sorrow, all-pervading death of our mortal existence; by the knowledge of the one Brahman in all beings and in all the various movement of the cosmos we attain beyond these things to the infinity, the omnipotent being, the omniscient light, the pure beatitude of that divine existence.

This great achievement must be done here in this mortal world, in this limited body; for if we do it, we arrive at our true existence and are no longer bound down to our phenomenal becoming. But if here we find it not, great is the loss and perdition; for we remain continually immersed in the phenomenal life of the mind and body and do not rise above it into the true supramental existence. Nor, if we miss it here, will death give it to us by our passage to another and less difficult world. Only those who use their awakened self and enlightened powers to distinguish and discover that One and Immortal in all existences, the all-originating self, the all-inhabiting Lord, can make the real passage which transcends life and death, can pass out of this mortal status, can press beyond and rise upward into a world-transcending immortality.

This, then, and no other is the means to be seized on and the goal to be reached. "There is no other path for the great journey." The Self and the Lord are that indeterminable, unknowable, ineffable Parabrahman and when we seek rather that which is indeterminable and unknowable to us, it is still the Self and the Lord always that we find, though by an attempt which is not the straight and possible road intended for the embodied soul seeking here to accomplish its true existence.[4] They are the self-manifested Reality which so places itself before man as the object of his highest aspiration and the fulfilment of all his activities.

_____

[4] Gita.

XIII

The Parable of the Gods

FROM its assertion of the relative knowableness of the unknowable Brahman and the justification of the soul's aspiration towards that which is beyond its present capacity and status the Upanishad turns to the question of the means by which that high-reaching aspiration can put itself into relation with the object of its search. How is the veil to be penetrated and the subject consciousness of man to enter into the master-consciousness of the Lord? What bridge is there over this gulf? Knowledge has already been pointed out as the supreme means open to us, a knowledge which begins by a sort of reflection of the true existence in the awakened mental understanding. But Mind is one of the gods; the Light behind it is indeed the greatest of the gods, Indra. Then, an awakening of all the gods through their greatest to the essence of that which they are, the one Godhead which they represent. By the mentality opening itself to the Mind of our mind, the sense and speech also will open themselves to the Sense of our sense and to the Word behind our speech and the life to the Life of our life. The Upanishad proceeds to develop this consequence of its central suggestion by a striking parable or apologue.

The gods, the powers that affirm the Good, the Light, the Joy and Beauty, the Strength and Mastery have found themselves victorious in their eternal battle with the powers that deny. It is Brahman that has stood behind the gods and conquered for them; the Master of all who guides all has thrown His deciding will into the balance, put down his darkened children and exalted the children of Light. In this victory of the Master of all the gods are conscious of a mighty development of themselves, a splendid efflorescence of their greatness in man, their joy, their light, their glory, their power and pleasure. But their vision is as yet sealed to their own deeper truth; they know of themselves, they know not the Eternal; they know the godheads, they do not know God. Therefore they see the victory as their own, the greatness as their own. This opulent efflorescence of the gods and uplifting of their greatness and light is the advance of man to his ordinary ideal of a perfectly enlightened mentality, a strong and sane vitality, a well-ordered body and senses, a harmonious, rich, active and happy life, the Hellenic ideal which the modern world holds to be our ultimate potentiality. When such an efflorescence takes place whether in the individual or the kind, the gods in man grow luminous, strong, happy; they feel they have conquered the world and they proceed to divide it among themselves and enjoy it.

But such is not the full intention of Brahman in the universe or in the creature. The greatness of the gods is His own victory and greatness, but it is only given in order that man may grow nearer to the point at which his faculties will be strong enough to go beyond themselves and realise the Transcendent. Therefore Brahman manifests Himself before the exultant gods in their well-ordered world and puts to them by His silence the heart-shaking, the world-shaking question, "If ye are all, then what am I? for see, I am and I am here." Though He manifests, He does not reveal Himself, but is seen and felt by them as a vague and tremendous presence, the Yaksha, the Daemon, the Spirit, the unknown Power, the Terrible beyond good and evil for whom good and evil are instruments towards His final self-expression. Then there is alarm and confusion in the divine assembly; they feel a demand and a menace; on the side of the evil the possibility of monstrous and appalling powers yet unknown and unmastered which may wreck the fair world they have built, upheave and shatter to pieces the brilliant harmony of the intellect, the aesthetic mind, the moral nature, the vital desires, the body and senses which they have with such labour established; on the side of the good the demand of things unknown which are beyond all these and therefore are equally a menace, since the little which is realised cannot stand against the much that is unrealised, cannot shut out the vast, the infinite that presses against the fragile walls we have erected to define and shelter our limited being and pleasure. Brahman presents itself to them as the Unknown; the gods knew not what was this Daemon. Therefore Agni first arises at their bidding to discover its nature, limits, identity. The gods of the Upanishad differ in one all-important respect from the gods of the Rig Veda; for the latter are not only powers of the One, but conscious of their source and true identity; they know the Brahman, they dwell in the supreme Godhead, their origin, home and proper plane is the superconscient Truth. It is true they manifest themselves in man in the form of human faculties and assume the appearance of human limitations, manifest themselves in the lower cosmos and assume the mould of its cosmic operations; but this is only their lesser and lower movement and beyond it they are for ever the One, the Transcendent and Wonderful, the Master of Force and Delight and Knowledge and Being. But in the Upanishads the Brahman idea has grown and cast down the gods from this high preeminence so that they appear only in their lesser human and cosmic workings. Much of their other Vedic aspects they keep. Here the three gods Indra, Vayu, Agni represent the cosmic Divine on each of its three planes, Indra on the mental, Vayu on the vital, Agni on the material. In that order, therefore, beginning from the material they approach the Brahman.

Agni is the heat and flame of the conscious force in Matter which has built up the universe; it is he who has made life and mind possible and developed them in the material universe where he is the greatest deity. Especially he is the primary impeller of speech of which Vayu is the medium and Indra the lord. This heat of conscious force in Matter is Agni Jatavedas, the knower of all births: of all things born, of every cosmic phenomenon he knows the law, the process, the limit, the relation. If then it is some mighty Birth of the cosmos that stands before them, some new indeterminate developed in the cosmic struggle and process, who shall know him, determine his limits, strength, potentialities if not Agni Jatavedas?

Full of confidence he rushes towards the object of his search and is met by the challenge "Who art thou? What is the force in thee?" His name is Agni Jatavedas, the Power that is at the basis of all birth and process in the material universe and embraces and knows their workings and the force in him is this that all that is thus born, he as the flame of Time and Death can devour. All things are his food which he assimilates and turns into material of new birth and formation. But this all-devourer cannot devour with all his force a fragile blade of grass so long as it has behind it the power of the Eternal. Agni is compelled to return, not having discovered. One thing only is settled that this Daemon is no Birth of the material cosmos, no transient thing that is subject to the flame and breath of Time; it is too great for Agni.

Another god rises to the call. It is Vayu Matarishwan, the great Life-Principle, he who moves, breathes, expands infinitely in the mother element. All things in the universe are the movement of this mighty Life; it is he who has brought Agni and placed him secretly in all existence; for him the worlds have been upbuilded that Life may move in them, that it may act, that it may riot and enjoy. If this Daemon be no birth of Matter, but some stupendous Life-force active whether in the depths or on the heights of being, who shall know it, who shall seize it in his universal expansion if not Vayu Matarishwan?

There is the same confident advance upon the object, the same formidable challenge "Who art thou? What is the force in thee?" This is Vayu Matarishwan and the power in him is this that he, the Life, can take all things in his stride and growth and seize on them for his mastery and enjoyment. But even the veriest frailest trifle he cannot seize and master so long as it is protected against him by the shield of the Omnipotent. Vayu too returns, not having discovered. One thing only is settled that this is no form or force of cosmic Life which operates within the limits of the all-grasping vital impulse; it is too great for Vayu.

Indra next arises, the Puissant, the Opulent. Indra is the power of the Mind; the senses which the Life uses for enjoyment, are operations of Indra which he conducts for knowledge and all things that Agni has upbuilt and supports and destroys in the universe are Indra's field and the subject of his functioning. If then this unknown Existence is something that the senses can grasp or, if it is something that the mind can envisage, Indra shall know it and make it part of his opulent possessions. But it is nothing that the senses can grasp or the mind envisage, for as soon as Indra approaches it, it vanishes. The mind can only envisage what is limited by Time and Space and this Brahman is that which, as the Rig Veda has said, is neither today nor tomorrow and though it moves and can be approached in the conscious being of all conscious existences, yet when the mind tries to approach it and study it in itself, it vanishes from the view of the mind. The Omnipresent cannot be seized by the senses, the Omniscient cannot be known by the mentality.

But Indra does not turn back from the quest like Agni and Vayu; he pursues his way through the highest ether of the pure mentality and there he approaches the Woman, the many-shining, Uma Haimavati; from her he learns that this Daemon is the Brahman by whom alone the gods of mind and life and body conquer and affirm themselves, and in whom alone they are great. Uma is the supreme Nature from whom the whole cosmic action takes its birth; she is the pure summit and highest power of the One who here shines out in many forms. From this supreme Nature which is also the supreme Consciousness the gods must learn their own truth; they must proceed by reflecting it in themselves instead of limiting themselves to their own lower movement. For she has the knowledge and consciousness of the One, while the lower nature of mind, life and body can only envisage the many. Although therefore Indra, Vayu and Agni are the greatest of the gods, the first coming to know the existence of the Brahman, the others approaching and feeling the touch of it, yet it is only by entering into contact with the supreme consciousness and reflecting its nature and by the elimination of the vital, mental, physical egoism so that their whole function shall be to reflect the One and Supreme that Brahman can be known by the gods in us and possessed. The conscious force that supports our embodied life must become simply and purely a reflector of that supreme Consciousness and Power of which its highest ordinary action is only a twilight figure; the Life must become a passively potent reflection and pure image of that supreme Life which is greater than all our utmost actual and potential vitality; the Mind must resign itself to be no more than a faithful mirror of the image of the superconscient Existence. By this conscious surrender of mind, life and senses to the Master of our senses, life and mind who alone really governs their action, by this turning of the cosmic existence into a passive reflection of the eternal being and a faithful reproductor of the nature of the Eternal we may hope to know and through knowledge to rise into that which is superconscient to us; we shall enter into the Silence that is master of an eternal, infinite, free and all-blissful activity.

XIV

The Transfiguration of the Self and the Gods

THE MEANS of the knowledge of Brahman are, we have seen, to get back behind the forms of the universe to that which is essential in the cosmos — and that which is essential is twofold, the gods in Nature and the self in the individual, — and then to get behind these to the Beyond which they represent. The practical relation of the gods to Brahman in this process of divine knowledge has been already determined. The cosmic functionings through which the gods act, mind, life, speech, senses, body, must become aware of something beyond them which governs them, by which they are and move, by whose force they evolve, enlarge themselves and arrive at power and joy and capacity; to that they must turn from their ordinary operations; leaving these, leaving the false idea of independent action and self-ordering which is an egoism of mind and life and sense they must become consciously passive to the power, light and joy of something which is beyond themselves. What happens then is that this divine Unnameable reflects Himself openly in the gods. His light takes possession of the thinking mind, His power and joy of the life, His light and rapture of the emotional mind and the senses. Something of the supreme image of Brahman falls upon the world-nature and changes it into divine nature.

All this is not done by a sudden miracle. It comes by flashes, revelations, sudden touches and glimpses; there is as if a leap of the lightning of revelation flaming out from those heavens for a moment and then returning into its secret source; as if the lifting of the eyelid of an inner vision and its falling again because the eye cannot look long and steadily on the utter light. The repetition of these touches and visitings from the Beyond fixes the gods in their upward gaze and expectation, constant repetition fixes them in a constant passivity; not moving out any longer to grasp at the forms of the universe mind, life and senses will more and more be fixed in the memory, in the understanding, in the joy of the touch and vision of that transcendent glory which they have now resolved to make their sole object; to that only they will learn to respond and not to the touches of outward things. The silence which has fallen on them and which is now their foundation and status will become their knowledge of the eternal silence which is Brahman; the response of their functioning to a supernal light, power, joy will become their knowledge of the eternal activity which is Brahman. Other status, other response and activity they will not know. The mind will know nothing but the Brahman, think of nothing but the Brahman, the Life will move to, embrace, enjoy nothing but the Brahman, the eye will see, the ear hear, the other senses sense nothing but the Brahman.

But is then a complete oblivion of the external the goal? Must the mind and senses recede inward and fall into an unending trance and the life be for ever stilled? This is possible, if the soul so wills, but it is not inevitable and indispensable. The Mind is cosmic, one in all the universe; so too are the Life, and the Sense, so too is Matter of the body; and when they exist in and for the Brahman only, they will not only know this but will sense, feel and live in that universal unity. Therefore to whatever thing they turn which to the individual sense and mind and life seems now external to them, there also it is not the mere form of things which they will know, think of, sense, embrace and enjoy, but always and only the Brahman. Moreover, the external will cease to exist for them, because nothing will be external but all things internal to us, even the whole world and all that is in it. For the limit of ego, the wall of individuality will break; the individual Mind will cease to know itself as individual, it will be conscious only of universal Mind one everywhere in which individuals are only knots of the one mentality; so the individual life will lose its sense of separateness and live only in and as the one life in which all individuals are simply whirls of the indivisible flood of pranic activity; the very body and senses will be no longer conscious of a separated existence, but the real body which the man will feel himself to be physically will be the whole Earth and the whole universe and the whole indivisible form of things wheresoever existent, and the senses also will be converted to this principle of sensation so that even in what we call the external, the eye will see Brahman only in every sight, the ear will hear Brahman only in every sound, the inner and outer body will feel Brahman only in every touch and the touch itself as if internal in the greater body. The soul whose gods are thus converted to this supreme law and religion, will realise in the cosmos itself and in all its multiplicity the truth of the One besides whom there is no other or second. Moreover, becoming one with the formless and infinite, it will exceed the universe itself and see all the worlds not as external, not even as commensurate with itself, but as if within it.

And in fact, in the higher realisation it will not be Mind, Life, Sense of which even the mind, life and sense themselves will be originally aware, but rather that which constitutes them. By this process of constant visiting and divine touch and influence the Mind of the mind, that is to say, the superconscient Knowledge will take possession of the mental understanding and begin to turn all its vision and thinking into luminous stuff and vibration of light of the Supermind. So too the sense will be changed by the visitings of the Sense behind the sense and the whole sense-view of the universe itself will be altered so that the vital, mental and supramental will become visible to the senses with the physical only as their last, outermost and smallest result. So too the Life will become a superlife, a conscious movement of the infinite Conscious-Force; it will be impersonal, unlimited by any particular acts and enjoyment, unbound to their results, untroubled by the dualities or the touch of sin and suffering, grandiose, boundless, immortal. The material world itself will become for these gods a figure of the infinite, luminous and blissful Superconscient.

This will be the transfiguration of the gods, but what of the self? For we have seen that there are two fundamental entities, the gods and the self, and the self in us is greater than the cosmic Powers, its God-ward destination more vital to our perfection and self-fulfilment than any transfiguration of these lesser deities. Therefore not only must the gods find their one Godhead and resolve themselves into it; that is to say, not only must the cosmic principles working in us resolve themselves into the working of the One, the Principle of all principles, so that they shall become only a unified existence and single action of That in spite of all play of differentiation, but also and with a more fundamental necessity the self in us which supports the action of the gods must find and enter into the one Self of all individual existences, the indivisible Spirit to whom all souls are no more than dark or luminous centres of its consciousness.

This the self of man, since it is the essentiality of a mental being, will do through the mind. In the gods the transfiguration is effected by the Superconscient itself visiting their substance and opening their vision with its flashes until it has transformed them; but the mind is capable of another action which is only apparently movement of mind, but really the movement of the self towards its own reality. The mind seems to go to That, to attain to it; it is lifted out of itself into something beyond and, although it falls back, still by the mind the will of knowledge in the mental thought continually and at last continuously re-members that into which it has entered. On this the Self through the mind seizes and repeatedly dwells and so doing it is finally caught up into it and at last able to dwell securely in that transcendence. It transcends the mind, it transcends its own mental individualisation of the being, that which it now knows as itself; it ascends and takes foundation in the Self of all and in the status of self-joyous infinity which is the supreme manifestation of the Self. This is the transcendent immortality, this is the spiritual existence which the Upanishads declare to be the goal of man and by which we pass out of the mortal state into the heaven of the Spirit.

What then happens to the gods and the cosmos and all that the Lord develops in His being? Does it not all disappear? Is not the transfiguration of the gods even a mere secondary state through which we pass towards that culmination and which drops away from us as soon as we reach it? And with the disappearance of the gods and the cosmos does not the Lord too, the Master-Consciousness, disappear so that nothing is left but the one pure indeterminate Existence self-blissful in an eternal inaction and non-creation? Such was the conclusion of the later Vedanta in its extreme monistic form and such was the sense which it tried to read into all the Upanishads; but it must be recognised that in the language whether of the Isha or the Kena Upanishad there is absolutely nothing, not even a shade or a nuance pointing to it. If we want to find it there, we have to put it in by force; for the actual language used favours instead the conclusion of other Vedantic systems, which considered the goal to be the eternal joy of the soul in a Brahmaloka or world of the Brahman in which it is one with the infinite existence and yet in a sense still a soul able to enjoy differentiation in the oneness.

In the next verse we have the culmination of the teaching of the Upanishad, the result of the great transcendence which it has been setting forth and afterwards the description of the immortality to which the souls of knowledge attain when they pass beyond the mortal status. It declares that Brahman is in its nature "That Delight", Tadvanam. "Vana" is the Vedic word for delight or delightful, and "Tadvanam" means therefore the transcendent Delight, the all-blissful Ananda of which the Taittiriya Upanishad speaks as the highest Brahman from which all existences are born, by which all existences live and increase and into which all existences arrive in their passing out of death and birth. It is as this transcendent Delight that the Brahman must be worshipped and sought. It is this beatitude therefore which is meant by the immortality of the Upanishads. And what will be the result of knowing and possessing Brahman as the supreme Ananda? It is that towards the knower and possessor of the Brahman is directed the desire of all creatures. In other words, he becomes a centre of the divine Delight shedding it on all the world and attracting all to it as to a fountain of joy and love and self-fulfilment in the universe.

This is the culmination of the teaching of the Upanishad;

there was a demand for the secret teaching that enters into the ultimate truth, for the "Upanishad", and in response this doctrine has been given. It has been uttered, the Upanishad of the Brahman, the hidden ultimate truth of the supreme Existence; its beginning was the search for the Lord, Master of mind, life, speech and senses in whom is the absolute of mind, the absolute of life, the absolute of speech and senses and its close is the finding of Him as the transcendent Beatitude and the elevation of the soul that finds and possesses it into a living centre of that Delight towards which all creatures in the universe shall turn as to a fountain of its ecstasies.

*

* *

The Upanishad closes with two verses which seem to review and characterise the whole work in the manner of the ancient writings when they have drawn to their close. This Upanishad or gospel of the inmost Truth of things has for its foundation, it is said, the practice of self-mastery, action and the subdual of the sense-life to the power of the Spirit. In other words, life and works are to be used as a means of arriving out of the state of subjection proper to the soul in the ignorance into a state of mastery which brings it nearer to the absolute self-mastery and all-mastery of the supreme Soul seated in the knowledge. The Vedas, that is to say, the utterances of the inspired seers and the truths they hold, are described as all the limbs of the Upanishad; in other words, all the convergent lines and aspects, all the necessary elements of this great practice, this profound psychological self-training and spiritual aspiration are set forth in these great Scriptures, channels of supreme knowledge and indicators of a supreme discipline. Truth is its home; and this Truth is not merely intellectual verity, — for that is not the sense of the word in the Vedic writings, — but man's ultimate human state of true being, true consciousness, right knowledge, right works, right joy of existence, all indeed that is contrary to the falsehood of egoism and ignorance. It is by these means, by

using works and self-discipline for mastery of oneself and for
the generation of spiritual energy, by fathoming in all its parts
the knowledge and repeating the high example of the great Vedic
seers and by living in the Truth that one becomes capable of the
great ascent which the Upanishad opens to us.

The goal of the ascent is the world of the true and vast
existence of which the Veda speaks as the Truth that is the final
goal and home of man. It is described here as the greater infinite
heavenly world, (Swargaloka, Swarloka of the Veda), which is
not the lesser Swarga of the Puranas or the lesser Brahmaloka of
the Mundaka Upanishad, its world of the sun's rays to which the
soul arrives by works of virtue and piety, but falls from them by
the exhaustion of their merit; it is the higher Swarga or Brahman-
world of the Katha which is beyond the dual symbols of birth
and death, the higher Brahman-worlds of the Mundaka which
the soul enters by knowledge and renunciation. It is therefore a
state not belonging to the Ignorance, but to Knowledge. It is, in
fact, the infinite existence and beatitude of the soul in the being
of the all-blissful existence; it is too the higher status, the light
of the Mind beyond the mind, the joy and eternal mastery of the
Life beyond the life, the riches of the Sense beyond the senses.
And the soul finds in it not only its own largeness but finds too
and possesses the infinity of the One and it has firm foundation
in that immortal state because there a supreme Silence and eternal Peace are the secure foundation of eternal Knowledge and
absolute Joy.

XV

A Last Word

WE HAVE now completed our review of this Upanishad; we have considered minutely the bearings of its successive utterances and striven to make as precise as we can to the intelligence the sense of the puissant phrases in which it gives us its leading clues to that which can never be entirely expressed by human speech. We have some idea of what it means by that Brahman, by the Mind of mind, the Life of life, the Sense of sense, the Speech of speech, by the opposition of ourselves and the gods, by the Unknowable who is yet not utterly unknowable to us, by the transcendence of the mortal state and the conquest of immortality.

Fundamentally its teaching reposes on the assertion of three states of existence, the human and mortal, the Brahman-consciousness which is the absolute of our relativities, and the utter Absolute which is unknowable. The first is in a sense a false status of misrepresentation because it is a continual term of apparent opposites and balancings where the truth of things is a secret unity; we have here a bright or positive figure and a dark or negative figure and both are figures, neither the Truth; still in that we now live and through that we have to move to the Beyond. The second is the Lord of all this dual action who is beyond it; He is the truth of Brahman and not in any way a falsehood or misrepresentation, but the truth of it as attained by us in our eternal supramental being; in Him are the absolutes of all that here we experience in partial figures. The Unknowable is beyond our grasp because though it is the same Reality, yet it exceeds even our highest term of eternal being and is beyond Existence and Non-existence; it is therefore to the Brahman, the Lord who has a relation to what we are that we must direct our search if we would attain beyond what temporarily seems to what eternally is.

The attainment of the Brahman is our escape from the mortal status into Immortality, by which we understand not the survival of death, but the finding of our true self of eternal being and bliss beyond the dual symbols of birth and death. By immortality we mean the absolute life of the soul as opposed to the transient and mutable life in the body which it assumes by birth and death and rebirth and superior also to its life as the mere mental being who dwells in the world subjected helplessly to this law of death and birth or seems at least by his ignorance to be subjected to this and to other laws of the lower Nature. To know and possess its true nature, free, absolute, master of itself and its embodiments is the soul's means of transcendence, and to know and possess this is to know and possess the Brahman. It is also to rise out of mortal world into immortal world, out of world of bondage into world of largeness, out of finite world into infinite world. It is to ascend out of earthly joy and sorrow into a transcendent Beatitude.

This must be done by the abandonment of our attachment to the figure of things in the mortal world. We must put from us its death and dualities if we would compass the unity and immortality. Therefore it follows that we must cease to make the goods of this world or even its right, light and beauty our object of pursuit; we must go beyond these to a supreme Good, a transcendent Truth, Light and Beauty in which the opposite figures of what we call evil disappear. But still, being in this world, it is only through something in this world itself that we can transcend it; it is through its figures that we must find the absolute. Therefore, we scrutinise them and perceive that there are first these forms of mind, life, speech and sense, all of them figures and imperfect suggestions, and then behind them the cosmic principles through which the One acts. It is to these cosmic principles that we must proceed and turn them from their ordinary aim and movement in the world to find their own supreme aim and absolute movement in their own one Godhead, the Lord, the Brahman; they must be drawn to leave the workings of ordinary mind and find the superconscient Mind, to leave the workings of ordinary speech and sense and find the supra-mental Sense and original Word, to leave the apparent workings of mundane Life and find the transcendent Life.

Besides the gods, there is our self, the spirit within who supports all this action of the gods. Our spirit too must turn from its absorption in its figure of itself as it sees it involved in the movement of individual life, mind, body and subject to it and must direct its gaze upward to its own supreme Self who is beyond all this movement and master of it all. Therefore the mind must indeed become passive to the divine Mind, the sense to the divine Sense, the life to the divine Life and by receptivity to constant touches and visitings of the highest be transfigured into a reflection of these transcendences; but also the individual self must through the mind's aspiration upwards, through upliftings of itself beyond, through constant memory of the supreme Reality in which during these divine moments it has lived, ascend finally into that Bliss and Power and Light.

But this will not necessarily mean the immersion into an all-oblivious Being eternally absorbed in His own inactive self-existence. For the mind, sense, life going beyond their individual formations find that they are only one centre of the sole Mind, Life, Form of things and therefore they find Brahman in that also and not only in an individual transcendence; they bring down the vision of the superconscient into that also and not only into their own individual workings. The mind of the individual escapes from its limits and becomes the one universal mind, his life the one universal life, his bodily sense the sense of the whole universe and even more as his own indivisible Brahman-body. He perceives the universe in himself and he perceives also his self in all existences and knows it to be the one, the omnipresent, the single-multiple all-inhabiting Lord and Reality. Without this realisation he has not fulfilled the conditions of immortality. Therefore it is said that what the sages seek is to distinguish and see the Brahman in all existences; by that discovery, realisation and possession of Him everywhere and in all they attain to their immortal existence.

Still although the victory of the gods, that is to say, the progressive perfection of the mind, life, body in the positive terms of good, right, joy, knowledge, power is recognised as a victory of the Brahman and the necessity of using life and human works in the world as a means of preparation and self-mastery is admitted, yet a final passing away into the infinite heavenly world or status of the Brahman-consciousness is held out as the goal. And this would seem to imply a rejection of the life of the cosmos. Well then may we ask, we the modern humanity more and more conscious of the inner warning of that which created us, be it Nature or God, that there is a work for the race, a divine purpose in its creation which exceeds the salvation of the individual soul, because the universal is as real or even more real than the individual, we who feel more and more, in the language of the Koran, that the Lord did not create heaven and earth in a jest, that Brahman did not begin dreaming this world-dream in a moment of aberration and delirium, — well may we ask whether this gospel of individual salvation is all the message even of this purer, earlier, more catholic Vedanta. If so, then Vedanta at its best is a gospel for the saint, the ascetic, the monk, the solitary, but it has not a message which the widening consciousness of the world can joyfully accept as the word for which it was waiting. For there is evidently something vital that has escaped it, a profound word of the riddle of existence from which it has turned its eyes or which it was unable or thought it not worth while to solve.

Now certainly there is an emphasis in the Upanishads increasing steadily as time goes on into an over-emphasis, on the salvation of the individual, on his rejection of the lower cosmic life. This note increases in them as they become later in date, it swells afterwards into the rejection of all cosmic life whatever and that becomes finally in later Hinduism almost the one dominant and all-challenging cry. It does not exist in the earlier Vedic revelation where individual salvation is regarded as a means towards a great cosmic victory, the eventual conquest of heaven and earth by the superconscient Truth and Bliss and those who have achieved the victory in the past are the conscious helpers of their yet battling posterity. If this earlier note is missing in the Upanishads, then, — for great as are these Scriptures, luminous, profound, sublime in their unsurpassed truth, beauty and power, yet it is only the ignorant soul that will make itself the slave of a book, — then in using them as an aid to knowledge we must insistently call back that earlier missing note, we must seek elsewhere a solution for the word of the riddle that has been ignored. The Upanishad alone of extant scriptures gives us without veil or stinting, with plenitude and a noble catholicity the truth of the Brahman; its aid to humanity is therefore indispensable. Only, where anything essential is missing, we must go beyond the Upanishads to seek it, — as for instance when we add to its emphasis on divine knowledge the indispensable ardent emphasis of the later teachings upon divine love and the high emphasis of the Veda upon divine works.

The Vedic gospel of a supreme victory in heaven and on earth for the divine in man, the Christian gospel of a kingdom of God and divine city upon earth, the Puranic idea of progressing Avataras ending in the kingdom of the perfect and the restoration of the golden Age, not only contain behind their forms a profound truth, but they are necessary to the religious sense in mankind. Without it the teaching of the vanity of human life and of a passionate fleeing and renunciation can only be powerful in passing epochs or else on the few strong souls in each age that are really capable of these things. The rest of humanity will either reject the creed which makes that its foundation or ignore it in practice while professing it in precept or else must sink under the weight of its own impotence and the sense of the illusion of life or of the curse of God upon the world as mediaeval Christendom sank into ignorance and obscurantism or later India into stagnant torpor and the pettiness of a life of aimless egoism. The promise for the individual is well but the promise for the race is also needed. Our father Heaven must remain bright with the hope of deliverance, but also our mother Earth must not feel herself for ever accursed.

It was necessary at one time to insist even exclusively on the idea of individual salvation so that the sense of a Beyond might be driven into man's mentality, as it was necessary at one time to insist on a heaven of joys for the virtuous and pious so that man might be drawn by that shining bait towards the practice of religion and the suppression of his unbridled animality. But as the lures of earth have to be conquered, so also have the lures of heaven. The lure of a pleasant Paradise of the rewards of virtue has been rejected by man; the Upanishads belittled it ages ago in India and it is now no longer dominant in the mind of the people; the similar lure in popular Christianity and popular Islam has no meaning for the conscience of modern humanity. The lure of a release from birth and death and withdrawal from the cosmic labour must also be rejected, as it was rejected by Mahayanist Buddhism which held compassion and helpfulness to be greater than Nirvana. As the virtues we practise must be done without demand of earthly or heavenly reward, so the salvation we seek must be purely internal and impersonal; it must be the release from egoism, the union with the Divine, the realisation of our universality as well as our transcendence, and no salvation should be valued which takes us away from the love of God in his manifestation and the help we can give to the world. If need be, it must be taught for a time, "Better this hell with our other suffering selves than a solitary salvation."

Fortunately, there is no need to go to such lengths and deny one side of the truth in order to establish another. The Upanishad itself suggests the door of escape from any over-emphasis in its own statement of the truth. For the man who knows and possesses the supreme Brahman as the transcendent Beatitude becomes a centre of that delight to which all his fellows shall come, a well from which they can draw the divine waters. Here is the clue that we need. The connection with the universe is preserved for the one reason which supremely justifies that connection; it must subsist not from the desire of personal earthly joy, as with those who are still bound, but for help to all creatures. Two then are the objects of the high-reaching soul, to attain the Supreme and to be for ever for the good of all the world, — even as Brahman Himself; whether here or elsewhere, does not essentially matter. Still where the struggle is thickest, there should be the hero of the spirit, that is surely the highest choice of the son of Immortality; the earth calls most, because it has most need of him, to the soul that has become one with the universe.

And the nature of the highest good that can be done is also indicated, — though other lower forms of help are not therefore excluded. To assist in the lesser victories of the gods which must prepare the supreme victory of the Brahman may well be and must be in some way or other a part of our task; but the greatest helpfulness of all is this, to be a human centre of the Light, the Glory, the Bliss, the Strength, the Knowledge of the Divine Existence, one through whom it shall communicate itself lavishly to other men and attract by its magnet of delight their souls to that which is the Highest.

Katha Upanishad

The Katha Upanishad

of the Black Yajurveda

THE FIRST CYCLE; FIRST CHAPTER

उशन् ह वै वाजश्रवसः सर्ववेदसं ददौ । तस्य ह नचिकेता नाम पुत्र
आस ॥ १ ॥

1. Vajasravasa, desiring, gave all he had. Now Vajasravasa had
a son named Nachiketas.

तं ह कुमारं सन्तं दक्षिणासु नीयमानासु श्रद्धाविवेश सोऽमन्यत ॥ २ ॥

2. As the gifts were led past, faith took possession of him who
was yet a boy unwed and he pondered:

पीतोदका जग्धतृणा दुग्धदोहा निरिन्द्रियाः ।
अनन्दा नाम ते लोकास्तान् स गच्छति ता ददत् ॥ ३ ॥

3. "Cattle that have drunk their water, eaten their grass,
yielded their milk, worn out their organs, of undelight are
the worlds which he reaches who gives such as these."

स होवाच पितरं तत कस्मै मां दास्यसीति । द्वितीयं तृतीयं तं होवाच
मृत्यवे त्वा ददामीति ॥ ४ ॥

4. He said to his father, "Me, O my father, to whom wilt thou
give?" A second time and a third he said it, and he replied,
"To Death I give thee."

बहूनामेमि प्रथमो बहूनामेमि मध्यमः ।
किं स्विद्यमस्य कर्तव्यं यन्मयाद्य करिष्यति ॥ ५ ॥

5. "Among many I walk the first, among many I walk the
midmost; something Death means to do which today by me
he will accomplish.

अनुपश्य यथा पूर्वे प्रतिपश्य तथापरे ।
सस्यमिव मर्त्य: पच्यते सस्यमिवाजायते पुन: ॥ ६ ॥

6. "Look back and see, even as were the men of old, — look round! — even so are they that have come after. Mortal man withers like the fruits of the field and like the fruits of the field he is born again."

वैश्वानर: प्रविशत्यतिथिर्ब्राह्मणो गृहान् ।
तस्यैतां शान्तिं कुर्वन्ति हर वैवस्वतोदकम् ॥ ७ ॥

His attendants say to Yama:

7. "Fire is the Brahmin who enters as a guest the houses of men; him thus they appease. Bring, O son of Vivasvan,[1] the water of the guest-rite.

आशाप्रतीक्षे संगतं सूनृतां चेष्टापूर्ते पुत्रपशूंश्च सर्वान् ।
एतद् वृङ्क्ते पुरुषस्याल्पमेधसो यस्यानश्नन् वसति ब्राह्मणो गृहे ॥ ८ ॥

8. "That man of little understanding in whose house a Brahmin dwells fasting, all his hope and his expectation and all he has gained and the good and truth that he has spoken and the wells he has dug and the sacrifices he has offered and all his sons and his cattle are torn from him by that guest unhonoured."

तिस्रो रात्रीर्यदवात्सीर्गृहे मेऽनश्नन् ब्रह्मन्नतिथिर्नमस्य: ।
नमस्तेऽस्तु ब्रह्मन् स्वस्ति मेऽस्तु तस्मात्प्रति त्रीन्वरान्वृणीष्व ॥ ९ ॥

9. "Because for three nights thou hast dwelt in my house, O Brahmin, a guest worthy of reverence, — salutation to thee, O Brahmin, on me let there be the weal, — therefore three boons do thou choose; for each night a boon."

---

[1] Yama, lord of death, is also the master of the Law in the world, and he is therefore the child of the Sun, luminous Master of Truth from which the Law is born.

शान्तसंकल्पः सुमना यथा स्याद् वीतमन्युर्गौतमो माभि मृत्यो ।
त्वत्प्रसृष्टं माभिवदेत्प्रतीत एतत् त्रयाणां प्रथमं वरं वृणे ॥ १० ॥

10. "Tranquillised in his thought and serene of mind be the
Gautama, my father, let his passion over me pass away
from him; assured in heart let him greet me from thy grasp
delivered; this boon I choose, the first of three."

यथा पुरस्ताद् भविता प्रतीत औद्दालकिरारुणिर्मत्प्रसृष्टः ।
सुखं रात्रीः शयिता वीतमन्युस्त्वां ददृशिवान्मृत्युमुखात्प्रमुक्तम् ॥ ११ ॥

11. "Even as before assured in heart and by me released shall
he be, Auddalaki Aruni, thy father; sweetly shall he sleep
through the nights and his passion shall pass away from
him, having seen thee from death's jaws delivered."

स्वर्गे लोके न भयं किंचनास्ति न तत्र त्वं न जरया बिभेति ।
उभे तीर्त्वाशनायापिपासे शोकातिगो मोदते स्वर्गलोके ॥ १२ ॥

12. "In heaven fear is not at all, in heaven, O Death, thou art
not, nor old age and its terrors; crossing over hunger and
thirst as over two rivers, leaving sorrow behind the soul in
heaven rejoices.

स त्वमग्निं स्वर्ग्यमध्येषि मृत्यो प्रब्रूहि त्वं श्रद्दधानाय मह्यम् ।
स्वर्गलोका अमृतत्वं भजन्त एतद् द्वितीयेन वृणे वरेण ॥ १३ ॥

13. "Therefore that heavenly Flame[2] which thou, O Death, stud-
iest, expound unto me, for I believe. They who win their
world of heaven, have immortality for their portion. This
for the second boon I have chosen."

प्र ते ब्रवीमि तदु मे निबोध स्वर्ग्यमग्निं नचिकेतः प्रजानन् ।
अनन्तलोकाप्तिमथो प्रतिष्ठां विद्धि त्वमेतं निहितं गुहायाम् ॥ १४ ॥

---

[2] The celestial force concealed subsciently in man's mortality by the kindling of
which and its right ordering man transcends his earthly nature; not the physical flame
of the external sacrifice to which these profound phrases are inapplicable.

14. "Hearken to me and understand, O Nachiketas; I declare
to thee that heavenly Flame, for I know it. Know this to be
the possession of infinite existence and the foundation and
the thing hidden in the secret cave of our being."

लोकादिमग्निं तमुवाच तस्मै या इष्टका यावतीर्वा यथा वा ।
स चापि तत्प्रत्यवदद् यथोक्तमथास्य मृत्युः पुनरेवाह तुष्टः ॥ १५ ॥

15. Of the Flame that is the world's beginning[3] he told him and
what are the bricks to him and how many and the way of
their setting; and Nachiketas too repeated it even as it was
told; then Death was pleased and said to him yet farther;

तमब्रवीत्प्रीयमाणो महात्मा वरं तवेहाद्य ददामि भूयः ।
तवैव नाम्ना भवितायमग्निः सृङ्कां चेमामनेकरूपां गृहाण ॥ १६ ॥

16. Yea; the Great Soul was gratified and said to him, "Yet a
farther boon today I give thee; for even by thy name shall this
Fire be called; this necklace also take unto thee, a necklace[4]
of many figures.

त्रिणाचिकेतस्त्रिभिरेत्य संधिं त्रिकर्मकृत् तरति जन्ममृत्यू ।
ब्रह्मजज्ञं देवमीड्यं विदित्वा निचाय्येमां शान्तिमत्यन्तमेति ॥ १७ ॥

17. "Whoso lights the three fires[5] of Nachiketas and comes to
union with the Three[6] and does the triple works,[7] beyond
birth and death he crosses; for he finds the God of our

---

[3] The Divine Force concealed in the subconscient is that which has originated and built
up the worlds. At the other end in the superconscient it reveals itself as the Divine Being,
Lord and Knower who has manifested Himself out of the Brahman

[4] The necklace of many figures is Prakriti, creative Nature which comes under the
control of the soul that has attained to the divine existence.

[5] Probably, the divine force utilised to raise to divinity the triple being of man.

[6] Possibly, the three Purushas, soul-states or Personalities of the divine Being, indicated
by the three letters A U M. The highest Brahman is beyond the three letters of the mystic
syllable.

[7] The sacrifice of the lower existence to the divine, consummated on the three planes
of man's physical, vital and mental consciousness.

adoration, the Knower[8] who is born from the Brahman, whom having beheld he attains to surpassing peace.

त्रिणाचिकेतस्त्रयमेतद् विदित्वा य एवं विद्वांश्चिनुते नाचिकेतम् ।
स मृत्युपाशान्पुरतः प्रणोद्य शोकातिगो मोदते स्वर्गलोके ॥ १८ ॥

18. "When a man has the three flames of Nachiketas and knows this that is Triple, when so knowing he beholds the Flame of Nachiketas, then he thrusts from in front of him the meshes of the snare of death; leaving sorrow behind him he in heaven rejoices.

एष तेऽग्निनर्नंचिकेतः स्वर्ग्यो यमवृणीथा द्वितीयेन वरेण ।
एतमग्निं तवैव प्रवक्ष्यन्ति जनासस्तृतीयं वरं नचिकेतो वृणीष्व ॥ १९ ॥

19. "This is the heavenly Flame, O Nachiketas, which thou hast chosen for the second boon; of this Flame the peoples shall speak that it is thine indeed. A third boon choose, O Nachiketas."

येयं प्रेते विचिकित्सा मनुष्येऽस्तीत्येके नायमस्तीति चैके ।
एतद् विद्यामनुशिष्टस्त्वयाहं वराणामेष वरस्तृतीयः ॥ २० ॥

20. "This debate that there is over the man who has passed and some say 'This he is not' and some that he is, that, taught by thee, I would know; this is the third boon of the boons of my choosing."

देवैरत्रापि विचिकित्सितं पुरा न हि सुज्ञेयमणुरेष धर्मः ।
अन्यं वरं नचिकेतो वृणीष्व मा मोपरोत्सीरति मा सृजैनम् ॥ २१ ॥

21. "Even by the gods was this debated of old; for it is not easy of knowledge, since very subtle is the law of it. Another boon choose, O Nachiketas; importune me not, nor urge me; this, this abandon."

---

[8] The Purusha or Divine Being, Knower of the Field, who dwells within all and for whose pleasure Prakriti fulfils the cosmic play.

देवैरत्रापि विचिकित्सितं किल त्वं च मृत्यो यन्न सुज्ञेयमात्थ ।
वक्ता चास्य त्वादृगन्यो न लभ्यो नान्यो वरस्तुल्य एतस्य
कश्चित् ॥ २२ ॥

22. "Even by the gods was this debated, it is sure, and thou
    thyself hast said that it is not easy of knowledge; never shall
    I find another like thee[9] to tell of it, nor is there any other
    boon that is its equal."

शतायुषः पुत्रपौत्रान्वृणीष्व बहून्पशून् हस्तिहिरण्यमश्वान् ।
भूमेर्महदायतनं वृणीष्व स्वयं च जीव शरदो यावदिच्छसि ॥ २३ ॥

23. "Choose sons and grandsons who shall live each a hun-
    dred years, choose much cattle and elephants and gold and
    horses; choose a mighty reach of earth and thyself live for
    as many years as thou listest.

एतत्तुल्यं यदि मन्यसे वरं वृणीष्व वित्तं चिरजीविकां च ।
महाभूमौ नचिकेतस्त्वमेधि कामानां त्वा कामभाजं करोमि ॥ २४ ॥

24. "This boon if thou deemest equal to that of thy asking,
    choose wealth and long living; possess thou, O Nachiketas,
    a mighty country; I give thee thy desire of all desirable things
    for thy portion.

ये ये कामा दुर्लभा मर्त्यलोके सर्वान्कामांश्छन्दतः प्रार्थयस्व ।
इमा रामाः सरथाः सतूर्या न हीदृशा लम्भनीया मनुष्यैः ।
आभिर्मत्प्रत्ताभिः परिचारयस्व नचिकेतो मरणं मानुप्राक्षीः ॥ २५ ॥

25. "Yea, all desires that are hard to win in the world of mortals,
    all demand at thy pleasure; lo, these delectable women with
    their chariots and their bugles, whose like are not to be
    won by men, these I will give thee; live with them for thy
    handmaidens. But of death question not, O Nachiketas."

---

[9] Yama is the knower and keeper of the cosmic Law through which the soul has to rise
by death and life to the freedom of Immortality.

श्वोभावा मर्त्यस्य यदन्तकैतत् सर्वेन्द्रियाणां जरयन्ति तेजः ।
अपि सर्वं जीवितमल्पमेव तवैव वाहास्तव नृत्यगीते ॥ २६ ॥

26. "Until the morrow mortal man has these things, O Ender, and they wear away all this keenness and glory of his senses; nay, all life is even for a little. Thine are these chariots and thine the dancing of these women and their singing.

न वित्तेन तर्पणीयो मनुष्यो लप्स्यामहे वित्तमद्राक्ष्म चेत्त्वा ।
जीविष्यामो यावदीशिष्यसि त्वं वरस्तु मे वरणीयः स एव ॥ २७ ॥

27. "Man is not to be satisfied by riches, and riches we shall have if we have beheld thee and shall live as long as thou shalt be lord of us.[10] This boon and no other is for my choosing.

अजीर्यतामम्रृतानामुपेत्य जीर्यन्मर्त्यः क्वधःस्थः प्रजानन् ।
अभिध्यायन् वर्णरतिप्रमोदानतिदीर्घे जीविते को रमेत ॥ २८ ॥

28. "Who that is a mortal man and grows old and dwells down upon the unhappy earth, when he has come into the presence of the ageless Immortals and knows, yea, who when he looks very close at beauty and enjoyment and pleasure, can take delight in overlong living?

यस्मिन्निदं विचिकित्सन्ति मृत्यो यत्सांपराये महति ब्रूहि नस्तत् ।
योऽयं वरो गूढमनुप्रविष्टो नान्यं तस्मान्नचिकेता वृणीते ॥ २९ ॥

29. "This of which they thus debate, O Death, declare to me, even that which is in the great passage; than this boon which enters in into the secret that is hidden from us, no other chooses Nachiketas."

---

[10] Life being a figure of death and Death of life, the only true existence is the infinite, divine and immortal.

The First Cycle; Second Chapter

अन्यच्छ्रेयोऽन्यदुतैव प्रेयस्ते उभे नानार्थे पुरुषं सिनीतः ।
तयोः श्रेय आददानस्य साधु भवति हीयतेऽर्थाद्य उ प्रेयो वृणीते ॥ १ ॥

Yama speaks:

1. One thing is the good and quite another thing is the pleasant,
and both seize upon a man with different meanings. Of these
whoso takes the good, it is well with him; he falls from the
aim of life who chooses the pleasant.

श्रेयश्च प्रेयश्च मनुष्यमेतस्तौ संपरीत्य विविनक्ति धीरः ।
श्रेयो हि धीरोऽभि प्रेयसो वृणीते प्रेयो मन्दो योगक्षेमाद् वृणीते ॥ २ ॥

2. The good and the pleasant come to a man and the thought-
ful mind turns all around them and distinguishes. The wise
chooses out the good from the pleasant, but the dull soul
chooses the pleasant rather than the getting of his good and
its having.

स त्वं प्रियान्प्रियरूपांश्च कामानभिध्यायन् नचिकेतोऽत्यस्राक्षीः ।
नैतां सृङ्कां वित्तमयीमवाप्तो यस्यां मज्जन्ति बहवो मनुष्याः ॥ ३ ॥

3. And thou, O Nachiketas, hast looked close at the objects of
desire, at pleasant things and beautiful, and thou hast cast
them from thee; thou hast not entered into the net of riches
in which many men sink to perdition.

दूरमेते विपरीते विषूची अविद्या या च विद्येति ज्ञाता ।
विद्याभीप्सिनं नचिकेतसं मन्ये न त्वा कामा बहवोऽलोलुपन्त ॥ ४ ॥

4. For far apart are these, opposite, divergent, the one that
is known as the Ignorance and the other the Knowledge.
But Nachiketas I deem truly desirous of the knowledge
whom so many desirable things could not make to lust after
them.

अविद्यायामन्तरे वर्तमानाः स्वयं धीराः पण्डितंमन्यमानाः ।
दन्द्रम्यमाणाः परियन्ति मूढा अन्धेनैव नीयमाना यथान्धाः ॥ ५ ॥

5. They who dwell in the ignorance, within it, wise in their own wit and deeming themselves very learned, men bewildered are they who wander about round and round circling like blind men led by the blind.

न सांपरायः प्रतिभाति बालं प्रमाद्यन्तं वित्तमोहेन मूढम् ।
अयं लोको नास्ति पर इति मानी पुनः पुनर्वशमापद्यते मे ॥ ६ ॥

6. The childish wit bewildered and drunken with the illusion of riches cannot open its eyes to see the passage to heaven; for he that thinks this world is and there is no other, comes again and again into Death's thraldom.

श्रवणायापि बहुभिर्यो न लभ्यः शृण्वन्तोऽपि बहवो यं न विद्युः ।
आश्चर्यो वक्ता कुशलोऽस्य लब्धाऽऽश्चर्यो ज्ञाता कुशलानुशिष्टः ॥ ७ ॥

7. He that is not easy even to be heard of by many, and even of those that have heard they are many who have not known Him, — a miracle is the man that can speak of Him wisely or is skilful to win Him, and when one is found, a miracle is the listener who can know God even when taught of Him by the knower.

न नरेणावरेण प्रोक्त एष सुविज्ञेयो बहुधा चिन्त्यमानः ।
अनन्यप्रोक्ते गतिरत्र नास्त्यणीयान् ह्यतर्क्यमणुप्रमाणात् ॥ ८ ॥

8. An inferior man cannot tell you of Him; for thus told thou canst not truly know Him, since He is thought of in many aspects. Yet unless told of Him by another thou canst not find thy way there to Him; for He is subtler than subtlety and that which logic cannot reach.

नैषा तर्केण मतिरापनेया प्रोक्तान्येनैव सुज्ञानाय प्रेष्ठ ।
यां त्वमापः सत्यधृतिर्बतासि त्वादृङ् नो भूयान्नचिकेतः प्रष्टा ॥ ९ ॥

9. This wisdom is not to be had by reasoning, O beloved Nachiketas; only when told thee by another it brings real knowledge, — the wisdom which thou hast gotten. Truly thou art steadfast in the Truth! Even such a questioner as thou art may I meet with always.

जानाम्यहं शेवधिरित्यनित्यं न ह्यध्रुवैः प्राप्यते हि ध्रुवं तत् ।
ततो मया नाचिकेतश्चितोऽग्निरनित्यैर्द्रव्यैः प्राप्तवानस्मि नित्यम् ॥१०॥

Nachiketas speaks:

10. I know of treasure that it is not for ever; for not by things unstable shall one attain That which is stable; therefore I heaped the fire of Nachiketas, and by the sacrifice of transitory things I won the Eternal.

कामस्याप्तिं जगतः प्रतिष्ठां क्रतोरनन्त्यमभयस्य पारम् ।
स्तोमं महदुरुगायं प्रतिष्ठां दृष्ट्वा धृत्या धीरो नचिकेतोऽत्यस्राक्षीः ॥११॥

Yama speaks:

11. When thou hast seen in thy grasp, O Nachiketas, the possession of desire and firm foundation of this world and an infinity of power and the other shore of security and praise and scope and wide moving and firm foundation,[11] wise and strong in steadfastness thou didst cast these things from thee.

तं दुर्दर्शं गूढमनुप्रविष्टं गुहाहितं गह्वरेष्ठं पुराणम् ।
अध्यात्मयोगाधिगमेन देवं मत्वा धीरो हर्षशोकौ जहाति ॥१२॥

12. Realising God by attainment to Him through spiritual Yoga, even the Ancient of Days who hath entered deep into that which is hidden and is hard to see, for he is established in our secret being and lodged in the cavern heart of things, the wise and steadfast man casts far from him joy and sorrow.

---

[11] Or, "and great fame chanted through widest regions".

एतच्छ्रुत्वा संपरिगृह्य मर्त्यः प्रवृह्य धर्म्यमणुमेतमाप्य ।
स मोदते मोदनीयं हि लब्ध्वा विवृतं सद्म नचिकेतसं मन्ये ॥ १३ ॥

13. When mortal man has heard, when he has grasped, when he has forcefully separated the Righteous One from his body and won that subtle Being, then he has delight, for he has got that which one can indeed delight in. Verily I deem of Nachiketas as a house wide open.

अन्यत्र धर्मादन्यत्राधर्मादन्यत्रास्मात् कृताकृतात् ।
अन्यत्र भूताच्च भव्याच्च यत्तत्पश्यसि तद्वद ॥ १४ ॥

Nachiketas speaks:

14. Tell me of That which thou seest otherwhere than in virtue and otherwhere than in unrighteousness, otherwhere than in the created and the uncreated, otherwhere than in that which has been and that which shall be.

सर्वे वेदा यत्पदमामनन्ति तपांसि सर्वाणि च यद्वदन्ति ।
यदिच्छन्तो ब्रह्मचर्यं चरन्ति तत्ते पदं संग्रहेण ब्रवीम्योमित्येतत् ॥ १५ ॥

Yama speaks:

15. The seat and goal that all the Vedas glorify and which all austerities declare, for the desire of which men practise holy living, of That will I tell thee in brief compass. OM is that goal, O Nachiketas.

एतद्ध्येवाक्षरं ब्रह्म एतद्ध्येवाक्षरं परम् ।
एतद्ध्येवाक्षरं ज्ञात्वा यो यदिच्छति तस्य तत् ॥ १६ ॥

16. For this Syllable is Brahman, this Syllable is the Most High: this Syllable if one know, whatsoever one shall desire, it is his.

एतदालम्बनं श्रेष्ठमेतदालम्बनं परम् ।
एतदालम्बनं ज्ञात्वा ब्रह्मलोके महीयते ॥ १७ ॥

17. This support is the best, this support is the highest, knowing

this support one grows great in the world of the Brahman.

न जायते म्रियते वा विपश्चिन्नायं कुतश्चिन्न बभूव कश्चित् ।
अजो नित्यः शाश्वतोऽयं पुराणो न हन्यते हन्यमाने शरीरे ॥ १८ ॥

18. That Wise One is not born, neither does he die; he came
not from anywhere, neither is he anyone; he is unborn, he
is everlasting, he is ancient and sempiternal, he is not slain
in the slaying of the body.

हन्ता चेन्मन्यते हन्तुं हतश्चेन्मन्यते हतम् ।
उभौ तौ न विजानीतो नायं हन्ति न हन्यते ॥ १९ ॥

19. If the slayer think that he slays, if the slain think that he is
slain, both of these have not the knowledge. This slays not,
neither is He slain.

अणोरणीयान्महतो महीयानात्मास्य जन्तोर्निहितो गुहायाम् ।
तमक्रतुः पश्यति वीतशोको धातुप्रसादान्महिमानमात्मनः ॥ २० ॥

20. Finer than the fine, huger than the huge the Self hides in
the secret heart of the creature: when a man strips himself
of will and is weaned from sorrow, then he beholds Him,
purified from the mental elements he sees the greatness of
the Self-being.

आसीनो दूरं व्रजति शयानो याति सर्वतः ।
कस्तं मदामदं देवं मदन्यो ज्ञातुमर्हति ॥ २१ ॥

21. Seated He journeys far off, lying down He goes everywhere.
Who other than I is fit to know God, even Him who is
rapture and the transcendence of rapture?

अशरीरं शरीरेष्वनवस्थेष्ववस्थितम् ।
महान्तं विभुमात्मानं मत्वा धीरो न शोचति ॥ २२ ॥

22. Realising the Bodiless in bodies, the Established in things
unsettled, the Great and Omnipresent Self, the wise and
steadfast soul grieves no longer.

नायमात्मा प्रवचनेन लभ्यो न मेधया न बहुना श्रुतेन ।
यमेवैष वृणुते तेन लभ्यस्तस्यैष आत्मा विवृणुते तनूं स्वाम् ॥ २३ ॥

23. The Self is not to be won by eloquent teaching, nor by brain
power, nor by much learning: but only he whom this being
chooses can win Him, for to him this Self bares His body.

नाविरतो दुश्चरितान्नाशान्तो नासमाहितः ।
नाशान्तमानसो वापि प्रज्ञानेनैनमाप्नुयात् ॥ २४ ॥

24. None who has not ceased from doing evil, or who is not
calm, or not concentrated in his being, or whose mind has
not been tranquillised, can by wisdom attain to Him.

यस्य ब्रह्म च क्षत्रं च उभे भवत ओदनः ।
मृत्युर्यस्योपसेचनं क इत्था वेद यत्र सः ॥ २५ ॥

25. He to whom the sages are as meat and heroes as food for
His eating and Death is an ingredient of His banquet, how
thus shall one know of Him where He abideth?

THE FIRST CYCLE; THIRD CHAPTER

ऋतं पिबन्तौ सुकृतस्य लोके गुहां प्रविष्टौ परमे परार्धे ।
छायातपौ ब्रह्मविदो वदन्ति पञ्चाग्नयो ये च त्रिणाचिकेताः ॥ १ ॥

Yama speaks:

1. There are two that drink deep of the Truth in the world
of work well accomplished: they are lodged in the secret
plane of being and in the highest kingdom of the most High
is their dwelling: as of light and shade the knowers of the
Brahman speak of them and those of the five fires and those
who have the three fires of Nachiketas.

यः सेतुरीजानानामक्षरं ब्रह्म यत्परम् ।
अभयं तितीर्षतां पारं नाचिकेतं शकेमहि ॥ २ ॥

2. May we have strength to kindle Agni Nachiketas, for he
   is the bridge of those who do sacrifice and he is Brahman
   supreme and imperishable, and the far shore of security to
   those who would cross this ocean.

आत्मानं रथिनं विद्धि शरीरं रथमेव तु।
बुद्धिं तु सारथिं विद्धि मनः प्रग्रहमेव च ॥ ३ ॥

3. Know the body for a chariot and the soul for the master of
   the chariot: know Reason for the charioteer and the mind
   for the reins only.

इन्द्रियाणि हयानाहुर्विषयांस्तेषु गोचरान्।
आत्मेन्द्रियमनोयुक्तं भोक्तेत्याहुर्मनीषिणः ॥ ४ ॥

4. The senses they speak of as the steeds and the objects of sense
   as the paths in which they move; and One yoked with Self
   and the mind and the senses is the enjoyer, say the thinkers.

यस्त्वविज्ञानवान् भवत्ययुक्तेन मनसा सदा।
तस्येन्द्रियाण्यवश्यानि दुष्टाश्वा इव सारथेः ॥ ५ ॥

5. Now he that is without knowledge with his mind ever
   unapplied, his senses are to him as wild horses and will
   not obey the driver of the chariot.

यस्तु विज्ञानवान् भवति युक्तेन मनसा सदा।
तस्येन्द्रियाणि वश्यानि सदश्वा इव सारथेः ॥ ६ ॥

6. But he that has knowledge with his mind ever applied, his
   senses are to him as noble steeds and they obey the driver.

यस्त्वविज्ञानवान् भवत्यमनस्कः सदाऽशुचिः।
न स तत्पदमाप्नोति संसारं चाधिगच्छति ॥ ७ ॥

7. Yea, he that is without knowledge and is unmindful and is
   ever unclean, reaches not that goal, but wanders in the cycle
   of phenomena.

यस्तु विज्ञानवान् भवति समनस्कः सदा शुचिः ।
स तु तत्पदमाप्नोति यस्माद् भूयो न जायते ॥ ८ ॥

8. But he that has knowledge and is mindful and pure always, reaches that goal whence he is not born again.

विज्ञानसारथिर्यस्तु मनःप्रग्रहवान् नरः ।
सोऽध्वनः पारमाप्नोति तद्विष्णोः परमं पदम् ॥ ९ ॥

9. That man who uses the mind for reins and the knowledge for the driver, reaches the end of his road, the highest seat of Vishnu.

इन्द्रियेभ्यः परा ह्यर्था अर्थेभ्यश्च परं मनः ।
मनसस्तु परा बुद्धिर्बुद्धेरात्मा महान्परः ॥ १० ॥

10. Than the senses the objects of sense are higher; and higher than the objects of sense is the Mind; and higher than the Mind is the faculty of knowledge; and than that is the Great Self higher.

महतः परमव्यक्तमव्यक्तात् पुरुषः परः ।
पुरुषान्न परं किंचित्सा काष्ठा सा परा गतिः ॥ ११ ॥

11. And higher than the Great Self is the Unmanifest and higher than the Unmanifest is the Purusha: than the Purusha there is none higher: He is the culmination, He is the highest goal of the journey.

एष सर्वेषु भूतेषु गूढोऽऽत्मा न प्रकाशते ।
दृश्यते त्वग्र्यया बुद्धा सूक्ष्मया सूक्ष्मदर्शिभिः ॥ १२ ॥

12. The secret Self in all existences does not manifest Himself to the vision: yet is He seen by the seers of the subtle by a subtle and perfect understanding.

यच्छेद् वाङ्मनसी प्राज्ञस्तद्यच्छेज्ज्ञान आत्मनि ।
ज्ञानमात्मनि महति नियच्छेत् तद्यच्छेच्छान्त आत्मनि ॥ १३ ॥

13. Let the wise man restrain speech in his mind and mind in his self of knowledge, and knowledge in the Great Self, and that again let him restrain in the Self that is at peace.

उत्तिष्ठत जाग्रत प्राप्य वरान्निबोधत ।
क्षुरस्य धारा निशिता दुरत्यया दुर्गं पथस्तत् कवयो वदन्ति ॥ १४ ॥

14. Arise, awake, find out the great ones and learn of them; for sharp as a razor's edge, hard to traverse, difficult of going is that path, say the sages.

अशब्दमस्पर्शमरूपमव्ययं तथारसं नित्यमगन्धवच्च यत् ।
अनाद्यनन्तं महतः परं ध्रुवं निचाय्य तन्मृत्युमुखात् प्रमुच्यते ॥ १५ ॥

15. That in which sound is not, nor touch, nor shape, nor diminution, nor taste, nor smell, that which is eternal, and It is without end or beginning, higher than the Great Self and stable, — that having seen, from the mouth of death there is deliverance.

नाचिकेतमुपाख्यानं मृत्युप्रोक्तं सनातनम् ।
उक्त्वा श्रुत्वा च मेधावी ब्रह्मलोके महीयते ॥ १६ ॥

16. The man of intelligence having spoken or heard the eternal story of Nachiketas wherein Death was the speaker, grows great in the world of the Brahman.

य इमं परमं गुह्यं श्रावयेद् ब्रह्मसंसदि ।
प्रयतः श्राद्धकाले वा तदानन्त्याय कल्पते ।
तदानन्त्याय कल्पत इति ॥ १७ ॥

17. He who being pure recites this supreme secret at the time of the Shraddha in the assembly of the Brahmins, that turns for him to infinite existence.

THE SECOND CYCLE; FIRST CHAPTER

परांञ्चि खानि व्यतृणत् स्वयम्भूस्तस्मात्पराङ् पश्यति नान्तरात्मन् ।
कश्चिद्धीरः प्रत्यगात्मानमैक्षदावृत्तचक्षुरमृतत्वमिच्छन् ॥ १ ॥

Yama said:

1. The Self-born hath set the doors of the body to face outward, therefore the soul of a man gazeth outward and not
   at the Self within; hardly a wise man here and there desiring
   immortality turneth his eyes inward and seeth the Self within
   him.

परांचः कामाननुयन्ति बालास्ते मृत्योर्यन्ति विततस्य पाशम् ।
अथ धीरा अमृतत्वं विदित्वा ध्रुवमध्रुवेष्विह न प्रार्थयन्ते ॥ २ ॥

2. The rest childishly follow after desire and pleasure and walk
   into the snare of Death who gapeth wide for them. But calm
   souls having learned of immortality seek not for permanence
   in the things of this world that pass and are not.

येन रूपं रसं गन्धं शब्दान् स्पर्शांश्च मैथुनान् ।
एतेनैव विजानाति किमत्र परिशिष्यते । एतद्वै तत् ॥ ३ ॥

3. By the Self one knoweth taste and form and smell, by the
   Self one knoweth sound and touch and the joy of man with
   woman; what is there left in this world of which the Self not
   knoweth? This is the thing thou seekest.

स्वप्नान्तं जागरितान्तं चोभौ येनानुपश्यति ।
महान्तं विभुमात्मानं मत्वा धीरो न शोचति ॥ ४ ॥

4. The calm soul having comprehended the great Lord, the
   omnipresent Self by whom one beholdeth both to the end
   of dream and to the end of waking, ceaseth from grieving.

य इमं मध्वदं वेद आत्मानं जीवमन्तिकात् ।
ईशानं भूतभव्यस्य न ततो विजुगुप्सते । एतद्वै तत् ॥ ५ ॥

5. He that hath known from very close this Eater of sweetness, the Jiva, the Self within that is lord of what was and what shall be, shrinketh not thereafter from aught nor abhorreth any. This is the thing thou seekest.

यः पूर्वं तपसो जातमद्भ्यः पूर्वमजायत ।
गुहां प्रविश्य तिष्ठन्तं यो भूतेभिर्व्यपश्यत । एतद्वै तत् ॥ ६ ॥

6. He is the seer that seeth Him who came into being before austerity and was before the waters; deep in the heart of the creature he seeth Him, for there He standeth by the mingling of the elements. This is the thing thou seekest.

या प्राणेन संभवत्यदितिर्देवतामयी ।
गुहां प्रविश्य तिष्ठन्तीं या भूतेभिर्व्यजायत । एतद्वै तत् ॥ ७ ॥

7. This is Aditi, the mother of the Gods, who was born through the Prana and by the mingling of the elements had her being; deep in the heart of things she has entered, there she is seated. This is the thing thou seekest.

अरण्योर्निहितो जातवेदा गर्भ इव सुभृतो गर्भिणीभिः ।
दिवे दिव ईड्यो जागृवद्भिर्हविष्मद्भिर्मनुष्येभिरग्निः ।

एतद्वै तत् ॥ ८ ॥

8. As a woman carrieth with care the unborn child in her womb, so is the Master of knowledge lodged in the tinders, and day by day should men worship him who live their waking life and stand before him with sacrifice; for he is that Agni. This is the thing thou seekest.

यतश्चोदेति सूर्योऽस्तं यत्र च गच्छति ।
तं देवाः सर्वेऽर्पितास्तदु नात्येति कश्चन । एतद्वै तत् ॥ ९ ॥

9. He from whom the sun riseth and to whom the sun returneth, and in Him are all the Gods established, — none passeth beyond Him. This is the thing thou seekest.

यदेवेह तदमुत्र यदमुत्र तदन्विह ।
मृत्योः स मृत्युमाप्नोति य इह नानेव पश्यति ॥ १० ॥

10. What is in this world is also in the other, and what is in the other, that again is in this; who thinketh he sees difference here, from death to death he goeth.

मनसैवेदमाप्तव्यं नेह नानास्ति किंचन ।
मृत्योः स मृत्युं गच्छति य इह नानेव पश्यति ॥ ११ ॥

11. Through the mind must we understand that there is nothing in this world that is really various; who thinketh he sees difference here, from death to death he goeth.

अङ्गुष्ठमात्रः पुरुषो मध्य आत्मनि तिष्ठति ।
ईशानो भूतभव्यस्य न ततो विजुगुप्सते । एतद्वै तत् ॥ १२ ॥

12. The Purusha who is seated in the midst of ourself is no larger than the finger of a man. He is the lord of what was and what shall be; Him having seen one shrinketh not from aught nor abhorreth any. This is the thing thou seekest.

अङ्गुष्ठमात्रः पुरुषो ज्योतिरिवाधूमकः ।
ईशानो भूतभव्यस्य स एवाद्य स उ श्वः । एतद्वै तत् ॥ १३ ॥

13. The Purusha that is within is no larger than the finger of a man; He is like a blazing fire that is without smoke, He is lord of His past and His future. He alone is today and He alone shall be tomorrow. This is the thing thou seekest.

यथोदकं दुर्गे वृष्टं पर्वतेषु विधावति ।
एवं धर्मान्पृथक् पश्यंस्तानेवानुविधावति ॥ १४ ॥

14. As water that raineth in the rough and difficult places, runneth to many sides on the mountain-tops, so he that seeth separate law and action of the one Spirit, followeth in the track of what he seeth.

यथोदकं शुद्धे शुद्धमासिक्तं तादृगेव भवति ।
एवं मुनेर्विजानत आत्मा भवति गौतम ॥ १५ ॥

15. But as pure water that is poured into pure water, even as it was such it remaineth, so is it with the soul of the thinker who knoweth God, O seed of Gotama.

THE SECOND CYCLE; SECOND CHAPTER

पुरमेकादशद्वारमजस्यावक्रचेतसः ।
अनुष्ठाय न शोचति विमुक्तश्च विमुच्यते । एतद्वै तत् ॥ १ ॥

Yama said:

1. The Unborn who is not devious-minded hath a city with eleven gates; when He taketh up his abode in it, He grieveth not, but when He is set free from it, that is His deliverance. This is the thing thou seekest.

हंसः शुचिषद् वसुरन्तरिक्षसद्धोता वेदिषदतिथिर्दुरोणसत् ।
नृषद्वरसदृतसद् व्योमसदब्जा गोजा ऋतजा अद्रिजा ऋतं बृहत् ॥ २ ॥

2. Lo, the Swan whose dwelling is in the purity, He is the Vasu in the interregions, the Sacrificer at the altar, the Guest in the vessel of the drinking; He is in man and in the Great Ones and His home is in the Law and His dwelling is in the firmament; He is all that is born of water and all that is born of earth and all that is born of the mountains. He is the Truth and He is the Mighty One.

ऊर्ध्वं प्राणमुन्नयत्यपानं प्रत्यगस्यति ।
मध्ये वामनमासीनं विश्वे देवा उपासते ॥ ३ ॥

3. This is He that draweth the main breath upward and casteth the lower breath downward. The Dwarf that sitteth in the centre, to Him all the Gods do homage.

अस्य विस्रंसमानस्य शरीरस्थस्य देहिनः ।
देहाद् विमुच्यमानस्य किमत्र परिशिष्यते । एतद्वै तत् ॥ ४ ॥

4. When this encased spirit that is in the body falleth away
from it, when He is freed from its casing, what is there then
that remaineth? This is the thing thou seekest.

न प्राणेन नापानेन मर्त्यो जीवति कश्चन ।
इतरेण तु जीवन्ति यस्मिन्नेतावुपाश्रितौ ॥ ५ ॥

5. Man that is mortal liveth not by the breath, no, nor by the
lower breath; but by something else we live in which both
these have their being.

हन्त त इदं प्रवक्ष्यामि गुह्यं ब्रह्म सनातनम् ।
यथा च मरणं प्राप्य आत्मा भवति गौतम ॥ ६ ॥

6. Surely, O Gautama, I will tell thee of this secret and eternal
Brahman and likewise what becometh of the soul when one
dieth.

योनिमन्ये प्रपद्यन्ते शरीरत्वाय देहिनः ।
स्थाणुमन्येऽनुसंयन्ति यथाकर्म यथाश्रुतम् ॥ ७ ॥

7. For some enter a womb to the embodying of the Spirit
and others follow after the Immovable; according to their
deeds is their goal and after the measure of their revealed
knowledge.

य एष सुप्तेषु जागर्ति कामं कामं पुरुषो निर्मिमाणः ।
तदेव शुक्रं तद् ब्रह्म तदेवामृतमुच्यते ।
तस्मिँल्लोकाः श्रिताः सर्वे तदु नात्येति कश्चन । एतद्वै तत् ॥ ८ ॥

8. This that waketh in the sleepers creating desire upon desire,
this Purusha, Him they call the Bright One, Him Brahman,
Him Immortality, and in Him are all the worlds established;
none goeth beyond Him. This is the thing thou seekest.

अग्निर्यथैको भुवनं प्रविष्टो रूपं रूपं प्रतिरूपो बभूव ।
एकस्तथा सर्वभूतान्तरात्मा रूपं रूपं प्रतिरूपो बहिश्च ॥ ९ ॥

9. Even as one Fire hath entered into the world but it shapeth
   itself to the forms it meeteth, so there is one Spirit within all
   creatures but it shapeth itself to form and form; it is likewise
   outside these.

वायुर्यथैको भुवनं प्रविष्टो रूपं रूपं प्रतिरूपो बभूव ।
एकस्तथा सर्वभूतान्तरात्मा रूपं रूपं प्रतिरूपो बहिश्च ॥ १० ॥

10. Even as one Air hath entered into the world but it shapeth
    itself to the forms it meeteth, so there is one Spirit within all
    creatures but it shapeth itself to form and form; it is likewise
    outside these.

सूर्यो यथा सर्वलोकस्य चक्षुर्न लिप्यते चाक्षुषैर्बाह्यदोषैः ।
एकस्तथा सर्वभूतान्तरात्मा न लिप्यते लोकदुःखेन बाह्यः ॥ ११ ॥

11. Even as the Sun is the eye of all this world, yet it is not soiled
    by the outward blemishes of the visual, so there is one Spirit
    within all creatures, but the sorrow of this world soils it not,
    for it is beyond grief and his danger.

एको वशी सर्वभूतान्तरात्मा एकं रूपं बहुधा यः करोति ।
तमात्मस्थं येऽनुपश्यन्ति धीरास्तेषां सुखं शाश्वतं नेतरेषाम् ॥ १२ ॥

12. One calm and controlling Spirit within all creatures that
    maketh one form into many fashions; the calm and strong
    who see Him in the self as in a mirror, theirs is eternal felicity
    and 'tis not for others.

नित्योऽनित्यानां चेतनश्चेतनानामेको बहूनां यो विदधाति कामान् ।
तमात्मस्थं येऽनुपश्यन्ति धीरास्तेषां शान्तिः शाश्वती नेतरेषाम् ॥ १३ ॥

13. The One Eternal in many transient, the One Conscious in
    many conscious beings, who being One ordereth the desires
    of many; the calm and strong who behold Him in the self
    as in a mirror, theirs is eternal peace and 'tis not for others.

तदेतदिति मन्यन्तेऽनिर्देश्यं परमं सुखम् ।
कथं नु तद्विजानीयां किमु भाति विभाति वा ॥ १४ ॥

14. "This is He," is all they can realise of Him, a highest felicity which none can point to nor any define it. How shall I know of Him whether He shineth or reflecteth one light and another?

न तत्र सूर्यो भाति न चन्द्रतारकं नेमा विद्युतो भान्ति कुतोऽयमग्निः ।
तमेव भान्तमनुभाति सर्वं तस्य भासा सर्वमिदं विभाति ॥ १५ ॥

15. There the Sun cannot shine and the moon has no lustre; all the stars are blind; there our lightnings flash not, neither any earthly fire. For all that is bright is but the shadow of His brightness and by His shining all this shineth.

THE SECOND CYCLE; THIRD CHAPTER

ऊर्ध्वमूलोऽवाक्शाख एषोऽश्वत्थः सनातनः ।
तदेव शुक्रं तद् ब्रह्म तदेवामृतमुच्यते ।
तस्मिँल्लोकाः श्रिताः सर्वे तदु नात्येति कश्चन । एतद्वै तत् ॥ १ ॥

Yama said:

1. This is the eternal uswattha tree whose roots are aloft, but its branches are downward. It is He that is called the Bright One and Brahman and Immortality, and in Him are all the worlds established; none goeth beyond Him. This is the thing thou seekest.

यदिदं किंच जगत्सर्वं प्राण एजति निःसृतम् ।
महद् भयं वज्रमुद्यतं य एतद् विदुरमृतास्ते भवन्ति ॥ २ ॥

2. All this universe of motion moveth in the Prana and from the Prana also it proceeded; a mighty terror is He, yea, a thunderbolt uplifted. Who know Him are the immortals.

भयादस्याग्निस्तपति भयात्तपति सूर्यः ।
भयादिन्द्रश्च वायुश्च मृत्युर्धावति पञ्चमः ॥ ३ ॥

3. For fear of Him the fire burneth, for fear of Him the sun giveth heat, for fear of Him Indra and Vayu and Death hasten in their courses.

इह चेदशकद्बोद्धुं प्राक् शरीरस्य विस्रसः ।
ततः सर्गेषु लोकेषु शरीरत्वाय कल्पते ॥ ४ ॥

4. If in this world of men and before thy body fall from thee, thou art able to apprehend it, then thou availest for embodiment in the worlds that are His creations.

यथादर्शे तथात्मनि यथा स्वप्ने तथा पितृलोके ।
यथाप्सु परीव ददृशे तथा गन्धर्वलोके छायातपयोरिव ब्रह्मलोके ॥ ५ ॥

5. In the self one seeth God as in a mirror but as in a dream in the world of the fathers, and as in water one seeth the surface of an object, so one seeth Him in the world of the Gandharvas; but He is seen as light and shade in the heaven of the Spirit.

इन्द्रियाणां पृथग्भावमुदयास्तमयौ च यत् ।
पृथगुत्पद्यमानानां मत्वा धीरो न शोचति ॥ ६ ॥

6. The calm soul having comprehended the separateness of the senses and the rising of them and their setting and their separate emergence putteth from him pain and sorrow.

इन्द्रियेभ्यः परं मनो मनसः सत्त्वमुत्तमम् ।
सत्त्वादधि गहानात्मा महतोऽव्यक्तमुत्तमम् ॥ ७ ॥

7. The mind is higher than the senses, and above the mind is the thought, and above the thought is the mighty Spirit, and above the Mighty One is the Unmanifest.

अव्यक्तात्तु परः पुरुषो व्यापकोऽलिङ्ग एव च ।
यं ज्ञात्वा मुच्यते जन्तुरमृतत्वं च गच्छति ॥ ८ ॥

8. But highest above the Unmanifest is the Purusha who pervadeth all and alone hath no sign nor feature. Mortal man knowing Him is released into immortality.

न संदृशे तिष्ठति रूपमस्य न चक्षुषा पश्यति कश्चनैनम् ।
हृदा मनीषा मनसाभिक्लृप्तो य एतद् विदुरमृतास्ते भवन्ति ॥ ९ ॥

9. He hath not set His body within the ken of seeing, neither doth any man with the eye behold Him, but to the heart and mind and the supermind He is manifest. Who know Him are the immortals.

यदा पञ्चावतिष्ठन्ते ज्ञानानि मनसा सह ।
बुद्धिश्च न विचेष्टति तामाहुः परमां गतिम् ॥ १० ॥

10. When the five senses cease and are at rest and the mind resteth with them and the Thought ceaseth from its workings, that is the highest state, say thinkers.

तां योगमिति मन्यन्ते स्थिरामिन्द्रियधारणाम् ।
अप्रमत्तस्तदा भवति योगो हि प्रभवाप्ययौ ॥ ११ ॥

11. The state unperturbed when the senses are imprisoned in the mind, of this they say "it is Yoga". Then man becomes very vigilant, for Yoga is the birth of things and their ending.[12]

नैव वाचा न मनसा प्राप्तुं शक्यो न चक्षुषा ।
अस्तीति ब्रुवतोऽन्यत्र कथं तदुपलभ्यते ॥ १२ ॥

12. Not with the mind hath man the power to see God, no, nor by speech nor with the eye. Unless one saith "He is," how can one become sensible of Him?

---

[12] Shankara interprets, "As Yoga hath a beginning (birth) so hath it an ending." But this is not what the Sruti says.

अस्तित्येवोपलब्ध्यव्यस्तत्त्वभावेन चोभयो: ।
अस्तित्येवोपलब्धस्य तत्त्वभाव: प्रसीदति ॥ १३ ॥

13. One must apprehend Him in the concept "He is" and also in His essential principle, but when he hath grasped Him as the Is, then the essential of Him dawneth upon a man.

यदा सर्वे प्रमुच्यन्ते कामा येऽस्य हृदि श्रिता: ।
अथ मर्त्योऽमृतो भवत्यत्र ब्रह्म समश्नुते ॥ १४ ॥

14. When every desire that harboureth in the heart of a man hath been loosened from its moorings, then this mortal putteth on immortality; even here he enjoyeth Brahman in this human body.

यदा सर्वे प्रभिद्यन्ते हृदयस्येह ग्रन्थय: ।
अथ मर्त्योऽमृतो भवत्येतावद्ध्यनुशासनम् ॥ १५ ॥

15. When all the strings of the heart are rent asunder, even here in this human birth, then the mortal becometh immortal. This is the whole teaching of the Scriptures.

शतं चैका च हृदयस्य नाड्यस्तासां मूर्धानमभिनि:सृतैका ।
तयोर्ध्वमायन्नमृतत्वमेति विश्वङ्ङन्या उत्क्रमणे भवन्ति ॥ १६ ॥

16. A hundred and one are the nerves of the heart and of all these only one issueth out through the head of a man; by this the soul mounteth up to its immortal home but the rest lead him to all sorts and conditions of births in his passing.

अङ्गुष्ठमात्र: पुरुषोऽन्तरात्मा सदा जनानां हृदये संनिविष्ट: ।
तं स्वाच्छरीरात् प्रवृहेन्मुञ्जादिवेषीकां धैर्येण ।
तं विद्याच्छुक्रममृतं तं विद्याच्छुक्रममृतमिति ॥ १७ ॥

17. The Purusha, the Spirit within, who is no larger than the finger of a man is seated for ever in the heart of creatures; one must separate Him with patience from one's own body as one separates from a blade of grass its main fibre. Thou

shalt know Him for the Bright Immortal, yea, for the Bright Immortal.

मृत्युप्रोक्तां नचिकेतोऽथ लब्ध्वा विद्यामेतां योगविधिं च कृत्स्नम् ।
ब्रह्मप्राप्तो विरजोऽभूद् विमृत्युरन्योऽप्येवं यो विदध्यात्ममेव ॥ १८ ॥

18. Thus did Nachiketas with Death for his teacher win the God-knowledge; he learned likewise the whole ordinance of the Yoga: thereafter he obtained Brahman and became void of stain and void of death. So shall another be who cometh likewise to the science of the Spirit.

shall know Him for the Bright Immortal, yea, for the bright
Immortal.

नाचिकेतमुपाख्यानं मृत्युप्रोक्तं सनातनम् ।
उक्त्वा श्रुत्वा च मेधावी ब्रह्मलोके महीयते ॥ १८ ॥

18. Thus did Nachiketas with Death for his teacher win the
God-knowledge; he learned likewise the whole ordinance
of the Yoga; thereafter he obtained Brahman, and became
void of stain and void of death. So shall another be who
cometh likewise to the science of the spirit.

Mundaka Upanishad

Mundaka Upanishad

CHAPTER ONE: SECTION I

ब्रह्मा देवानां प्रथमः संबभूव विश्वस्य कर्ता भुवनस्य गोप्ता ।
स ब्रह्मविद्यां सर्वविद्याप्रतिष्ठामथर्वाय ज्येष्ठपुत्राय प्राह ॥ १ ॥

1. Brahma first of the Gods was born, the creator of all, the
   world's protector; he to Atharvan, his eldest son, declared
   the God-knowledge in which all sciences have their foundation.

अथर्वणे यां प्रवदेत ब्रह्माथर्वा तां पुरोवाचाङ्गिरे ब्रह्मविद्याम् ।
स भारद्वाजाय सत्यवहाय प्राह भारद्वाजोऽङ्गिरसे परावराम् ॥ २ ॥

2. The God-knowledge by Brahma declared to Atharvan,
   Atharvan of old declared to Angir; he to Satyavaha the
   Bharadwaja told it, the Bharadwaja to Angiras, both the
   higher and the lower knowledge.

शौनको ह वै महाशालोऽङ्गिरसं विधिवदुपसन्नः पप्रच्छ । कस्मिन्नु
भगवो विज्ञाते सर्वमिदं विज्ञातं भवतीति ॥ ३ ॥

3. Shaunaka, the great house-lord, came to Angiras in the due
   way of the disciple and asked of him, "Lord, by knowing
   what does all this that is become known?"

तस्मै स होवाच । द्वे विद्ये वेदितव्ये इति ह स्म यद् ब्रह्मविदो वदन्ति
परा चैवापरा च ॥ ४ ॥

4. To him thus spoke Angiras: Twofold is the knowledge that
   must be known of which the knowers of the Brahman tell,
   the higher and the lower knowledge.

तत्रापरा ऋग्वेदो यजुर्वेदः सामवेदोऽथर्ववेदः शिक्षा कल्पो व्याकरणं
निरुक्तं छन्दो ज्योतिषमिति । अथ परा यया तदक्षरमधिगम्यते ॥ ५ ॥

5. Of which the lower, the Rig Veda and the Yajur Veda and the Sama Veda and the Atharva Veda, chanting, ritual, grammar, etymological interpretation, and prosody and astronomy. And then the higher by which is known the Immutable.

यत् तददृश्यमग्राह्यमगोत्रमवर्णमचक्षुःश्रोत्रं तदपाणिपादम् । नित्यं विभुं सर्वगतं सुसूक्ष्मं तदव्ययं यद् भूतयोनिं परिपश्यन्ति धीराः ॥ ६ ॥

6. That the invisible, that the unseizable, without connections, without hue, without eye or ear, that which is without hands or feet, eternal, pervading, which is in all things and impalpable, that which is Imperishable, that which is the womb of creatures sages behold everywhere.

यथोर्णनाभिः सृजते गृह्णते च यथा पृथिव्यामोषधयः संभवन्ति । यथा सतः पुरुषात्केशलोमानि तथाक्षरात्संभवतीह विश्वम् ॥ ७ ॥

7. As the spider puts out and gathers in, as herbs spring up upon the earth, as hair of head and body grow from a living man, so here all is born from the Immutable.

तपसा चीयते ब्रह्म ततोऽन्नमभिजायते । अन्नात्प्राणो मनः सत्यं लोकाः कर्मसु चामृतम् ॥ ८ ॥

8. Brahman grows by his energy at work, and then from Him is Matter born, and out of Matter life, and mind and truth and the worlds, and in works immortality.

यः सर्वज्ञः सर्वविद् यस्य ज्ञानमयं तपः । तस्मादेतद् ब्रह्म नाम रूपमन्नं च जायते ॥ ९ ॥

9. He who is the Omniscient, the all-wise, He whose energy is all made of knowledge, from Him is born this that is Brahman here, this Name and Form and Matter.

CHAPTER ONE: SECTION II

तदेतत्सत्यं मन्त्रेषु कर्माणि कवयो यान्यपश्यंस्तानि त्रेतायां बहुधा
संततानि ।
तान्याचरथ नियतं सत्यकामा एष वः पन्थाः सुकृतस्य लोके ॥ १ ॥

1. This is That, the Truth of things: works which the sages beheld in the Mantras[1] were in the Treta[2] manifoldly extended. Works do ye perform religiously with one passion for the Truth; this is your road to the heaven of good deeds.

यदा लेलायते ह्यर्चिः समिद्धे हव्यवाहने ।
तदाज्यभागावन्तरेणाहुतीः प्रतिपादयेच्छ्रद्धया हुतम् ॥ २ ॥

2. When the fire of the sacrifice is kindled and the flame sways and quivers, then between the double pourings of butter cast therein with faith thy offerings.

यस्याग्निहोत्रमदर्शमपौर्णमासमचातुर्मास्यमनाग्रयणमतिथिवर्जितं च ।
अहुतमवैश्वदेवमविधिना हुतमासप्तमांस्तस्य लोकान् हिनस्ति ॥ ३ ॥

3. For he whose altar-fires are empty of the new-moon offering and the full-moon offering and the offering of the rains and the offering of the first fruits, or unfed, or fed without right ritual, or without guests or without the dues to the Vishwa-Devas, destroys his hope of all the seven worlds.

काली कराली च मनोजवा च सुलोहिता या च सुधूम्रवर्णा ।
स्फुलिङ्गिनी विश्वरुची च देवी लेलायमाना इति सप्त जिह्वाः ॥ ४ ॥

4. Kali, the black, Karali, the terrible, Manojava, thought-swift, Sulohita, blood-red, Sudhumravarna, smoke-hued, Sphulingini, scattering sparks, Vishwaruchi, the all-beautiful, these are the seven swaying tongues of the fire.

---

[1] The inspired verses of the Veda.
[2] The second of the four ages.

एतेषु यन्नरते भ्राजमानेषु यथाकालं चाहुतयो ह्याददायन् ।
तं नयन्त्येताः सूर्यस्य रश्मयो यत्र देवानां पतिरेकोऽधिवासः ॥ ५ ॥

5. He who in these when they are blazing bright performs
the rites, in their due season, him his fires of sacrifice take
and they lead him, these rays of the Sun, there where the
Overlord of the gods is the Inhabitant on high.

एह्येहीति तमाहुतयः सुवर्चसः सूर्यस्य रश्मिभिर्यजमानं वहन्ति ।
प्रियां वाचमभिवदन्त्योऽर्चयन्त्य एष वः पुण्यः सुकृतो ब्रह्मलोकः ॥ ६ ॥

6. "Come with us", "Come with us", they cry to him, these
luminous fires of sacrifice, and they bear him by the rays of
the Sun speaking to him pleasant words of sweetness, doing
him homage, "This is your holy world of Brahman and the
heaven of your righteousness."

प्लवा ह्येते अदृढा यज्ञरूपा अष्टादशोक्तमवरं येषु कर्म ।
एतच्छ्रेयो येऽभिनन्दन्ति मूढा जरामृत्युं ते पुनरेवापि यन्ति ॥ ७ ॥

7. But frail are the ships of sacrifice, frail these forms of sacrifice, all the eighteen of them, in which are declared the lower
works; fools are they who hail them as the highest good and
they come yet again to this world of age and death.

अविद्यायामन्तरे वर्तमानाः स्वयं धीराः पण्डितंमन्यमानाः ।
जङ्घन्यमानाः परियन्ति मूढा अन्धेनैव नीयमाना यथान्धाः ॥ ८ ॥

8. They who dwell shut within the Ignorance and they hold
themselves for learned men thinking "We, even we are
the wise and the sages" — fools are they and they wander
around beaten and stumbling like blind men led by the
blind.

अविद्यायां बहुधा वर्तमाना वयं कृतार्था इत्यभिमन्यन्ति बालाः ।
यत्कर्मिणो न प्रवेदयन्ति रागात् तेनातुराः क्षीणलोकाश्च्यवन्ते ॥ ९ ॥

9. They dwell in many bonds of the Ignorance, children thinking, "We have achieved our aim of Paradise"; for when the

men of works are held by their affections, and arrive not at the Knowledge, then they are overtaken by anguish, then their Paradise wastes by enjoying and they fall from their heavens.

इष्टापूर्तं मन्यमाना वरिष्ठं नान्यच्छ्रेयो वेदयन्ते प्रमूढाः ।
नाकस्य पृष्ठे ते सुकृतेऽनुभूत्वेमं लोकं हीनतरं वा विशन्ति ॥ १० ॥

10. Minds bewildered who hold the oblation offered and the well dug for the greatest righteousness and know not any other highest good, on the back of heaven they enjoy the world won by their righteousness and enter again this or even a lower world.

तपःश्रद्धे ये ह्युपवसन्त्यरण्ये शान्ता विद्वांसो भैक्ष्यचर्यां चरन्तः ।
सूर्यद्वारेण ते विरजाः प्रयान्ति यत्रामृतः स पुरुषो ह्यव्ययात्मा ॥ ११ ॥

11. But they who in the forest follow after faith and self-discipline, calm and full of knowledge, living upon alms, cast from them the dust of their passions, and through the gate of the Sun they pass on there where is the Immortal, the Spirit, the Self undecaying and imperishable.

परीक्ष्य लोकान्कर्मचितान् ब्राह्मणो निर्वेदमायान्नास्त्यकृतः कृतेन ।
तद्विज्ञानार्थं स गुरुमेवाभिगच्छेत् समित्पाणिः श्रोत्रियं ब्रह्मनिष्ठम् ॥१२॥

12. The seeker of the Brahman, having put to the test the worlds piled up by works, arrives at world-distaste, for not by work done is reached He who is Uncreated.[3] For the knowledge of That, let him approach, fuel in hand, a Guru, one who is learned in the Veda and is devoted to contemplation of the Brahman.

तस्मै स विद्वानुपसन्नाय सम्यक् प्रशान्तचित्ताय शमान्विताय ।
येनाक्षरं पुरुषं वेद सत्यं प्रोवाच तां तत्त्वतो ब्रह्मविद्याम् ॥ १३ ॥

---

[3] Or, "He, the uncreated, lives not by that which is made." Literally, "not by the made (or, by that which is done) the Unmade (He who is uncreated)".

13. To him because he has taken entire refuge with him, with a heart tranquillised and a spirit at peace, that man of knowledge declares in its principles the science of the Brahman by which one comes to know the Immutable Spirit, the True and Real.

CHAPTER TWO: SECTION I

तदेतत्सत्यं यथा सुदीप्तात्पावकाद् विस्फुलिङ्गाः सहस्रशः प्रभवन्ते
सरूपाः ।
तथाक्षराद् विविधाः सोम्य भावाः प्रजायन्ते तत्र चैवापि यन्ति ॥ १ ॥

1. This is That, the Truth of things: as from one high-kindled fire thousands of different sparks are born and all have the same form of fire, so, O fair son, from the immutable manifold becomings are born and even into that they depart.

दिव्यो ह्यमूर्तः पुरुषः स बाह्याभ्यन्तरो ह्यजः ।
अप्राणो ह्यमनाः शुभ्रो ह्यक्षरात्परतः परः ॥ २ ॥

2. He, the divine, the formless Spirit, even he is the outward and the inward and he the Unborn; he is beyond life, beyond mind, luminous, Supreme beyond the immutable.

एतस्माज्जायते प्राणो मनः सर्वेन्द्रियाणि च ।
खं वायुज्योतिरापः पृथिवी विश्वस्य धारिणी ॥ ३ ॥

3. Life and mind and the senses are born from Him and the sky, and the wind, and light, and the waters and earth upholding all that is.

अग्निर्मूर्धा चक्षुषी चन्द्रसूर्यौ दिशः श्रोत्रे वाग् विवृताश्च वेदाः ।
वायुः प्राणो हृदयं विश्वमस्य पद्भ्यां पृथिवी ह्येष
सर्वभूतान्तरात्मा ॥ ४ ॥

4. Fire is the head of Him and his eyes are the Sun and Moon, the quarters his organs of hearing and the revealed Vedas are his voice, air is his breath, the universe is his heart, Earth lies at his feet. He is the inner Self in all beings.

तस्मादग्निः समिधो यस्य सूर्यः सोमात्पर्जन्य ओषधयः पृथिव्याम् ।
पुमान् रेतः सिञ्चति योषितायां बह्वीः प्रजाः पुरुषात्संप्रसूताः ॥ ५ ॥

5. From Him is fire, of which the Sun is the fuel, then rain

from the Soma, herbs upon the earth, and the male casts his
seed into woman: thus are these many peoples born from
the Spirit.

तस्मादृचः साम यजूंषि दीक्षा यज्ञाश्च सर्वे क्रतवो दक्षिणाश्च ।
संवत्सरश्च यजमानश्च लोकाः सोमो यत्र पवते यत्र सूर्यः ॥ ६ ॥

6. From Him are the hymns of the Rig Veda, the Sama and the
Yajur, initiation, and all sacrifices and works of sacrifice,
and dues given, the year and the giver of the sacrifice and
the worlds, on which the moon shines and the sun.

तस्माच्च देवा बहुधा संप्रसूताः साध्या मनुष्याः पशवो वयांसि ।
प्राणापानौ व्रीहियवौ तपश्च श्रद्धा सत्यं ब्रह्मचर्यं विधिश्च ॥ ७ ॥

7. And from Him have issued many gods, and demi-gods and
men and beasts and birds, the main breath and downward
breath, and rice and barley, and askesis and faith and Truth,
and chastity and rule of right practice.

सप्त प्राणाः प्रभवन्ति तस्मात्सप्तार्चिषः समिधः सप्त होमाः ।
सप्त इमे लोका येषु चरन्ति प्राणा गुहाशया निहिताः सप्त सप्त ॥ ८ ॥

8. The seven breaths are born from Him and the seven lights
and kinds of fuel and the seven oblations and these seven
worlds in which move the life-breaths set within with the
secret heart for their dwelling-place, seven and seven.

अतः समुद्रा गिरयश्च सर्वेऽस्मात्स्यन्दन्ते सिन्धवः सर्वरूपाः ।
अतश्च सर्वा ओषधयो रसश्च येनैष भूतैस्तिष्ठते ह्यन्तरात्मा ॥ ९ ॥

9. From Him are the oceans and all these mountains and from
Him flow rivers of all forms, and from Him are all plants,
and sensible delight which makes the soul to abide with the
material elements.

पुरुष एवेदं विश्वं कर्म तपो ब्रह्म परामृतम् ।
एतद्यो वेद निहितं गुहायां सोऽविद्याग्रन्थिं विकिरतीह सोम्य ॥ १० ॥

10. The Spirit is all this universe; He is works and askesis and the Brahman, supreme and immortal. O fair son, he who knows this hidden in the secret heart, scatters even here in this world the knot of the Ignorance.

CHAPTER TWO: SECTION II

आविः संनिहितं गुहाचरं नाम महत्पदमत्रैतत् समर्पितम् ।
एजत्प्राणन्निमिषच्च यदेतज्जानथ सदसद्वरेण्यं परं विज्ञानाद् यद्वरिष्ठं
प्रजानाम् ॥ १ ॥

1. Manifested, it is here set close within, moving in the secret heart, this is the mighty foundation and into it is consigned all that moves and breathes and sees. This that is that great foundation here, know, as the Is and Is-not, the supremely desirable, greatest and the Most High, beyond the knowledge of creatures.

यदर्चिमद् यदणुभ्योऽणु च यस्मिँल्लोका निहिता लोकिनश्च ।
तदेतदक्षरं ब्रह्म स प्राणस्तदु वाङ्मनः । तदेतत्सत्यं तदमृतं तद्वेद्धव्यं
सोम्य विद्धि ॥ २ ॥

2. That which is the Luminous, that which is smaller than the atoms, that in which are set the worlds and their peoples, That is This, — it is Brahman immutable: life is That, it is speech and mind. That is This, the True and Real, it is That which is immortal: it is into That that thou must pierce, O fair son, into That penetrate.

धनुर्गृहीत्वौपनिषदं महास्त्रं शरं ह्युपासानिशितं संधयीत ।
आयम्य तद्भावगतेन चेतसा लक्ष्यं तदेवाक्षरं सोम्य विद्धि ॥ ३ ॥

3. Take up the bow of the Upanishad, that mighty weapon, set to it an arrow sharpened by adoration, draw the bow with a heart wholly devoted to the contemplation of That, and O fair son, penetrate into That as thy target, even into the Immutable.

प्रणवो धनुः शरो ह्यात्मा ब्रह्म तल्लक्ष्यमुच्यते ।
अप्रमत्तेन वेद्धव्यं शरवत् तन्मयो भवेत् ॥ ४ ॥

4. OM is the bow and the soul is the arrow, and That, even the
Brahman, is spoken of as the target. That must be pierced
with an unfaltering aim; one must be absorbed into That as
an arrow is lost in its target.

यस्मिन्द्यौः पृथिवी चान्तरिक्षमोतं मनः सह प्राणैश्च सर्वैः ।
तमेवैकं जानथ आत्मानमन्या वाचो विमुञ्चथामृतस्यैष सेतुः ॥ ५ ॥

5. He in whom are inwoven heaven and earth and the mid-
region, and mind with all the life-currents, Him know to
be the one Self; other words put away from you: this is the
bridge to immortality.

अरा इव रथनाभौ संहता यत्र नाड्यः स एषोऽन्तश्चरते बहुधा
जायमानः ।
ओमित्येवं ध्यायथ आत्मानं स्वस्ति वः पाराय तमसः परस्तात् ॥ ६ ॥

6. Where the nerves are brought close together like the spokes
in the nave of a chariot-wheel, this is He that moves within,
— there is He manifoldly born. Meditate on the Self as OM
and happy be your passage to the other shore beyond the
darkness.

यः सर्वज्ञः सर्वविद् यस्यैष महिमा भुवि ।
दिव्ये ब्रह्मपुरे ह्येष व्योम्न्यात्मा प्रतिष्ठितः ॥ ७ ॥

7. The Omniscient, the All-wise, whose is this might and
majesty upon the earth, is this self enthroned in the divine
city of the Brahman, in his ethereal heaven.

मनोमयः प्राणशरीरनेता प्रतिष्ठितोऽन्ने हृदयं संनिधाय ।
तद्विज्ञानेन परिपश्यन्ति धीरा आनन्दरूपममृतं यद्विभाति ॥ ८ ॥

8. A mental being, leader of the life and the body, has set a
heart in matter, in matter he has taken his firm foundation.

By its knowing the wise see everywhere around them That which shines in its effulgence, a shape of Bliss and immortal.

भिद्यते हृदयग्रन्थिश्छिद्यन्ते सर्वसंशयाः ।
क्षीयन्ते चास्य कर्माणि तस्मिन्दृष्टे परावरे ॥ ९ ॥

9. The knot of the heart-strings is rent, cut away are all doubts, and a man's works are spent and perish, when is seen That which is at once the being below and the Supreme.

हिरण्मये परे कोशे विरजं ब्रह्म निष्कलम् ।
तच्छुभ्रं ज्योतिषां ज्योतिस्तद्यदात्मविदो विदुः ॥ १० ॥

10. In a supreme golden sheath the Brahman lies, stainless, without parts. A Splendour is That, It is the Light of Lights, It is That which the self-knowers know.

न तत्र सूर्यो भाति न चन्द्रतारकं नेमा विद्युतो भान्ति कुतोऽयमग्निः ।
तमेव भान्तमनुभाति सर्वं तस्य भासा सर्वमिदं विभाति ॥ ११ ॥

11. There the sun shines not and the moon has no splendour and the stars are blind; there these lightnings flash not, how then shall burn this earthly fire? All that shines is but the shadow of his shining; all this universe is effulgent with his light.

ब्रह्मैवेदममृतं पुरस्तात् ब्रह्म पश्चाद् ब्रह्म दक्षिणतश्चोत्तरेण ।
अधश्चोर्ध्वं च प्रसृतं ब्रह्मैवेदं विश्वमिदं वरिष्ठम् ॥ १२ ॥

12. All this is Brahman immortal, naught else; Brahman is in front of us, Brahman behind us, and to the south of us and to the north of us[4] and below us and above us; it stretches everywhere. All this is Brahman alone, all this magnificent universe.

---

[4] Or, "to the right and the left of us".

CHAPTER THREE: SECTION I

द्वा सुपर्णा सयुजा सखाया समानं वृक्षं परिषस्वजाते ।
तयोरन्यः पिप्पलं स्वाद्वत्त्यनश्नन्नन्यो अभिचाकशीति ॥ १ ॥

1. Two birds, beautiful of wing, close companions, cling to one
common tree: of the two one eats the sweet fruit of the tree,
the other eats not but watches his fellow.

समाने वृक्षे पुरुषो निमग्नोऽनीशया शोचति मुह्यमानः ।
जुष्टं यदा पश्यत्यन्यमीशमस्य महिमानमिति वीतशोकः ॥ २ ॥

2. The soul is the bird that sits immersed on the one common
tree; but because he is not lord he is bewildered and has
sorrow. But when he sees that other who is the Lord and
beloved, he knows that all is His greatness and his sorrow
passes away from him.

यदा पश्यः पश्यते रुक्मवर्णं कर्तारमीशं पुरुषं ब्रह्मयोनिम् ।
तदा विद्वान्पुण्यपापे विधूय निरञ्जनः परमं साम्यमुपैति ॥ ३ ॥

3. When, a seer, he sees the Golden-hued, the maker, the Lord,
the Spirit who is the source of Brahman,[5] then he becomes
the knower and shakes from his wings sin and virtue; pure
of all stain he reaches the supreme identity.[6]

प्राणो ह्येष यः सर्वभूतैर्विभाति विजानन् विद्वान्भवते नातिवादी ।
आत्मक्रीड आत्मरतिः क्रियावानेष ब्रह्मविदां वरिष्ठः ॥ ४ ॥

4. This is the life in things that shines manifested by all these
beings; a man of knowledge coming wholly to know this,
draws back from creeds and too much disputings. In the
Self his delight, at play in the Self, doing works, — the best
is he among the knowers of the Eternal.

---

[5] Or, "whose source is Brahman"; Shankara admits the other meaning as an alternative,
but explains it as "the source of the lower Brahman".
[6] Or, "pure of all staining tinge he reaches to a supreme equality."

सत्येन लभ्यस्तपसा ह्येष आत्मा सम्यग्ज्ञानेन ब्रह्मचर्येण नित्यम् ।
अन्तःशरीरे ज्योतिर्मयो हि शुभ्रो यं पश्यन्ति यतयः क्षीणदोषाः ॥ ५ ॥

5. The Self can always be won by truth, by self-discipline, by
   integral knowledge, by a life of purity, — this Self that is
   in the inner body, radiant, made all of light whom by the
   perishing of their blemishes the doers of askesis behold.

सत्यमेव जयते नानृतं सत्येन पन्था विततो देवयानः ।
येनाक्रमन्त्यृषयो ह्याप्तकामा यत्र तत्सत्यस्य परमं निधानम् ॥ ६ ॥

6. It is Truth that conquers and not falsehood; by Truth was
   stretched out the path of the journey of the gods, by which
   the sages winning their desire ascend there where Truth has
   its supreme abode.

बृहच्च तद्दिव्यमचिन्त्यरूपं सूक्ष्माच्च तत्सूक्ष्मतरं विभाति ।
दूरात्सुदूरे तदिहान्तिके च पश्यत्स्विहैव निहितं गुहायाम् ॥ ७ ॥

7. Vast is That, divine, its form unthinkable; it shines out subtler than the subtle:[7] very far and farther than farness, it is
   here close to us, for those who have vision it is even here in
   this world; it is here, hidden in the secret heart.

न चक्षुषा गृह्यते नापि वाचा नान्यैर्देवैस्तपसा कर्मणा वा ।
ज्ञानप्रसादेन विशुद्धसत्त्वस्ततस्तु तं पश्यते निष्कलं ध्यायमानः ॥ ८ ॥

8. Eye cannot seize, speech cannot grasp Him, nor these other
   godheads; not by austerity can he be held nor by works:
   only when the inner being is purified by a glad serenity of
   knowledge, then indeed, meditating, one beholds the Spirit
   indivisible.

एषोऽणुरात्मा चेतसा वेदितव्यो यस्मिन्प्राणः पञ्चधा संविवेश ।
प्राणैश्चित्तं सर्वमोतं प्रजानां यस्मिन्विशुद्धे विभवत्येष आत्मा ॥ ९ ॥

9. This Self is subtle and has to be known by a thought-mind

---

[7] Or, "minuter than the minute".

into which the life-force has made its fivefold entry: all the conscious heart of creatures is shot through and inwoven with the currents of the life-force and only when it is purified can this Self manifest its power.[8]

यं यं लोकं मनसा संविभाति विशुद्धसत्त्वः कामयते यांश्च कामान् ।
तं तं लोकं जयते तांश्च कामांस्तस्मादात्मज्ञं ह्यर्चयेद् भूतिकामः ॥ १० ॥

10. Whatever world the man whose inner being is purified sheds the light of his mind upon, and whatsoever desires he cherishes, that world he takes by conquest, and those desires. Then, let whosoever seeks for success and well-being approach with homage a self-knower.

CHAPTER THREE: SECTION II

स वेदैतत्परमं ब्रह्म धाम यत्र विश्वं निहितं भाति शुभ्रम् ।
उपासते पुरुषं ये ह्यकामास्ते शुक्रमेतदतिवर्तन्ति धीराः ॥ १ ॥

1. He knows this supreme Brahman as the highest abiding place in which shines out, inset, the radiant world. The wise who are without desire and worship the Spirit pass beyond this sperm.[9]

कामान् यः कामयते मन्यमानः स कामभिर्जायते तत्र तत्र ।
पर्याप्तकामस्य कृतात्मनस्तु इहैव सर्वे प्रविलीयन्ति कामाः ॥ २ ॥

2. He who cherishes desires and his mind dwells with his longings, is by his desires born again wherever they lead him, but the man who has won all his desire[10] and has found his soul, for him even here in this world vanish away all desires.

---

[8] The verb *vibhavati* seems here to have a complex sense and to mean, "to manifest its full power and pervading presence".

[9] Shankara takes it so in the sense of semen virile, which is the cause of birth into the cosmos. But it is possible that it means rather "pass beyond this brilliant universe", the radiant world which has just been spoken of, to the greater Light which is its abiding place and source, the supreme Brahman.

[10] Or, "finished with desires".

नायमात्मा प्रवचनेन लभ्यो न मेधया न बहुना श्रुतेन ।
यमेवैष वृणुते तेन लभ्यस्तस्यैष आत्मा विवृणुते तनुं स्वाम् ॥ ३ ॥

3. This Self is not won by exegesis, nor by brain-power, nor by much learning of Scripture. Only by him whom It chooses can It be won; to him this Self unveils its own body.

नायमात्मा बलहीनेन लभ्यो न च प्रमादात्तपसो वाप्यलिङ्गात् ।
एतैरुपायैर्यतते यस्तु विद्वांस्तस्यैष आत्मा विशते ब्रह्मधाम ॥ ४ ॥

4. This Self cannot be won by any who is without strength, nor with error in the seeking, nor by an askesis without the true mark: but when a man of knowledge strives by these means his self enters into Brahman, his abiding place.

संप्राप्यैनमृषयो ज्ञानतृप्ताः कृतात्मानो वीतरागाः प्रशान्ताः ।
ते सर्वगं सर्वतः प्राप्य धीरा युक्तात्मानः सर्वमेवाविशन्ति ॥ ५ ॥

5. Attaining to him, seers glad with fullness of knowledge, perfected in the Self, all passions cast from them, tranquillised, — these, the wise, come to the all-pervading from every side, and, uniting themselves with him, enter utterly the All.

वेदान्तविज्ञानसुनिश्चितार्थाः संन्यासयोगाद् यतयः शुद्धसत्त्वाः ।
ते ब्रह्मलोकेषु परान्तकाले परामृताः परिमुच्यन्ति सर्वे ॥ ६ ॥

6. Doers of askesis who have made sure of the aim[11] of the whole-knowledge of Vedanta, the inner being purified by the Yoga of renunciation, all in the hour of their last end passing beyond death are released into the worlds of the Brahman.

गताः कलाः पञ्चदश प्रतिष्ठा देवाश्च सर्वे प्रतिदेवतासु ।
कर्माणि विज्ञानमयश्च आत्मा परेऽव्यये सर्व एकीभवन्ति ॥ ७ ॥

---

[11] Or, "meaning".

7. The fifteen parts return into their foundations, and all the gods pass into their proper godheads, works and the Self of Knowledge, — all become one in the Supreme and Imperishable.

यथा नद्यः स्यन्दमानाः समुद्रेऽस्तं गच्छन्ति नामरूपे विहाय।
तथा विद्वान् नामरूपाद्विमुक्तः परात्परं पुरुषमुपैति दिव्यम् ॥ ८ ॥

8. As rivers in their flowing reach their home[12] in the ocean and cast off their names and forms, even so one who knows is delivered from name and form and reaches the Supreme beyond the Most High, even the Divine Person.

स यो ह वै तत्परमं ब्रह्म वेद ब्रह्मैव भवति नास्याब्रह्मवित् कुले भवति।
तरति शोकं तरति पाप्मानं गुहाग्रन्थिभ्यो विमुक्तोऽमृतो भवति ॥ ९ ॥

9. He, verily, who knows that Supreme Brahman becomes himself Brahman; in his lineage none is born who knows not the Brahman. He crosses beyond sorrow, he crosses beyond sin, he is delivered from the knotted cord of the secret heart and becomes immortal.

तदेतदृचाभ्युक्तम् —
क्रियावन्तः श्रोत्रिया ब्रह्मनिष्ठाः स्वयं जुह्वत एकर्षिं श्रद्धयन्तः।
तेषामेवैतां ब्रह्मविद्यां वदेत शिरोव्रतं विधिवद् यैस्तु चीर्णम् ॥ १० ॥

10. This is That declared by the Rig Veda. Doers of works, versed in the Veda, men absorbed in the Brahman, who putting their faith in the sole-seer offer themselves to him sacrifice, — to them one should speak this Brahman-knowledge, men by whom the Vow of the Head has been done according to the rite.

तदेतत्सत्यमृषिरङ्गिराः पुरोवाच नैतदचीर्णव्रतोऽधीते।
नमः परमऋषिभ्यो नमः परमऋषिभ्यः ॥ ११ ॥

---

[12] Or, "come to their end".

11. This is That, the Truth of things, which the seer Angiras spoke of old. This none learns who has not performed the Vow of the Head. Salutation to the seers supreme! Salutation to the seers supreme!

Readings in the Taittiriya Upanishad

The Knowledge of Brahman

The knower of Brahman reacheth that which is supreme.
This is that verse which was spoken; "Truth, Knowledge,
  Infinity the Brahman,
He who knoweth that hidden in the secrecy in the supreme
  ether,
Enjoyeth all desires along with the wise-thinking Brahman."

This is the burden of the opening sentences of the Taittiriya
Upanishad's second section; they begin its elucidation of the
highest truth. Or in the Sanskrit,

*brahmavid āpnoti param —
tad eṣābhyuktā — satyaṁ jñānam anantaṁ brahma —
yo veda nihitaṁ guhāyām — parame vyoman —
so 'śnute sarvān kāmān saha — brahmaṇā vipaściteti.*

But what is Brahman?

Whatever reality is in existence, by which all the rest subsists,
that is Brahman. An Eternal behind all instabilities, a Truth
of things which is implied, if it is hidden in all appearances,
a Constant which supports all mutations, but is not increased,
diminished, abrogated, — there is such an unknown *x* which
makes existence a problem, our own self a mystery, the universe
a riddle. If we were only what we seem to be to our normal self-
awareness, there would be no mystery; if the world were only
what it can be made out to be by the perceptions of the senses
and their strict analysis in the reason, there would be no riddle;
and if to take our life as it is now and the world as it has so
far developed to our experience were the whole possibility of
our knowing and doing, there would be no problem. Or at best

there would be but a shallow mystery, an easily solved riddle, the problem only of a child's puzzle. But there is more, and that more is the hidden head of the Infinite and the secret heart of the Eternal. It is the highest and this highest is the all; there is none beyond and there is none other than it. To know it is to know the highest and by knowing the highest to know all. For as it is the beginning and source of all things, so everything else is its consequence; as it is the support and constituent of all things, so the secret of everything else is explained by its secret; as it is the sum and end of all things, so everything else amounts to it and by throwing itself into it achieves the sense of its own existence.

 This is the Brahman.

*
* *

If this unknown be solely an indecipherable, only indefinable *x*, always unknown and unknowable, the hidden never revealed, the secret never opened to us, then our mystery would for ever remain a mystery, our riddle insoluble, our problem intangible. Its existence, even while it determines all we are, know and do, could yet make no practical difference to us; for our relation to it would then be a blind and helpless dependence, a relation binding us to ignorance and maintainable only by that ignorance. Or again, if it be in some way knowable, but the sole result of knowledge were an extinction or cessation of our being, then within our being it could have no consequences; the very act and fructuation of knowledge would bring the annihilation of all that we now are, not its completion or fulfilment. The mystery, riddle, problem would not be so much solved as abolished, for it would lose all its data. In effect we should have to suppose that there is an eternal and irreconcilable opposition between Brahman and what we now are, between the supreme cause and all its effects or between the supreme source and all its derivations. And it would then seem that all that the Eternal originates, all he supports, all he takes back to himself is a denial or contradiction of his being which, though in itself a negative of that which alone is, has yet in some way become a positive. The two could not coexist in consciousness; if he allowed the world to know him, it would disappear from being.

But the Eternal is knowable, He defines himself so that we may seize him, and man can become, even while he exists as man and in this world and in this body, a knower of the Brahman.

The knowledge of the Brahman is not a thing luminous but otiose, informing to the intellectual view of things but without consequence to the soul of the individual or his living; it is a knowledge that is a power and a divine compulsion to change; by it his existence gains something that now he does not possess in consciousness. What is this gain? it is this that he is conscious now in a lower state only of his being, but by knowledge he gains his highest being.

The highest state of our being is not a denial, contradiction and annihilation of all that we now are; it is a supreme accomplishment of all things that our present existence means and aims at, but in their highest sense and in the eternal values.

*

* *

To live in our present state of self-consciousness is to live and to act in ignorance. We are ignorant of ourselves, because we know as yet only that in us which changes always, from moment to moment, from hour to hour, from period to period, from life to life, and not that in us which is eternal. We are ignorant of the world because we do not know God; we are aware of the law of appearances, but not of the law and truth of being.

Our highest wisdom, our minutest most accurate science, our most effective application of knowledge can be at most a thinning of the veil of ignorance, but not a going beyond it, so long as we do not get at the fundamental knowledge and the consciousness to which that is native. The rest are effective for their own temporal purposes, but prove ineffective in the end, because they do not bring to the highest good; they lead to no permanent solution of the problem of existence.

The ignorance in which we live is not a baseless and wholesale falsehood, but at its lowest the misrepresentation of a Truth, at its highest an imperfect representation and translation into inferior and to that extent misleading values. It is a knowledge of the superficial only and therefore a missing of the secret essential which is the key to all that the superficial is striving for; a knowledge of the finite and apparent, but a missing of all that the apparent symbolises and the finite suggests; a knowledge of inferior forms, but a missing of all that our inferior life and being has above it and to which it must aspire if it is to fulfil its greatest possibilities. The true knowledge is that of the highest, the inmost, the infinite. The knower of the Brahman sees all these lower things in the light of the Highest, the external and superficial as a translation of the internal and essential, the finite from the view of the Infinite. He begins to see and know existence no longer as the thinking animal, but as the Eternal sees and knows it. Therefore he is glad and rich in being, luminous in joy, satisfied of existence.

*
* *

Knowledge does not end with knowing, nor is it pursued and found for the sake of knowing alone. It has its full value only when it leads to some greater gain than itself, some gain of being. Simply to know the eternal and to remain in the pain, struggle and inferiority of our present way of being, would be a poor and lame advantage.

A greater knowledge opens the possibility and, if really possessed, brings the actuality of a greater being. To be is the first verb which contains all the others; knowledge, action, creation, enjoyment are only a fulfilment of being. Since we are incomplete in being, to grow is our aim, and that knowledge, action, creation, enjoyment are the best which most help us to expand, grow, feel our existence.

Mere existence is not fullness of being. Being knows itself as power, consciousness, delight; a greater being means a greater power, consciousness and delight.

If by greater being we incurred only a greater pain and suffering, this good would not be worth having. Those who say that it is, mean simply that we get by it a greater sense of fulfilment which brings of itself a greater joy of the power of existence, and an extension of suffering or a loss of other enjoyment is worth having as a price for this greater sense of wideness, height and power. But this could not be the perfection of being or the highest height of its fulfilment; suffering is the seal of a lower status. The highest consciousness is integrally fulfilled in wideness and power of its existence, but also it is integrally fulfilled in delight.

The knower of Brahman has not only the joy of light, but gains something immense as the result of his knowledge, *brahmavid āpnoti.*

What he gains is that highest, that which is supreme; he gains the highest being, the highest consciousness, the highest wideness and power of being, the highest delight; *brahmavid āpnoti param.*

*
* *

The Supreme is not something aloof and shut up in itself. It is not a mere indefinable, prisoner of its own featureless absoluteness, impotent to define, create, know itself variously, eternally buried in a sleep or a swoon of self-absorption. The Highest is the Infinite and the Infinite contains the All. Whoever attains the highest consciousness, becomes infinite in being and embraces the All.

To make this clear the Upanishad has defined the Brahman as the Truth, Knowledge, Infinity and has defined the result of the knowledge of Him in the secrecy, in the cave of being, in the supreme ether as the enjoyment of all its desires by the soul of the individual in the attainment of its highest self-existence.

Our highest state of being is indeed a becoming one with Brahman in his eternity and infinity, but it is also an association

with him in delight of self-fulfilment, *aśnute saha brahmaṇā.*
And that principle of the Eternal by which this association is
possible, is the principle of his knowledge, his self-discernment
and all-discernment, the wisdom by which he knows himself
perfectly in all the world and all beings, *brahmaṇā vipaścitā.*

Delight of being is the continent of all the fulfilled values
of existence which we now seek after in the forms of desire. To
know its conditions and possess it purely and perfectly is the
infinite privilege of the eternal Wisdom.

Truth, Knowledge, Infinity

Truth, Knowledge, Infinity, not as three separate things, but in their inseparable unity, are the supernal conscious being of the Eternal. It is an infinite being, an infinite truth of being, an infinite self-knowledge of self-being. Take one of these away and the idea of the Eternal fails us; we land ourselves in half-lights, in dark or shining paradoxes without issue or in a vain exaggeration and apotheosis of isolated intellectual conceptions.

Infinity is the timeless and spaceless and causeless infinity of the eternal containing all the infinities of space and time and the endless succession which humanly we call causality. But in fact causality is only an inferior aspect and translation into mental and vital terms of something which is not mechanical causality, but the harmonies of a free self-determination of the being of the Eternal.

Truth is truth of the infinite and eternal, truth of being, and truth of becoming only as a self-expression of the being. The circumstances of the self-expression appear to the mind as the finite, but nothing is really finite except the way the mind has of experiencing all that appears to its view. All things are, each thing is the Brahman.

Knowledge is the Eternal's inalienable self-knowledge of his infinite self-existence and of all its truth and reality and, in that truth, of all things as seen not by the mind, but by the self-view of the Spirit. This knowledge is not possible to the mind; it can only be reflected inadequately by it when it is touched by a ray from the secret luminous cavern of our superconscient being; yet of that ray we can make a shining ladder to climb into the source of this supreme self-viewing wisdom.

To know the eternal Truth, Knowledge, Infinity is to know the Brahman.

*

* *

Part Two

Translations and Commentaries
from Manuscripts

These texts written between c. 1900 and 1914 were found among Sri Aurobindo's manuscripts and typescripts. He did not revise them for publication.

Section One

Introduction

On Translating the Upanishads

OM TAT SAT

This translation of a few of the simpler & more exoteric Upanishads to be followed by other sacred and philosophical writings of the Hindus not included in the Revealed Scriptures, all under the one title of the Book of God, has been effected on one definite and unvarying principle, to present to England and through England to Europe the religious message of India only in those parts of her written thought which the West is fit to hear and to present these in such a form as should be attractive & suggestive to the Occidental intellect. The first branch of this principle necessitated a rigid selection on definite lines, the second dictated the choice of a style & method of rendering which should be literary rather than literal.

The series of translations called the Sacred Books of the East, edited by the late Professor Max Muller, was executed in a scholastic and peculiar spirit. Professor Max Muller, a scholar of wide attainments, great versatility and a refreshingly active, ingenious & irresponsible fancy, has won considerable respect in India by his attachment to Vedic studies, but it must fairly be recognized that he was more of a grammarian and philologist, than a sound Sanscrit scholar. He could construe Sanscrit well enough, but he could not feel the language or realise the spirit behind the letter. Accordingly he committed two serious errors of judgment; he imagined that by sitting in Oxford and evolving new meanings out of his own brilliant fancy he could understand the Upanishads better than Shankaracharya or any other Hindu of parts and learning; and he also imagined that what was important for Europe to know about the Upanishads was what he and other European scholars considered they ought to mean. This, however, is a matter of no importance to anybody but the scholars themselves. What it is really important for Europe to know is in the first place what the Upanishads really do mean, so far as their exoteric teaching extends, and in a less degree what philosophic Hinduism took them to mean. The latter knowledge may be gathered from the commentaries of Shankaracharya and other philosophers which may be studied in the original or in the translations which the Dravidian Presidency, ignorantly called benighted by the materialists, has been issuing with a truly noble learning & high-minded enterprise. The former this book makes some attempt to convey.

But it may be asked, why these particular Upanishads alone, when there are so many others far larger in plan and of a not inferior importance? In answer I may quote a sentence from Professor Max Muller's Preface to the Sacred Books of the East. "I confess" he says "it has been for many years a problem to me, aye, and to a great extent is so still, how the Sacred Books of the East should, by the side of so much that is fresh, natural, simple, beautiful and true, contain so much that is not only unmeaning, artificial and silly, but even hideous and repellent." Now I am myself only a poor coarseminded Oriental and therefore not disposed to deny the gross physical facts of life & nature or able to see why we should scuttle them out of sight and put on a smug, respectable expression which suggests while it affects to hide their existence. This perhaps is the reason why I am somewhat at a loss to imagine what the Professor found in the Upanishads that is hideous and repellent. Still I was brought up almost from my infancy in England and received an English education, so that sometimes I have glimmerings. But as to what he intends by the unmeaning, artificial and silly elements, there can be no doubt. Everything is unmeaning in the Upanishads which the Europeans cannot understand, everything is artificial which does not come within the circle of their mental experience and everything is silly which is not explicable by European science and wisdom. Now this attitude is almost inevitable on the part of an European, for we all judge according to our lights and those who keep their minds really open, who can realise that there may be lights which are not theirs and yet as illuminating or more illuminating than theirs, are in any nation a very small handful. For the most part men are the slaves of their associations.

Let us suppose that the ceremonies & services of the Roman Catholic were not mere ceremonies and formularies, borrowed for the most part from Eastern occultisms without understanding them, — that they had been arranged so as to be perfect symbols of certain deep metaphysical truths and to produce certain effects spiritual and material according to a scientific knowledge of the power of sound over both mind and matter; let us suppose that deep philosophical works had been written in the terminology of these symbols and often in a veiled allusive language; and let us suppose finally that these were translated into Bengali or Hindustani and presented to an educated Pundit who had studied both at Calcutta & at Nuddea or Benares. What would he make of them? It will be as well to take a concrete instance. Jesus Christ was a great thinker, a man who had caught, apparently by his unaided power, though this is not certain, something of the divine knowledge, but the writers who recorded his sayings were for the most part ordinary men of a very narrow culture and scope of thought and they seem grossly to have misunderstood his deepest sayings. For instance when he said "I and my Father are one" expressing the deep truth that the human self and the divine self are identical, they imagined that he was setting up an individual claim to be God; hence the extraordinary legend of the Virgin Mary & all that followed from it. Well, we all know the story of the Last Supper and Jesus' marvellously pregnant utterance as he broke the bread and gave of the wine to his disciples "This is my body and this is my blood" and the remarkable rite of the Eucharist and the doctrine of Transubstantiation which the Roman Catholic Church has founded upon it. "Corruption! superstition! blasphemous nonsense!" cries the Protestant. "Only a vivid Oriental metaphor and nothing more." If so, it was certainly an "unmeaning, artificial and silly" metaphor, nay, "even a hideous and repellent" one. But I prefer to believe that Jesus' words had always a meaning & generally a true & beautiful one. On the other hand the Transubstantiation doctrine is one which the Catholics themselves do not understand, it is to them a "mystery". And yet how plain the meaning is to an Oriental intelligence! The plasm of matter, the foodsheath of the universe to which bread and wine belong, is indeed the blood and body of God and typifies the great primal sacrifice by which God crucified himself so that the world might exist. The Infinite had to become finite, the Unconditioned to condition himself, Spirit to evolve matter. In the bread and the wine which the communicant eats, God actually is but he is not present to our consciousness, and he only becomes so present by an act of faith; this is the whole doctrine of the Transubstantiation. For as the Upanishad says, we must believe in God before we can know him; we must realise him as the "He is" before we realise him in his essential. And indeed if the child had not believed in what his teacher or his book told him, how could the grown man know anything? But if a deep philosophical work were written on the Eucharist hinting at great truths but always using the symbol of the bread and wine and making its terminology from the symbol & from the doctrine of Transubstantiation based upon the symbol, what would our Hindu Pundit make of it? Being a scholar & philosopher, he would find there undoubtedly much that was fresh, natural, simple, beautiful & true but also a great deal that was unmeaning, artificial & silly & even to his vegetarian imagination hideous & repellent. As for the symbol itself, its probable effect on the poor vegetarian would be to make him vomit. "What hideous nonsense," says the Protestant, "we are to believe that we are eating God!" But that is exactly what the Protestant himself does believe if he is sincere & not a parrot when he says "God is everywhere", which is true enough, though it would be truer to say everything is in God. If God is everywhere, He must be in the food we eat. Not only is God the eaten, but He is the eater and eventually, says the Vedanta, when you come to the bottom fact of existence there is neither eaten or eater, but all is God. These are hard sayings for the rationalist who insists on limiting knowledge within the circle of the five senses. "God to whom the sages are as meat & princes as excellent eating & Death is the spice of his banquet, how shall such an one know of Him where He abideth?"

Many of the Upanishads are similarly written round symbols and in a phraseology and figures which have or had once a deep meaning and a sacred association to the Hindus but must be unintelligible and repellent to the European. What possible use can be served by presenting to Europe such works as the Chandogya or Aitareya Upanishads in which even the majority of Hindus find it difficult or impossible to penetrate every symbol to its underlying truth? Only the few Upanishads have been selected which contain the kernel of the matter in the least technical and most poetical form; the one exception is the Upanishad of the Questions which will be necessarily strange and not quite penetrable to the European mind. It was, however, necessary to include it for the sake of a due presentation of Upanishad philosophy in some of its details as well as in its main ideas, and its technical element has a more universal appeal than that of the Chandogya or Taittiriya.

An objection may be urged to the method of translation that has been adopted. Professor Max Muller in his translation did not make any attempt to render into English the precise shades of Aryan philosophical terms like Atman & Prana which do not correspond to any philosophical conception familiar to the West; he believed that the very unfamiliarity of the terms he used to translate them would be like a bracing splash of cold water to the mind forcing it to rouse itself and think. In this I think the Professor was in error; his proposition may be true of undaunted philosophical intellects such as Schopenhauer's or of those who are already somewhat familiar with the Sanscrit language, but to the ordinary reader the unfamiliar terminology forms a high & thick hedge of brambles shutting him off from the noble palace & beautiful gardens of the Upanishads. Moreover the result of a scholastic faithfulness to the letter has been to make the style of the translation intolerably uncouth and unworthy of the solemn rhythmic grandeur and ineffable poetical depth and beauty of these great religious poems. I do not say that this translation is worthy of them, for in no other human tongue than Sanscrit is such grandeur & beauty possible. But there are ways and their degrees. For instance *Étadwaitad*, the refrain of the

Katha Upanishad has a deep & solemn ring in Sanscrit because *étad* and *tad* so used have in Sanscrit a profound and grandiose philosophical signification which everybody at once feels; but in English "This truly is That" can be nothing but a juggling with demonstrative pronouns; it is far better and renders more nearly both rhythm & meaning to translate "This is the God of your seeking" however inadequate such a translation may be.

It may, however, fairly be said that a version managed on these lines cannot give a precise & accurate idea of the meaning. It is misleading to translate Prâna sometimes by life, sometimes by breath, sometimes by life breath or breath of life, because breath & life are merely subordinate aspects of the Prâna. Atman again rendered indifferently by soul, spirit & self, must mislead, because what the West calls the soul is really the Atman yoked with mind & intelligence, and spirit is a word of variable connotation often synonymous with soul; even "self" cannot be used precisely in that way in English. Again the Hindu idea of "immortality" is different from the European; it implies not life after death, but freedom from both life and death, for what we call life is after all impossible without death. Similarly Being does not render *Purusha*, nor "matter" *rayi*, nor askesis the whole idea of "tapas". To a certain extent all this may be admitted, but at the same time I do not think that any reader who can think & feel will be seriously misled, and at any rate he will catch more of the meaning from imperfect English substitutes than from Sanscrit terms which will be a blank to his intelligence. The mind of man demands, and the demand is legitimate, that new ideas shall be presented to him in words which convey to him some association, with which he will not feel like a foreigner in a strange country where no one knows his language nor he theirs. The new must be presented to him in the terms of the old; new wine must be put to some extent in old bottles. What is the use of avoiding the word "God" and speaking always of the Supreme as "It" simply because the Sanscrit usually, — but not, be it observed, invariably — employs the neuter gender? The neuter in Sanscrit applies not only to what is inanimate but to what is beyond such terms as animate and inanimate, not only to what is below gender but to what is above gender. In English this is not the case. The use of "It" may therefore lead to far more serious misconceptions than to use the term "God" & the pronoun "He". When Matthew Arnold said that God was a stream of tendency making towards righteousness, men naturally scoffed because it seemed to turn God into an inanimate force; yet surely such was not Arnold's meaning. On the other side if the new ideas are presented with force and power, a reader of intelligence will soon come to understand that something different is meant by "God" from the ideas he attaches to that word. And in the meanwhile we gain this distinct advantage that he has not been repelled at the outset by what would naturally seem to him bizarre, repulsive or irreverent.

It is true however that this translation will not convey a precise, full and categorical knowledge of the truths which underlie the Upanishads. To convey such knowledge is not the object of this translation, neither was it the object of the Upanishads themselves. It must always be remembered that these great treatises are simply the gate of the Higher Knowledge; there is much that lies behind the gate. Srikrishna has indeed said that the knowledge in the Vedas is sufficient for a holy mind that is capable of knowing God, just as the water in a well is sufficient for a man's purpose though there may be whole floods of water all around. But this does not apply to ordinary men. The ordinary man who wishes to reach God through knowledge, must undergo an elaborate training. He must begin by becoming absolutely pure, he must cleanse thoroughly his body, his heart and his intellect, he must get himself a new heart and be born again; for only the twiceborn can understand or teach the Vedas. When he has done this he needs yet four things before he can succeed, the Sruti or recorded revelation, the Sacred Teacher, the practice of Yoga and the Grace of God. The business of the Sruti and especially of the Upanishads is to seize the mind and draw it into a magic circle, to accustom it to the thought of God and aspirations after the Supreme, to bathe it in certain ideas, surround it with a certain spiritual atmosphere; for this purpose it plunges & rolls the mind over & over in an ocean of marvellous sound thro' which a certain train of associations goes ever rolling. In other words it appeals through the intellect, the ear and the imagination to the soul. The purpose of the Upanishad cannot therefore be served by a translation; a translation at best prepares him for & attracts him to the original. But even when he has steeped himself in the original, he may have understood what the Upanishad suggests, but he has not understood all that it implies, the great mass of religious truth that lies behind, of which the Upanishad is but a hint or an echo. For this he must go to the Teacher. "Awake ye, arise & learn of God seeking out the Best who have the knowledge." Hard is it in these days to find the Best; for the Best do not come to us, we have to show our sincerity, patience and perseverance by seeking them. And when we have heard the whole of the Brahmavidya from the Teacher, we still know of God by theory only; we must farther learn from a preceptor the practical knowledge of God, the vision of Him and attainment of Him which is Yoga and the goal of Yoga. And even in that we cannot succeed unless we have the Grace of God, for Yoga is beset with temptations not the least of which are the powers it gives us, powers which the ignorant call supernatural. "Then must a man be very vigilant for Yoga, as it hath a beginning, so hath it an ending." Only the Grace of God, the blessing of triumphant self-mastery that comes from long and patient accumulation of soul-experience, can keep us firm and help us over these temptations. "The Spirit is not to be won by eloquent teaching, nor by brain power, nor by much learning: but he whom the Spirit chooseth, he getteth the Spirit, and to him God discovereth His body." Truly does the Upanishad say "for sharp as a razor's edge is the path, difficult & hard to traverse, say the seers." Fortunately it is not necessary & indeed it is not possible for all to measure the whole journey in a single life, nor can we, or should we abandon our daily duties like Buddha and flee into the mountain or the forest. It is enough for us to make a beginning.

Section Two

Complete Translations

Circa 1900–1902

                    The Upanishads

rendered into simple and rhythmic English.

(comprising six Upanishads namely the Isha, Kena,Katha,

Moondaca,Prusna, and Mandoukya).

Swulpumupyusya dhurmusya trayate mahato bhayat

                            Bhagavudgeta.

Even a little of this Law delivereth one out of great fear

                    X

Quãl chella par quand un poco sorride
Non si pйò dicer ne tener a mente,
Si è novo miracolo gentile.

                    Dante

What She appears when She smiles a little,
Cannot be spoken of, neither can the mind lay hold on it,
It is so sweet and strange and sublime a miracle.

                ---0:0:0:---------

The Prusna Upanishad
of the Athurvaveda

being the Upanishad of the Six Questions.

Before which one repeats the Mantra.

ॐ भद्रं कर्णेभिः शृणुयाम देवा भद्रं पश्येमाक्षभिर्यजत्राः ।
स्थिरैरङ्गैस्तुष्टुवांसस्तनूभिर्व्यशेम देवहितं यदायुः ॥
स्वस्ति न इन्द्रो वृद्धश्रवाः स्वस्ति नः पूषा विश्ववेदाः ।
स्वस्ति नस्ताक्ष्यर्यो अरिष्टनेमिः स्वस्ति नो बृहस्पतिर्दधातु ॥
ॐ शान्तिः शान्तिः शान्तिः ॥

OM. May we hear what is auspicious with our ears, O ye Gods;
may we see what is auspicious with our eyes, O ye of the sacrifice;
giving praise with steady limbs, with motionless bodies, may we
enter into that life which is founded in the Gods.

Ordain weal unto us Indra of high-heaped glories; ordain
weal unto us Pushan, the all-knowing Sun; ordain weal unto
us Tarkshya Arishtanemi; Brihaspati ordain weal unto us. OM.
Peace! peace! peace!

Then the Chapter of the First Question.

ॐ नमः परमात्मने । हरिः ॐ ॥ सुकेशा च भारद्वाजः शैव्यश्च
सत्यकामः सौर्यायणी च गार्ग्यः कौसल्यश्चाश्वलायनो भार्गवो वैदर्भिः
कबन्धी कात्यायनस्ते हैते ब्रह्मपरा ब्रह्मनिष्ठाः परं ब्रह्मान्वेषमाणा
एष ह वै तत्सर्वं वक्ष्यतीति ते ह समित्पाणयो भगवन्तं पिप्पलादमुप -
सन्नाः ॥ १ ॥

1. OM! Salutation to the Supreme Spirit. The Supreme is
OM.
Sukesha the Bharadwaja; the Shaivya, Satyakama; Gargya,

son of the Solar race; the Coshalan, son of Uswal; the Bhargove of Vidurbha; and Cobundhy Catyaian; — these sought the Most High God, believing in the Supreme and to the Supreme devoted. Therefore they came to the Lord Pippalada, for they said "This is he that shall tell us of that Universal."

तान् ह स ऋषिरुवाच भूय एव तपसा ब्रह्मचर्येण श्रद्धया संवत्सरं संवत्स्यथ यथाकामं प्रश्नान्पृच्छत यदि विज्ञास्यामः सर्वं ह वो वक्ष्याम इति ॥ २ ॥

2. The Rishi said to them, "Another year do ye dwell in holiness and faith and askesis; then ask what ye will, and if I know, surely I will conceal nothing."

अथ कबन्धी कात्यायन उपेत्य पप्रच्छ। भगवन् कुतो ह वा इमाः प्रजाः प्रजायन्त इति ॥ ३ ॥

3. Then came Cobundhy, son of Katya, to him and asked: "Lord, whence are all these creatures born?"

तस्मै स होवाच प्रजाकामो वै प्रजापतिः स तपोऽतप्यत स तपस्तप्त्वा स मिथुनमुत्पादयते रयिं च प्राणं चेत्येतौ मे बहुधा प्रजाः करिष्यत इति ॥ ४ ॥

4. To him answered the Rishi Pippalada: "The Eternal Father desired children, therefore he put forth his energy and by the heat of his energy produced twin creatures, Prana the Life, who is Male, and Rayi the Matter, who is Female. 'These' said he 'shall make for me children of many natures.'

आदित्यो ह वै प्राणो रयिरेव चन्द्रमा रयिर्वा एतत्सर्वं यन्मूर्तं चामूर्तं च तस्मान्मूर्तिरेव रयिः ॥ ५ ॥

5. "The Sun verily is Life and the Moon is no more than Matter; yet truly all this Universe formed and formless is Matter; therefore Form and Matter are One.

अथादित्य उदयन् यत्प्राचीं दिशं प्रविशति तेन प्राच्यान्प्राणान् रश्मिषु
संनिधत्ते । यद्दक्षिणां यत्प्रतीचीं यदुदीचीं यदधो यदूर्ध्वं यदन्तरा दिशो
यत्सर्वं प्रकाशयति तेन सर्वान्प्राणान् रश्मिषु संनिधत्ते ॥ ६ ॥

6. "Now when the Sun rising entereth the East, then absorbeth
he the eastern breaths into his rays. But when he illumineth
the south and west and north, and below and above and all
the angles of space, yea, all that is, then he taketh all the
breaths into his rays.

स एष वैश्वानरो विश्वरूपः प्राणोऽग्निरुदयते । तदेतदृचाभ्युक्तम् ॥ ७ ॥

7. "Therefore is this fire that riseth, this Universal Male, of
whom all things are the bodies, Prana the breath of existence. This is that which was said in the Rigveda.

विश्वरूपं हरिणं जातवेदसं परायणं ज्योतिरेकं तपन्तम् ।
सहस्ररश्मिः शतधा वर्तमानः प्राणः प्रजानामुदयत्येष सूर्यः ॥ ८ ॥

8. "'Fire is this burning and radiant Sun, he is the One lustre
and all-knowing Light, he is the highest heaven of spirits.
With a thousand rays he burneth and existeth in a hundred
existences; lo this Sun that riseth, he is the Life of all his
creatures.'

संवत्सरो वै प्रजापतिस्तस्यायने दक्षिणं चोत्तरं च । तद्ये ह वै तदिष्टापूर्ते
कृतमित्युपासते ते चान्द्रमसमेव लोकमभिजयन्ते । त एव पुनरावर्तन्ते
तस्मादेत ऋषयः प्रजाकामा दक्षिणं प्रतिपद्यन्ते । एष ह वै रयिर्यः
पितृयाणः ॥ ९ ॥

9. "The year also is that Eternal Father and of the year there
are two paths, the northern solstice and the southern. Now
they who worship God with the well dug and the oblation
offered, deeming these to be righteousness, conquer their
heavens of the Moon; these return again to the world of
birth. Therefore do the souls of sages who have not yet
put from them the desire of offspring, take the way of the
southern solstice which is the road of the Fathers. And this
also is Matter, the Female.

अथोत्तरेण तपसा ब्रह्मचर्येण श्रद्धया विद्ययात्मानमन्विष्यादित्यमभि-
जयन्ते। एतद्वै प्राणानामायतनमेतदमृतमभयमेतत् परायणमेतस्मान्न
पुनरावर्तन्त इत्येष निरोधस्तदेष श्लोकः॥ १०॥

10. "But by the way of the northern solstice go the souls that
have sought the Spirit through holiness and knowledge and
faith and askesis; for they conquer their heavens of the Sun.
There is the resting place of the breaths, there immortality
casteth out fear, there is the highest heaven of spirits; thence
no soul returneth; therefore is the wall and barrier. Whereof
this is the Scripture.

पञ्चपादं पितरं द्वादशाकृतिं दिव आहुः परे अर्धे पुरीषिणम्।
अथेमे अन्य उ परे विचक्षणं सप्तचक्रे षडर आहुरर्पितमिति॥ ११॥

11. "'Five-portioned, some say, is the Father and hath twelve
figures and he floweth in the upper hemisphere beyond
the heavens; but others speak of him as the Wisdom who
standeth in a chariot of six spokes and seven wheels.'

मासो वै प्रजापतिस्तस्य कृष्णपक्ष एव रयिः शुक्लः प्राणस्तस्मादेत
ऋषयः शुक्ल इष्टं कुर्वन्तीतर इतरस्मिन्॥ १२॥

12. "The month also is that Eternal Father, whereof the dark
fortnight is Matter the Female and the bright fortnight is Life
the Male. Therefore do one manner of sages offer sacrifice
in the bright fortnight and another in the dark.

अहोरात्रो वै प्रजापतिस्तस्याहरेव प्राणो रात्रिरेव रयिः प्राणं वा एते
प्रस्कन्दन्ति ये दिवा रत्या संयुज्यन्ते ब्रह्मचर्यमेव तद्यद् रात्रौ रत्या
संयुज्यन्ते॥ १३॥

13. "Day and night also are the Eternal Father, whereof the day
is Life and the night is Matter. Therefore do they offend
against their own life who take joy with woman by day; by
night who take joy, enact holiness.

अन्नं वै प्रजापतिस्ततो ह वै तद् रेतस्तस्मादिमाः प्रजाः प्रजायन्त
इति॥ १४॥

14. "Food is the Eternal Father; for of this came the seed and of the seed is the world of creatures born.

तद्ये ह वै तत्प्रजापतिव्रतं चरन्ति ते मिथुनमुत्पादयन्ते । तेषामेवैष ब्रह्मलोको येषां तपो ब्रह्मचर्यं येषु सत्यं प्रतिष्ठितम् ॥ १५ ॥

15. "They therefore who perform the vow of the Eternal Father produce the twin creature. But theirs is the heaven of the spirit in whom are established askesis and holiness and in whom Truth has her dwelling.

तेषामसौ विरजो ब्रह्मलोको न येषु जिह्ममनृतं न माया चेति ॥ १६ ॥

16. "Theirs is the heaven of the Spirit, the world all spotless, in whom there is neither crookedness nor lying nor any illusion."

And afterwards
The Chapter of the Second Question.

अथ हैनं भार्गवो वैदर्भिः पप्रच्छ । भगवन् कत्येव देवाः प्रजां वि-धारयन्ते कतर एतत्प्रकाशयन्ते कः पुनरेषां वरिष्ठ इति ॥ १ ॥

1. Then the Bhargove, the Vidurbhan, asked him: "Lord, how many Gods maintain this creature, and how many illumine it, and which of these again is the mightiest?"

तस्मै स होवाचाकाशो ह वा एष देवो वायुरग्निरापः पृथिवी वाङ्मनश्चक्षुः श्रोत्रं च । ते प्रकाश्याभिवदन्ति वयमेतद् बाणमवष्टभ्य विधारयामः ॥ २ ॥

2. To him answered the Rishi Pippalada: "These are the Gods, even Ether and Wind and Fire and Water and Earth and Speech and Mind and Sight and Hearing. These nine illumine the creature; therefore they vaunted themselves, — We, even we support this harp of God and we are the preservers.

तान् वरिष्ठः प्राण उवाच । मा मोहमापद्यथाहमेवैतत् पञ्चधात्मानं प्रविभज्यैतद् बाणमवष्टभ्य विधारयामीति तेऽश्रद्धाना बभूवुः ॥ ३ ॥

3. "Then answered Breath, their mightiest: 'Yield not unto delusion; I dividing myself into this fivefold support this harp of God, I am its preserver.' But they believed him not.

सोऽभिमानादूर्ध्वमुत्क्रमत इव तस्मिन्नुत्क्रामत्यथेतरे सर्व एवोत्क्रामन्ते तस्मिंश्च प्रतिष्ठमाने सर्व एव प्रातिष्ठन्ते । तद्यथा मक्षिका मधुकर-राजानमुत्क्रामन्तं सर्वा एवोत्क्रामन्ते तस्मिंश्च प्रतिष्ठमाने सर्वा एव प्रातिष्ठन्त एवं वाङ्मनश्चक्षुः श्रोत्रं च ते प्रीताः प्राणं स्तुवन्ति ॥ ४ ॥

4. "Therefore offended he rose up, he was issuing out from the body. But when the Breath goeth out, then go all the others with him, and when the Breath abideth all the others abide; therefore as bees with the kingbee: when he goeth out all go out with him, and when he abideth all abide, even so was it with Speech and Mind and Sight and Hearing; then were they well-pleased and hymned the Breath to adore him.

एषोऽग्निस्तपत्येष सूर्य एष पर्जन्यो मघवानेष वायुः ।
एष पृथिवी रयिर्देवः सदसच्चामृतं च यत् ॥ ५ ॥

5. "'Lo this is he that is Fire and the Sun that burneth, Rain and Indra and Earth and Air, Matter and Deity, Form and Formless, and Immortality.

अरा इव रथनाभौ प्राणे सर्वं प्रतिष्ठितम् ।
ऋचो यजूंषि सामानि यज्ञः क्षत्रं ब्रह्म च ॥ ६ ॥

6. "'As the spokes meet in the nave of a wheel, so are all things in the Breath established, the Rigveda and the Yajur and the Sama, and Sacrifice and Brahminhood and Kshatriyahood.

प्रजापतिश्चरसि गर्भे त्वमेव प्रतिजायसे ।
तुभ्यं प्राण प्रजास्त्विमा बलिं हरन्ति यः प्राणैः प्रतितिष्ठसि ॥ ७ ॥

7. "'As the Eternal Father thou movest in the womb and art born in the likeness of the parents. To thee, O Life, the world of creatures offer the burnt offering, who by the breaths abidest.

देवानामसि वह्नितमः पितॄणां प्रथमा स्वधा ।
ऋषीणां चरितं सत्यमथर्वाङ्गिरसामसि ॥ ८ ॥

8. "'Of all the Gods thou art the strongest and fiercest and to
the fathers thou art the first oblation; thou art the truth and
virtue of the sages and thou art Athurvan among the sons
of Ungirus.

इन्द्रस्त्वं प्राण तेजसा रुद्रोऽसि परिरक्षिता ।
त्वमन्तरिक्षे चरसि सूर्यस्त्वं ज्योतिषां पतिः ॥ ९ ॥

9. "'Thou art Indra, O Breath, by thy splendour and energy
and Rudra because thou preservest; thou walkest in the
welkin as the Sun, that imperial lustre.

यदा त्वमभिवर्षस्यथेमाः प्राण ते प्रजाः ।
आनन्दरूपास्तिष्ठन्ति कामायान्नं भविष्यतीति ॥ १० ॥

10. "'When thou, O Breath, rainest, thy creatures stand all joy
because there shall be grain to the heart's desire.

व्रात्यस्त्वं प्राणैकर्षिरत्ता विश्वस्य सत्पतिः ।
वयमाद्यस्य दातारः पिता त्वं मातरिश्व नः ॥ ११ ॥

11. "'Thou art, O Breath, the unpurified and thou art Fire, the
only purity, the devourer of all and the lord of existences. We
are the givers to thee of thy eating; for thou, O Matariswun,
art our Father.

या ते तनूर्वाचि प्रतिष्ठिता या श्रोत्रे या च चक्षुषि ।
या च मनसि संतता शिवां तां कुरु मोत्क्रमीः ॥ १२ ॥

12. "'That body of thine which is established in the speech,
sight and hearing, and in the mind is extended, that make
propitious; O Life, go not out from our midst!

प्राणस्येदं वशे सर्वं त्रिदिवे यत्प्रतिष्ठितम् ।
मातेव पुत्रान् रक्षस्व श्रीश्च प्रज्ञां च विधेहि न इति ॥ १३ ॥

13. "'For all this Universe, yea, all that is established in the heavens to the Breath is subject; guard us as a mother watches over her little children; give us fortune and beauty, give us Wisdom.'"

And afterwards
The Chapter of the Third Question.

अथ हैनं कौसल्यश्चाश्वलायनः पप्रच्छ। भगवन् कुत एष प्राणो
जायते कथमायात्यस्मिञ्शरीर आत्मानं वा प्रविभज्य कथं प्रतिष्ठते
केनोत्क्रमते कथं बाह्यमभिधत्ते कथमध्यात्ममिति ॥ १ ॥

1. Then the Coshalan, the son of Uswal, asked him: "Lord, whence is this Life born? How comes it in this body or how stands by self-division? By what departeth, or how maintaineth the outward and how the inward spiritual?"

तस्मै स होवाचातिप्रश्नान् पृच्छसि ब्रह्मिष्ठोऽसीति तस्मात् तेऽहं
ब्रवीमि ॥ २ ॥

2. To him answered the Rishi Pippalada: "Many and difficult things thou askest; but because thou art very holy, therefore will I tell thee.

आत्मन एष प्राणो जायते। यथैषा पुरुषे छायैतस्मिन्नेतदाततं
मनोकृतेनायात्यस्मिञ्शरीरे ॥ ३ ॥

3. "Of the Spirit is this breath of Life born; even as a shadow is cast by a man, so is this Life extended in the Spirit and by the action of the Mind it entereth into this body.

गथा सग्राडेवापिवृत्तान् विनियुङ्क्ते। एतान्ग्रामानेतान्ग्रामानधितिष्ठ -
स्वेत्येवमेवैष प्राण इतरान्प्राणान् पृथक्पृथगेव संनिधत्ते ॥ ४ ॥

4. "As an Emperor commandeth his officers, and he sayeth to one 'Govern for me these villages', and to another 'Govern for me these others', so this breath, the Life, appointeth the other breaths each in his province.

पायूपस्थेऽपानं चक्षुःश्रोत्रे मुखनासिकाभ्यां प्राणः स्वयं प्रातिष्ठते मध्ये
तु समानः। एष ह्येतद्धुतमन्नं समं नयति तस्मादेताः सप्तार्चिषो
भवन्ति॥ ५॥

5. "In the anus and the organ of pleasure is the lower breath,
   and in the eyes and the ears, the mouth and the nose, the
   main breath itself is seated; but the medial breath is in the
   middle. This is he that equally distributeth the burnt offering
   of food; for from this are the seven fires born.

हृदि ह्येष आत्मा। अत्रैतदेकशतं नाडीनां तासां शतं शतमेकैक-
स्यां द्वासप्ततिर्द्वासप्ततिः प्रतिशाखानाडीसहस्राणि भवन्त्यासु व्यान-
श्चरति॥ ६॥

6. "The Spirit in the heart abideth, and in the heart there
   are one hundred and one nerves, and each nerve hath a
   hundred branch-nerves and each branch-nerve hath seventy
   two thousand sub-branch-nerves; through these the breath
   pervasor moveth.

अथैकयोर्ध्व उदानः पुण्येन पुण्यं लोकं नयति पापेन पापमुभाभ्यामेव
मनुष्यलोकम्॥ ७॥

7. "Of these many there is one by which the upper breath
   departeth that by virtue taketh to the heaven of virtue, by
   sin to the hell of sin, and by mingled sin and righteousness
   back to the world of men restoreth.

आदित्यो ह वै बाह्यः प्राण उदयत्येष ह्येनं चाक्षुषं प्राणमनुगृह्णानः।
पृथिव्यां या देवता सैषा पुरुषस्यापानमवष्टभ्यान्तरा यदाकाशः स
समानो वायुर्व्यानः॥ ८॥

8. "The Sun is the main breath outside this body, for it cherisheth the eye in its rising. The divinity in the earth, she
   attracteth the lower breath of man, and the ether between
   is the medial breath; air is the breath pervasor.

तेजो ह वा उदानस्तस्मादुपशान्ततेजाः। पुनर्भवमिन्द्रियैर्मनसि सं-
पद्यमानैः॥ ९॥

9. "Light, the primal energy, is the upper breath; therefore when the light and heat in a man hath dwindled, his senses retire into the mind and with these he departeth into another birth.

यच्चित्तस्तेनैष प्राणमायाति प्राणस्तेजसा युक्तः । सहात्मना यथा-
संकल्पितं लोकं नयति ॥ १० ॥

10. "Whatsoever be the mind of a man, with that mind he seeketh refuge with the breath when he dieth, and the breath and the upper breath lead him with the Spirit within him to the world of his imaginings.

य एवं विद्वान् प्राणं वेद । न हास्य प्रजा हीयतेऽमृतो भवति तदेष
श्लोकः ॥ ११ ॥

11. "The wise man that knoweth thus of the breath, his progeny wasteth not and he becometh immortal. Whereof this is the Scripture.

उत्पत्तिमायतिं स्थानं विभुत्वं चैव पञ्चधा ।
अध्यात्मं चैव प्राणस्य विज्ञायामृतमश्नुत इति ॥ १२ ॥

12. "'By knowing the origin of the Breath, his coming and his staying and his lordship in the five provinces, likewise his relation to the Spirit, one shall taste immortality.'"

And afterwards
    The Chapter of the Fourth Question.

अथ हैनं सौर्यायणी गार्ग्यः पप्रच्छ । भगवन्नेतस्मिन् पुरुषे कानि
स्वपन्ति कान्यस्मिञ्जाग्रति कतर एष देवः स्वप्नान्पश्यति कस्यैतत्
सुखं भवति कस्मिन्नु सर्वे संप्रतिष्ठिता भवन्तीति ॥ १ ॥

1. Then Gargya of the Solar race asked him, "Lord, what are they that slumber in this Existing and what that keep vigil? Who is this god who seeth dreams or whose is this felicity? Into whom do all they vanish?"

तस्मै स होवाच। यथा गार्ग्य मरीचयोऽर्कस्यास्तं गच्छतः सर्वा
एतस्मिंस्तेजोमण्डल एकीभवन्ति। ताः पुनः पुनरुदयतः प्रचरन्त्येवं ह
वै तत्सर्वं परे देवे मनस्येकीभवति। तेन तर्ह्येष पुरुषो न शृणोति न
पश्यति न जिघ्रति न रसयते न स्पृशते नाभिवदते नादत्ते नानन्दयते
न विसृजते नेयायते स्वपितीत्याचक्षते ॥ २ ॥

2. To him answered the Rishi Pippalada: "O Gargya, as are the
rays of the sun in its setting, for they retire and all become
one in yonder circle of splendour, but when he riseth again
once more they walk abroad, so all the man becomes one
in the highest god, even the mind. Then indeed this being
seeth not, neither heareth, nor doth he smell, nor taste, nor
touch, nor speaketh he aught, nor taketh in or giveth out,
nor cometh nor goeth; he feeleth not any felicity. Then they
say of him, 'He sleepeth'.

प्राणाग्नय एवैतस्मिन् पुरे जाग्रति। गार्हपत्यो ह वा एषोऽपानो
व्यानोऽन्वाहार्यपचनो यद् गार्हपत्यात् प्रणीयते प्रणयनादाहवनीयः
प्राणः ॥ ३ ॥

3. "But the fires of the breath keep watch in that sleeping city.
The lower breath is the householder's fire and the breath
pervasor the fire of the Lares that burneth to the south-
ward. The main breath is the orient fire of the sacrifice; and
even as the eastern fire taketh its fuel from the western, so
in the slumber of a man the main breath taketh from the
lower.

यदुच्छ्वासनिश्वासावेतावाहुती समं नयतीति स समानः। मनो ह वाव
यजमान इष्टफलमेवोदानः स एनं यजमानमहरहर्ब्रह्म गमयति ॥ ४ ॥

4. "But the medial breath is the priest, the sacrificant; for
he equaliseth the offering of the inbreath and the offering
of the outbreath. The Mind is the giver of the sacrifice
and the upper breath is the fruit of the sacrifice, for it
taketh the sacrificer day by day into the presence of the
Eternal.

अत्रैष देवः स्वप्ने महिमानमनुभवति। यद् दृष्टं दृष्टमनुपश्यति श्रुतं
श्रुतमेवार्थमनुशृणोति देशदिगन्तरैश्च प्रत्यनुभूतं पुनः पुनः प्रत्यनुभवति
दृष्टं चादृष्टं च श्रुतं चाश्रुतं चानुभूतं चाननुभूतं च सच्चासच्च सर्वं
पश्यति सर्वः पश्यति ॥ ५ ॥

5. "Now the Mind in dream revelleth in the glory of his imaginings. All that it hath seen it seemeth to see over again, and
of all that it hath heard it repeateth the hearing; yea, all that
it hath felt and thought and known in many lands and in
various regions, these it liveth over again in its dreaming.
What it hath seen and what it hath not seen, what it hath
heard and what it hath not heard, what it hath known and
what it hath not known, what is and what is not, all, all it
seeth; for the Mind is the Universe.

स यदा तेजसाभिभूतो भवति। अत्रैष देवः स्वप्नान् न पश्यत्यथ
तदैतस्मिञ्छरीर एतत्सुखं भवति ॥ ६ ॥

6. "But when he is overwhelmed with light, then Mind, the
God, dreameth no longer; then in this body he hath felicity.

स यथा सोम्य वयांसि वासोवृक्षं संप्रतिष्ठन्ते। एवं ह वै तत्सर्वं पर
आत्मनि संप्रतिष्ठते ॥ ७ ॥

7. "O fair son, as birds wing towards their resting tree, so do
all these depart into the Supreme Spirit:

पृथिवी च पृथिवीमात्रा चापश्चापोमात्रा च तेजश्च तेजोमात्रा च वायुश्च
वायुमात्रा चाकाशश्चाकाशमात्रा च चक्षुश्च द्रष्टव्यं च श्रोत्रं च श्रोतव्यं
च घ्राणं च घ्रातव्यं च रसश्च रसयितव्यं च त्वक् च स्पर्शयितव्यं च
वाक् च वक्तव्यं च हस्तौ चादातव्यं चोपस्थश्चानन्दयितव्यं च पायुश्च
विसर्जयितव्यं च पादौ च गन्तव्यं च मनश्च मन्तव्यं च बुद्धिश्च बोद्धव्यं
चाहंकारश्चाहंकर्तव्यं च चित्तं च चेतयितव्यं च तेजश्च विद्योतयितव्यं
च प्राणश्च विधारयितव्यं च ॥ ८ ॥

8. "Earth and the inner things of earth; water and the inner
things of water; light and the inner things of light; air and

the inner things of air; ether and the inner things of ether;
the eye and its seeings; the ear and its hearings; smell and
the objects of smell; taste and the objects of taste; the skin
and the objects of touch; speech and the things to be spoken; the two hands and their takings; the organ of pleasure
and its enjoyings; the anus and its excretions; the feet and
their goings; the mind and its feelings; the intelligence and
what it understandeth; the sense of Ego and that which is
felt to be Ego; the conscious heart and that of which it is
conscious; light and what it lighteneth; Life and the things
it maintaineth.

एष हि द्रष्टा स्रष्टा श्रोता घ्राता रसयिता मन्ता बोद्धा कर्ता विज्ञानात्मा
पुरुषः । स परेऽक्षर आत्मनि संप्रतिष्ठते ॥ ९ ॥

9. "For this that seeth and toucheth, heareth, smelleth, tasteth,
feeleth, understandeth, acteth, is the reasoning self, the Male
within. This too departeth into the Higher Self which is
Imperishable.

परमेवाक्षरं प्रतिपद्यते स यो ह वै तदच्छायमशरीरमलोहितं शुभ्रमक्षरं
वेदयते यस्तु सोम्य । स सर्वज्ञः सर्वो भवति तदेष श्लोकः ॥ १० ॥

10. "He that knoweth the shadowless, colourless, bodiless,
luminous and imperishable Spirit, attaineth to the Imperishable, even to the Most High. O fair son, he knoweth the
All and becometh the All. Whereof this is the Scripture.

विज्ञानात्मा सह देवैश्च सर्वैः प्राणा भूतानि संप्रतिष्ठन्ति यत्र ।
तदक्षरं वेदयते यस्तु सोम्य स सर्वज्ञः सर्वमेवाविवेशेति ॥ ११ ॥

11. "'He, O fair son, that knoweth the Imperishable into whom
the understanding self departeth, and all the Gods, and the
life-breaths and the elements, he knoweth the Universe!'"

And afterwards

The Chapter of the Fifth Question.

अथ हैनं शैव्यः सत्यकामः पप्रच्छ। स यो ह वै तद् भगवन् मनुष्येषु
प्रायणान्तमोंकारमभिध्यायीत। कतमं वाव स तेन लोकं जयतीति ॥१॥

1. Then the Shaivya Satyakama asked him: "Lord, he among
men that meditate unto death on OM the syllable, which of
the worlds doth he conquer by its puissance?"

तस्मै स होवाच। एतद्वै सत्यकाम परं चापरं च ब्रह्म यदोंकारः।
तस्माद् विद्वानेतेनैवायतनेनैकतरमन्वेति ॥२॥

2. To him answered the Rishi Pippalada: "This imperishable
Word that is OM, O Satyakama, is the Higher Brahman and
also the Lower. Therefore the wise man by making his home
in the Word, winneth to one of these.

स यद्येकमात्रमभिध्यायीत स तेनैव संवेदितस्तूर्णमेव जगत्यामभि-
संपद्यते। तमृचो मनुष्यलोकमुपनयन्ते स तत्र तपसा ब्रह्मचर्येण श्रद्धया
संपन्नो महिमानमनुभवति ॥३॥

3. "If he meditate on the one letter of OM the syllable, by that
enlightened he attaineth swiftly in the material universe,
and the hymns of the Rigveda escort him to the world of
men; there endowed with askesis and faith and holiness he
experienceth majesty.

अथ यदि द्विमात्रेण मनसि संपद्यते सोऽन्तरिक्षं यजुर्भिरुन्नीयते
सोमलोकम्। स सोमलोके विभूतिमनुभूय पुनरावर्तते ॥४॥

4. "Now if by the two letters of the syllable he in the mind
attaineth, to the skies he is exalted and the hymns of the
Yajur escort him to the Lunar World. In the heavens of
the Moon he feeleth his soul's majesty; then once more he
returneth.

यः पुनरेतं त्रिमात्रेणोमित्येतेनैवाक्षरेण परं पुरुषमभिध्यायीत स तेजसि
सूर्ये संपन्नः । यथा पादोदरस्त्वचा विनिर्मुच्यत एवं ह वै स पाप्मना
विनिर्मुक्तः स सामभिरुन्नीयते ब्रह्मलोकं स एतस्माज्जीवघनात्परात्परं
पुरिशयं पुरुषमीक्षते तदेतौ श्लोकौ भवतः ॥ ५ ॥

5. "But he who by all the three letters meditateth by this syllable, even by OM on the Most High Being, he in the Solar
World of light and energy is secured in his attainings; as a
snake casteth off its slough, so he casteth off sin, and the
hymns of the Samaveda escort him to the heaven of the
Spirit. He from that Lower who is the density of existence
beholdeth the Higher than the Highest of whom every form
is one city. Whereof these are the verses.

तिस्रो मात्रा मृत्युमत्यः प्रयुक्ता अन्योन्यसक्ता अनविप्रयुक्ताः ।
क्रियासु बाह्याभ्यन्तरमध्यमासु सम्यक्प्रयुक्तासु न कम्पते ज्ञः ॥ ६ ॥

6. "'Children of death are the letters when they are used as
three, the embracing and the inseparable letters; but the wise
man is not shaken; for there are three kinds of works, outward deed and inward action and another which is blended
of the two, and all these he doeth rightly without fear and
without trembling.

ऋग्भिरेतं यजुर्भिरन्तरिक्षं सामभिर्यत्तत्कवयो वेदयन्ते ।
तमोंकारेणैवायतनेनान्वेति विद्वान् यत्तच्छान्तमजरममृतमभयं
                                                    परं चेति ॥ ७ ॥

7. "'To the earth the Rigveda leadeth, to the skies the Yajur,
but the Sama to That of which the sages know. Thither the
wise man by resting on OM the syllable attaineth, even to
that Supreme Quietude where age is not and fear is cast out
by immortality.'"

And afterwards
The Chapter of the Sixth Question.

अथ हैनं सुकेशा भारद्वाजः पप्रच्छ। भगवन् हिरण्यनाभः कौसल्यो
राजपुत्रो मामुपेत्यैतं प्रश्नमपृच्छत। षोडशकलं भारद्वाज पुरुषं वेत्थ।
तमहं कुमारमब्रुवं नाहमिमं वेद। यद्यहमिममवेदिषं कथं ते नावक्ष्य-
मिति। समूलो वा एष परिशुष्यति योऽनृतमभिवदति तस्मान्ना-
र्हाम्यनृतं वक्तुम्। स तूष्णीं रथमारुह्य प्रवव्राज। तं त्वा पृच्छामि
क्वासौ पुरुष इति ॥ १ ॥

1. Then Sukesha the Bharadwaja asked him, "Lord, Hiranyan-
   abha of Coshala, the king's son, came to me and put me this
   question, 'O Bharadwaja, knowest thou the Being and the
   sixteen parts of Him?' and I answered the boy, 'I know Him
   not; for if I knew Him, surely I should tell thee of Him: but I
   cannot tell thee a lie; for from the roots he shall wither who
   speaketh falsehood.' But he mounted his chariot in silence
   and departed from me. Of Him I ask thee, who is the Being?"

तस्मै स होवाच। इहैवान्तःशरीरे सोम्य स पुरुषो यस्मिन्नेताः षोडश
कलाः प्रभवन्तीति ॥ २ ॥

2. To him answered the Rishi Pippalada: "O fair son, even here
   is that Being, in the inner body of every creature for in Him
   are the sixteen members born.

स ईक्षांचक्रे। कस्मिन्नहमुत्क्रान्त उत्क्रान्तो भविष्यामि कस्मिन् वा
प्रतिष्ठिते प्रतिष्ठास्यामीति ॥ ३ ॥

3. "He bethought Him. 'What shall that be in whose issuing
   forth I shall issue forth from the body and in his abiding I
   shall abide?'

स प्राणमसृजत प्राणाच्छ्रद्धां खं वायुर्ज्योतिरापः पृथिवीन्द्रियं मनः।
अन्नमन्नाद्वीर्यं तपो मन्त्राः कर्म लोका लोकेषु च नाम च ॥ ४ ॥

4. "Then he put forth the Life, and from the Life faith, next
   ether and then air, and then light, and then water, and then
   earth, the senses and mind and food, and from food virility

and from virility askesis, and from askesis the mighty verses and from these action, and the worlds from action and name in the worlds; in this wise were all things born from the Spirit.

स यथेमा नद्यः स्यन्दमानाः समुद्रायणाः समुद्रं प्राप्यास्तं गच्छन्ति भिद्येते तासां नामरूपे समुद्र इत्येवं प्रोच्यते । एवमेवास्य परिद्रष्टुरिमाः षोडश कलाः पुरुषायणाः पुरुषं प्राप्यास्तं गच्छन्ति भिद्येते चासां नामरूपे पुरुष इत्येवं प्रोच्यते स एषोऽकलोऽमृतो भवति तदेष श्लोकः ॥ ५ ॥

5. "Therefore as all these flowing rivers move towards the sea, but when they reach the sea they are lost in it and name and form break away from them and all is called only the sea, so all the sixteen members of the silent witnessing Spirit move towards the Being, and when they have attained the Being they are lost in Him and name and form break away from them and all is called only the Being; then is He without members and immortal. Whereof this is the Scripture.

अरा इव रथनाभौ कला यस्मिन्प्रतिष्ठिताः ।
तं वेद्यं पुरुषं वेद यथा मा वो मृत्युः परिव्यथा इति ॥ ६ ॥

6. "'He in whom the members are set as the spokes of a wheel are set in its nave, Him know for the Being who is the goal of knowledge, so shall death pass away from you and his anguish.'"

तान् होवाचैतावदेवाहमेतत् परं ब्रह्म वेद । नातः परमस्तीति ॥ ७ ॥

7. And Pippalada said to them: "Thus far do I know the Most High God; than He there is none Higher."

ते तमर्चयन्तस्त्वं हि नः पिता योऽस्माकमविद्यायाः परं पारं तारयसीति । नमः परमऋषिभ्यो नमः परमऋषिभ्यः ॥ ८ ॥

8. And they worshipping him: "For thou art our father who hast carried us over to the other side of the Ignorance."

Salutation to the mighty sages, salutation!

After which one repeats the Mantra.

ॐ भद्रं कर्णेभिः शृणुयाम देवा भद्रं पश्येमाक्षभिर्यजत्राः ।
स्थिरैरङ्गैस्तुष्टुवांसस्तनूभिर्व्यशेम देवहितं यदायुः ॥
स्वस्ति न इन्द्रो वृद्धश्रवाः स्वस्ति नः पूषा विश्ववेदाः ।
स्वस्ति नस्ताक्ष्र्यो अरिष्टनेमिः स्वस्ति नो बृहस्पतिर्दधातु ॥
ॐ शान्तिः शान्तिः शान्तिः ॥

OM. May we hear what is auspicious with our ears, O ye Gods;
may we see what is auspicious with our eyes, O ye of the sacrifice;
giving praise with steady limbs, with motionless bodies, may we
enter into that life which is founded in the Gods.

Ordain weal unto us Indra of high-heaped glories; ordain
weal unto us Pushan, the all-knowing Sun; ordain weal unto
us Tarkshya Arishtanemi; Brihaspati ordain weal unto us. OM.
Peace! peace! peace!

The Mandoukya Upanishad

Before which one repeats the Mantra.

ॐ भद्रं कर्णेभिः शृणुयाम देवा भद्रं पश्येमाक्षभिर्यजत्राः ।
स्थिरैरङ्गैस्तुष्टुवांसस्तनूभिर्व्यशेम देवहितं यदायुः ॥
स्वस्ति न इन्द्रो वृद्धश्रवाः स्वस्ति नः पूषा विश्ववेदाः ।
स्वस्ति नस्ताक्ष्यों अरिष्टनेमिः स्वस्ति नो बृहस्पतिर्दधातु ॥
ॐ शान्तिः शान्तिः शान्तिः ॥

OM. May we hear what is auspicious with our ears, O ye Gods; may we see what is auspicious with our eyes, O ye of the sacrifice; giving praise with steady limbs, with motionless bodies, may we enter into that life which is founded in the Gods.

Ordain weal unto us Indra of high-heaped glories; ordain weal unto us Pushan, the all-knowing Sun; ordain weal unto us Tarkshya Arishtanemi; Brihaspati ordain weal unto us. OM. Peace! peace! peace!

ओमित्येतदक्षरमिदं सर्वं तस्योपव्याख्यानं भूतं भवद् भविष्यदिति
सर्वमोंकार एव । यच्चान्यत् त्रिकालातीतं तदप्योंकार एव ॥ १ ॥

1. OM is this imperishable Word, OM is the Universe, and this is the exposition of OM. The past, the present and the future, all that was, all that is, all that will be, is OM. Likewise all else that may exist beyond the bounds of Time, that too is OM.

सर्वं ह्येतद् ब्रह्मायमात्मा ब्रह्म सोऽयमात्मा चतुष्पात् ॥ २ ॥

2. All this Universe is the Eternal Brahman, this Self is the Eternal, and the Self is fourfold.

जागरितस्थानो बहिष्प्रज्ञः सप्ताङ्ग एकोनविंशतिमुखः स्थूलभुग् वैश्वा-
नरः प्रथमः पादः ॥ ३ ॥

3. He whose place is the wakefulness, who is wise of the outward, who has seven limbs, to whom there are nineteen doors, who feeleth and enjoyeth gross objects, Vaiswanor, the Universal Male, He is the first.

स्वप्नस्थानोऽन्तःप्रज्ञः सप्ताङ्ग एकोनविंशतिमुखः प्रविविक्तभुक् तैजसो द्वितीयः पादः ॥ ४ ॥

4. He whose place is the dream, who is wise of the inward, who has seven limbs, to whom there are nineteen doors, who feeleth and enjoyeth subtle objects, Taijasa, the Inhabitant in Luminous Mind, He is the second.

यत्र सुप्तो न कंचन कामं कामयते न कंचन स्वप्नं पश्यति तत्सुषुप्तम् ।
सुषुप्तस्थान एकीभूतः प्रज्ञानघन एवानन्दमयो ह्यानन्दभुक् चेतोमुखः
प्राज्ञस्तृतीयः पादः ॥ ५ ॥

5. When one sleepeth and yearneth not with any desire, nor seeth any dream, that is the perfect slumber. He whose place is the perfect slumber, who is become Oneness, who is wisdom gathered into itself, who is made of mere delight, who enjoyeth delight unrelated, to whom conscious mind is the door, Prajna, the Lord of Wisdom, He is the third.

एष सर्वेश्वर एष सर्वज्ञ एषोऽन्तर्याम्येष योनिः सर्वस्य प्रभवाप्ययौ हि
भूतानाम् ॥ ६ ॥

6. This is the Almighty, this is the Omniscient, this is the Inner Soul, this is the Womb of the Universe, this is the Birth and Destruction of creatures.

नान्तःप्रज्ञं न बहिष्प्रज्ञं नोभयतःप्रज्ञं न प्रज्ञानघनं न प्रज्ञं नाप्रज्ञम् ।
अदृष्टमव्यवहार्यमग्राह्यमलक्षणमचिन्त्यमव्यपदेश्यमेकात्मप्रत्ययसारं
प्रपञ्चोपशमं शान्तं शिवमद्वैतं चतुर्थं मन्यन्ते स आत्मा स वि-
ज्ञेयः ॥ ७ ॥

7. He who is neither inward-wise, nor outward-wise, nor both inward and outward wise, nor wisdom self-gathered, nor possessed of wisdom, nor unpossessed of wisdom, He Who

is unseen and incommunicable, unseizable, featureless, unthinkable, and unnameable, Whose essentiality is awareness of the Self in its single existence, in Whom all phenomena dissolve, Who is Calm, Who is Good, Who is the One than Whom there is no other, Him they deem the fourth; He is the Self, He is the object of Knowledge.

सोऽयमात्माध्यक्षरमोंकारोऽधिमात्रं पादा मात्रा मात्राश्च पादा अकार उकारो मकार इति ॥ ८ ॥

8. Now this the Self, as to the imperishable Word, is OM; and as to the letters, His parts are the letters and the letters are His parts, namely, A U M.

जागरितस्थानो वैश्वानरोऽकार: प्रथमा मात्राप्तेरादिमत्त्वाद्वाप्नोति ह वै सर्वान्कामानादिश्च भवति य एवं वेद ॥ ९ ॥

9. The Waker, Vaiswanor, the Universal Male, He is A, the first letter, because of Initiality and Pervasiveness; he that knoweth Him for such pervadeth and attaineth all his desires; he becometh the source and first.

स्वप्नस्थानस्तैजस उकारो द्वितीया मात्रोत्कर्षाद्उभयत्वाद्वोत्कर्षति ह वै ज्ञानसंततिं समानश्च भवति नास्याब्रह्मवित् कुले भवति य एवं वेद ॥ १० ॥

10. The Dreamer, Taijasa, the Inhabitant in Luminous Mind, He is U, the second letter, because of Advance and Centrality; he that knoweth Him for such, advanceth the bounds of his knowledge and riseth above difference; nor of his seed is any born that knoweth not the Eternal.

सुषुप्तस्थान: प्राज्ञो मकारस्तृतीया मात्रा मितेरपीतेर्वा मिनोति ह वा इदं सर्वमपीतिश्च भवति य एवं वेद ॥ ११ ॥

11. The Sleeper, Prajna, the Lord of Wisdom, He is M, the third letter, because of Measure and Finality; he that knoweth Him for such measureth with himself the Universe and becometh the departure into the Eternal.

अमात्रश्चतुर्थोऽव्यवहार्यः प्रपञ्चोपशमः शिवोऽद्वैत एवमोंकार आत्मैव
संविशत्यात्मनात्मानं य एवं वेद य एवं वेद ॥ १२ ॥

12. Letterless is the fourth, the Incommunicable, the end of phe-
     nomena, the Good, the One than Whom there is no other;
     thus is OM. He that knoweth is the Self and entereth by his
     self into the Self, he that knoweth, he that knoweth.

Here ends the Mandoukya Upanishad.

After which one repeats the Mantra.

ॐ भद्रं कर्णेभिः शृणुयाम देवा भद्रं पश्येमाक्षभिर्यजत्राः ।
स्थिरैरङ्गैस्तुष्टुवांसस्तनूभिर्व्यशेम देवहितं यदायुः ॥
स्वस्ति न इन्द्रो वृद्धश्रवाः स्वस्ति नः पूषा विश्ववेदाः ।
स्वस्ति नस्ताक्ष्र्यो अरिष्टनेमिः स्वस्ति नो बृहस्पतिर्दधातु ॥
ॐ शान्तिः शान्तिः शान्तिः ॥

OM. May we hear what is auspicious with our ears, O ye Gods;
may we see what is auspicious with our eyes, O ye of the sacrifice;
giving praise with steady limbs, with motionless bodies, may we
enter into that life which is founded in the Gods.

Ordain weal unto us Indra of high-heaped glories; ordain
weal unto us Pushan, the all-knowing Sun; ordain weal unto
us Tarkshya Arishtanemi; Brihaspati ordain weal unto us. OM.
Peace! peace! peace!

The Aitereya Upanishad

Chapter I

आत्मा वा इदमेक एवाग्र आसीत्। नान्यत्किंचन मिषत्। स ईक्षत
लोकान्नु सृजा इति ॥ १ ॥

1. In the beginning the Spirit was One and all this (universe)
   was the Spirit; there was nought else that saw. The Spirit
   thought, "Lo, I will make me worlds from out my being."

स इमाँल्लोकानसृजत। अम्भो मरीचीर्मरमापोऽदोऽम्भः परेण दिवं द्यौः
प्रतिष्ठान्तरिक्षं मरीचयः पृथिवी मरो या अधस्तात् ता आपः ॥ २ ॥

2. These were the worlds he made; Ambhah, of the ethereal
   waters, Marichih of light, Mara, of death and mortal things,
   Apah, of the lower waters. Beyond the shining firmament
   are the ethereal waters and the firmament is their base and
   resting-place; Space is the world of light; the earth is the
   world mortal; and below the earth are the lower waters.

स ईक्षतेमे नु लोका लोकपालान्नु सृजा इति। सोऽद्भ्य एव पुरुषं
समुद्धृत्यामूर्छयत् ॥ ३ ॥

3. The Spirit thought, "Lo, these are the worlds; and now will I
   make me guardians for my worlds." Therefore he gathered
   the Purusha out of the waters and gave Him shape and
   substance.

तमभ्यतपत् तस्याभितप्तस्य मुखं निरभिद्यत यथाण्डम्। मुखाद्वाग्
वाचोऽग्निर्नासिके निरभिद्येतां नासिकाभ्यां प्राणः प्राणाद्वायुरक्षिणी
निरभिद्येतामक्षिभ्यां चक्षुश्चक्षुष आदित्यः कर्णौ निरभिद्येतां कर्णाभ्यां
श्रोत्रं श्रोत्रादिशस्त्वङ् निरभिद्यत त्वचो लोमानि लोमभ्य ओषधिवन-
स्पतयो हृदयं निरभिद्यत हृदयान्मनो मनसश्चन्द्रमा नाभिर्निरभिद्यत
नाभ्या अपानोऽपानान्मृत्युः शिश्नं निरभिद्यत शिश्नादेतो रेतस
आपः ॥ ४ ॥

4. Yea, the Spirit brooded over Him and of Him thus brooded over the mouth broke forth, as when an egg is hatched and breaketh; from the mouth brake Speech and of Speech fire was born. The nostrils brake forth and from the nostrils Breath and of Breath air was born. The eyes brake forth and from the eyes Sight and of Sight the Sun was born. The ears brake forth and from the ears Hearing and of Hearing the regions were born. The skin brake forth and from the skin hairs and from the hairs herbs of healing and all trees and plants were born. The heart brake forth and from the heart Mind and of Mind the moon was born. The navel brake forth and from the navel Apana and of Apana Death was born. The organ of pleasure brake forth and from the organ seed and of seed the waters were born.

Chapter II

ता एता देवताः सृष्टा अस्मिन्महत्यर्णवे प्रापतन् । तमशनायापिपासा-
भ्यामन्ववार्जत् । ता एनमब्रुवन्नायतनं नः प्रजानीहि यस्मिन्प्रतिष्ठिता
अन्नमदामेति ॥ १ ॥

1. These were the Gods that He created; they fell into this great Ocean, and Hunger and Thirst leaped upon them. Then they said to Him, "Command unto us an habitation that we may dwell secure and eat of food."

ताभ्यो गामानयत् ता अब्रुवन्न वै नोऽयमलमिति । ताभ्योऽश्वमानयत्
ता अब्रुवन्न वै नोऽयमलमिति ॥ २ ॥

2. He brought unto them the cow, but they said, "Verily, it is not sufficient for us." He brought unto them the horse, but they said, "Verily, it is not enough for us."

ताभ्यः पुरुषमानयत् ता अब्रुवन सुकृतं बतेति पुरुषो वाव सुकृतम् ।
ता अब्रवीदथायतनं प्रविशतेति ॥ ३ ॥

3. He brought unto them Man, and they said, "O well fashioned truly! Man indeed is well and beautifully made." Then

the Spirit said unto them, "Enter ye in each according to his habitation."

अग्निर्वाग्भूत्वा मुखं प्राविशद् वायुः प्राणो भूत्वा नासिके प्राविश-
दादित्यश्चक्षुर्भूत्वाक्षिणी प्राविशद् दिशः श्रोत्रं भूत्वा कर्णौ प्राविश-
न्नोषधिवनस्पतयो लोमानि भूत्वा त्वचं प्राविशंश्चन्द्रमा मनो भूत्वा
हृदयं प्राविशन्मृत्युरपानो भूत्वा नाभिं प्राविशदापो रेतो भूत्वा शिश्नं
प्राविशन् ॥ ४ ॥

4. Fire became Speech and entered into the mouth; Air became Breath and entered into the nostrils; the Sun became Sight and entered into the eyes; the Quarters became Hearing and entered into the ears; Herbs of healing and the plants and trees became Hairs and entered into the skin; the Moon became Mind and entered into the heart; Death became Apana, the lower breathing, and entered into the navel; the Waters became Seed and entered into the organ.

तमशनायापिपासे अब्रूतामावाभ्यामभिप्रजानीहीति ते अब्रवीदेता-
स्वेव वां देवतास्वाभजाम्येतासु भागिन्यौ करोमीति । तस्माद्यस्यै कस्यै
च देवतायै हविर्गृह्यते भागिन्यावेवास्यामशनायापिपासे भवतः ॥ ५ ॥

5. Then Hunger and Thirst said unto the Spirit, "Unto us too command an habitation." But He said unto them, "Even among these gods do I apportion you; lo! I have made you sharers in their godhead." Therefore to whatever god the oblation is offered, Hunger and Thirst surely have their share in the offering.

Chapter III

स ईक्षतेमे नु लोकाश्च लोकपालाश्चान्नमेभ्यः सृजा इति ॥ १ ॥

1. The Spirit thought, "These verily are my worlds and their guardians; and now will I make me food for these."

सोऽपोऽभ्यतपत् ताभ्योऽभितप्ताभ्यो मूर्तिरजायत । या वै सा मूर्तिर-
जायतान्नं वै तत् ॥ २ ॥

2. The Spirit brooded in might upon the waters and from the waters brooded mightily over Form was born. Lo, all this that was born as form, is no other than Food.

तदेनत्सृष्टं पराङत्यजिघांसत् तद्वाचाजिघृक्षत् तन्नाशक्नोद्वाचा ग्रहीतुं
स यद्धैनद् वाचाग्रहैष्यदभिव्याहृत्य हैवान्नमत्रप्स्यत् ॥ ३ ॥

3. Food being created fled back from his grasp. By speech He would have seized it, but He could not seize it by speech. Had He seized it by speech, then would a man be satisfied by merely speaking food.

तत्प्राणेनाजिघृक्षत् तन्नाशक्नोत्प्राणेन ग्रहीतुं स यद्धैनत् प्राणेनाग्रहैष्य-
दभिप्राण्य हैवान्नमत्रप्स्यत् ॥ ४ ॥

4. By the breath He would have seized it, but He could not seize it by the breath. Had He seized it by the breath, then would a man be satisfied by merely breathing food.

तच्चक्षुषाजिघृक्षत् तन्नाशक्नोच्चक्षुषा ग्रहीतुं स यद्धैनच्चक्षुषाग्रहैष्यद्
दृष्ट्वा हैवान्नमत्रप्स्यत् ॥ ५ ॥

5. By the eye He would have seized it, but He could not seize it by the eye. Had He seized it by the eye, then would a man be satisfied by merely seeing food.

तच्छ्रोत्रेणाजिघृक्षत् तन्नाशक्नोच्छ्रोत्रेण ग्रहीतुं स यद्धैनच्छ्रोत्रेणाग्रहै-
ष्यच्छ्रुत्वा हैवान्नमत्रप्स्यत् ॥ ६ ॥

6. By the ear He would have seized it, but He could not seize it by the ear. Had He seized it by the ear, then would a man be satisfied by merely hearing food.

तत्त्वचाजिघृक्षत् तन्नाशक्नोत्त्वचा ग्रहीतुं स यद्धैनत्त्वचाग्रहैष्यत् स्पृष्ट्वा
हैवान्नमत्रप्स्यत् ॥ ७ ॥

7. By the skin He would have seized it, but He could not seize it by the skin. Had He seized it by the skin, then would a man be satisfied by merely touching food.

तन्मनसाजिघृक्षत् तन्नाशक्कोन्मनसा ग्रहीतुं स यद्धैनन्मनसाग्रहैष्यद्
ध्यात्वा हैवान्नमत्रप्स्यत् ॥ ८ ॥

8. By the mind He would have seized it, but He could not seize
it by the mind. Had He seized it by the mind, then would a
man be satisfied by merely thinking food.

तच्छिछ्नेनाजिघृक्षत् तन्नाशक्कोच्छिछ्नेन ग्रहीतुं स यद्धैनच्छिछ्नेना-
ग्रहैष्यद् विसृज्य हैवान्नमत्रप्स्यत् ॥ ९ ॥

9. By the organ He would have seized it, but He could not
seize it by the organ. Had He seized it by the organ, then
would a man be satisfied by merely emitting food.

तदपानेनाजिघृक्षत् तदावयत् सैषोऽन्नस्य ग्रहो यद्वायुरन्नायुर्वा एष
यद्वायुः ॥ १० ॥

10. By the Apana He would have seized it, and it was seized.
Lo this is the seizer of food which is also Breath of the Life,
and therefore all that is Breath hath its life in food.

स ईक्षत कथं न्विदं मदृते स्यादिति स ईक्षत कतरेण प्रपद्या इति । स
ईक्षत यदि वाचाभिव्याहृतं यदि प्राणेनाभिप्राणितं यदि चक्षुषा दृष्टं यदि
श्रोत्रेण श्रुतं यदि त्वचा स्पृष्टं यदि मनसा ध्यातं यद्यपानेनाभ्यपानितं
यदि शिछ्नेन विसृष्टमथ कोऽहमिति ॥ ११ ॥

11. The Spirit thought, "Without Me how should all this be?"
and He thought, "By what way shall I enter in?" He thought
also, "If utterance is by Speech, if breathing is by the Breath,
if sight is by the Eye, if hearing is by the Ear, if thought is by
the Mind, if the lower workings are by Apana, if emission
is by the organ, who then am I?"

स एतमेव सीमानं विदार्यैतया द्वारा प्रापद्यत । सैषा विदृतिर्नाम
द्वास्तदेतन्नान्दनम् । तस्य त्रय आवसथास्त्रयः स्वप्ना अयमावसथो
ऽयमावसथोऽयमावसथ इति ॥ १२ ॥

12. It was this bound that He cleft, it was by this door that He
entered in. 'Tis this that is called the gate of the cleaving; this
is the door of His coming and here is the place of His delight.

He hath three mansions in His city, three dreams wherein He dwelleth, and of each in turn He saith, "Lo, this is my habitation" and "This is my habitation" and "This is my habitation."

स जातो भूतान्यभिव्यैख्यत् किमिहान्यं वावदिषदिति । स एतमेव पुरुषं ब्रह्म ततममपश्यत् । इदमदर्शमिती३ ॥ १३ ॥

13. Now when He was born, He thought and spoke only of Nature and her creations; in this world of matter of what else should He speak or reason? Thereafter He beheld that Being who is the Brahman and the last Essence. He said, "Yea, this is He; verily, I have beheld Him."

तस्मादिदिन्द्रो नामेदन्द्रो ह वै नाम । तमिदन्द्रं सन्तमिन्द्र इत्याचक्षते परोक्षेण । परोक्षप्रिया इव हि देवाः परोक्षप्रिया इव हि देवाः ॥ १४ ॥

14. Therefore is He Idandra; for Idandra is the true name of Him. But though He is Idandra, they call Him Indra because of the veil of the Unrevelation; for the gods love the veil of the Unrevelation, yea, verily, the gods love the Unrevelation.

Chapter IV

पुरुषे ह वा अयमादितो गर्भो भवति यदेतद् रेतः । तदेतत् सर्वेभ्यो ऽङ्गेभ्यस्तेजः संभूतमात्मन्येवात्मानं बिभर्ति तद्यदा स्त्रियां सिञ्च-त्यथैनज्जनयति तदस्य प्रथमं जन्म ॥ १ ॥

1. In the male first the unborn child becometh. This which is seed is the force and heat of him that from all parts of the creature draweth together for becoming; therefore he beareth himself in himself, and when he casteth it into the woman, 'tis himself he begetteth. And this is the first birth of the Spirit.

तत् स्त्रिया आत्मभूयं गच्छति यथा स्वमङ्गं तथा । तस्मादेनां न हिनस्ति । सास्यैतमात्मानमत्र गतं भावयति ॥ २ ॥

2. It becometh one self with the woman, therefore it doeth her no hurt and she cherisheth this self of her husband that hath got into her womb.

सा भावयित्री भावयितव्या भवति । तं स्त्री गर्भं बिभर्ति । सोऽग्र एव कुमारं जन्मनोऽग्रेऽधिभावयति । स यत्कुमारं जन्मनोऽग्रेऽधिभावय - त्यात्मानमेव तद् भावयत्येषां लोकानां संतत्या एवं संतता ह्रीमे लोकास्तदस्य द्वितीयं जन्म ॥ ३ ॥

3. She the cherisher must be cherished. So the woman beareth the unborn child and the man cherisheth the boy even from the beginning ere it is born. And whereas he cherisheth the boy ere it is born, 'tis verily himself that he cherisheth for the continuance of these worlds and their peoples; for 'tis even thus the thread of these worlds spinneth on unbroken. And this is the second birth of the Spirit.

सोऽस्यायमात्मा पुण्येभ्यः कर्मभ्यः प्रतिधीयते । अथास्यायमितर आत्मा कृतकृत्यो वयोगतः प्रैति । स इतः प्रयन्नेव पुनर्जायते तदस्य तृतीयं जन्म ॥ ४ ॥

4. Lo this is the spirit and self of him and he maketh it his vicegerent for the works of righteousness. Now this his other self when it hath done the works it came to do and hath reached its age, lo! it goeth hence, and even as it departeth, it is born again. And this is the third birth of the Spirit.

तदुक्तमृषिणा —
गर्भे नु सन्नन्वेषामवेदमहं देवानां जनिमानि विश्वा ।
शतं मा पुर आयसीररक्षन्नधः श्येनो जवसा निरदीयमिति ।
गर्भ एवैतच्छयानो वामदेव एवमुवाच ॥ ५ ॥

5. Therefore it was said by the sage Vamadeva: "I, Vamadeva, being yet in the womb, knew all the births of these gods and their causes. In a hundred cities of iron they held me down and kept me; I broke through them all with might & violence, like a hawk I soared up into my heavens." While yet he lay in the womb, thus said Vamadeva.

स एवं विद्वानस्माच्छरीरभेदादूर्ध्व उत्क्रम्यामुष्मिन् स्वर्गे लोके सर्वान्
कामानाप्त्वामृतः समभवत्समभवत् ॥ ६ ॥

6. And because he knew this, therefore when the strings of the
body were snapped asunder, lo he soared forth into yonder
world of Paradise & there having possessed all desires, put
death behind him, yea, he put death behind him.

Chapter V

कोऽयमात्मेति वयमुपास्महे कतरः स आत्मा । येन वा पश्यति येन
वा शृणोति येन वा गन्धानाजिघ्रति येन वा वाचं व्याकरोति येन वा
स्वादु चास्वादु च विजानाति ॥ १ ॥

1. Who is this Spirit that we may adore Him? and which of
all these is the Spirit? by whom one seeth or by whom one
heareth or by whom one smelleth all kinds of perfume or
by whom one uttereth clearness of speech or by whom one
knoweth the sweet and bitter.

यदेतद्धृदयं मनश्चैतत् । संज्ञानमाज्ञानं विज्ञानं प्रज्ञानं मेधा दृष्टिर्धृति-
र्मतिर्मनीषा जूतिः स्मृतिः संकल्पः क्रतुरसुः कामो वश इति । सर्वा-
ण्येवैतानि प्रज्ञानस्य नामधेयानि भवन्ति ॥ २ ॥

2. This which is the heart, is mind also. Concept and will and
analysis and wisdom and intellect and vision and continuity
of purpose and feeling and understanding, pain and memory
and volition and operation of thought and vitality and desire
and passion, all these, yea all, are but names of the Eternal
Wisdom.

एष ब्रह्मैष इन्द्र एष प्रजापतिरेते सर्वे देवा इमानि च पञ्च महाभूतानि
पृथिवी वायुराकाश आपो ज्योतींषीत्येतानीमानि च क्षुद्रमिश्राणीव ।
बीजानीतराणि चेतराणि चाण्डजानि च जारुजानि च स्वेदजानि
चोद्भिज्जानि चाश्वा गावः पुरुषा हस्तिनो यत्किंचेदं प्राणि जङ्गमं च
पतत्रि च यच्च स्थावरं सर्वं तत् प्रज्ञानेत्रं प्रज्ञाने प्रतिष्ठितं प्रज्ञानेत्रो
लोकः प्रज्ञा प्रतिष्ठा प्रज्ञानं ब्रह्म ॥ ३ ॥

3. This creating Brahma; this ruling Indra; this Prajapati Father
   of his peoples; all these Gods and these five elemental substances, even earth, air, ether, water and the shining principles; and these great creatures and those small; and seeds
   of either sort; and things egg-born and things sweat-born
   and things born of the womb and plants that sprout; and
   horses and cattle and men and elephants; yea, whatsoever
   thing here breatheth and all that moveth and everything that
   hath wings and whatso moveth not; by Wisdom all these are
   guided and have their firm abiding in Wisdom. For Wisdom
   is the eye of the world, Wisdom is the sure foundation,
   Wisdom is Brahman Eternal.

स एतेन प्रज्ञेनात्मनास्माल्लोकादुत्क्रम्यामुष्मिन् स्वर्गे लोके सर्वान्
कामानाश्वामृतः समभवत्समभवत् ॥ ४ ॥

4. By the strength of the wise and seeing Self the sage having
   soared up from this world ascended into his other world
   of Paradise; and there having possessed desire, put death
   behind him, yea, he put death behind him.

Taittiriya Upanishad

Shiksha Valli

Chapter I

हरिः ॐ । शं नो मित्रः शं वरुणः । शं नो भवत्वर्यमा । शं न इन्द्रो
बृहस्पतिः । शं नो विष्णुरुरुक्रमः । नमो ब्रह्मणे । नमस्ते वायो । त्वमेव
प्रत्यक्षं ब्रह्मासि । त्वामेव प्रत्यक्षं ब्रह्म वदिष्यामि । ऋतं वदिष्यामि ।
सत्यं वदिष्यामि । तन्मामवतु । तद्वक्तारमवतु । अवतु माम् । अवतु
वक्तारम् । ॐ शान्तिः शान्तिः शान्तिः ॥

Hari OM. Be peace to us Mitra. Be peace to us Varouna. Be
peace to us Aryaman. Be peace to us Indra & Brihaspati. May
far-striding Vishnu be peace to us. Adoration to the Eternal.
Adoration to thee, O Vaiou. Thou, thou art the visible Eternal
and as the visible Eternal I will declare thee. I will declare Righteousness! I will declare Truth! May that protect me! May that
protect the Speaker! Yea, may it protect me! May it protect the
Speaker. OM Peace! Peace! Peace!

Chapter II

ॐ शीक्षां व्याख्यास्यामः । वर्णः स्वरः । मात्रा बलम् । साम संतानः ।
इत्युक्तः शीक्षाध्यायः ॥

OM. We will expound Shiksha, the elements. Syllable and Ac-
cent, Pitch and Effort, Even Tone and Continuity, in these six
we have declared the chapter of the elements.

Chapter III

सह नौ यशः । सह नौ ब्रह्मवर्चसम् । अथातः संहिताया उपनिषदं
व्याख्यास्यामः । पञ्चस्वधिकरणेषु । अधिलोकमधिज्यौतिषमधिविद्य-
मधिप्रजमध्यात्मम् । ता महासंहिता इत्याचक्षते ।

अथाधिलोकम् । पृथिवी पूर्वरूपम् । द्यौरुत्तररूपम् । आकाश:
संधि: । वायु: संधानम् । इत्यधिलोकम् ।

अथाधिज्यौतिषम् । अग्नि: पूर्वरूपम् । आदित्य उत्तररूपम् ।
आप: संधि: । वैद्युत: संधानम् । इत्यधिज्यौतिषम् ।

अथाधिविद्यम् । आचार्य: पूर्वरूपम् । अन्तेवास्युत्तररूपम् । विद्या
संधि: । प्रवचनं संधानम् । इत्यधिविद्यम् ।

अथाधिप्रजम् । माता पूर्वरूपम् । पितोत्तररूपम् । प्रजा संधि: ।
प्रजननं संधानम् । इत्यधिप्रजम् ।

अथाध्यात्मम् । अधरा हनु: पूर्वरूपम् । उत्तरा हनुरुत्तररूपम् ।
वाक् संधि: । जिह्वा संधानम् । इत्यध्यात्मम् ।

इतीमा महासंहिता: । य एवमेता महासंहिता व्याख्याता वेद ।
संधीयते प्रजया पशुभि: । ब्रह्मवर्चसेनान्नाद्येन सुवर्ग्येण लोकेन ॥

Together may we attain glory, together to the radiance of ho-
liness. Hereupon we will expound next the secret meaning of
Sanhita whereof there are five capitals; Concerning the Worlds:
Concerning the Shining Fires: Concerning the Knowledge: Con-
cerning Progeny: Concerning Self. These are called the great
Sanhitas.

Now concerning the worlds. Earth is the first form; the
heavens are the second form; ether is the linking; air is the joint
of the linking. Thus far concerning the worlds.

Next concerning the shining fires. Fire is the first form; the
Sun is the latter form; the waters are the linking; electricity is
the joint of the linking. Thus far concerning the shining fires.

Next concerning the Knowledge. The Master is the first
form; the disciple is the latter form; Knowledge is the linking;
exposition is the joint of the linking. Thus far concerning the
Knowledge.

Next concerning progeny. The mother is the first form; the
father is the latter form; progeny is the linking; act of procreation
is the joint of the linking. Thus far concerning progeny.

Next concerning Self. The upper jaw is the first form; the
lower jaw is the latter form; speech is the linking; the tongue is
the joint of the linking. Thus far concerning Self.

These are the great Sanhitas. He who knoweth thus the great
Sanhitas as we have expounded them, to him are linked progeny

and wealth of cattle and the radiance of holiness and food and all that is of food and the world of his high estate in heaven.

Chapter IV

यश्छन्दसामृषभो विश्वरूपः। छन्दोभ्योऽध्यमृतात्संबभूव। स मेन्द्रो मेधया स्पृणोतु। अमृतस्य देव धारणो भूयासम्। शरीरं मे विचर्षणम्। जिह्वा मे मधुमत्तमा। कर्णाभ्यां भूरि विश्रुवम्। ब्रह्मणः कोशोऽसि मेधया पिहितः। श्रुतं मे गोपाय।

आवहन्ती वितन्वाना। कुर्वाणाचीरमात्मनः। वासांसि मम गावश्च। अन्नपाने च सर्वदा। ततो मे श्रियमावह। लोमशं पशुभिः सह स्वाहा।

आ मा यन्तु ब्रह्मचारिणः स्वाहा।

वि मायन्तु ब्रह्मचारिणः स्वाहा।

प्र मायन्तु ब्रह्मचारिणः स्वाहा।

दमायन्तु ब्रह्मचारिणः स्वाहा।

शमायन्तु ब्रह्मचारिणः स्वाहा।

यशो जनेऽसानि स्वाहा।

श्रेयान् वस्यसोऽसानि स्वाहा।

तं त्वा भग प्रविशानि स्वाहा।

स मा भग प्रविश स्वाहा।

तस्मिन् सहस्रशाखे। नि भगाहं त्वयि मृजे स्वाहा।

यथापः प्रवता यन्ति। यथा मासा अहर्जरम्। एवं मां ब्रह्म-चारिणः। धातरायन्तु सर्वतः स्वाहा।

प्रतिवेशोऽसि प्र मा भाहि प्र मा पद्यस्व॥

The bull of the hymns of Veda whose visible form is all this Universe, he above the Vedas who sprang from that which is deathless, may Indra increase intellect unto me for my strengthening. O God, may I become a vessel of immortality. May my body be swift to all works, may my tongue drop pure honey. May I hear vast and manifold lore with my ears. O Indra, thou art the sheath of the Eternal and the veil that the workings of brain have drawn over Him; preserve whole unto me the sacred lore that I have studied.

She bringeth unto me wealth and extendeth it, yea, she

maketh speedily my own raiment and cattle and drink and food now and always; therefore carry to me Fortune of much fleecy wealth and cattle with her. Swaha!

May the Brahmacharins come unto me. Swaha!

From here and there may the Brahmacharins come unto me. Swaha!

May the Brahmacharins set forth unto me. Swaha!

May the Brahmacharins attain self-mastery. Swaha!

May the Brahmacharins attain to peace of soul. Swaha!

May I be a name among the folk! Swaha!

May I be the first of the wealthy! Swaha!

O Glorious Lord, into That which is Thou may I enter. Swaha!

Do thou also enter into me, O Shining One. Swaha!

Thou art a river with a hundred branching streams, O Lord of Grace, in thee may I wash me clean. Swaha!

As the waters of a river pour down the steep, as the months of the year hasten to the old age of days, O Lord that cherisheth, so may the Brahmacharins come to me from all the regions. Swaha!

O Lord, thou art my neighbour, thou dwellest very near me. Come to me, be my light and sun.

Chapter V

भूर्भुवः सुवरिति वा एतास्तिस्रो व्याहृतयः । तासामु ह स्मैतां चतुर्थीम् । माहाचमस्यः प्रवेदयते । मह इति । तद् ब्रह्म । स आत्मा । अङ्गान्यन्या देवताः ।

भूरिति वा अयं लोकः । भुव इत्यन्तरिक्षम् । सुवरित्यसौ लोकः । मह इत्यादित्यः । आदित्येन वाव सर्वे लोका महीयन्ते ।

भूरिति वा अग्निः । भुव इति वायुः । सुवरित्यादित्यः । मह इति चन्द्रमाः । चन्द्रमसा वाव सर्वाणि ज्योतींषि महीयन्ते ।

भूरिति वा ऋचः । भुव इति सामानि । सुवरिति यजूंषि । मह इति ब्रह्म । ब्रह्मणा वाव सर्वे वेदा महीयन्ते ।

भूरिति वै प्राणः । भुव इत्यपानः । सुवरिति व्यानः । मह इत्यन्नम् । अन्नेन वाव सर्वे प्राणा महीयन्ते ।

ता वा एताश्चतस्रश्चतुर्धा । चतस्रश्चतस्रो व्याहृतयः । ता यो वेद ।
स वेद ब्रह्म । सर्वेऽस्मै देवा बलिमावहन्ति ॥

Bhûr, Bhuvar and Suvar, these are the three Words of His naming.
Verily the Rishi Mahachamasya made known a fourth to these,
which is Mahas. It is Brahman, it is the Self, and the other gods
are his members.

Bhûr, it is this world; Bhuvar, it is the sky; Suvar, it is the
other world: but Mahas is the Sun. By the Sun all these worlds
increase and prosper.

Bhûr, it is Fire; Bhuvar, it is Air; Suvar, it is the Sun: but
Mahas is the Moon. By the Moon all these shining fires increase
and prosper.

Bhûr, it is the hymns of the Rigveda; Bhuvar, it is the hymns
of the Sâma; Suvar, it is the hymns of the Yajur: but Mahas is
the Eternal. By the Eternal all these Vedas increase and prosper.

Bhûr, it is the main breath; Bhuvar, it is the lower breath;
Suvar, it is the breath pervasor: but Mahas is food. By food all
these breaths increase and prosper.

These are the four & they are fourfold; — four Words of His
naming and each is four again. He who knoweth these knoweth
the Eternal, and to him all the Gods carry the offering.

Chapter VI

स य एषोऽन्तर्हृदय आकाशः । तस्मिन्नयं पुरुषो मनोमयः । अमृतो
हिरण्मयः । अन्तरेण तालुके । य एष स्तन इवावलम्बते । सेन्द्रयोनिः ।
यत्रासौ केशान्तो विवर्तते । व्यपोह्य शीर्षकपाले ।

भूरित्यग्नौ प्रतितिष्ठति । भुव इति वायौ । सुवरित्यादित्ये ।
मह इति ब्रह्मणि । आप्नोति स्वाराज्यम् । आप्नोति मनसस्पतिम् ।
वाक्पतिश्चक्षुष्पतिः । श्रोत्रपतिर्विज्ञानपतिः । एतत्ततो भवति । आकाश-
शरीरं ब्रह्म । सत्यात्म प्राणारामं मनआनन्दम् । शान्तिसमृद्धममृतम् ।
इति प्राचीनयोग्योपास्व ॥

Lo this heaven of ether which is in the heart within, there
dwelleth the Being who is all Mind, the radiant & golden Immortal. Between the two palates, this that hangeth down like

the breast of a woman, is the womb of Indra; yea where the hair at its end whirleth round like an eddy, there it divideth the skull and pusheth through it.

As Bhûr He is established in Agni, as Bhuvar in Vaiou, as Suvar in the Sun, as Mahas in the Eternal. He attaineth to the kingdom of Himself; He attaineth to be the Lord of Mind; He becometh Lord of Speech, Lord of Sight, Lord of Hearing, Lord of the Knowledge. Thereafter this too He becometh, — the Eternal whose body is all ethereal space, whose soul is Truth, whose bliss is in Mind, who taketh His ease in Prana, the Rich in Peace, the Immortal. As such, O son of the ancient Yoga, do thou adore Him.

Chapter VII

पृथिव्यन्तरिक्षं द्यौर्दिशोऽवान्तरदिशः । अग्निर्वायुरादित्यश्चन्द्रमा नक्ष-
त्राणि । आप ओषधयो वनस्पतय आकाश आत्मा । इत्यधिभूतम् ।
अथाध्यात्मम् । प्राणो व्यानोऽपान उदानः समानः । चक्षुः श्रोत्रं
मनो वाक् त्वक् । चर्म मांसं स्नावास्थि मज्जा । एतदधिविधाय
ऋषिरवोचत् । पाङ्क्तं वा इदं सर्वम् । पाङ्क्तेनैव पाङ्क्तं स्पृणोतीति ॥

Earth, sky, heaven, the quarters and the lesser quarters; Fire, Air, Sun, Moon and the Constellations; Waters, herbs of healing, trees of the forest, ether and the Self in all; these three concerning this outer creation.

Then concerning the Self. The main breath, the middle breath, the nether breath, the upper breath and the breath pervasor; eye, ear, mind, speech and the skin; hide, flesh, muscle, bone and marrow. Thus the Rishi divided them and said, "In sets of five is this universe; five and five with five and five He relateth."

Chapter VIII

ओमिति ब्रह्म । ओमितीदं सर्वम् । ओमित्येतदनुकृतिर्ह स्म वा अप्यो
श्रावयेत्याश्रावयन्ति । ओमिति सामानि गायन्ति । ओं शोमिति
शस्त्राणि शंसन्ति । ओमित्यध्वर्युः प्रतिगरं प्रतिगृणाति । ओमिति ब्रह्मा

प्रसौति । ओमित्यग्निहोत्रमनुजानाति । ओमिति ब्राह्मणः प्रवक्ष्यन्नाह ब्रह्योपाप्नवानीति । ब्रह्मैवोपाप्नोति ॥

OM is the Eternal, OM is all this universe. OM is the syllable of assent: saying OM! let us hear, they begin the citation. With OM they sing the hymns of the Sama; with OM SHOM they pronounce the Shastra. With OM the priest officiating at the sacrifice sayeth the response. With OM Brahma beginneth creation (or With OM the chief priest giveth sanction). With OM one sanctioneth the burnt offering. With OM the Brahmin ere he expound the Knowledge, crieth "May I attain the Eternal." The Eternal verily he attaineth.

Chapter IX

ऋतं च स्वाध्यायप्रवचने च । सत्यं च स्वाध्यायप्रवचने च । तपश्च स्वाध्यायप्रवचने च । दमश्च स्वाध्यायप्रवचने च । शमश्च स्वाध्याय- प्रवचने च । अग्नयश्च स्वाध्यायप्रवचने च । अग्निहोत्रं च स्वाध्याय- प्रवचने च । अतिथयश्च स्वाध्यायप्रवचने च । मानुषं च स्वाध्याय- प्रवचने च । प्रजा च स्वाध्यायप्रवचने च । प्रजनश्च स्वाध्यायप्रवचने च । प्रजातिश्च स्वाध्यायप्रवचने च । सत्यमिति सत्यवचा राथीतरः । तप इति तपोनित्यः पौरुशिष्टिः । स्वाध्यायप्रवचने एवेति नाको मौद्गल्यः । तद्धि तपस्तद्धि तपः ॥

Righteousness with the study & teaching of Veda; Truth with the study and teaching of Veda; askesis with the study and teaching of Veda; self-mastery with the study and teaching of Veda. Peace of soul with the study and teaching of Veda. The household fires with the study and teaching of Veda. The burnt offering with the study and teaching of Veda. Progeny with the study and teaching of Veda. Act of procreation with the study and teaching of Veda. Children of thy children with the study and teaching of Veda — *these duties.* "Truth is first" said the truth-speaker, the Rishi son of Rathitar. "Askesis is first" said the constant in austerity, the Rishi son of Purushishta. "Study and teaching of Veda is first" said Naka son of Mudgala. For this too is austerity and this too is askesis.

Chapter X

अहं वृक्षस्य रेरिवा। कीर्तिः पृष्ठं गिरेरिव। ऊर्ध्वपवित्रो वाजिनीव
स्वमृतमस्मि। द्रविणं सवर्चसम्। सुमेधा अमृतोऽक्षितः। इति त्रिशङ्कोे -
र्वेदानुवचनम्।

"I am He that moveth the Tree of the Universe & my glory is like
the shoulders of a high mountain. I am lofty and pure like sweet
nectar in the strong, I am the shining riches of the world, I am
the deep thinker, the deathless One who decayeth not from the
beginning." This is Trishanku's voicing of Veda and the hymn
of his self-knowledge.

Chapter XI

वेदमनूच्याचार्योऽन्तेवासिनमनुशास्ति।
    सत्यं वद। धर्मं चर। स्वाध्यायान्मा प्रमदः। आचार्याय प्रियं
धनमाहृत्य प्रजातन्तुं मा व्यवच्छेत्सीः। सत्यान्न प्रमदितव्यम्।
धर्मान्न प्रमदितव्यम्। कुशलान्न प्रमदितव्यम्। भूत्यै न प्रमदितव्यम्।
स्वाध्यायप्रवचनाभ्यां न प्रमदितव्यम्।
    देवपितृकार्याभ्यां न प्रमदितव्यम्। मातृदेवो भव। पितृदेवो
भव। आचार्यदेवो भव। अतिथिदेवो भव। यान्यनवद्यानि कर्माणि।
तानि सेवितव्यानि। नो इतराणि। यान्यस्माकं सुचरितानि। तानि
त्वयोपास्यानि। नो इतराणि।
    ये के चास्मच्छ्रेयांसो ब्राह्मणाः। तेषां त्वयासनेन प्रश्वसितव्यम्।
श्रद्धया देयम्। अश्रद्धयाऽदेयम्। श्रिया देयम्। ह्रिया देयम्। भिया
देयम्।संविदा देयम्।अथ यदि ते कर्मविचिकित्सा वा वृत्तविचिकित्सा
वा स्यात्। ये तत्र ब्राह्मणाः संमर्शिनः। युक्ता आयुक्ताः। अलूक्षा
धर्मकामाः स्युः। यथा ते तत्र वर्तेरन्। तथा तत्र वर्तेथाः। अथाभ्या-
ख्यातेषु। ये तत्र ब्राह्मणाः संमर्शिनः। युक्ता आयुक्ताः। अलूक्षा
धर्मकामाः स्युः। यथा ते तेषु वर्तेरन्। तथा तेषु वर्तेथाः।
    एष आदेशः। एष उपदेशः। एषा वेदोपनिषत्। एतदनुशासनम्।
एवमुपासितव्यम्। एवमु चैतदुपास्यम् ॥

When the Master hath declared Veda, then he giveth the com-
mandments to his disciple.

    Speak truth, walk in the way of thy duty, neglect not the

study of Veda. When thou hast brought to the Master the wealth
that he desireth, thou shalt not cut short the long thread of
thy race. Thou shalt not be negligent of truth; thou shalt not
be negligent of thy duty; thou shalt not be negligent of welfare; thou shalt not be negligent towards thy increase and thy
thriving; thou shalt not be negligent of the study & teaching of
Veda.

Thou shalt not be negligent of thy works unto the Gods
or thy works unto the Fathers. Let thy father be unto thee as
thy God and thy mother as thy Goddess whom thou adorest.
Serve the Master as a God and as a God the stranger within thy
dwelling. The works that are without blame before the people,
thou shalt do these with diligence and no others. The deeds we
have done that are good and righteous, thou shalt practise these
as a religion and no others.

Whosoever are better and nobler than we among the Brahmins, thou shalt refresh with a seat to honour them. Thou shalt
give with faith and reverence; without faith thou shalt not give.
Thou shalt give with shame, thou shalt give with fear; thou
shalt give with fellow-feeling. Moreover if thou doubt of thy
course or of thy action, then whatsoever Brahmins be there
who are careful thinkers, devout, not moved by others, lovers
of virtue, not severe or cruel, even as they do in that thing, so
do thou. Then as to men accused & arraigned by their fellows,
whatsoever Brahmins be there who are careful thinkers, devout,
not moved by others, lovers of virtue, not severe or cruel, even
as they are towards these, so be thou.

This is the law & the teaching. These are the Command-
ments. In such wise shalt thou practise religion, yea, verily in
such wise do ever religiously.

Chapter XII

शं नो मित्रः शं वरुणः । शं नो भवत्वर्यमा । शं न इन्द्रो बृहस्पतिः । शं
नो विष्णुरुरुक्रमः । नमो ब्रह्मणे । नमस्ते वायो । त्वमेव प्रत्यक्षं ब्रह्मा -
सि । त्वामेव प्रत्यक्षं ब्रह्मावादिषम् । ऋतमवादिषम् । सत्यमवादिषम् ।

तन्मामावीत्। तद्वक्तारमावीत्। आवीन्माम्। आवीद्वक्तारम्। ॐ
शान्ति: शान्ति: शान्ति:। हरि: ॐ ॥

Be peace to us Mitra. Be peace to us Varouna. Be peace to us
Aryaman. Be peace to us Indra and Brihaspati. May far-striding
Vishnu be peace to us. Adoration to the Eternal. Adoration to
thee, O Vaiou. Thou, thou art the visible Eternal & as the visible
Eternal I have declared thee. I have declared Righteousness; I
have declared Truth. That has protected me. That has protected
the Speaker. Yea it protected me; it protected the Speaker. OM.
Peace. Peace. Peace. Hari OM.

Brahmananda Valli

हरिः ॐ । सह नाववतु । सह नौ भुनक्तु । सह वीर्यं करवावहै । तेजस्वि
नावधीतमस्तु मा विद्विषावहै । ॐ शान्तिः शान्तिः शान्तिः ॥

Hari OM. Together may He protect us, together may He possess us, together may we make unto us strength and virility. May our study be full to us of light and power. May we never hate. OM! Peace, peace, peace.

Chapter I

ॐ ब्रह्मविदाप्नोति परम् । तदेषाभ्युक्ता । सत्यं ज्ञानमनन्तं ब्रह्म । यो
वेद निहितं गुहायां परमे व्योमन् । सोऽश्नुते सर्वान्कामान् सह । ब्रह्मणा
विपश्चितेति ।
तस्माद्वा एतस्मादात्मन आकाशः संभूतः । आकाशाद् वायुः ।
वायोरग्निः । अग्नेरापः । अद्भ्यः पृथिवी । पृथिव्या ओषधयः ।
ओषधीभ्योऽन्नम् । अन्नात्पुरुषः । स वा एष पुरुषोऽन्नरसमयः । तस्येद-
मेव शिरः । अयं दक्षिणः पक्षः । अयमुत्तरः पक्षः । अयमात्मा । इदं
पुच्छं प्रतिष्ठा । तदप्येष श्लोको भवति ॥

OM. The knower of Brahman attaineth the Highest; for this is the verse that was declared of old, "Brahman is Truth, Brahman is Knowledge, Brahman is the Infinite, he that findeth Him hidden in the cavern heart of being; in the highest heaven of His creatures, lo he enjoyeth all desire and he abideth with the Eternal, even with that cognisant and understanding Spirit."

This is the Self, the Spirit, and from the Spirit ether was born; and from the ether, air; and from the air, fire; and from the fire, the waters; and from the waters, earth; and from the earth, herbs and plants; and from the herbs and plants, food; and from food man was born. Verily, man, this human being, is made of the essential substance of food. And this that we see is the head of him, and this is his right side and this is his left; and this is his spirit & the self of him; and this is his lower member whereon he resteth abidingly. Whereof this is the Scripture.

Chapter II

अन्नाद्वै प्रजाः प्रजायन्ते। याः काश्च पृथिवीं श्रिताः। अथो अन्नेनैव जीवन्ति। अथैनदपि यन्त्यन्ततः। अन्नं हि भूतानां ज्येष्ठम्। तस्मात् सर्वौषधमुच्यते। सर्वं वै तेऽन्नमाप्नुवन्ति। येऽन्नं ब्रह्मोपासते। अन्नं हि भूतानां ज्येष्ठम्। तस्मात्सर्वौषधमुच्यते। अन्नाद् भूतानि जायन्ते। जातान्यन्नेन वर्धन्ते। अद्यतेऽत्ति च भूतानि। तस्मादन्नं तदुच्यत इति। तस्माद्वा एतस्मादन्नरसमयात्। अन्योऽन्तर आत्मा प्राणमयः। तेनैष पूर्णः। स वा एष पुरुषविध एव। तस्य पुरुषविधताम्। अन्वयं पुरुषविधः। तस्य प्राण एव शिरः। व्यानो दक्षिणः पक्षः। अपान उत्तरः पक्षः। आकाश आत्मा। पृथिवी पुच्छं प्रतिष्ठा। तदप्येष श्लोको भवति ॥

Verily all sorts and races of creatures that have their refuge upon earth, are begotten from food; thereafter they live also by food and 'tis to food again that they return at the end and last. For food is the eldest of created things and therefore they name it the Green Stuff of the Universe. Verily they who worship the Eternal as food, attain the mastery of food to the uttermost; for food is the eldest of created things and therefore they name it the Green Stuff of the Universe. From food all creatures are born and being born they increase by food. Lo it is eaten and it eateth; yea it devoureth the creatures that feed upon it, therefore it is called food from the eating.

Now there is a second and inner Self which is other than this that is of the substance of food; and it is made of the vital stuff called Prana. And the Self of Prana filleth the Self of food. Now the Self of Prana is made in the image of a man; according as is the human image of the other, so is it in the image of the man. The main Breath is the head of him, the breath pervasor is his right side and the lower breath is his left side; ether is his spirit which is the self of him, earth is his lower member whereon he resteth abidingly. Whereof this is the Scripture.

Chapter III

प्राणं देवा अनु प्राणन्ति । मनुष्याः पशवश्च ये । प्राणो हि भूतानामायुः ।
तस्मात्सर्वायुषमुच्यते । सर्वमेव त आयुर्यन्ति । ये प्राणं ब्रह्मोपासते ।
प्राणो हि भूतानामायुः । तस्मात्सर्वायुषमुच्यत इति । तस्यैष एव शारीर
आत्मा । यः पूर्वस्य ।

तस्माद्वा एतस्मात्प्राणमयात् । अन्योऽन्तर आत्मा मनोमयः ।
तेनैष पूर्णः । स वा एष पुरुषविध एव । तस्य पुरुषविधताम् । अन्वयं
पुरुषविधः । तस्य यजुरेव शिरः । ऋग्दक्षिणः पक्षः । सामोत्तरः पक्षः ।
आदेश आत्मा । अथर्वाङ्गिरसः पुच्छं प्रतिष्ठा । तदप्येष श्लोको भवति ॥

The Gods live and breathe under the dominion of Prana and
men and all these that are beasts; for Prana is the life of created
things & therefore they name it the Life-Stuff of the All. Verily
they who worship the Eternal as Prana attain mastery of Life to
the uttermost; for Prana is the life of created things and therefore
they name it the Life-Stuff of the All. And this Self of Prana is
the soul in the body of the former one which was of food.

Now there is yet a second and inner Self which is other
than this that is of Prana, and it is made of Mind. And the
Self of Mind filleth the Self of Prana. Now the Self of Mind is
made in the image of a man; according as is the human image
of the other, so is it in the image of the man. Yajur is the head
of him and the Rigveda is his right side and the Samaveda is
his left side: the Commandment is his spirit which is the self of
him, Atharvan Ungirus is his lower member whereon he resteth
abidingly. Whereof this is the Scripture.

Chapter IV

गतो बाजो निवर्तन्ते । अप्राप्य मनसा सह । आनन्दं ब्रह्मणो विद्वान् ।
न बिभेति कदाचनेति । तस्यैष एव शारीर आत्मा । यः पूर्वस्य ।
तस्माद्वा एतस्मान्मनोमयात् । अन्योऽन्तर आत्मा विज्ञानमयः ।
तेनैष पूर्णः । स वा एष पुरुषविध एव । तस्य पुरुषविधताम् । अन्वयं
पुरुषविधः । तस्य श्रद्धैव शिरः । ऋतं दक्षिणः पक्षः । सत्यमुत्तरः पक्षः ।
योग आत्मा । महः पुच्छं प्रतिष्ठा । तदप्येष श्लोको भवति ॥

The delight of the Eternal from which words turn away without attaining and the mind also returneth baffled, who knoweth the delight of the Eternal? He shall fear nought now or hereafter. And this Self of Mind is the soul in the body to the former one which was of Prana.

Now there is yet a second and inner Self which is other than this which is of Mind and it is made of Knowledge. And the Self of Knowledge filleth the Self of Mind. Now the Knowledge-Self is made in the image of a man; according as is the human image of the other, so is it in the image of the man. Faith is the head of him, Law is his right side, Truth is his left side; Yoga is his spirit which is the self of him; Mahas (the material world) is his lower member whereon he resteth abidingly. Whereof this is the Scripture.

Chapter V

विज्ञानं यज्ञं तनुते। कर्माणि तनुतेऽपि च। विज्ञानं देवाः सर्वे। ब्रह्म ज्येष्ठमुपासते। विज्ञानं ब्रह्म चेद्वेद। तस्माच्चेन्न प्रमाद्यति। शरीरे पाप्मनो हित्वा। सर्वान्कामान् समश्नुत इति। तस्यैष एव शारीर आत्मा। यः पूर्वस्य।

तस्माद्वा एतस्माद्विज्ञानमयात्। अन्योऽन्तर आत्मानन्दमयः। तेनैष पूर्णः। स वा एष पुरुषविध एव। तस्य पुरुषविधताम्। अन्वयं पुरुषविधः। तस्य प्रियमेव शिरः। मोदो दक्षिणः पक्षः। प्रमोद उत्तरः पक्षः। आनन्द आत्मा। ब्रह्म पुच्छं प्रतिष्ठा। तदप्येष श्लोको भवति॥

Knowledge spreadeth the feast of sacrifice and knowledge spreadeth also the feast of works; all the gods offer adoration to him as to Brahman and the Elder of the Universe. For if one worship Brahman as the knowledge and if one swerve not from it neither falter, then he casteth sin from him in this body and tasteth all desire. And this Self of Knowledge is the soul in the body to the former one which was of Mind.

Now there is yet a second and inner self which is other than this which is of Knowledge and it is fashioned out of Bliss. And the Self of Bliss filleth the Self of Knowledge. Now the Bliss

Self is made in the image of a man; according as is the human image of the other, so is it made in the image of the man. Love is the head of Him; Joy is His right side; pleasure is His left side; Bliss is His spirit which is the self of Him; the Eternal is His lower member wherein He resteth abidingly. Whereof this is the Scripture.

Chapter VI

असन्नेव स भवति। असद् ब्रह्मेति वेद चेत्। अस्ति ब्रह्मेति चेद्वेद।
सन्तमेनं ततो विदुरिति। तस्यैष एव शारीर आत्मा। यः पूर्वस्य।
अथातोऽनुप्रश्नः। उताविद्वानमुं लोकं प्रेत्य। कश्चन गच्छतीऽ। आहो
विद्वानमुं लोकं प्रेत्य। कश्चित्समश्नुता३ उ।

सोऽकामयत। बहु स्यां प्रजायेयेति। स तपोऽतप्यत। स
तपस्तप्त्वा। इदं सर्वमसृजत। यदिदं किंच। तत्सृष्ट्वा। तदेवानुप्राविशत्।
तदनुप्रविश्य। सच्च त्यच्चाभवत्। निरुक्तं चानिरुक्तं च। निलयनं
चानिलयनं च। विज्ञानं चाविज्ञानं च। सत्यं चानृतं च सत्यमभवत्।
यदिदं किंच। तत्सत्यमित्याचक्षते। तदप्येष श्लोको भवति॥

One becometh as the unexisting, if he know the Eternal as negation; but if one knoweth of the Eternal that He is, then men know him for the saint & the one reality. And this Self of Bliss is the soul in the body to the former one which was of Knowledge. And thereupon there arise these questions. "When one who hath not the Knowledge, passeth over to that other world, doth any such travel farther? Or when one who knoweth, hath passed over to the other world, doth any such enjoy possession?"

The Spirit desired of old "I would be manifold for the birth of peoples." Therefore He concentrated all Himself in thought, and by the force of His brooding He created all this universe, yea all whatsoever existeth. Now when He had brought it forth, He entered into that He had created, He entering in became the Is here and the May Be there; He became that which is defined and that which hath no feature; He became this housèd thing and that houseless; He became Knowledge and He became Ignorance; He became Truth and He became falsehood. Yea He became all truth, even whatsoever here existeth. Therefore they say of Him that He is Truth. Whereof this is the Scripture.

Chapter VII

असद्वा इदमग्र आसीत्। ततो वै सदजायत। तदात्मानं स्वयम् -
कुरुत। तस्मात् तत्सुकृतमुच्यत इति। यद्वै तत्सुकृतम्। रसो वै
सः। रसं ह्येवायं लब्ध्वानन्दी भवति। को ह्येवान्यात्कः प्राण्यात्।
यदेष आकाश आनन्दो न स्यात्। एष ह्येवानन्दयाति। यदा ह्येवैष
एतस्मिन्नदृश्येऽनात्म्येऽनिरुक्तेऽनिलयनेऽभयं प्रतिष्ठां विन्दते। अथ
सोऽभयं गतो भवति। यदा ह्येवैष एतस्मिन्नुदरमन्तरं कुरुते। अथ
तस्य भयं भवति। तत् त्वेव भयं विदुषोऽमन्वानस्य। तदप्येष श्लोको
भवति ॥

In the beginning all this Universe was Non-Existent and Unmanifest, from which this manifest Existence was born. Itself created itself; none other created it. Therefore they say of it the well and beautifully made. Lo this that is well and beautifully made, verily it is no other than the delight behind existence. When he hath gotten him this delight, then it is that this creature becometh a thing of bliss; for who could labour to draw in the breath or who could have strength to breathe it out, if there were not that Bliss in the heaven of his heart, the ether within his being? It is He that is the fountain of bliss; for when the Spirit that is within us findeth his refuge and firm foundation in the Invisible Bodiless Undefinable and Unhoused Eternal, then he hath passed beyond the reach of Fear. But when the Spirit that is within us maketh for himself even a little difference in the Eternal, then he hath fear, yea the Eternal himself becometh a terror to such a knower who thinketh not. Whereof this is the Scripture.

Chapter VIII

भीषास्मात् वातः पवते। भीषोदेति सूर्यः। भीषास्मादग्निश्चेन्द्रश्च।
मृत्युर्धावति पञ्चम इति। सैषानन्दस्य मीमांसा भवति। युवा स्यात्
साधुयुवाध्यायकः। आशिष्ठो दृढिष्ठो बलिष्ठः। तस्येयं पृथिवी सर्वा

वित्तस्य पूर्णा स्यात् । स एको मानुष आनन्दः । ते ये शतं मानुषा
आनन्दाः । स एको मनुष्यगन्धर्वाणामानन्दः । श्रोत्रियस्य चाकाम-
हतस्य । ते ये शतं मनुष्यगन्धर्वाणामानन्दाः । स एको देवगन्धर्वाणा-
मानन्दः । श्रोत्रियस्य चाकामहतस्य । ते ये शतं देवगन्धर्वाणामानन्दाः ।
स एकः पितृणां चिरलोकलोकानामानन्दः । श्रोत्रियस्य चाकामहतस्य ।
ते ये शतं पितृणां चिरलोकलोकानामानन्दाः । स एक आजानजानां
देवानामानन्दः । श्रोत्रियस्य चाकामहतस्य । ते ये शतमाजानजानां
देवानामानन्दाः । स एकः कर्मदेवानां देवानामानन्दः । ये कर्मणा
देवानपियन्ति । श्रोत्रियस्य चाकामहतस्य । ते ये शतं कर्मदेवानां
देवानामानन्दाः । स एको देवानामानन्दः । श्रोत्रियस्य चाकामहतस्य ।
ते ये शतं देवानामानन्दाः । स एक इन्द्रस्यानन्दः । श्रोत्रियस्य
चाकामहतस्य । ते ये शतमिन्द्रस्यानन्दाः । स एको बृहस्पतेरानन्दः ।
श्रोत्रियस्य चाकामहतस्य । ते ये शतं बृहस्पतेरानन्दाः । स एकः प्रजा-
पतेरानन्दः । श्रोत्रियस्य चाकामहतस्य । ते ये शतं प्रजापतेरानन्दाः ।
स एको ब्रह्मण आनन्दः । श्रोत्रियस्य चाकामहतस्य ।

स यश्चायं पुरुषे । यश्चासावादित्ये । स एकः । स य एवंवित् ।
अस्माल्लोकात् प्रेत्य । एतमन्नमयमात्मानमुपसंक्रामति । एतं प्राणमय-
मात्मानमुपसंक्रामति । एतं मनोमयमात्मानमुपसंक्रामति । एतं वि-
ज्ञानमयमात्मानमुपसंक्रामति । एतमानन्दमयमात्मानमुपसंक्रामति ।
तदप्येष श्लोको भवति ॥

Through the fear of Him the Wind bloweth; through the fear of
Him the Sun riseth; through the fear of Him Indra and Agni and
Death hasten in their courses. Behold this exposition of the Bliss
to which ye shall hearken. Let there be a young man, excellent
& lovely in his youth, a great student; let him have fair manners
and a most firm heart and great strength of body, and let all this
wide earth be full of wealth for his enjoying. That is the measure
of bliss of one human being. Now a hundred and a hundredfold
of the human measure of bliss, is one bliss of men that have
become angels in heaven. And this is the bliss of the Vedawise
whose soul the blight of desire not toucheth. A hundred and a
hundredfold of this measure of angelic bliss is one bliss of Gods
that are angels in heaven. And this is the bliss of the Vedawise
whose soul the blight of desire not toucheth. A hundred and a
hundredfold of this measure of divine angelic bliss is one bliss of
the Fathers whose world of heaven is their world for ever. And

this is the bliss of the Vedawise whose soul the blight of desire not toucheth. A hundred and a hundredfold of this measure of bliss of the Fathers whose worlds are for ever, is one bliss of the Gods who are born as Gods in heaven. And this is the bliss of the Vedawise whose soul the blight of desire not toucheth. A hundred and a hundredfold of this measure of bliss of the firstborn in heaven, is one bliss of the Gods of work who are Gods, for by the strength of their deeds they depart and are Gods in heaven. And this is the bliss of the Vedawise whose soul the blight of desire not toucheth. A hundred and a hundredfold of this measure of bliss of the Gods of work, is one bliss of the great Gods who are Gods for ever. And this is the bliss of the Vedawise whose soul the blight of desire not toucheth. A hundred and a hundredfold of this measure of divine bliss, is one bliss of Indra, the King in Heaven. And this is the bliss of the Vedawise whose soul the blight of desire not toucheth. A hundred and a hundredfold of this measure of Indra's bliss is one bliss of Brihaspati, who taught the Gods in heaven. And this is the bliss of the Vedawise whose soul the blight of desire not toucheth. A hundred and a hundredfold of this measure of Brihaspati's bliss, is one bliss of Prajapati, the Almighty Father. And this is the bliss of the Vedawise whose soul the blight of desire not toucheth. A hundred and a hundredfold of this measure of Prajapati's bliss, is one bliss of the Eternal Spirit. And this is the bliss of the Vedawise whose soul the blight of desire not toucheth.

The Spirit who is here in a man and the Spirit who is there in the Sun, it is one Spirit and there is no other. He who knoweth this, when he hath gone away from this world, passeth to this Self which is of food; he passeth to this Self which is of Prana; he passeth to this Self which is of Mind; he passeth to this Self which is of Knowledge; he passeth to this Self which is of Bliss. Whereof this is the Scripture.

Chapter IX

यतो वाचो निवर्तन्ते । अप्राप्य मनसा सह । आनन्दं ब्रह्मणो विद्वान् ।
न बिभेति कुतश्चनेति । एतं ह वाव न तपति । किमहं साधु नाकरवम् ।
किमहं पापमकरवमिति । स य एवं विद्वानेते आत्मानं स्पृणुते । उभे
ह्येवैष एते आत्मानं स्पृणुते । य एवं वेद । इत्युपनिषत् ।
सह नाववतु । सह नौ भुनक्तु । सह वीर्यं करवावहै । तेजस्वि
नावधीतमस्तु मा विद्विषावहै । ॐ शान्तिः शान्तिः शान्तिः । हरिः
ॐ ॥

The Bliss of the Eternal from which words turn back without
attaining and mind also returneth baffled, who knoweth the
Bliss of the Eternal? He feareth not for aught in this world or
elsewhere. Verily to him cometh not remorse and her torment
saying "Why have I left undone the good & why have I done
that which was evil?" For he who knoweth the Eternal, knoweth
these that they are alike his Spirit; yea, he knoweth both evil and
good for what they are and delivereth Spirit, who knoweth the
Eternal. And this is Upanishad, the secret of the Veda.

Together may He protect us, together may He possess us,
together may we make unto us strength & virility. May our
reading be full of light and power. May we never hate. OM
Peace! Peace! Peace! Hari OM!

Bhrigu Valli

हरिः ॐ । सह नाववतु । सह नौ भुनक्तु । सह वीर्यं करवावहै । तेजस्वि
नावधीतमस्तु मा विद्विषावहै । ॐ शान्तिः शान्तिः शान्तिः ॥

Hari OM. Together may He protect us, together may He possess us, together may we make unto us force & virility. May our reading be full of light and power. May we never hate. OM Peace! Peace! Peace!

Chapter I

भृगुर्वै वारुणिः । वरुणं पितरमुपससार । अधीहि भगवो ब्रह्मेति । तस्मा
एतत् प्रोवाच । अन्नं प्राणं चक्षुः श्रोत्रं मनो वाचमिति । तं होवाच ।
यतो वा इमानि भूतानि जायन्ते । येन जातानि जीवन्ति । यत्
प्रयन्त्यभिसंविशन्ति । तद् विजिज्ञासस्व । तद् ब्रह्मेति । स तपोऽतप्यत ।
स तपस्तप्त्वा ॥

Bhrigu, Varouna's son, came unto his father Varouna and said "Lord, teach me the Eternal." And his father declared it unto him thus "Food and Prana and Eye and Ear and Mind — even these." Verily he said unto him "Seek thou to know that from which these creatures are born, whereby being born they live and to which they go hence and enter again; for that is the Eternal." And Bhrigu concentrated himself in thought and by the askesis of his brooding

Chapter II

अन्नं ब्रह्मेति व्यजानात् । अन्नाद्ध्येव खल्विमानि भूतानि जायन्ते । अन्नेन
जातानि जीवन्ति । अन्नं प्रयन्त्यभिसंविशन्तीति । तद्विज्ञाय । पुनरेव
वरुणं पितरमुपससार । अधीहि भगवो ब्रह्मेति । तं होवाच । तपसा ब्रह्म
विजिज्ञासस्व । तपो ब्रह्मेति । स तपोऽतप्यत । स तपस्तप्त्वा ॥

He knew food for the Eternal. For from food alone, it appeareth, are these creatures born and being born they live by food, and into food they depart and enter again. And when he had known this, he came again to Varouna his father and said "Lord, teach me the Eternal." And his father said to him "By askesis do thou seek to know the Eternal, for concentration in thought is the Eternal." He concentrated himself in thought and by the energy of his brooding

Chapter III

प्राणो ब्रह्मेति व्यजानात्। प्राणाद्ध्येव खल्विमानि भूतानि जायन्ते। प्राणेन जातानि जीवन्ति। प्राणं प्रयन्त्यभिसंविशन्तीति। तद्विज्ञाय। पुनरेव वरुणं पितरमुपससार। अधीहि भगवो ब्रह्मेति। तं होवाच। तपसा ब्रह्म विजिज्ञासस्व। तपो ब्रह्मेति। स तपोऽतप्यत। स तप-स्तत्त्वा॥

He knew Prana for the Eternal. For from Prana alone, it appeareth, are these creatures born and being born they live by Prana and to Prana they go hence and return. And when he had known this, he came again to Varouna his father and said "Lord, teach me the Eternal." But his father said to him "By askesis do thou seek to know the Eternal, for askesis in thought is the Eternal." He concentrated himself in thought and by the energy of his brooding

Chapter IV

मनो ब्रह्मेति व्यजानात्। मनसो ह्येव खल्विमानि भूतानि जायन्ते। मनसा जातानि जीवन्ति। मनः प्रयन्त्यभिगिरांविशन्तीति। तद्विज्ञाय। पुनरेव वरुणं पितरमुपससार। अधीहि भगवो ब्रह्मेति। तं होवाच। तपसा ब्रह्म विजिज्ञासस्व। तपो ब्रह्मेति। स तपोऽतप्यत। स तप-स्तत्त्वा॥

He knew mind for the Eternal. For from mind alone, it appeareth, are these creatures born and being born they live by

mind, and to mind they go hence and return. And when he had
known this, he came again to Varouna his father and said "Lord,
teach me the Eternal." But his father said to him "By askesis do
thou seek to know the Eternal, for concentration of force is the
Eternal." He concentrated himself in thought and by the energy
of his brooding

Chapter V

विज्ञानं ब्रह्मेति व्यजानात्। विज्ञानाद्ध्येव खल्विमानि भूतानि जायन्ते।
विज्ञानेन जातानि जीवन्ति। विज्ञानं प्रयन्त्यभिसंविशन्तीति। तद्विज्ञा-
ज्ञाय। पुनरेव वरुणं पितरमुपससार। अधीहि भगवो ब्रह्मेति। तं
होवाच। तपसा ब्रह्म विजिज्ञासस्व। तपो ब्रह्मेति। स तपोऽतप्यत। स
तपस्तप्त्वा॥

He knew Knowledge for the Eternal. For from Knowledge alone,
it appeareth, are these creatures born and being born they live
by Knowledge and to Knowledge they go hence and return. And
when he had known this, he came again to Varouna his father
and said "Lord, teach me the Eternal." But his father said to him
"By askesis do thou seek to know the Eternal, for concentration
of force is the Eternal." He concentrated himself in thought and
by the energy of his brooding

Chapter VI

आनन्दो ब्रह्मेति व्यजानात्। आनन्दाद्ध्येव खल्विमानि भूतानि जायन्ते।
आनन्देन जातानि जीवन्ति। आनन्दं प्रयन्त्यभिसंविशन्तीति। सैषा
भार्गवी वारुणी विद्या। परमे व्योमन्प्रतिष्ठिता। स य एवं वेद प्रति-
तिष्ठति। अन्नवानन्नादो भवति। महान्भवति प्रजया पशुभिर्ब्रह्मवर्चसेन।
महान्कीर्त्या॥

He knew Bliss for the Eternal. For from Bliss alone, it appeareth,
are these creatures born and being born they live by Bliss and
to Bliss they go hence and return. This is the lore of Bhrigu, the
lore of Varouna, which hath its firm base in the highest heaven.

Who knoweth, getteth his firm base, he becometh the master of food and its eater, great in progeny, great in cattle, great in the splendour of holiness, great in glory.

Chapter VII

अन्नं न निन्द्यात्। तद् व्रतम्। प्राणो वा अन्नम्। शरीरमन्नादम्। प्राणे शरीरं प्रतिष्ठितम्। शरीरे प्राणः प्रतिष्ठितः। तदेतदन्नमन्ने प्रतिष्ठितम्। स य एतदन्नमन्ने प्रतिष्ठितं वेद प्रतितिष्ठति। अन्नवानन्नादो भवति। महान्भवति प्रजया पशुभिर्ब्रह्मवर्चसेन। महान्कीर्त्या ॥

Thou shalt not blame food; for that is thy commandment unto labour. Verily Prana also is food, and the body is the eater. The body is established upon Prana and Prana is established upon the body. Therefore food here is established upon food. He who knoweth this food that is established upon food, getteth his firm base, he becometh the master of food and its eater, great in progeny, great in cattle, great in the radiance of holiness, great in glory.

Chapter VIII

अन्नं न परिचक्षीत। तद् व्रतम्। आपो वा अन्नम्। ज्योतिरन्नादम्। अप्सु ज्योतिः प्रतिष्ठितम्। ज्योतिष्यापः प्रतिष्ठिताः। तदेतदन्नमन्ने प्रतिष्ठितम्। स य एतदन्नमन्ने प्रतिष्ठितं वेद प्रतितिष्ठति। अन्नवानन्नादो भवति। महान्भवति प्रजया पशुभिर्ब्रह्मवर्चसेन। महान्कीर्त्या ॥

Thou shalt not reject food; for that too is the vow of thy labour. Verily the waters also are food, and the bright fire is the eater. The fire is established upon the waters and the waters are established upon the fires. Here too is food established upon food. He who knoweth this food that is established upon food, getteth his firm base, he becometh the master of food and its eater, great in progeny, great in cattle, great in the radiance of holiness, great in glory.

Chapter IX

अन्नं बहु कुर्वीत। तद् व्रतम्। पृथिवी वा अन्नम्। आकाशोऽन्नादः।
पृथिव्यामाकाशः प्रतिष्ठितः। आकाशे पृथिवी प्रतिष्ठिता। तदेतदन्नमन्ने
प्रतिष्ठितम्। स य एतदन्नमन्ने प्रतिष्ठितं वेद प्रतितिष्ठति। अन्नवानन्नादो
भवति। महान्भवति प्रजया पशुभिर्ब्रह्मवर्चसेन। महान्कीर्त्या ॥

Thou shalt increase and amass food; for that too is thy commandment unto labour. Verily, earth also is food and ether is the
eater. Ether is established upon earth and earth is established
upon ether. Here too is food established upon food. He who
knoweth this food that is established upon food, getteth his firm
base. He becometh the master of food and its eater, great in
progeny, great in cattle, great in the radiance of holiness, great
in glory.

Chapter X

न कंचन वसतौ प्रत्याचक्षीत। तद् व्रतम्। तस्माद् यया कया
च विधया बह्वन्नं प्राप्नुयात्। अराध्यस्मा अन्नमित्याचक्षते। एतद्वै
मुखतोऽन्नं राद्धम्। मुखतोऽस्मा अन्नं राध्यते। एतद्वै मध्यतोऽन्नं
राद्धम्। मध्यतोऽस्मा अन्नं राध्यते। एतद्वा अन्ततोऽन्नं राद्धम्।
अन्ततोऽस्मा अन्नं राध्यते। य एवं वेद। क्षेम इति वाचि। योगक्षेम इति
प्राणापानयोः। कर्मेति हस्तयोः। गतिरिति पादयोः। विमुक्तिरिति
पायौ। इति मानुषीः समाज्ञाः। अथ दैवीः। तृप्तिरिति वृष्टौ। बलमिति
विद्युति। यश इति पशुषु। ज्योतिरिति नक्षत्रेषु। प्रजातिरमृतमानन्द
इत्युपस्थे। सर्वमित्याकाशे। तत्प्रतिष्ठेत्युपासीत। प्रतिष्ठावान् भवति।
तन्मह इत्युपासीत। महान् भवति। तन्मन इत्युपासीत। मानवान्
भवति। तन्नम इत्युपासीत। नम्यन्तेऽस्मै कामाः। तद् ब्रह्मेत्युपासीत।
ब्रह्मवान् भवति। तद् ब्रह्मणः परिमर इत्युपासीत। पर्येणं म्रियन्ते
द्विषन्तः सपत्नाः। परि येऽप्रिया भ्रातृव्याः। स यश्चायं पुरुषे।
यश्चासावादित्ये। स एकः। स य एवंवित्। अस्माल्लोकात् प्रेत्य।
एतमन्नमयमात्मानमुपसंक्रम्य। एतं प्राणमयमात्मानमुपसंक्रम्य। एतं
मनोमयमात्मानमुपसंक्रम्य। एतं विज्ञानमयमात्मानमुपसंक्रम्य। एत-
मानन्दमयमात्मानमुपसंक्रम्य। इमाँल्लोकान् कामान्नी कामरूप्यनुसं-
चरन्। एतत् साम गायन्नास्ते। हाउवु हाउवु हाउवु। अहमन्नमह-
मन्नमहमन्नम्। अहमन्नादोऽ३हमन्नादोऽ३हमन्नादः। अहं श्लोककृदहं

श्लोककृदहं श्लोककृत् । अहमस्मि प्रथमजा ऋताऽस्य । पूर्वं देवेभ्यो
अमृतस्य नाऽभायि । यो मा ददाति स इदेव माऽवा: । अहमन्नमन्न-
मदन्तमाऽद्मि । अहं विश्वं भुवनमभ्यभवाऽम् । सुवर्न ज्योती: । य एवं
वेद । इत्युपनिषत् ॥
     सह नाववतु । सह नौ भुनक्तु । सह वीर्यं करवावहै । तेजस्वि
नावधीतमस्तु मा विद्विषावहै । ॐ शान्ति: शान्ति: शान्ति: । हरि:
ॐ ॥

Thou shalt not reject any man in thy habitation, for that too
is thy commandment unto labour. Therefore in whatsoever sort
do thou get thee great store of food. They say unto the stranger
in their dwelling "Arise, the food is ready." Was the food made
ready at the beginning? To him also is food made ready in the
beginning. Was the food made ready in the middle? To him also
is food made ready in the middle. Was the food made ready at
the end & last? To him also is the food made ready at the end
and last, who hath this knowledge. As prosperity in speech, as
getting & having in the main breath and the nether, as work in
the hands, as movement in the feet, as discharge in the anus,
these are the cognitions in the human. Then in the divine; as
satisfaction in the rain, as force in the lightning, as splendour in
the beasts, as brightness in the constellations, as procreation and
bliss and death conquered in the organ of pleasure, as the All in
Ether. Pursue thou Him as the firm foundation of things & thou
shalt get thee firm foundation. Pursue Him as Mahas, thou shalt
become Mighty; pursue Him as Mind, thou shalt become full
of mind; pursue Him as adoration, thy desires shall bow down
before thee; pursue Him as the Eternal, thou shalt become full
of the Spirit; pursue Him as the destruction of the Eternal that
rangeth abroad, thou shalt see thy rivals and thy haters perish
thick around thee and thy kin who loved thee not. The Spirit
who is here in man & the Spirit who is there in the Sun, lo, it is
One Spirit and there is no other. He who hath this knowledge,
when he goeth from this world having passed to the Self which
is of food; having passed to the Self which is of Prana; having
passed to the Self which is of Mind; having passed to the Self
which is of Knowledge; having passed to the Self which is of

Bliss, lo he rangeth about the worlds & eateth what he will and taketh what shape he will and ever he singeth the mighty Sama. "Ho! ho! ho! I am food! I am food! I am food! I am the eater of food! I am the eater! I am the eater! I am he who maketh Scripture! I am he who maketh! I am he who maketh! I am the firstborn of the Law; before the gods were, I am, yea at the very heart of immortality. He who giveth me, verily he preserveth me; for I being food, eat him that eateth. I have conquered the whole world and possessed it, my light is as the sun in its glory." Thus he singeth, who hath the knowledge. This verily is Upanishad, the secret of the Veda.

Together may He protect us, together may He possess us, together may we make unto us strength and virility! May our study be full of light and power! May we never hate! OM Peace! Peace! Peace! Hari OM!

Section Three

Incomplete Translations
and Commentaries

Circa 1902–1912

Svetasvatara Upanishad

Chapter IV

य एकोऽवर्णो बहुधा शक्तियोगाद् वर्णाननेकान्निहितार्थो दधाति ।
वि चैति चान्ते विश्वमादौ स देवः स नो बुद्धया शुभया संयुनक्तु ॥ १ ॥

1. He who is one and without hue, but has ordained manifoldly
   many hues by the Yoga of his Force and holds within himself
   all objects, and in Him the universe dissolves in the end, that
   Godhead was in the beginning. May He yoke us with a good
   and bright understanding.

तदेवाग्निस्तदादित्यस्तद्वायुस्तदु चन्द्रमाः ।
तदेव शुक्रं तद् ब्रह्म तदापस्तत्प्रजापतिः ॥ २ ॥

2. That alone is the fire and That the sun and That the wind
   and That too the moon; That is the Luminous, That the
   Brahman, That the waters, That the Father and Lord of
   creatures.

त्वं स्त्री त्वं पुमानसि त्वं कुमार उत वा कुमारी ।
त्वं जीर्णो दण्डेन वञ्चसि त्वं जातो भवसि विश्वतोमुखः ॥ ३ ॥

3. Thou art the woman and Thou the man; Thou art a boy
   and again a young virgin; Thou art yonder worn and aged
   man that walkest bent with thy staff. Lo, Thou becomest
   born and the world is full of thy faces.

नीलः पतङ्गो हरितो लोहिताक्षस्तडिद्गर्भ ऋतवः समुद्राः ।
अनादिमत् त्वं विभुत्वेन वर्तसे यतो जातानि भुवनानि विश्वा ॥ ४ ॥

4. Thou art the blue bird and the green and the scarlet-eyed,
   the womb of lightning and the seasons and the oceans. Thou

art that which is without beginning and thou movest with
thy pervasive extension whence all the worlds are born.

अजामेकां लोहितशुक्लकृष्णां बह्वीः प्रजाः सृजमानां सरूपाः ।
अजो ह्येको जुषमाणोऽनुशेते जहात्येनां भुक्तभोगामजोऽन्यः ॥ ५ ॥

5. There is One, unborn, white and black and red, who is ever
bringing forth many creatures with forms and her one unborn loves and cleaves to and lies with her; another unborn
abandons, when all her enjoyments have been enjoyed.

द्वा सुपर्णा सयुजा सखाया समानं वृक्षं परिषस्वजाते ।
तयोरन्यः पिप्पलं स्वाद्वत्त्यनश्नन्नन्यो अभिचाकशीति ॥ ६ ॥

6. Two winged birds cling about a common tree, comrades,
yoke-fellows; and one eats the sweet fruit of the tree, the
other eats not, but watches.

समाने वृक्षे पुरुषो निमग्नोऽनीशया शोचति मुह्यमानः ।
जुष्टं यदा पश्यत्यन्यमीशमस्य महिमानमिति वीतशोकः ॥ ७ ॥

7. The Soul upon a common tree is absorbed and because he
is not lord, grieves and is bewildered; but when he sees and
cleaves to that other who is the Lord, he knows that all is
His greatness and his sorrow passes away from him.

ऋचो अक्षरे परमे व्योमन् यस्मिन्देवा अधि विश्वे निषेदुः ।
यस्तं न वेद किमृचा करिष्यति य इत् तद्विदुस्त इमे समासते ॥ ८ ॥

8. In the highest immutable Heaven where all the gods have
taken up their session, there are the verses of the Rigveda,
and he who knows Him not, what shall he do with the Rik?
They who know That, lo, it is they who thus are seated.

छन्दांसि यज्ञाः क्रतवो व्रतानि भूतं भव्यं यच्च वेदा वदन्ति ।
अस्मान्मायी सृजते विश्वमेतत् तस्मिंश्चान्यो मायया सन्निरुद्धः ॥ ९ ॥

9. Rhythms and sacrifices and ritual and vows, what has been
and what is to be and what the Vedas declare, — the Master

of Maya brings forth from that all this that is and there is another whom within it his Maya holds imprisoned.

मायां तु प्रकृतिं विद्यान्मायिनं तु महेश्वरम् ।
तस्यावयवभूतैस्तु व्याप्तं सर्वमिदं जगत् ॥ १० ॥

10. Thou shalt know Maya to be Force of Nature and the Master of Maya to be the great Lord; this whole universe is occupied by His becomings that are His members.

यो योनिं योनिमधितिष्ठत्येको यस्मिन्निदं सं च वि चैति सर्वम् ।
तमीशानं वरदं देवमीड्यं निचाय्येमां शान्तिमत्यन्तमेति ॥ ११ ॥

11. He who being One enters every womb and in whom all this comes together and goes apart, the adorable Godhead who rules as lord and gives us our desirable boons, one having seen comes exceedingly unto this peace.

यो देवानां प्रभवश्चोद्भवश्च विश्वाधिपो रुद्रो महर्षिः ।
हिरण्यगर्भं पश्यत जायमानं स नो बुद्ध्या शुभया संयुनक्तु ॥ १२ ॥

12. He who is the coming to birth of the gods and the arising of their being, the master of the universe, the Violent One, the Great Seer and beheld Hiranyagarbha born, — may he yoke us with a bright and good understanding.

यो देवानामधिपो यस्मिँल्लोका अधिश्रिताः ।
य ईशे अस्य द्विपदश्चतुष्पदः कस्मै देवाय हविषा विधेम ॥ १३ ॥

13. He who is the master of the gods, in whom the worlds are lodged and who rules over this two-footed and four-footed, to what god should we offer the worship of our oblation?

सूक्ष्मातिसूक्ष्मं कलिलस्य मध्ये विश्वस्य स्रष्टारमनेकरूपम् ।
विश्वस्यैकं परिवेष्टितारं ज्ञात्वा शिवं शान्तिमत्यन्तमेति ॥ १४ ॥

14. Subtle beyond the subtle in the midst of the hurtling chaos, the creator of the universe who has many forms and being

one encompasses all, knowing as the Benign, one comes
exceedingly to the peace.

स एव काले भुवनस्य गोप्ता विश्वाधिपः सर्वभूतेषु गूढः।
यस्मिन् युक्ता ब्रह्मर्षयो देवताश्च तमेवं ज्ञात्वा मृत्युपाशां -
छिन्दन्ति ॥ १५ ॥

15. He in Time is the guardian of the world of existence and the
master of the universe secret in all existences, — in whom
have union of Yoga the holy sages and the gods; thus knowing him one cuts asunder the snares of Death.

घृतात्परं मण्डमिवातिसूक्ष्मं ज्ञात्वा शिवं सर्वभूतेषु गूढम्।
विश्वस्यैकं परिवेष्टितारं ज्ञात्वा देवं मुच्यते सर्वपाशैः ॥ १६ ॥

16. Knowing him who is exceedingly subtle like the cream above
the clarified butter, the Benign secret in all existences, knowing the God who being one encompasses all, one is released
from every bondage.

एष देवो विश्वकर्मा महात्मा सदा जनानां हृदये सन्निविष्टः।
हृदा मनीषा मनसाभिक्लृप्तो य एतद् विदुरमृतास्ते भवन्ति ॥ १७ ॥

17. This is the God, the mighty Soul, the Architect of all, seated
for ever in the hearts of creatures and he is realised by the
heart and the intellect and the mind; who know this, they
become immortal.

यदाऽतमस्तन्न दिवा न रात्रिर्न सन्न चासच्छिव एव केवलः।
तदक्षरं तत्सवितुर्वरेण्यं प्रज्ञा च तस्मात्प्रसृता पुराणी ॥ १८ ॥

18. When there is no darkness, that is neither day nor night, nor
being nor non-being, it is the absolute Benign alone; That is
the immutable, that the supreme light of the Creating Sun
and from it the Wisdom went forth that is of old.

नैनमूर्ध्वं न तिर्यञ्चं न मध्ये परिजग्रभत्।
न तस्य प्रतिमा अस्ति यस्य नाम महद्यशः ॥ १९ ॥

19. Him one shall not seize as on high nor as one on a level plane nor in the middle; there is no image for him whose name is a mighty glory.

न संदृशे तिष्ठति रूपमस्य न चक्षुषा पश्यति कश्चनैनम् ।
हृदा हृदिस्थं मनसा य एनमेवं विदुरमृतास्ते भवन्ति ॥ २० ॥

20. The form of Him stands not within the vision and none beholdeth Him by the eye; but by the heart and the mind, for in the heart is His station; who thus know Him, they become immortal.

अजात इत्येवं कश्चिद् भीरुः प्रपद्यते ।
रुद्र यत्ते दक्षिणं मुखं तेन मां पाहि नित्यम् ॥ २१ ॥

21. One here and there approaches him with awe thinking of him as the Unborn. O Violent One, that which is thy auspicious right-hand face, with that protect me ever.

मा नस्तोके तनये मा न आयुषि मा नो गोषु मा नो अश्वेषु रीरिषः ।
वीरान् मा नो रुद्र भामितो वधीर्हविष्मन्तः सदमित् त्वा हवामहे ॥२२॥

22. Do no hurt to our son nor our grandson nor our life nor our cattle nor our horses. O Violent One, slay not in thy anger our heroes; ever to Thee with the oblation we call.

Chapter V

द्वे अक्षरे ब्रह्मपरे त्वनन्ते विद्याविद्ये निहिते यत्र गूढे ।
क्षरं त्वविद्या ह्यमृतं तु विद्या विद्याविद्ये ईशते यस्तु सोऽन्यः ॥ १ ॥

1. Both of these in the Transcendent, the Knowledge & the
   Ignorance, yea both have their hidden being in the Eternal &
   Infinite Who dwelleth beyond Brahman of the Veda, & are
   set in it for ever. But of these Ignorance dieth and Knowledge
   liveth for ever; and He who is master of both is other than
   they.

यो योनिं योनिमधितिष्ठत्येको विश्वानि रूपाणि योनीश्च सर्वाः ।
ऋषिं प्रसूतं कपिलं यस्तमग्रे ज्ञानैर्बिभर्ति जायमानं च पश्येत् ॥ २ ॥

2. He being One entereth upon womb & womb, yea upon
   all forms of being and upon all wombs of creatures. This
   was He that of old filled with many sorts of Knowledge
   Kapila, the seer, after his mother bore him; yea He saw
   Kapila shaping.

एकैकं जालं बहुधा विकुर्वन्नस्मिन्क्षेत्रे संहरत्येष देवः ।
भूयः सृष्ट्वा यतयस्तथेशः सर्वाधिपत्यं कुरुते महात्मा ॥ ३ ॥

3. God weaveth Him one net or He weaveth Him another and
   He maketh it of manifold meshes & casteth it abroad in
   this field of the body; then He draweth it in again. Also
   He created Yatis, great Seekers, & thus the Mighty Mind
   wieldeth the sceptre of His universal Lordship.

सर्वा दिश ऊर्ध्वमधश्च तिर्यक् प्रकाशयन्भ्राजते यद्वनड्वान् ।
एवं स देवो भगवान्वरेण्यो योनिस्वभावानधितिष्ठत्येकः ॥ ४ ॥

4. The Sun riseth & driveth the world's wain, then he blazeth
   illumining all the regions and above and below and the level
   grow one lustre, even so this glorious & shining God, being
   One, entereth upon & ruleth nature that clingeth to the
   womb, to each womb its nature.

यच्च स्वभावं पचति विश्वयोनि: पाच्यांश्च सर्वान् परिणामयेद्य: ।
सर्वमेतद् विश्वमधितिष्ठत्येको गुणांश्च सर्वान् विनियोजयेद्य: ॥ ५ ॥

5. For He who is the Womb of the World bringeth each nature
   to its perfection and He matureth all those that are yet to be
   perfected. He indwelleth & presideth over all this His world
   and setteth all the modes of Nature to their workings.

तद् वेदगुह्योपनिषत्सु गूढं तद् ब्रह्मा वेदते ब्रह्मयोनिम् ।
ये पूर्वदेवा ऋषयश्च तद्विदुस्ते तन्मया अमृता वै बभूवु: ॥ ६ ॥

6. This is that secret mystery which is hidden in Upanishads;
   for the Upanishad is the secret of the Veda. This is that
   which Brahma knoweth for the Womb of the Eternal and
   the older Gods and the sages who knew of This, became
   This & were immortal.

गुणान्वयो य: फलकर्मकर्ता कृतस्य तस्यैव स चोपभोक्ता ।
स विश्वरूपस्त्रिगुणस्त्रिवर्त्मा प्राणाधिप: संचरति स्वकर्मभि: ॥ ७ ॥

7. There is One who maketh works and their fruits to them, for
   the moods of Nature cleave to Him; this is He that enjoyeth
   the works He hath done; and the World is His body and He
   hath three modes of His natures & the roads of His travel
   are likewise three. Lo, the Master of Life, by the momentum
   of His own works He moveth in the centuries.

अङ्गुष्ठमात्रो रवितुल्यरूप: संकल्पाहंकारसमन्वितो य: ।
बुद्धेर्गुणेनात्मगुणेन चैव आराग्रमात्रो ह्यपरोऽपि दृष्ट: ॥ ८ ॥

8. His size is as the size of a man's thumb but His aspect as
   the Sun in its glory; and He hath Volition and He hath
   Personality; but there is another whom we see by virtue of
   the Understanding & by virtue of the Spirit for the point of
   a cobbler's awl is not finer to vision.

वालाग्रशतभागस्य शतधा कल्पितस्य च ।
भागो जीव: स विज्ञेय: स चानन्त्याय कल्पते ॥ ९ ॥

9. Take thou the hundredth part of the point of a hair, divide it into a hundred parts again; then as is a part of this hundredth part of a hundredth, such shalt thou find this Spirit in man, if thou seek to separate Him; yet 'tis this in thee that availeth towards Infinity.

नैव स्त्री न पुमानेष न चैवायं नपुंसकः ।
यद्यच्छरीरमादत्ते तेन तेन स रक्ष्यते ॥ १० ॥

10. Not woman is He, nor man either, nor yet sexless; but whatsoever body He take, that confineth & preserveth Him.

संकल्पनस्पर्शनदृष्टिमोहैर्ग्रासाम्बुवृष्ट्या चात्मविवृद्धिजन्म ।
कर्मानुगान्यनुक्रमेण देही स्थानेषु रूपाण्यभिसंप्रपद्यते ॥ ११ ॥

11. As body is born and groweth by food and drink and plenty, so also the Spirit in body progressively attaineth to successive forms in their fit places — by the allurements of sight, by the witcheries of touch, by the magic of volition, for according to his works he progresseth and his forms shape themselves to his works.

स्थूलानि सूक्ष्माणि बहूनि चैव रूपाणि देही स्वगुणैर्वृणोति ।
क्रियागुणैरात्मगुणैश्च तेषां संयोगहेतुरपरोऽपि दृष्टः ॥ १२ ॥

12. Forms gross and forms subtle, forms many, — the Spirit in body evolveth them all by his own nature in its working; by the law of action of his works & the law of action of the Spirit in man, by these he evolveth them. But there is Another in Whom we behold Cause whereby all these meet together.

अनाद्यनन्तं कलिलस्य मध्ये विश्वस्य स्रष्टारमनेकरूपम् ।
विश्वस्यैकं परिवेष्टितारं ज्ञात्वा देवं मुच्यते सर्वपाशैः ॥ १३ ॥

13. Without beginning, without end in the welter and the chaos, who createth the world by taking many figures & as the One girdeth & encompasseth it. He is the Lord &

if thou know Him thou shalt break free from all kinds of bondage.

भावग्राह्यमनीडाख्यं भावाभावकरं शिवम् ।
कलासर्गकरं देवं ये विदुस्ते जहुस्तनुम् ॥ १४ ॥

14. Shiva the Master of all becomings and not-becomings and from Him this whole creation floweth and it is only one part of Shiva; but He is not named after any nest of the wingèd Spirit, and the heart alone can apprehend Him. They who know Shiva, the Blessed One, abandon body for ever.

Chapter VI

स्वभावमेके कवयो वदन्ति कालं तथान्ये परिमुह्यमानाः ।
देवस्यैष महिमा तु लोके येनेदं भ्राम्यते ब्रह्मचक्रम् ॥ १ ॥

1. 'Tis Nature and Self-existence, say one school of the Seers.
   Nay, 'tis Time, say another; both are deceived and bewildered. 'Tis the Majesty of the Lord in the world of His
   creatures whereby the Wheel of the Eternal whirleth about
   continually.

येनावृतं नित्यमिदं हि सर्वं ज्ञः कालकारो गुणी सर्वविद्यः ।
तेनेशितं कर्म विवर्तते ह पृथ्व्याप्यतेजोऽनिलखानि चिन्त्यम् ॥ २ ॥

2. He envelopeth this whole Universe with Himself for ever, He
   that knoweth, Maker of Time, & the Modes of Nature dwell
   in Him; yea, all things He discerneth and by His governance
   the Law of Works revolveth in its cycle. Earth, water, fire, air,
   ether, of these thou shalt consider (as the substance wherein
   it turneth).

तत्कर्म कृत्वा विनिवर्त्य भूयस्तत्त्वस्य तत्त्वेन समेत्य योगम् ।
एकेन द्वाभ्यां त्रिभिरष्टभिर्वा कालेन चैवात्मगुणैश्च सूक्ष्मैः ॥ ३ ॥

3. The Lord doeth works and resteth again from His works,
   one or two or three or eight He yoketh Himself with the
   Principle of things in their essence & with Time He yoketh
   Himself and with Self in its subtle workings.

आरभ्य कर्माणि गुणान्वितानि भावांश्च सर्वान् विनियोजयेद्यः ।
तेषामभावे कृतकर्मनाशः कर्मक्षये याति स तत्त्वतोऽन्यः ॥ ४ ॥

4. So He beginneth works, that are subject to the modes of
   Nature, and setteth all existences to their workings: & when
   these things are not, thereby cometh annihilation of work
   that hath been done; and with the perishing of work, He
   departeth out of them; for in His final truth He is other than
   they.

आदिः स संयोगनिमित्तहेतुः परस्त्रिकालादकलोऽपि दृष्टः ।
तं विश्वरूपं भवभूतमीड्यं देवं स्वचित्तस्थमुपास्य पूर्वम् ॥ ५ ॥

5. Lo we have beheld Him & He is the Beginning and the
Cause of all Causes whereby these elements meet together
& form ariseth; the past, the present and the future are this
side of Him and Time hath no part in Him. Let us worship
the Ancient of Days in our own hearts who sitteth. Let us
wait upon God who must be adored, for the world is His
shape and the Universe is but His becoming.

स वृक्षकालाकृतिभिः परोऽन्यो यस्मात्प्रपञ्चः परिवर्ततेऽयम् ।
धर्मावहं पापनुदं भगेशं ज्ञात्वात्मस्थममृतं विश्वधाम ॥ ६ ॥

6. Time & Form and the Tree of Things, none of these is He
for He is more than they & it is from Him that this Cosmos
beginneth. We will know this Master of grace & glory for
He cometh to us carrying righteousness in His hand & He
driveth Sin from its strong places. We will know Him for
He is in our Self & immortal & the World's foundation.

तमीश्वराणां परमं महेश्वरं तं देवतानां परमं च दैवतम् ।
पतिं पतीनां परमं परस्ताद् विदाम देवं भुवनेशमीड्यम् ॥ ७ ॥

7. We will know this Mightiest one who is far above all the
mighty — this summit of the gods & their godhead, King
of Kings and Lord of Lords, who towereth high above all
summits & greatnesses. Let us learn of God for He is this
World's Master & all shall adore Him.

न तस्य कार्यं करणं च विद्यते न तत्समश्चाभ्यधिकश्च दृश्यते ।
परास्य शक्तिर्विविधैव श्रूयते स्वाभाविकी ज्ञानबलक्रिया च ॥ ८ ॥

8. God needeth not to do anything neither hath He any organ of doing; there is none greater than He nor do we
see any that is His equal — for His power is far over all,
only men hear of it under a thousand names & various
fashions. Lo the strength of Him and the works of Him and

His Knowledge, they are self-efficient & their own cause & nature.

न तस्य कश्चित् पतिरस्ति लोके न चेशिता नैव च तस्य लिङ्गम् ।
स कारणं करणाधिपाधिपो न चास्य कश्चिज्जनिता न चाधिपः ॥ ९ ॥

9. He hath no master in all this world, there is none that shall rule over Him. Nor feature nor distinction hath He; for He is begetting cause and sovran over the lords of these natural organs, but Himself hath no begetter neither any sovran.

यस्तन्तुनाभ इव तन्तुभिः प्रधानजैः स्वभावतः ।
देव एकः स्वमावृणोत् स नो दधाद् ब्रह्माप्ययम् ॥ १० ॥

10. Even as is the spider that out of himself fashioneth his own web, so is God One & nought else existeth but by his own nature covereth Himself up in the threads He hath spun out of primal matter. May the One God ordain unto us departure into His Eternal.

एको देवः सर्वभूतेषु गूढः सर्वव्यापी सर्वभूतान्तरात्मा ।
कर्माध्यक्षः सर्वभूताधिवासः साक्षी चेता केवलो निर्गुणश्च ॥ ११ ॥

11. One God who alone is & He lurketh hidden in every creature for He pervadeth and is the inmost Self of all beings, He presideth over all work and is the home of all things living. He is the Mighty Witness who relateth thought with thought and again He is the Absolute in whom mood is not nor any attribute.

एको वशी निष्क्रियाणां बहूनामेकं बीजं बहुधा यः करोति ।
तमात्मस्थं येऽनुपश्यन्ति धीरास्तेषां सुखं शाश्वतं नेतरेषाम् ॥ १२ ॥

12. One God & alone He controlleth the many who have themselves no separate work nor purpose; and He developeth one seed into many kinds of creatures; the strong-hearted behold God in their own Self, therefore for them is everlasting bliss and not for others.

नित्योऽनित्यानां चेतनश्चेतनानामेको बहूनां यो विदधाति कामान् ।
तत्कारणं सांख्ययोगाधिगम्यं ज्ञात्वा देवं मुच्यते सर्वपाशैः ॥ १३ ॥

13. One Eternal of all these that pass & are not, One conscious
in all consciousnesses; He being One ordereth the desires of
many; He alone is the great Source to which Sankhya and
Yoga bring us. If thou know God thou shalt break free from
every sort of bondage.

न तत्र सूर्यो भाति न चन्द्रतारकं नेमा विद्युतो भान्ति कुतोऽयमग्निः ।
तमेव भान्तमनुभाति सर्वं तस्य भासा सर्वमिदं विभाति ॥ १४ ॥

14. There the sun cannot shine and the moon has no splendour;
the stars are blind; there our lightnings flash not neither
any earthly fire; all that is bright is but the shadow of His
brightness and by His shining all this shineth.

एको हंसो भुवनस्यास्य मध्ये स एवाग्निः सलिले संनिविष्टः ।
तमेव विदित्वाति मृत्युमेति नान्यः पन्था विद्यतेऽयनाय ॥ १५ ॥

15. One Swan of Being in the heart of all this Universe & He
is Fire that lieth deep in the heart of water. By Knowledge
of Him, the soul passeth beyond the pursuit of Death and
there is no other road for the great passage.

स विश्वकृद् विश्वविदात्मयोनिर्ज्ञः कालकारो गुणी सर्वविद्यः ।
प्रधानक्षेत्रज्ञपतिर्गुणेशः संसारमोक्षस्थितिबन्धहेतुः ॥ १६ ॥

16. He hath made all and knoweth all; for He is the womb out of
which Self ariseth, & being possessed of the Nature Moods
He becometh Time's Maker and discerneth all things. And
Matter is subject to Him & the Spirit in Man that cogniseth
His field of matter & the modes of Nature are His servants.
He therefore is the cause of this coming into phenomena &
of the release from phenomena — & because of Him is their
endurance & because of Him is their bondage.

स तन्मयो ह्यमृत ईशसंस्थो ज्ञः सर्वगो भुवनस्यास्य गोप्ता ।
य ईशोऽस्य जगतो नित्यमेव नान्यो हेतुर्विद्यत ईशनाय ॥ १७ ॥

17. Lo He is Immortal because He is utter existence; but He
houseth Himself in the Lord & is the Knower, the Omnipresent that standeth on guard over this His universe, yea
He ruleth all this moving world for ever and for ever, and
there is no other source of lordship and kingliness.

यो ब्रह्माणं विदधाति पूर्वं यो वै वेदांश्च प्रहिणोति तस्मै ।
तं ह देवमात्मबुद्धिप्रकाशं मुमुक्षुर्वै शरणमहं प्रपद्ये ॥ १८ ॥

18. He ordained Brahma the Creator from of old and sent forth
unto him the Veda, I will hasten unto God who standeth
self-revealed in the Spirit & in the Understanding. I will
take refuge in the Lord for my salvation;

निष्कलं निष्क्रियं शान्तं निरवद्यं निरञ्जनम् ।
अमृतस्य परं सेतुं दग्धेन्धनमिवानलम् ॥ १९ ॥

19. Who hath neither parts nor works for He is utterly tranquil,
faultless, stainless, therefore He is the one great bridge that
carrieth us over to Immortality, even as when a fire hath
burnt all its fuel.

यदा चर्मवदाकाशं वेष्टयिष्यन्ति मानवाः ।
तदा देवमविज्ञाय दुःखस्यान्तो भविष्यति ॥ २० ॥

20. When the sons of men shall fold up ether like a skin and
wrap the heavens round them like a garment, then alone
without knowledge of the Lord our God shall the misery of
the World have an ending.

तपःप्रभावाद् देवप्रसादाच्च ब्रह्म ह श्वेताश्वतरोऽथ विद्वान् ।
अत्याश्रमिभ्यः परमं पवित्रं प्रोवाच सम्यगृषिसङ्घजुष्टम् ॥ २१ ॥

21. By the might of his devotion & the grace of God in his being
Svetasvatara hereafter knew the Eternal & he came to the

renouncers of the worldly life and truly declared unto them
the Most High & Pure God, to whom the companies of
seers resort for ever.

वेदान्ते परमं गुह्यं पुराकल्पे प्रचोदितम् ।
नाप्रशान्ताय दातव्यं नापुत्रायाशिष्याय वा पुनः ॥ २२ ॥

22. This is the great secret of the Vedanta which was declared in
former times, not on hearts untranquilled to be squandered
nor men sonless nor on one who hath no disciples.

यस्य देवे परा भक्तिर्यथा देवे तथा गुरौ ।
तस्यैते कथिता ह्यर्थाः प्रकाशन्ते महात्मनः प्रकाशन्ते महात्मनः ॥ २३ ॥

23. But whosoever hath supreme love & adoration for the Lord
and as for the Lord, so likewise for the Master, to that
Mighty Soul these great matters when they are told become
clear of themselves, yea to the Great Soul of him they are
manifest.

Chhandogya Upanishad

Chapter I

and the first section

ओमित्येतदक्षरमुद्गीथमुपासीत। ओमिति ह्युद्गायति तस्योपव्या-
ख्यानम् ॥ १ ॥

1. Worship ye OM, the eternal syllable. OM is Udgitha, the chant of Samaveda; for with OM they begin the chant of Sama. And this is the exposition of OM.

एषां भूतानां पृथिवी रसः पृथिव्या आपो रसः। अपामोषधयो रस
ओषधीनां पुरुषो रसः पुरुषस्य वाग्रसो वाच ऋग्रस ऋचः साम रसः
साम्न उद्गीथो रसः ॥ २ ॥

2. Earth is the substantial essence of all these creatures and the waters are the essence of earth; herbs of the field are the essence of the waters; man is the essence of the herbs. Speech is the essence of man, Rigveda the essence of Speech, Sama the essence of Rik. Of Sama OM is the essence.

स एष रसानां रसतमः परमः पराध्यॉऽष्टमो यदुद्गीथः ॥ ३ ॥

3. This is the eighth essence of the essences and the really essential, the highest and it belongeth to the upper hemisphere of things.

कतमा कतमर्क् कतमत् कतमत्साम कतमः कतम उद्गीथ इति विमृष्टं
भवति ॥ ४ ॥

4. Which among things & which again is Rik; which among things and which again is Sama; which among things and which again is OM of the Udgitha — this is now pondered.

वागेवर्कं प्राणः सामोमित्येतदक्षरमुद्गीथः । तद्वा एतन्मिथुनं यद्वाक् च
प्राणश्चर्कं च साम च ॥ ५ ॥

5. Speech is Rik, Breath is Sama; the Imperishable is OM of
Udgitha. These are the divine lovers, Speech & Breath, Rik
& Sama.

तदेतन्मिथुनमोमित्येतस्मिन्नक्षरे संसृज्यते यदा वै मिथुनौ समागच्छत
आपयतो वै तावन्योन्यस्य कामम् ॥ ६ ॥

6. As a pair of lovers are these and they cling together in OM
the eternal syllable; now when the beloved and her lover
meet, verily they gratify each the desire of the other.

आपयिता ह वै कामानां भवति य एतदेवं विद्वानक्षरमुद्गीथमुपा-
स्ते ॥ ७ ॥

7. He becometh a gratifier of the desires of men who with this
knowledge worshippeth OM the eternal syllable.

तद् वा एतदनुज्ञाक्षरं यद्धि किंचानुजानात्योमित्येव तदाहैषो एव
समृद्धिर्यदनुज्ञा समर्धयिता ह वै कामानां भवति य एतदेवं विद्वानक्षर-
मुद्गीथमुपास्ते ॥ ८ ॥

8. Now this OM is the syllable of Assent; for to whatsoever
one assenteth, one sayeth OM; and assent is blessing of
increase. Verily he becometh a blesser and increaser of the
desires of men who with this knowledge worshippeth OM
the eternal syllable.

तेनेयं त्रयी विद्या वर्तत ओमित्याश्रावयत्योमिति शंसत्योमित्युद्गाय-
त्येतस्यैवाक्षरस्यापचित्यै महिम्ना रसेन ॥ ९ ॥

9. By OM the triple knowledge proceedeth; with OM the priest
reciteth the Rik, with OM he pronounceth the Yajur, with
OM he chanteth the Sama. And all this is for the heaping
up of the Imperishable and by the greatness of It and the
delightfulness.

तेनोभौ कुरुतो यश्चैतदेवं वेद यश्च न वेद । नाना तु विद्या चाविद्या
च यदेव विद्यया करोति श्रद्धयोपनिषदा तदेव वीर्यवत्तरं भवतीति
खल्वेतस्यैवाक्षरस्योपव्याख्यानं भवति ॥ १० ॥

10. He doeth works by OM who hath the knowledge, and he
also who hath it not; but these are diverse, the Knowledge
and the Ignorance. Whatso work one doeth with knowledge,
with faith and with the secret of Veda, it becometh to him
more virile and mighty. This is the exposition of the eternal
letters.

And the second section

देवासुरा ह वै यत्र संयेतिर उभये प्राजापत्यास्तद्ध देवा उद्गीथमा-
जह्नुरनेनैनानभिभविष्याम इति ॥ १ ॥

1. The Gods and the Demons strove together and both were
children of the Almighty Father. Then the Gods took up for
weapon OM of Udgitha, for they said "With this we shall
overcome these Titans."

ते ह नासिकं प्राणमुद्गीथमुपासांचक्रिरे तं हासुराः पाप्मना विविधु-
स्तस्मात्तेनोभयं जिघ्रति सुरभि च दुर्गन्धि च पाप्मना ह्येष विद्धः ॥ २ ॥

2. The Gods worshipped OM as Breath in the nostrils; but the
Demons came and smote it with the arrow of Evil; therefore
it smelleth both alike, the sweet scent and the evil odour.
For it is smitten through and through with Evil.

अथ ह वाचमुद्गीथमुपासांचक्रिरे तां हासुराः पाप्मना विविधुस्तस्मात्
तयोभयं वदति सत्यं चानृतं च पाप्मना ह्येषा विद्धा ॥ ३ ॥

3. Then the Gods worshipped OM as Speech; but the Demons
came and smote it with the arrow of Evil; therefore it
speaketh both alike, Truth and Falsehood. For it is smitten
through and through with Evil.

अथ ह चक्षुरुद्गीथमुपासांचक्रिरे तद्धासुराः पाप्मना विविधुस्तस्मात्
तेनोभयं पश्यति दर्शनीयं चादर्शनीयं च पाप्मना ह्येतद् विद्धम् ॥ ४ ॥

4. Then the Gods worshipped OM as the Eye; but the Demons
came and smote it with the arrow of Evil; therefore it beholdeth both alike, the fair to see and the foul of favour. For
it is smitten through and through with Evil.

अथ ह श्रोत्रमुद्गीथमुपासांचक्रिरे तद्धासुराः पाप्मना विविधुस्तस्मात्
तेनोभयं शृणोति श्रवणीयं चाश्रवणीयं च पाप्मना ह्येतद् विद्धम् ॥ ५ ॥

5. Then the Gods worshipped OM as the Ear; but the Demons
came and smote it with the arrow of Evil; therefore it heareth
both alike, that which is well to hear and that which is harsh
and unseemly. For it is smitten through and through with
Evil.

अथ ह मन उद्गीथमुपासांचक्रिरे तद्धासुराः पाप्मना विविधुस्तस्मात्
तेनोभयं संकल्पयते संकल्पनीयं चासंकल्पनीयं च पाप्मना ह्येतद्
विद्धम् ॥ ६ ॥

6. Then the Gods worshipped Udgitha as Mind; but the
Demons came and smote it with the arrow of Evil; therefore it conceiveth both alike, right thoughts and unlawful
imaginations. For it is smitten through and through with
Evil.

अथ ह य एवायं मुख्यः प्राणस्तमुद्गीथमुपासांचक्रिरे तं हासुरा ऋत्वा
विदध्वंसुर्यथाश्मानमाखणमृत्वा विध्वंसेत ॥ ७ ॥

7. Then the Gods worshipped OM as this which is Breath in the
mouth and the Demons rushing against it dashed themselves
to pieces; as when an object striketh against firm and solid
rock, it dasheth to pieces upon the rock.

एवं यथाश्मानमाखणमृत्वा विध्वंसत एवं हैव स विध्वंसते य एवंविदि
पापं कामयते यश्चैनमभिदासति स एषोऽश्माखणः ॥ ८ ॥

8. And even as an object hurling against firm and solid rock

dasheth itself to pieces, so he hurleth himself upon destruction whoso desireth evil against the Knower or whoso doeth
him hurt; for the Knower is as that firm and solid rock.

नैवैतेन सुरभि न दुर्गन्धि विजानात्यपहतपाप्मा ह्येष तेन यदश्नाति
यत्पिबति तेनेतरान् प्राणानवति। एतमु एवान्ततोऽविच्त्वोत्क्रामति
व्याददात्येवान्तत इति ॥ ९ ॥

9. With this Breath one cogniseth neither sweet scent nor ill
   odour, for it hath flung Evil from it. Whatsoever one eateth
   with this or drinketh, thereby it cherisheth the other breaths.
   At the end and last when he findeth not the breath, the Spirit
   goeth out from the body; verily he openeth wide the mouth
   as he goeth.

तं हाङ्गिरा उद्गीथमुपासांचक्र एतमु एवाङ्गिरसं मन्यन्तेऽङ्गानां यद्
रस: ॥ १० ॥

10. Angiras worshipped OM of Udgitha as Breath in the mouth
    and men think of Breath in the mouth as Angiras because it
    is essence of the members of the body.

तेन तं ह बृहस्पतिरुद्गीथमुपासांचक्र एतमु एव बृहस्पतिं मन्यन्ते वाग्घि
बृहती तस्या एष पति: ॥ ११ ॥

11. By the strength of Angiras, Brihaspati worshipped OM as
    Breath in the mouth, and men think of the Breath as Brihas-
    pati, because Speech is the great goddess and Breath is the
    lord of Speech.

तेन तं हायास्य उद्गीथमुपासांचक्र एतमु एवायास्यं मन्यन्त आस्याद्
यदयते ॥ १२ ॥

12. By the strength of Brihaspati, Ayasya worshipped OM as
    Breath in the mouth and men think of the Breath as Ayasya,
    because 'tis from the mouth it cometh.

तेन तं ह बको दाल्भ्यो विदांचकार। स ह नैमिषीयाणामुद्गाता बभूव
स ह स्मैभ्य: कामानागायति ॥ १३ ॥

13. By the strength of Ayasya, Baka the son of Dalbha knew the Breath. And he became the Chanter of the Sama among the Naimishiyas and he chanteth their desires for them unto fulfilment.

आगाता ह वै कामानां भवति य एतदेवं विद्वानक्षरमुद्गीथमुपास्त इत्यध्यात्मम् ॥ १४ ॥

14. Verily he becometh a chanter unto fulfilment of the desires of men who with this knowledge worshippeth OM of Udgitha, the eternal syllable. Thus far concerning Self is the exposition.

And the third section

अथाधिदैवतं य एवासौ तपति तमुद्गीथमुपासीतोद्यन्वा एष प्रजाभ्य उद्गायति । उद्यंस्तमो भयमपहन्त्यपहन्ता ह वै भयस्य तमसो भवति य एवं वेद ॥ १ ॥

1. Thereafter concerning the Gods. Lo yonder burning fire in the heavens, worship ye Him as the Udgitha; for the Sun riseth & singeth his bright hymn unto the peoples. Yea he riseth, & darkness is slain & its terror — therefore shall he be a slayer of the terror & the darkness, he who thus knoweth.

समान उ एवायं चासौ चोष्णोऽयमुष्णोऽसौ स्वर इतीममाचक्षते स्वर इति प्रत्यास्वर इत्यमुं तस्माद्वा एतमिममममुं चोद्गीथमुपासीत ॥ २ ॥

2. Breath & the Sun are one & alike — for the one is heat & the other is heat, and they call Breath the mover and the Sun too they call the mover & they call him also the mover that returneth upon his paths — therefore ye shall worship both the one & the other as Udgitha.

अथ खलु व्यानमेवोद्गीथमुपासीत यद्वै प्राणिति स प्राणो यदपानिति सोऽपानः । अथ यः प्राणापानयोः संधिः स व्यानो यो व्यानः सा वाक् । तस्मादप्राणन्ननपानन् वाचमभिव्याहरति ॥ ३ ॥

3. Thereafter verily ye shall worship Vyana the middle breath
as Udgitha. For when one breathes forth it is Prana, the
Main Breath, & when one breathes down it is Apana, the
lower breath. Now this which is the joint & linking of
the main breath & the lower breath, is Vyana — & Vyana,
it is Speech. Therefore 'tis when one neither breatheth
forth nor breatheth down that one giveth utterance to
Speech.

या वाक् सर्कं तस्मादप्राणन्ननपानन्नृचमभिव्याहरति यर्कं तत्साम
तस्मादप्राणन्ननपानन् साम गायति यत्साम स उद्गीथस्तस्मादप्राणन्नन -
पानन्नुद्गायति ॥ ४ ॥

4. But Speech is the Rik — therefore 'tis when one neither
breatheth out nor breatheth in that one uttereth the Rik. And
Rik it is Sama — therefore 'tis when one neither breatheth
out nor breatheth in that one chanteth the Sama. But Sama
it is Udgitha — therefore 'tis when one neither breatheth out
nor breatheth in that one singeth Udgitha.

अतो यान्यन्यानि वीर्यंवन्ति कर्माणि यथाग्नेर्मन्थनमाजे: सरणं दृढस्य
धनुष आयमनमप्राणन्ननपानंस्तानि करोत्येतस्य हेतोर्व्यानमेवोद्गीथ -
मुपासीत ॥ ५ ॥

5. Hence whatsoever actions there be that are of might &
forcefulness as smiting out fire from the tinder or leaping a
great barrier or bending a stark & mighty bow, it is when
one neither breatheth out nor breatheth in that one doeth
these. And for this cause ye shall worship the middle breath
as Udgitha.

अथ खलूद्गीथाक्षराण्युपासीतोद्गीथ इति प्राण एवोत् प्राणेन ह्युत्तिष्ठति
वाग् गीर्वाचो ह गिर इत्याचक्षतेऽन्नं थमन्ने हीदं सर्वं स्थितम् ॥ ६ ॥

6. Thereafter verily ye shall worship the syllables of the
Udgitha saying Udgitha & Prana is the first syllable, because
one riseth up with the main breath & Speech is the second
syllable, because they call Speech that which goeth forth &

food is the third syllable, because in food all this Universe is established.

द्यौरेवोदन्तरिक्षं गीः पृथिवी थमादित्य एवोद् वायुर्गीरग्निस्थं
सामवेद एवोद् यजुर्वेदो गीर्ऋग्वेदस्थं दुग्धेऽस्मै वाग् दोहं यो वाचो
दोहोऽन्नवानन्नादो भवति य एतान्येवं विद्वानुद्गीथाक्षराण्युपास्त उद्गीथ
इति ॥ ७ ॥

7. Heaven is the first syllable, the middle air is the second syllable, earth is the third syllable. The Sun is the first syllable, Air is the second syllable, Fire is the third syllable. The Samaveda is the first syllable, Yajurveda is the second syllable, Rigveda is the third syllable. To him Speech is a cow that yieldeth sweet milk — & what is this milking of Speech? — even that he becometh rich in food & the eater of food who knoweth these & worshippeth the syllables of Udgitha saying lo even this is Udgitha.

Notes on the Chhandogya Upanishad

First Adhyaya

ओमित्येतदक्षरमुद्गीथमुपासीत । ओमिति ह्युद्गायति तस्योपव्या-
ख्यानम् ॥ १ ॥

OM is the syllable (the Imperishable One); one should follow after it as the upward Song (movement); for with OM one sings (goes) upwards; of which this is the analytical explanation.

So, literally translated in its double meaning, both its exoteric, physical and symbolic sense and its esoteric symbolised reality, runs the initial sentence of the Upanishad. These opening lines or passages of the Vedanta are always of great importance; they are always so designed as to suggest or even sum up, if not all that comes afterwards, yet the central and pervading idea of the Upanishad. The Isha Vasyam of the Vajasaneyi, the Keneshitam manas of the Talavakara, the Sacrificial Horse of the Brihad Aranyaka, the solitary Atman with its hint of the future world vibrations in the Aitareya are of this type. The Chhandogya, we see from its first and introductory sentence, is to be a work on the right & perfect way of devoting oneself to the Brahman; the spirit, the methods, the formulae are to be given to us. Its subject is the Brahman, but the Brahman as symbolised in the OM, the sacred syllable of the Veda; not, therefore, the pure state of the Universal Existence only, but that Existence in all its parts, the waking world & the dream self and the sleeping, the manifest, half-manifest and hidden, Bhurloka, Bhuvar & Swar, the right means to win all of them, enjoy all of them, transcend all of them, is the subject of the Chhandogya. OM is the symbol and the thing symbolised. It is the symbol, aksharam, the syllable in which all sound of speech is brought back to its wide, pure indeterminate state; it is the symbolised, aksharam, the changeless, undiminishing, unincreasing, unappearing, undying Reality which shows itself to experience in all the change, increase, diminution, appearance, departure which in a particular sum & harmony of them we call the world, just as OM the pure eternal sound-basis of speech shows itself to the ear in the variations and combinations of impure sound which in a particular sum and harmony of them we call the Veda. We are to follow after this OM with all our souls, upásíta, — to apply ourselves to it and devote ourselves to its knowledge and possession, but always to OM as the Udgitha. Again in this word we have the symbolic sense and the truth symbolised expressed, as in aksharam and OM, in a single vocable with a double function and significance.

The Sanscrit has always been a language in which one word is naturally capable of several meanings and therefore carries with it a number of varied associations. It lends itself, therefore, with peculiar ease and naturalness to the figure called slesha or embrace, the marriage of different meanings in a single form of words. Paronomasia in English is mere punning, a tour-de-force, an incongruity, a grotesque and artificial play of humour. Paronomasia, slesha, in Sanscrit, though in form precisely the same thing, is not punning, not incongruous but easily appropriate, not grotesque or artificial, but natural and often inevitable, not used for intellectual horseplay, but with a serious, often a high and worthy purpose. It has been abused by rhetorical writers; yet great and noble poetical effects have been obtained by its aid, as, for instance, when the same form of words has been used to convey open blame & cover secret praise. Nevertheless in classical Sanscrit, the language has become a little too rigid for the perfect use of the figure; it is too literary, too minutely grammatised; it has lost the memory of its origins. A sense of cleverness and artifice suggests itself to us because meanings known to be distinct and widely separate are brought together in a single activity of the word which usually suggests them only in different contexts. But in the Vedic slesha we have no sense of cleverness or artifice, because the writers themselves had none. The language was still near to its origins and had, not perhaps an intellectual, but still an instinctive memory of them. With less grammatical and as little etymological knowledge as

Panini and the other classical grammarians, the Rishis had better possession of the soul of Sanscrit speech. The different meanings of a word, though distinct, were not yet entirely separate; many links yet survived between them which were afterwards lost; the gradations of sense remained, the hint of the word's history, the shading off from one sense to another. Ardha now means half and it means nothing else. To the Vedic man it carried other associations. Derived from the root ridh which meant originally to go and join, then to add, to increase, to prosper, it bore the sense of place of destination, the person to whom I direct myself, or simply place; increase, also addition, a part added and so simply a part or half. To have used it in any other sense than "place of destination" or as at once "half, part" and "a place of destination" would not be a violence to the Vedic mind, but a natural association of ideas. So when they spoke of the higher worlds of Sacchidananda as Parardha, they meant at once the higher half of man's inner existence & the param dháma or high seat of Vishnou in other worlds and, in addition, thought of that high seat as the destination of our upward movement. All this rose at once to their mind when the word was uttered, naturally, easily and, by long association, inevitably.

OM is a word in instance. When the word was spoken as a solemn affirmation, everyone thought of the Pranava in the Veda, but no one could listen to the word OM without thinking also of the Brahman in Its triple manifestation and in Its transcendent being. The word, aksharam, meaning both syllable & unshifting, when coupled with OM, is a word in instance; "OM the syllable" meant also, inevitably, to the Vedic mind "Brahman, who changes not nor perishes". The words udgítha and udgáyati are words in instance. In classical Sanscrit the prepositional prefix to the verb was dead and bore only a conventional significance or had no force at all; udgáyati or pragáyati is not very different from the simple gáyati; all mean merely sing or chant. But in Veda the preposition is still living & joins its verb or separates itself as it pleases; therefore it keeps its full meaning always. In Vedanta the power of separation is lost, but the separate force remains. Again the roots gí and gá in classical Sanscrit mean to sing and have resigned the sense of going to their kinsman gam; but in Vedic times, the sense of going was still active and common. They meant also to express, to possess, to hold; but these meanings once common to the family are now entrusted to particular members of it, gir, for expression, grih, for holding. Gáthá, gíthá, gána, gáyati, gátá, gátu, meant to the Vedic mind both going and singing, udgítha meant ascension as well as casting upward the voice or the soul in song. When the Vedic singer said Ud gáyámi, the physical idea was that, perhaps, of the song rising upward, but he had also the psychical idea of the soul rising up in song to the gods and fulfilling in its meeting with them and entering into them its expressed aspiration. To show that this idea is not a modern etymological fancy of my own, it is sufficient to cite the evidence of the Chhandogya Upanishad itself in this very chapter where Baka Dalbhya is spoken of as the Udgata of the Naimishiyas who obtained their desires for them by the Vedic chant, ebhya ágáyati kámán; so, adds the Upanishad, shall everyone be a "singer to" & a "bringer to" of desires, ágátá kámánám, who with this knowledge follows after OM, the Brahman, as the Udgitha.

This then is the meaning of the Upanishad that OM, the syllable, technically called the Udgitha, is to be meditated on as a symbol of the fourfold Brahman with two objects, the "singing to" of one's desires & aspirations in the triple manifestation and the spiritual ascension into the Brahman Itself so as to meet and enter into heaven after heaven & even into Its transcendent felicity. For, it says, with the syllable OM one begins the chant of the Samaveda, or, in the esoteric sense, by means of the meditation on OM one makes this soul-ascension and becomes master of all the soul desires. It is in this aspect & to this end that the Upanishad will expound OM. To explain Brahman in Its nature & workings, to teach the right worship and meditation on Brahman, to establish what are the different means of attainment of different results and the formulae of the meditation and worship, is its purpose. All this work of explanation has to be done in reference to Veda & Vedic sacrifice and ritual of which OM is the substance. In a certain sense, therefore,

the Upanishad is an explanation of the purpose & symbology of
Vedic formulae & ritual; it sums up the results of the long travail
of seeking by which the first founders & pioneers of Vedantism
in an age when the secret & true sense of Veda had been largely
submerged in the ceremonialism & formalism of the close of the
Dwapara Yuga, attempted to recover their lost heritage partly
by reference to the adepts who still remained in possession of
it, partly by the traditions of the great seekers of the past Yuga,
Janaka, Yajnavalkya, Krishna and others, partly by their own
illuminations and spiritual experience. The Chhandogya Upanishad is thus the summary history of one of the greatest & most
interesting ages of human thought.

Satyakama Jabala

The story of Satyakama Jabala occupies five sections, the third to the eighth, of the fourth chapter in the Chhandogya Upanishad. The Chhandogya seems to be the most ancient of the extant Upanishads. It speaks of Krishna, son of Devaki, and Dhritarashtra Vaichitravirya in a tone that would justify us in assuming that it regarded them not as ancient and far-off names but as men who had walked the earth in living memory. The movement of philosophic speculation of which the Upanishads are the extant record, was an attempt to pass from the old ritualistic *karma* to the freedom of the *jnanamarga*. According to the writer of the Gita, this was not a new movement, but a return to a past and lost discipline; for Sri Krishna says to Arjuna of the true or *sajnan karmamarga* he reveals to him, "This is the imperishable Yoga I declared unto Vivaswan, Vivaswan revealed it to Manu and Manu to Ixvacu told it. Thus was it known to the royal sages by hereditary transmission, till by the great lapse of time this yoga was lost, O scourge of thy foes. This is the same ancient Yoga that I have told unto [thee] today, because thou art my lover and my friend; for this is the highest of all the inner truths."

The Dwapara Yuga was the age of Kuru preeminence and the Kurus were a great practical, warlike, ritualistic, juristic race of the Roman type, with little of the speculative temper or moral enthusiasm of the eastern Coshalas, Videhas, Kashis, Chedis. The West of India has always been noted for its practical, soldierly, commercial bent of mind in comparison with the imaginative and idealistic Eastern races and the scholastic, logical and metaphysical South. According to the Hindu theory of the Yugas, it is in the Dwapara that everything is codified, ritualised, formalised. In the Satya Vishnu descends among men as Yajna. Yajna is the spirit of adoration and sacrifice, and in the Satya yajna reigns in the hearts of men, and there is no need of external ritual, external sacrifices, elaborate law, government, castes, classes and creeds. Men follow the law by the necessity of their purified nature and their complete knowledge. The kingdom of God & the Veda are in the hearts of His people. In the Treta the old perfect order begins to break and Vishnu descends as the *chakravarti raja*, the warrior and ruler, Kartavirya, Parsurama, Rama, and the sword, the law and the written Veda are instituted to govern men. But there is still great elasticity and freedom and within certain limits men follow the healthy impulse of their nature, only slightly corrupted by the first descent from purity. It is in the Dwapara that form and rule have to take the place of the idea and the spirit as the true governors of religion, ethics and society. Vishnu then descends as Vyasa, the great codifier and systematiser of knowledge.

At the end of the Dwapara, when Sri Krishna came, this tendency had reached its extreme development, and the form tended to take the place of the idea and the rule to take the place of the spirit not only in the outward conduct but in the hearts of men. Nevertheless an opposite tendency had already begun. Dhritarashtra himself was an earnest inquirer into the inner meaning of things. Great Vedantists were living and teaching, such as the rishi Ghora to whom Sri Krishna himself went for the word of illumination. Sri Krishna was the intellectual force that took up all these scattered tendencies and, by breaking down the strong formalism of the Dwapara, prepared the work of the Kali. In the Gita he denounces those who will not go outside the four corners of the Veda and philosophises the whole theory of the sacrificial system; he contemptuously dismisses the guidance of the set ethical systems and establishes an inward and spiritual rule of conduct. To many of his time he seems to have appeared as a baneful and destructive portent; like all great revolutionary innovators, he is denounced by Bhurisravas as a well known misleader of men and corrupter of morals. It is the work of the Kali Yuga to destroy everything by questioning everything in order to establish after a struggle between the forces of purity and impurity a new harmony of life and knowledge in another Satyayuga.

After the destruction of the conservative Kurus and Pan-
chalas at Kurukshetra, the development of the Vedanta com-
menced and went on progressing till in its turn it reached its
extreme & excessive development in the teachings of Buddha
and Shankaracharya. But at the period of the Chhandogya it
is in its early stage of development. The first sections of the
Upanishad are taken up with an esoteric development of the
inner meaning of certain parts of the sacrificial formulae, which
in itself is sufficient to show that the work belongs to the first
stratum of Vedantic formation.

The story of Satyakama is one of the most typical in the Upanishad. It is full of sidelights on early Vedantic teaching, Yogic
sadhan and that deep psychical knowledge which the writer
took for granted in the hearers of his work. So much knowledge, indeed, is thus taken for granted that it is impossible for
anyone not himself a practiser of Yoga, to understand anything
but its broad conclusions. The modern commentators, Shankara
included, have approached it in order to establish particular
metaphysical doctrines, not to elucidate its entire significance.
I shall take the side that has been neglected; for what to the
European inquirer are merely "the babblings of children", bear
to the Yogin an aspect of infinite truth, value and significance.

Chapter II

"Now Satyakama Jabala spoke unto his mother Jabala and said
'Mother, I shall go and lead the life of the Brahmacharin; tell
me what is my *gotra.*' But she answered him, 'This I know
not, my son, of what gotra thou art; resorting to many as a
serving woman in my youth I got thee, therefore I know not
of what gotra thou art. But Jabala is my name and Satyakama
is thine, Satyakama Jabala therefore call thyself.' So he came
to Haridrumata the Gautama and said, 'I would stay with my
Lord as a Brahmacharin, let me therefore enter under thee.' And
he said to him, 'My son, of what gotra art thou?' But the other
answered, 'This, alas, I know not of what gotra I am; I asked my

mother and she answered me, Resorting to many in my youth
as a serving woman I got thee, therefore I know not of what
gotra thou art, but Jabala is my name and Satyakama is thine;
Satyakama Jabala therefore am I.' And he said to him, 'None
who is not a Brahmin can be strong enough to say this; gather
the firewood, my son, I will take thee under me, for thou didst
not depart from the truth.' He admitted him and put forth four
hundred cows weak and lean and said, 'These, my son, do thou
follow as a herd,' and he set the cows in motion and said, 'Return
not until they are a thousand.' And he fared abroad with them
during the years till they were a thousand."

So the story opens, and simple as it seems, it already contains several points of capital importance in understanding the
ideas of the time and the principles of the old Vedantic *sadhana*.
Satyakama, as we gather from other passages, was one of the
great Vedantic teachers of the time immediately previous to the
composition of the Chhandogya Upanishad. But his birth is the
meanest possible. His mother is a serving girl, not a *dasi* attached to a permanent household whose son could have named
his father and his gotra, but a *paricharika*, serving for hire at
various houses, "resorting to many", and therefore unable to
name her son's father. Satyakama has, therefore, neither caste,
nor gotra, nor any position in life. It appears from this story
as from others that, although the system of the four castes
was firmly established, it counted as no obstacle in the pursuit
of knowledge and spiritual advancement. The Kshatriya could
teach the Brahmin, the illegitimate and fatherless son of the
serving girl could be guru to the purest and highest blood in
the land. This is nothing new or improbable, for it has been
so throughout the history of Hinduism and the shutting out of
anyone from spiritual truth and culture on the ground of caste
is an invention of later times. In the nature of things the usual
rule would be for the greater number of spiritual preceptors to
be found in the higher castes, but this was the result of natural
laws and not of a fixed prohibition. It is noticeable also from this
and other instances that it was the father's position that fixed
the son's, and the mother's seems to have been of very minor

importance. The question about the gotra was of importance, probably, with regard to the rites and other circumstances of initiation. Satyakama must have known perfectly well that he was the illegitimate son of a serving woman, but he wished to know his father's name and gotra because he would have to tell it to his guru. Even after knowing the worst, he persisted in his intention of taking up spiritual studies, so that he can have had no fear of being rejected on account of his base origin. His guru, impressed by his truthfulness, says, "None but a Brahmin would have the moral strength to make such an avowal." It can hardly be meant by this that Satyakama's father must have been a Brahmin, but that since he had the Brahmin qualities, he must be accepted as a Brahmin. Even the Kshatriya would have hesitated to speak so truthfully, because the Kshatriya is by nature a lover of honour and shuns dishonour, he has the sense of *mana* and *apamana*; but the true Brahmin is *samo manapamanayoh*, he accepts indifferently worldly honour and dishonour and cares only for the truth and the right. In short the Gautama concludes that, whatever may be Satyakama's physical birth, spiritually he is of the highest order and especially fitted for a sadhaka; *na satyad agat*, he did not depart from the truth.

The second point is the first action of the guru after the ceremony of initiation. Instead of beginning the instruction of this promising disciple he sends him out with four hundred miserable kine, more likely to die than prosper and increase, and forbids him to return till he has increased them to a thousand. Wherefore this singular arrangement? Was it a test? Was it a discipline? But Haridrumata had already seen that his new disciple had the high Brahmin qualities. What more did he require?

The perfect man is a fourfold being and one object of Vedantic discipline is to be the perfect man, *siddha*. When Christ said, "Be ye perfect as your Father in heaven is perfect," he was only repeating in popular language the Vedantic teaching of *sadharmya*, likeness to God.

The Brihad Aranyak Upanishad

Chapter One: Section I

उषा वा अश्वस्य मेध्यस्य शिरः। सूर्यश्चक्षुर्वातः प्राणो व्यात्तमग्नि-
र्वैश्वानरः संवत्सर आत्माश्वस्य मेध्यस्य। द्यौः पृष्ठमन्तरिक्षमुदरं
पृथिवी पाजस्यं दिशः पार्श्वे अवान्तरदिशः पर्शव ऋतवोऽङ्गानि
मासाश्चार्धमासाश्च पर्वाण्यहोरात्राणि प्रतिष्ठा नक्षत्राण्यस्थीनि नभो
मांसानि। ऊवध्यं सिकताः सिन्धवो गुदा यकृच्च क्लोमानश्च पर्वता
ओषधयश्च वनस्पतयश्च लोमान्युद्यन्पूर्वार्धो निम्लोचञ्जघनार्धो यद्
विजृम्भते तद्विद्योतते यद्विधूनुते तत्स्तनयति यन्मेहति तद्वर्षति
वागेवास्य वाक् ॥ १ ॥

1. Dawn is the head[1] of the horse sacrificial.[2] The sun is his
eye,[3] his breath is the wind, his wide open mouth is Fire,
the master might universal, Time is the self of the horse
sacrificial.[4] Heaven is his back & the midworld his belly,
earth is his footing, — the regions are his flanks & the lesser
regions their ribs, the seasons his members, the months &
the half months are their joints, the days & nights are his
standing place, the stars his bones & the sky is the flesh of
his body. The strands are the food in his belly, the rivers are
his veins, his liver & his lungs are the mountains, herbs &
plants are his hairs, the rising is his front & the setting his
hinder portion, when he stretches himself, then it lightens,

---

[1] Because it is the front and beginning.
[2] Aswa meant originally "being, existence, substance". From the sense of speed &
strength it came to mean "horse". The word is therefore used to indicate material
existence & the horse (the image usually conveyed by this name) is taken as the symbol
of universal existence in annam.
　The horse is symbolic & the sacrifice is symbolic. We have in it an image of the Virat
Purusha, of Yajniya Purusha, God expressing himself in the material universe.
[3] Because the sun is the master of sight.
[4] Air is the basis of life, Fire of strength & expansion. Time is that which upholds
existence in material space & is the soul of it.

when he shakes his frame, then it thunders, when he urines, then it rains. Speech, verily, is the sound of him.

अहर्वा अश्वं पुरस्तान्महिमान्वजायत तस्य पूर्वे समुद्रे योनी रात्रिरेनं पश्चान्महिमान्वजायत तस्यापरे समुद्रे योनिरेतौ वा अश्वं महिमाना-वभितः संबभूवतुः । हयो भूत्वा देवानवहद् वाजी गन्धर्वानर्वासुरानश्वो मनुष्यान् समुद्र एवास्य बन्धुः समुद्रो योनिः ॥ २ ॥

2. Day was the grandeur that was born before the horse as he galloped, the eastern ocean gave it birth; night was the grandeur that was born behind him & its birth was from the other waters. These are the grandeurs that came into being on either side of the horse. He became Haya & bore the gods, Vaja & bore the Gandharvas, Arvan & bore the Titans, Aswa & bore mankind. The sea was his brother & the sea was his birthplace.

Chapter One: Section II

नैवेह किंचनाग्र आसीन्मृत्युनैवेदमावृतमासीत् । अशनाययाशनाया हि मृत्युस्तन्मनोऽकुरुतात्मन्वी स्यामिति । सोऽर्चन्नचरत् तस्यार्चत आपोऽजायन्तार्चते वै मे कमभूदिति तदेवार्कस्यार्कत्वं कं ह वा अस्मै भवति य एवमेतदर्कस्यार्कत्वं वेद ॥ १ ॥

1. Formerly there was nothing here; this was concealed by Death — by Hunger, for it is Hunger that is Death. That created Mind, & he said, Let me have substance. He moved about working & as he worked the waters were born & he said, Felicity was born to me as I worked. This verily is the activity in action. Therefore felicity cometh to him who thus knoweth this soul of activity in action.

आपो वा अर्कस्तद्यदपां शर आसीत् तत्समहन्यत । सा पृथिव्यभवत् तस्यामश्राम्यत तस्य श्रान्तस्य तप्तस्य तेजोरसो निरवर्ततागिनिः ॥ २ ॥

2. The waters verily (in their movement) are action; that which was a lake of waters was contracted & became compact. This became earth — upon earth he grew weary — in his

weariness he was heated & the Essence of energy went out
from him, even Fire.

स त्रेधात्मानं व्यकुरुतादित्यं तृतीयं वायुं तृतीयं स एष प्राणस्त्रेधा
विहितः । तस्य प्राची दिक् शिरोऽसौ चासौ चेर्मौ । अथास्य प्रतीची
दिक् पुच्छमसौ चासौ च सक्थ्यौ दक्षिणा चोदीची च पार्श्वे द्वौ:
पृष्ठमन्तरिक्षमुदरमियमुरः स एषोऽप्सु प्रतिष्ठितो यत्र क्व चैति तदेव
प्रतितिष्ठत्येवं विद्वान् ॥ ३ ॥

3. Fire divided himself into three — the sun one of the three
& Vayu one of the three; this is that force of life arranged
triply. The east is his head and the northeast & the southeast
are his arms. Now the west is his seat & the southwest &
the northwest are his thighs; his sides are the south & the
north; heaven is his back & the middle region is his belly;
this earth is his bosom. This is he that is established in the
waters wheresoever thou turn. And as that is he established
who thus knoweth.

सोऽकामयत द्वितीयो म आत्मा जायेतेति स मनसा वाचं मिथुनं
समभवदशनाया मृत्युस्तद्यद्रेत आसीत् स संवत्सरोऽभवत् । न ह पुरा
ततः संवत्सर आस तमेतावन्तं कालमबिभः । यावान् संवत्सरस्तमे-
तावतः कालस्य परस्तादसृजत । तं जातमभिव्याददात् स भाणकरोत्
सैव वागभवत् ॥ ४ ॥

4. He desired "Let a second self be born to me." He by mind
had intercourse with speech, even Hunger that is Death; the
seed that was of that union became Time. For before this
Time was not (period of Time) but so long He had borne
him in Himself. So long as is Time's period, after so long He
gave it birth. He yawned upon him as soon as it was born;
it cried out & that became speech.

स ऐक्षत यदि वा इममभिमंस्ये कनीयोऽन्नं करिष्य इति स तया
वाचा तेनात्मनेदं सर्वमसृजत यदिदं किंचर्चो यजूंषि सामानि छन्दांसि
यज्ञान्प्रजाः पशून् । स यद्यदेवासृजत तत्तदत्तुमध्रियत सर्वं वा अत्तीति
तददितेरदितित्वं सर्वस्यैतस्याचा भवति सर्वमस्यान्नं भवति य एव-
मेतददितेरदितित्वं वेद ॥ ५ ॥

5. He saw, If I devour this, I shall diminish food; therefore by
that speech & by that self he created all this that we see, the
Riks & the Yajus & the Samas & the rhythms & sacrifices &
animals & these nations. Whatsoever he created, that he set
about devouring, verily he devoureth all; this is the substantiality of being in substance (that it can be destroyed[5]). He
becometh the eater of all the world & everything becometh
his food who thus knoweth the substantiality of being in
substance.

सोऽकामयत भूयसा यज्ञेन भूयो यजेयेति । सोऽश्राम्यत् स तपोऽतप्यत
तस्य श्रान्तस्य तप्तस्य यशो वीर्यमुदक्रामत् । प्राणा वै यशो वीर्यं
तत्प्राणेषूत्क्रान्तेषु शरीरं श्वयितुमध्रियत तस्य शरीर एव मन
आसीत् ॥ ६ ॥

6. He desired "Let me sacrifice more richly with richer sacrifice." He laboured & put forth heat of force, & of him thus
laboured & heated splendour & strength came forth. The
life-forces are that splendour & strength, therefore when
the life-forces go forth, the body sets about to rot, yet in his
body even so mind was.

सोऽकामयत मेध्यं म इदं स्यादात्मन्व्यनेन स्यामिति । ततोऽश्वः
समभवद् यदश्वत् तन्मेध्यमभूदिति तदेवाश्वमेधस्याश्वमेधत्वम् । एष ह
वा अश्वमेधं वेद य एनमेवं वेद । तमनवरुध्यैवामन्यत । तं संवत्सरस्य
परस्तादात्मन आलभत । . . . ॥ ७ ॥

7. He desired "Let this have sacrificial capacity for me, by this
let me be provided with a body." That which has expressed
power & being, that is fit for the sacrifice. This verily is
the secret of the Aswamedha & he knoweth indeed the
Aswamedha who thus knoweth it. He gave him free course
& thought, then after a year (a fixed period of time) he
dedicated him to the self. [*The rest of this section was not
translated.*]

---

[5] Destroyed, ie enjoyed by absorption.

Chapter One: Section III

द्वया ह प्राजापत्या देवाश्चासुराश्च । ततः कानीयसा एव देवा ज्यायसा
असुरास्त एषु लोकेष्वस्पर्धन्त ते ह देवा ऊचुर्हन्तासुरान् यज्ञ
उद्गीथेनात्ययामेति ॥ १ ॥

1. Two were the races of the Sons of God, the gods & the
   Titans. Thereafter the gods were weaker, mightier the
   Titans. They in these worlds strove together, & the gods
   said, Let us by the udgitha overpass the Titans in the yajna.

ते ह वाचमूचुस्त्वं न उद्गायेति तथेति तेभ्यो वागुदगायत् । यो वाचि
भोगस्तं देवेभ्य आगायद् यत्कल्याणं वदति तदात्मने । ते विदुरनेन
वै न उद्गात्रात्येष्यन्तीति तमभिद्रुत्य पाप्मनाविध्यन् स य: स पाप्मा
यदेवेदमप्रतिरूपं वदति स एव स पाप्मा ॥ २ ॥

2. They said to Speech, Do thou go upward (by the udgitha)
   for us. "So be it" said Speech and he went upward for them;
   the enjoyment that is in speech, he reached for the gods, the
   good that it speaks, he reached for the self. They thought
   it was by this singer they would overpass them, but they
   ran at him and penetrated him with evil. The evil that one
   speaketh this that hath no correspondence (to the thing or
   fact to be expressed), — this is that evil.

The Great Aranyaka

A Commentary on the Brihad Aranyak Upanishad

Foreword

The Brihad Aranyak Upanishad, at once the most obscure and the profoundest of the Upanishads, offers peculiar difficulties to the modern mind. If its ideas are remote from us, its language is still more remote. Profound, subtle, extraordinarily rich in rare philosophical suggestions and delicate psychology, it has preferred to couch its ideas in a highly figurative and symbolical language, which to its contemporaries, accustomed to this suggestive dialect, must have seemed a noble frame for its riches, but meets us rather as an obscuring veil. To draw aside this curtain, to translate the old Vedic language and figures into the form contemporary thought prefers to give to its ideas is the sole object of this commentary. The task is necessarily a little hazardous. It would have been easy merely to reproduce the thoughts & interpretations of Shankara in the modern tongue — if there were an error, one could afford to err with so supreme an authority. But it seems to me that both the demands of truth and the spiritual need of mankind in this age call for a restoration of old Vedantic truth rather than for the prolonged dominion of that single side of it systematised by the mediaeval thinker. The great Shankaracharya needs no modern praise and can be hurt by no modern disagreement. Easily the first of metaphysical thinkers, the greatest genius in the history of philosophy, his commentary has also done an incalculable service to our race by bridging the intellectual gulf between the sages of the Upanishads and ourselves. It has protected them from the practical

oblivion in which our ignorance & inertia have allowed the
Veda to rest for so many centuries — only to be dragged out by
the rude hands of the daringly speculative Teuton. It has kept
these ancient grandeurs of thought, these high repositories of
spirituality under the safe-guard of that temple of metaphysics,
the Adwaita philosophy — a little in the background, a little
too much veiled & shrouded, but nevertheless safe from the
iconoclasm and the restless ingenuities of modern scholarship.
Nevertheless, it remains true that Shankara's commentary is interesting not so much for the light it sheds on the Upanishad
as for its digressions into his own philosophy. I do not think
that Shankara's rational intellect, subtle indeed to the extreme,
but avid of logical clearness and consistency, could penetrate
far into that mystic symbolism and that deep & elusive flex-
ibility which is characteristic of all the Upanishads, but rises
to an almost unattainable height in the Brihad Aranyaka. He
has done much, has shown often a readiness and quickness
astonishing in so different a type of intellectuality but more
is possible and needed. The time is fast coming when the human
intellect, aware of the mighty complexity of the universe, will
be more ready to learn & less prone to dispute & dictate; we
shall be willing then to read ancient documents of knowledge
for what they contain instead of attempting to force into them
our own truth or get them to serve our philosophic or scholastic
purposes. To enter passively into the thoughts of the old Rishis,
allow their words to sink into our souls, mould them & create
their own reverberations in a sympathetic & responsive material
— submissiveness, in short, to the Sruti — was the theory the
ancients themselves had of the method of Vedic knowledge —
giram upasrutim chara, stoman abhi swara, abhi grinihi, a ruva
— to listen in soul to the old voices and allow the Sruti in the soul
to respond, to vibrate first obscurely in answer to the Vedantic
hymn of knowledge, to give the response, the echo & last to
let that response gain in clarity, intensity & fullness. This is
the principle of interpretation that I have followed — mystical
perhaps but not necessarily more unsound than the insistence &
equally personal standards of the logician & the scholar. And

for the rest, where no inner experience of truth sheds light on the text, to abide faithfully by the wording of the Upanishad and trust my intuitions. For I hold it right to follow the intuitions especially in interpreting this Upanishad, even at the risk of being accused of reading mysticism into the Vedanta, because the early Vedantists, it seems to me, were mystics — not in the sense of being vague & loose-thoughted visionaries, but in the sense of being intuitional symbolists — who regarded the world as a movement of consciousness & all material forms & energies as external symbols & shadows of deeper & ever deeper internal realities. It is not my intention here nor is it in my limits possible to develop the philosophy of the Great Aranyaka Upanishad, but only to develop with just sufficient amplitude for entire clearness the ideas contained in its language & involved in its figures. The business of my commentary is to lay a foundation; it is for the thinker to build the superstructure.

The Horse of the Worlds

The Upanishad begins with a grandiose abruptness in an impetuous figure of the Horse of the Aswamedha. "OM" it begins "Dawn is the head of the horse sacrificial. The sun is his eye, his breath is the wind, his wide-open mouth is Fire, the universal energy; Time is the self of the horse sacrificial. Heaven is his back and the mid-region is his belly, earth is his footing, — the quarters are his flanks and their intermediate regions are his ribs; the seasons are his members, the months and the half months are their joints, the days and nights are that on which he stands, the stars are his bones and the sky is the flesh of his body. The strands are the food in his belly, the rivers are his veins, the mountains are his liver and lungs, herbs and plants are the hairs of his body; the rising day is his front portion and the setting day is his hinder portion. When he stretches himself, then it lightens; when he shakes himself, then it thunders; when he urines, then it rains. Speech verily is the voice of him. Day was the grandeur that was born before the horse as he galloped, the eastern ocean gave it birth. Night was the grandeur that was born in his rear and its birth was in the western waters. These were the grandeurs that arose to being on either side of the horse. He became Haya and carried the gods, — Vajin and bore the Gandharvas, — Arvan and bore the Titans, — Aswa and carried mankind. The sea was his brother and the sea his birthplace."

This passage, full of a gigantic imagery, sets the key to the Upanishad and only by entering into the meaning of its symbolism can we command the gates of this many-mansioned city of Vedantic thought. There is never anything merely poetic or ornamental in the language of the Upanishads. Even in this passage which would at first sight seem to be sheer imagery, there is a choice, a selecting eye, an intention in the images. They are all dependent not on the author's unfettered fancy, but on the common ideas of the early Vedantic theosophy. It is fortunate, also, that the attitude of the Upanishads to the Vedic sacrifices is perfectly plain from this opening. We shall not stand in danger of being accused of reading modern subtleties into primitive minds or of replacing barbarous superstitions by civilised mysticism. The Aswamedha or Horse-Sacrifice is, as we shall see, taken as the symbol of a great spiritual advance, an evolutionary movement, almost, out of the dominion of apparently material forces into a higher spiritual freedom. The Horse of the Aswamedha is, to the author, a physical figure representing, like some algebraical symbol, an unknown quantity of force & speed. From the imagery it is evident that this force, this speed, is something worldwide, something universal; it fills the regions with its body, it occupies Time, it gallops through Space, it bears on in its speed men and gods and the Titans. It is the Horse of the Worlds, — and yet the Horse sacrificial.

Let us regard first the word Aswa and consider whether it throws any light on the secret of this image. For we know that the early Vedantins attached great importance to words in both their apparent and their hidden meaning and no one who does not follow them in this path, can hope to enter into the associations with which their minds were full. Yet the importance of associations in colouring and often in determining our thoughts, determining even philosophic and scientific thought when it is most careful to be exact & free, should be obvious to the most superficial psychologist. Swami Dayananda's method with the Vedas, although it may have been too vigorously applied and more often out of the powerful mind of the modern Indian thinker than out of the recovered mentality of the old Aryan Rishis, would nevertheless, in its principle, have been approved by these Vedantins. Now the word Aswa must originally have implied strength or speed or both before it came to be applied to a horse. In its first or root significance it means to exist pervadingly and so to possess, have, obtain or enjoy. It is the Greek echo (OS. [*Old Sanskrit*] ashâ), the ordinary word in Greek for "I have". It means, also and even more commonly, to eat or enjoy. Beside this original sense inherent in the roots of its family it has its own peculiar significance of existence in force — strength, solidity, sharpness, speed, — in ashan and ashma, a stone, ashani, a thunderbolt, asri, a sharp edge or corner, (Latin acer, acris, sharp, acus, a point etc) and finally aswa, the strong, swift horse. Its fundamental meanings are, therefore, pervading existence, enjoyment, strength, solidity, speed. Shall we not say, therefore, that aswa to the Rishis meant the unknown power made up of force, strength, solidity, speed and enjoyment that pervades and constitutes the material world?

But there is a danger that etymological fancies may mislead us. It is necessary, therefore, to test our provisional conclusion from philology by a careful examination of the images of this parable. Yet before we proceed to this inquiry, it is as well to note that in the very opening of his second Brahmana, the Rishi passes on immediately from aswa the horse to Ashanaya mrityu, Hunger that is death and assigns this hunger that is death as the characteristic, indeed the very nature of the Force that has arranged and developed — evolved, as the moderns would say — the material worlds.

"Dawn" says the Rishi, "is the head of the horse sacrificial." Now the head is the front, the part of us that faces and looks out upon our world, — and Dawn is that part to the Horse of the worlds. This goddess must therefore be the opening out of

the world to the eye of being — for as day is the symbol of a
time of activity, night of a time of inactivity, so dawn images the
imperfect but pregnant beginnings of regular cosmic action; it
is the Being's movement forward, it is its impulse to look out
at the universe in which it finds itself and looking towards it,
to yearn, to desire to enter upon possession of a world which
looks so bright because of the brightness of the gaze that is
turned upon it. The word Ushas means etymologically coming
into manifested being; and it could mean also desire or yearning.
Ushas or Dawn to the early thinkers was the impulse towards
manifest existence, no longer a vague movement in the depths
of the Unmanifest, but already emerging and on the brink of its
satisfaction. For we must remember that we are dealing with a
book full of mystical imagery, which starts with & looks on psychological and philosophical truths in the most material things
and we shall miss its meaning altogether, if in our interpretation
we are afraid of mysticism.

The sun is the eye of this great Force, the wind is its life-
breath or vital energy, Fire is its open mouth. We are here in the
company of very familiar symbols. We shall have to return to
them hereafter but they are, in their surface application, obvious
and lucid. By themselves they are almost sufficient to reveal
the meaning of the symbol, — yet not altogether sufficient. For,
taken by themselves, they might mislead us into supposing the
Horse of the Worlds to be an image of the material universe
only, a figure for those movements of matter & in matter with
which modern Science is so exclusively preoccupied. But the next
image delivers us from passing by this side-gate into materialism.
"Time in its period is the self of the Horse Sacrificial." If we
accept for the word *atma* a significance which is also common
and is, indeed, used in the next chapter, if we understand by
it, as I think we ought here to understand by it, "substance"
or "body", the expression, in itself remarkable, will become
even more luminous and striking. Not Matter then, but Time,
a mental circumstance, is the body of this force of the material
universe whose eye is the sun and his breath the wind. Are we
then to infer that the Seer denies the essential materiality of

matter? does he assert it to be, as Huxley admitted it to be, "a state of consciousness"? We shall see. Meanwhile it is evident already that this Horse of the Worlds is not an image merely of matter or material force, but, as we had already supposed it to be, an image of the power which pervades and constitutes the material universe. We get also from this image about Time the idea of it as an unknown power — for Time which is its self or body, is itself an unknown quantity. The reality which expresses itself to us through Time — its body — but remains itself ungrasped, must be still what men have always felt it to be, the unknown God.

In the images that immediately follow we have the conception of Space added to the conception of Time and both are brought together side by side as constituents of the being of the horse. For the sky is the flesh of his body, the quarters his flanks & the intermediate regions his ribs — the sky, nabhas, the ether above us in which the stellar systems are placed, — and these stellar systems themselves, concentrations of ether, are the bones which support the flesh and of which life in this spatial infinity takes advantage in order more firmly to place & organise itself in matter. But side by side with this spatial image is that of the seasons reminding us immediately & intentionally of the connection of Time to Space. The seasons, determined for us by the movements of the sun & stars, are the flanks of the horse and he stands upon the months and the fortnights — the lunar divisions. Space, then, is the flesh constituting materially this body of Time which the Sage attributes to his Horse of the worlds, — by movement in Space its periods are shaped & determined. Therefore we return always to the full idea of the Horse — not as an image of matter, not as a symbol of the unknown supra-material Power in its supra-material reality, but of that Power expressing itself in matter — materially, we might almost say, pervading & constituting the universe. Time is its body, — yes, but sanvatsara not kala, Time in its periods determined by movement in Space, not Time in its essentiality.

Moreover, it is that Power imaging itself in Cosmos, it is the Horse of the Worlds. For, we read, "Heaven is its back, the mid-region is its belly, earth is its footing" — pajasyam, the four feet upon which it stands. We must be careful not to confuse the ancient Seer's conception of the universe with our modern conception. To us nothing exists except the system of gross material worlds — annamayam jagat, — this earth, this moon, this sun & its planets, these myriad suns and their systems. But to the Vedantic thinkers the universe, the manifest Brahman, was a harmony of worlds within worlds; they beheld a space within our space but linked with it, they were aware of a Time connected with our Time but different from it. This earth was Bhur. Rising in soul into the air above the earth, the antariksham, they thought they came into contact with other sevenfold earths in which just as here matter is the predominant principle, so there nervous or vital energy is the main principle or else manas, still dependent on matter & vital energy; these earths they called Bhuvar. And rising beyond this atmosphere into the ethereal void they believed themselves to be aware of other worlds which they called Swar or heaven, where again in its turn mind, free, blithe, delivered from its struggle to impose itself in a world not its own upon matter & nerve-life, is the medium of existence & the governing Force. If we keep in mind these ideas, we shall easily understand why the images are thus distributed in the sentence I have last quoted. Heaven is the back of the Horse, because it is on mind that we rest, mind that bears up the Gods & Gandharvas, Titans & men; — the mid-region is the belly because vital energy is that which hungers & devours, moves restlessly everywhere seizing everything and turning it into food or else because mind is the womb of all our higher consciousness; — earth is the footing because matter here, outward form, is the fundamental condition for the manifestation of life, mind and all higher forces. On Matter we rest and have our firm stand; out of Matter we rise to our fulfilment in Spirit.

Then once again, after these higher & more remote suggestions, we are reminded that it is some Force manifesting in matter which the Horse symbolises; the material manifestation constitutes the essence of its symbolism. The images used are of an almost gross materiality. Some of them are at the same time of a striking interest to the practical student of Yoga, for he recognises in them allusions to certain obscure but exceedingly common Yogic phenomena. The strands of the rivers are imaged as the undigested food in the horse's belly — earth not yet assimilated or of sufficient consistency for the habitual works of life; the rivers, distributing the water that is the life blood of earth's activities, are his veins; the mountains, breathing in health for us from the rarer altitudes and supporting by the streams born from them the works of life, are his lungs and liver; herbs and plants, springing up out of the sap of earth, are the hairs covering & clothing his body. All that is clear enough and designedly superficial. But then the Upanishad goes on to speak no longer of superficial circumstances but of the powers of the Horse. Some of these are material powers, the thunder, the lightning, the rain. When he stretches himself, then it lightens; when he shakes himself, then it thunders; when he urines, then it rains — vijrimbhate, extends himself by intensity, makes the most of his physical bulk & force; vidhunute, throws himself out by energy, converts his whole body into a motion & force; these two words are of a great impetuosity & vehemence, and taken in conjunction with what they image, extremely significant. The Yogin will at once recognise the reference to the electrical manifestations visible or felt which accompany so often the increase of concentration, thought & inner activity in the waking condition — electricity, vidyutas, the material symbol, medium & basis of all activities of knowledge, sarvani vijnanavijrimbhitani. He will recognise also the meghadhwani, one of the characteristic sounds heard in the concentration of Yoga, symbolical of kshatratejas and physically indicative of force gathering itself for action. The first image is therefore an image of knowledge expressing itself in matter, the second is an image of power expressing itself in matter. The third, the image of the rain, suggests that it is from the mere waste matter of his body that this great Power is able to fertilise the world & produce sustenance for the myriad nations of his creatures. "Speech verily is the voice of him." Vagevasya vak. Speech with its burden of definite thought, is the neighing of this mighty horse of sacrifice; by that this great Power in matter expresses materially the uprush of his thought & yearning & emotion, visible sparks of the secret universal fire that is in him — guhahitam.

But the real powers, the wonderful fundamental greatnesses of the Horse are, the Sage would have us remember, not the material. What are they then? The sunrise & sunset, day & night are their symbols, not the magnitudes of space, but the magnitudes of Time, — Time, that mysterious condition of universal mind which alone makes the ordering of the universe in Space possible, although its own particular relations to matter are necessarily determined by material events & movements — for itself subtle as well as infinite it offers no means by which it can be materially measured. Sunrise & sunset, that is to say birth & death, are the front & hind part of the body of the horse, Time expressed in matter. But on Day & Night the sage fixes a deeper significance. Day is the symbol of the continual manifestation of material things [in] the vyakta, the manifest or fundamentally in Sat, in infinite being; Night is the symbol of their continual disappearance in Avyakta, the unmanifest or finally into Asat, into infinite non-being. They appear according to the swift movement of this Horse of the Worlds, anu ajayata, or, as I have written, translating the idea & rhythm of the Upanishad rather than the exact words, as he gallops. Day is the greatness that appears in his front, Night is the greatness that appears in his rear, — whatever this Time-Spirit, this Zeitgeist, turns his face towards or arrives at as he gallops through Time, that appears or, as we say, comes into being, whatever he passes away from & leaves, that disappears out of being or, as we say, perishes. Not that things are really destroyed, for nothing that is can be destroyed — nabhavo vidyate satah, but they no longer appear, they are swallowed up in this darkness of his refusal of consciousness; for the purposes of manifestation they cease to exist. All things exist already in Parabrahman, but all are not here manifest. They are already there in Being, not in Time. The universal Thought expressing itself as Time reaches them, they seem to be born; It passes away from them, they seem to perish; but there they still are, in Being, but not in Time. These two greatnesses of the appearance of things in Time & Space & their disappearance in Time & Space act always & continuously so long as the Horse is galloping, are his essential greatnesses. Etau vai mahimanau. The birth of one is in the eastern ocean, of the other in the western, that is to say in Sat & Asat, in the ocean of Being & the ocean of denial of Being or else in Vyakrita Prakriti & Avyakrita Prakriti, occult sea of Chaos, manifest sea of Cosmos.

Then the sage throws out briefly a description, not exhaustive but typical, of the relations of the Horse to the different natural types of being that seem to possess this universe. For all of them He is the vahana, He bears them up on His infinite strength & speed & motion. He bears all of them without respect of differences, samabhavena, with the divine impartiality and equality of soul — samam hi Brahma. To the type of each individual being this Universal Might adapts himself & seems to take upon himself their image. He is Haya to the Gods, Arvan to the Asura, Vajin to the Gandharvas, Aswa to men. Ye yatha mam prapadyante tans tathaiva bhajamyaham, mama vartmanuvartante manushyah Partha sarvashah. In reality, they are made in his image, not He in theirs, & though he seems to obey them & follow their needs & impulses, though they handle the whip, ply the spur & tug the reins, it is he who bears them on in the courses of Time that are marked out for him by his hidden Self; He is free & exults in the swiftness of his galloping.

But what are these names, Haya, Vajin, Arvan, Aswa? Certainly, they must suggest qualities which fit the Horse in each case to the peculiar type of its rider; but the meaning depends on associations & an etymology which in modern Sanscrit have gone below the surface & are no longer easily seizable. Haya is especially difficult. For this reason Shankara, relying too much on scholarship & intellectual inference & too little on his intuitions, is openly at a loss in this passage. He sees that the word haya for horse must arise from the radical sense of motion borne by the root *hi*; but every horse has motion for his chief characteristic & utility, Arvan & Vajin no less than Haya. Why then should Haya alone be suitable for riding by the gods, why

Arvan for the Asuras? He has, I think, the right intuition when he suggests that it is some peculiar & excelling kind of motion (visishtagati) which is the characteristic of Haya. But then, unable to fix on that peculiarity, unable to read any characteristic meaning in the names that follow, he draws back from his intuition and adds that after all, these names may have merely indicated particular kinds of horses attributed mythologically to these various families of riders. But this suggestion would make the passage mere mythology; but the Upanishads, always intent on their deeper object, never waste time over mere mythology. We must therefore go deeper than Shankara and follow out the intuition he himself has abandoned.

I am dwelling on this passage at a length disproportionate to its immediate importance, not only because Shankara's failure in handling it shows the necessity & fruitfulness of trusting our intuitions when in contact with the Upanishads, but because the passage serves two other important uses. It illustrates the Vedantic use of the etymology of words and it throws light on the precise notions of the old thinkers about those super-terrestrial beings with whom the vision of the ancient Hindus peopled the universe. The Vedantic writers, we continually find, dwelt deeply & curiously on the innate & on the concealed meaning of words; vyakarana, always considered essential to the interpretation of the Vedas, they used not merely as scholars, but much more as intuitive thinkers. It was not only the actual etymological sense or the actual sense in use but the suggestions of the sound & syllables of the words which attracted them; for they found that by dwelling on them new & deep truths arose into their understandings. Let us see how they use this method in assigning the names assumed by the sacrificial Horse.

Here modern philology comes to our help, for, by the clue it has given, we can revive in its principle the Nirukta of our ancestors and discover by induction & inference the old meaning of the Vedic vocables. I will leave Haya alone for the present; because philology unaided does not help us very much in getting at the sense of its application, — in discovering the visishtagati which the word conveyed to the mind of the sage. But Vajin &

Arvan are very illuminative. Vaja & Vajin are common Vedic words; they recur perpetually in the Rigveda. The sense of Vaja is essentially substantiality of being attended with plenty, from which it came to signify full force, copiousness, strength, and by an easy transition substance & plenty in the sense of wealth and possessions. There can be no doubt about Vajin. But European scholarship has confused for us the approach to the sense of Arvan. *Ar* is a common Sanscrit root, the basis of ari, Arya, Aryama and a number of well known words. But the scholars tell us that it means to till or plough & the Aryans so called themselves because they were agriculturists and not nomads & hunters. Starting from this premise one may see in Arvan a horse for ploughing as opposed to a draught-animal or a warhorse, & support the derivation by instancing the Latin arvum, a tilled field! But even if the Aryans were ploughmen, the Titans surely were not — Hiranyakashipu & Prahlad did not pride themselves on the breaking of the glebe & the honest sweat of their brow! There is no trace of such an association in arvan here, — I know not whether there is any elsewhere in the Vedas. Indeed, this agriculturist theory of the Aryans seems one of the worst of the many irresponsible freaks which scholastic fancifulness has perpetrated in the field of Sanscrit learning. No ancient race would be likely so to designate itself. *Ar* signifies essentially any kind of preeminence in fact or force in act. It means therefore to be strong, high, swift or active, preeminent, noble, excellent or first; to raise, lead, begin or rule; it means also to struggle, fight, to drive, to labour, to plough. The sense of struggle & combat appears in ari, an enemy; the Greek Ares, the war-god, arete, virtue, meaning originally like the Latin virtus, valour; the Latin arma, weapons. Arya means strong, high, noble or warlike, as indeed its use in literature constantly indicates. We can now discover the true force of Arvan, — it is the strong one in command, it is the stallion, or the bull, ie master of the herd, the leader, master or fighter. The word Asura also means the strong or mighty one. The Gandharvas are cited here briefly, so as to suit the rapidity of the passage, as the type of a particular class of beings, Gandharvas, Yakshas, Kinnaras whose unifying characteristic is material ease, prosperity and a beautiful, happy & undisturbed self-indulgence; they are angels of joy, ease, art, beauty & pleasure. For them the Horse becomes full of ease & plenty, the support of these qualities, the vahana of the Gandharvas. The Asuras are, similarly, angels of might & force & violent struggle, — self-will is their characteristic, just as an undisciplined fury of self-indulgence is the characteristic of their kindred Rakshasas. It is a self-will capable of discipline, but always huge & impetuous even in discipline, always based on a colossal egoism. They struggle gigantically to impose that egoism on their surroundings. It is for these mighty but imperfect beings that the Horse adapts himself to their needs, becomes full of force & might and bears up their gigantic struggle, their unceasing effort. And Haya? In the light of these examples we can hazard a suggestion. The root meaning is motion; but from certain kindred words, *hil*, to swing, *hind*, to swing, *hiṇḍ*, to roam about freely & from another sense of *hi*, to exhilarate or gladden, we may, perhaps, infer that haya indicated to the sage a swift, free & joyous, bounding motion, fit movement for the bearer of the gods. For the Aryan gods were devas, angels of joy & brightness, fulfilled in being, in harmony with their functions & surroundings, not like the Titans imperfect, dispossessed, struggling. Firmly seated on the bounding joy of the Horse, they deliver themselves confidently to the exultation of his movements. The sense here is not so plain & certain as with Vajin & Arvan; but Haya must certainly have been one in character with the Deva in order to be his vahana; the sense I have given certainly belongs to the word Deva, is discoverable in Haya from its roots, & that this brightness & joyousness was the character of the Aryan gods, I think every reader of Veda & Purana must feel and admit. Last of all, the Horse becomes Aswa for men. But is he not Aswa for all? why particularly for men? The answer is that the Rishi is already moving forward in thought to the idea of Ashanaya Mrityu with which he opens the second Brahmana of the Upanishad. Man, first & supreme type of terrestrial creatures, is most of all subject to this mystery of wasting & death which the Titans bear with difficulty & the gods

& Gandharvas entirely overcome. For in man that characteristic of enjoyment which by enjoying devours & wastes both its object & itself is especially developed & he bears the consequent pressure of Ashanaya Mrityu which can only lighten & disappear if we rise upward in the scale of Being towards Brahman & become truly sons of immortality, Amritasya putrah. That form of force in matter that is self-wasting because it wastes or preys upon others, is man's vahana.

Of this Horse of the Worlds, who bears up all beings, the sea is the brother & the sea is the birthplace. There can be no doubt of the meaning of this symbol. It is the upper ocean of the Veda in which it imaged the superior & divine existence, these are the waters of supramaterial causality. From that this lower ocean of our manifestation derives its waters, its flowing energies, apah; from that when the Vritras are slain & the firmaments opened, it is perpetually replenished, prati samudram syandamanah and of that it is the shadow & the reproduction of its circumstances under the conditions of mental illusion, — Avidya, mother of limitation & death. This image not only consummates this passage but opens a door of escape from that which is to follow. Deliverance from the dominion of Ashanaya Mrityu is possible because of this circumstance that the sea of divine being is bandhu, kin & friend to the Horse. The aparardha proves to be of the same essential nature as the parardha, our mortal part is akin to our unlimited & immortal part, because the Horse of the Worlds comes to us from that divine source & in his essence partakes of its nature, & from what other except this Ocean can the Horse of the Worlds who is material yet supramaterial be said to have derived his being? We, appearing bound, mortal & limited, are manifestations of a free & infinite reality & from that from which we were born comes friendship & assistance for that which we are, towards making us that which we shall be. From our kindred heavens the Love descends always that works to raise up the lower to its brother, the higher.

The Kaivalya Upanishad

ॐ अथाश्वलायनो भगवन्तं परमेष्ठिनमुपसमेत्योवाच ।
अधीहि भगवन् ब्रह्मविद्यां वरिष्ठां सदा सद्भिः सेव्यमानां निगूढाम् ।
यथाचिरात् सर्वपापं व्यपोह्य परात्परं पुरुषं याति विद्वान् ॥ १ ॥

OM. Aswalayana to the Lord Parameshthi came and said, Teach me, Lord, the highest knowledge of Brahman, the secret knowledge ever followed by the saints, how the wise man swiftly putting from him all evil goeth to the Purusha who is higher than the highest.

Commentary

The Lord Parameshthi is Brahma — not the Creator Hiranyagarbha, but the soul who in this kalpa has climbed up to be the instrument of Creation, the first in time of the Gods, the Pitamaha or original & general Prajapati, the Pitamaha, because all the fathers or special Prajapatis, Daksha and others, are his mind born children. The confusion between the Grandsire and the Creator, who is also called Brahma, is common; but the distinction is clear. Thus in the Mundaka Upanishad ब्रह्मा देवानां प्रथमः संबभूव, it is the first of Gods, the earliest birth of Time, the father of Atharva, and not the unborn eternal Hiranyagarbha. In the Puranas Brahma is described as in fear of his life from Madhu and Kaitabha, and cannot be the fearless and immortal Hiranyagarbha. Nor would it be possible for Aswalayana to come to Hiranyagarbha and say "Teach me, Lord," for Hiranyagarbha has no form nor is He approachable nor does He manifest Himself to men as Shiva and Vishnu do. He is millionfold, Protean, intangible, and for that reason He places in each cycle a Brahma or divine Man between Him and the search and worship of men. It is Brahma or divine Man who is called Parameshthi or the one full of Parameshtham, that which is superlative and highest, — Hiranyagarbha. The power of Hiranyagarbha is in Brahma and creates through him the nama and rupa of things in this cycle.

To Brahma Parameshthi Aswalayana comes as a disciple to a master and says to him, Lord, teach me the Brahmavidya. He specifies the kind of knowledge he requires. It is varishtha, the best or highest, because it goes beyond the triple Brahman to the Purushottam or Most High God; it is secret, because even in the ordinary teaching of Vedanta, Purana and Tantra it is not expressed, it is always followed by the saints, the initiates. The *santah* or saints are those who are pure of desire and full of knowledge, and it is to these that the secret knowledge has been given सदा, from the beginning. He makes his meaning yet clearer by stating the substance of the knowledge — यथा, how, by what means won by knowledge, विद्वान्, one can swiftly put sin from him and reach Purushottam.

There are three necessary elements of the path to Kaivalya, — first, the starting point, vidya, right knowledge, implying the escape from ignorance, non-knowledge and false knowledge; next, the process or means, escape from सर्वपापं, all evil, ie, sin, pain and grief; last, the goal, Purushottam, the Being who is beyond the highest, that is, beyond Turiya, being the Highest. By the escape from sin, pain and grief one attains absolute ananda, and by ananda, the last term of existence, we reach that in which ananda exists. What is that? It is not Turiya who is shivam, shantam, adwaitam, sacchidanandam, but that which is beyond shivam and ashivam, good and evil, shantam and kalilam, calm and chaos, dwaitam and adwaitam, duality and unity. Sat, Chit and Ananda are in this Highest, but He is neither Sat, Chit nor Ananda nor any combination of these. He is All and yet He is neti, neti, He is One and yet He is many. He is Parabrahman and He is Parameswara. He is Male and He is Female. He is Tat and He is Sa. This is the Higher than the Highest. He is the Purusha, the Being in whose image the world and all the Jivas are made, who pervades all and underlies all the workings of Prakriti as its reality and self. It is this Purusha that Aswalayana seeks.

Nila Rudra Upanishad

First Part

Translation

ॐ अपश्यं त्वावरोहन्तं दिवितः पृथिवीमव: ।
अपश्यमस्यन्तं रुद्रं नीलग्रीवं शिखण्डिनम् ॥ १ ॥

1. OM. Thee I beheld in thy descending down from the heavens
to the earth, I saw Rudra, the Terrible, the azure-throated,
the peacock-feathered, as he hurled.

दिव उग्रो अवारुक्षत्प्रत्यष्ठाद् भूम्यामधि ।
जनासः पश्यते महं नीलग्रीवं विलोहितम् ॥ २ ॥

2. Fierce he came down from the sky, he stood facing me on
the earth as its lord, — the people behold a mass of strength,
azure-throated, scarlet-hued.

एष एत्यवीरहा रुद्रो जलासभेषजः ।
यत्तेऽक्षेममनीनशद् वातीकारोऽप्येतु ते ॥ ३ ॥

3. This that cometh is he that destroyeth evil, Rudra the Terrible, born of the tree that dwelleth in the waters; let the
globe of the stormwinds come too, that destroyeth for thee
all things of evil omen.

नमस्ते भवभावाय नमस्ते भाममन्यवे ।
नमस्ते अस्तु बाहुभ्यामुतो त इषवे नम: ॥ ४ ॥

4. Salutation to thee who bringeth the world into being, salutation to thee, the passionate with mighty wrath. Salutation
be to thy arms of might, salutation be to thy angry shaft.

यामिषुं गिरिशन्त हस्ते बिभर्ष्यस्तवे ।
शिवां गिरित्र तां कृणु मा हिंसीत्पुरुषान् मम ॥ ५ ॥

5. The arrow thou bearest in thy hand for the hurling, O thou that liest on the mountains, make an arrow of blessing, O keeper of the hills, let it not slay my armed men.

शिवेन वचसा त्वा गिरिशाच्छावदामसि ।
यथा नः सर्वमिज्जगदयक्ष्मं सुमना असत् ॥ ६ ॥

6. With fair speech, O mountain-dweller, we sue to thee in the assembly of the folk, that the whole world may be for us a friendly and sinless place.

या ते इषुः शिवतमा शिवं बभूव ते धनुः ।
शिवा शरव्या या तव तया नो मृड जीवसे ॥ ७ ॥

7. That thy arrow which is the kindliest of all and thy bow which is well-omened and that thy quiver which beareth blessing, by that thou livest for us, O lord of slaughter.

या ते रुद्र शिवा तनूरघोरा पापकाशिनी ।
तया नस्तन्वा शन्तमया गिरिश त्वाभिचाकशत् ॥ ८ ॥

8. That thy body, O Terrible One, which is fair and full of kindness and destroyeth sin, not thy shape of terrors, in that thy body full of peace, O mountaineer, thou art wont to be seen among our folk.

असौ यस्ताम्रो अरुण उत बभ्रुविलोहितः ।
ये चेमे अभितो रुद्रा दिक्षु श्रिताः सहस्रशो वैषां हेड ईमहे ॥ ९ ॥

9. This Aruna of the dawn that is tawny and copper-red and scarlet-hued, and these thy Violent Ones round about that dwell in the regions in their thousands, verily, it is these whom we desire.

Commentary

1. अपश्यं. I beheld. The speaker is the author of the Upanishad, a prince of the Aryan people, as we see from the fifth verse. He records a vision of Rudra descending from the heavens to the earth. अव:, down, is repeated for the sake of vividness. In the second half of the sloka the murti or image in which he beheld the Divine Manifestation is described, Rudra, the God of might and wrath, the neck and throat blue, a peacock's feather as a crest, in the act of hurling a shaft.

2. He proceeds to describe the descent. He descended fiercely, that is, with wrath in his face, gesture and motion and stood facing the seer, प्रत्यष्ठात्, on the earth, and over it, अधि, in a way expressive of command or control. This image of Divine Power, seen by the prince in Yoga, becomes visible to the people in general as a mass of strength, मह, scarlet in colour, deep blue in the neck and throat. मह is strength, bulk, greatness. The manifestation is that of wrath and might. The people see Rudra as a mass of brilliance, scarlet-ringed and crested with blue, the scarlet in Yoga denoting violent passion of anger or desire, the blue sraddha, bhakti, piety or religion.

3. Rudra, whom we know as the slayer of evil, comes. The Rajarshi describes him as born of the tree that is in the waters. भेष is by philology identical with the Latin ficus or figtree, aswattha. The aswattha is the Yogic emblem of the manifested world, as in the Gita, the tree of the two birds in the Swetaswatara Upanishad, the single tree in the blue expanse of the Song of Liberation. The jala is the apah or waters from which the world rises. The rishi then prays that the वातीकार:, mass of winds of which Rudra is lord and which in the tempest of their course blow away all calamity, such as pestilence etc, may come with him.

4. In the fourth verse he salutes the God. Rudra is the Supreme Ishwara, Creator of the World, He is the dreadful, wrathful and destroying Lord, swift to slay and punish. भाम is passionate

anger, and the word मन्युः denotes a violent disturbed state of mind, passion, either of grief or of anger. भाममन्यवे therefore means, one who is full of the passion of violent anger. Rudra is being saluted as a God of might and wrath, it is therefore to the arms as the seat of strength and the arrow as the weapon of destruction that salutation is made.

5. Rudra is coming in a new form of wrath and destruction in which the Aryans are not accustomed to see him. Apprehensive of the meaning of this vision, the King summons the people and in assembly prayer is offered to Rudra to avert possible calamity. The shaft is lifted to be hurled from the bow; it is prayed that it may be turned into a shaft of blessing, not of wrath. In this verse the Prince prays the God not to slay his men, meaning evidently, the armed warriors of the clan.

Section Four

Incomplete Commentaries
on the Kena Upanishad

Circa 1912–1914

Kena Upanishad

An Incomplete Commentary

Foreword

As the Isha Upanishad is concerned with the problem of God
& the world and consequently with the harmonising of spirituality & ordinary human action, so the Kena is occupied with
the problem of God & the Soul and the harmonising of our
personal activity with the movement of infinite energy & the
supremacy of the universal Will. We are not here in this universe
as independent existences. It is evident that we are limited beings
clashing with other limited beings, clashing with the forces of
material Nature, clashing too with forces of immaterial Nature
of which we are aware not with the senses but by the mind.
The Upanishad takes for granted that we are souls, not merely
life-inspired bodies — into that question it does not enter. But
this soul in us is in relation with the outside world through the
senses, through the vitality, through mind. It is entangled in the
mesh of its instruments, thinks they alone exist or is absorbed
in their action with which it identifies itself — it forgets itself in
its activities. To recall it to itself, to lift it above this life of the
senses, so that even while living in this world, it shall always
refer itself & its actions to the high universal Self & Deity which
we all are in the ultimate truth of our being — so that we may
be free, may be pure & joyous, may be immortal, that is the
object of the seer in the Kena Upanishad. Briefly to explain the
steps by which he develops and arrives at his point and the
principal philosophical positions underlying his great argument,
is as always the purpose of this commentary. There is much that
might & should be said for the full realisation of this ancient
gospel of submission & self-surrender to the Infinite, but it is left
to be said in a work of greater amplitude and capacity. Exegesis

in faithful subordination to the strict purport & connotation of the text will be here as always my principle.

=====

The First Part
The Self & the Senses

"By whom controlled, by whom commissioned & sent forth falleth the mind on its object, by whom yoked to its activity goeth abroad this chief of the vital forces? By whom controlled is this word that men speak, and what god set ear & eye to their workings? That which is hearing within hearing, mind of the mind, speech behind the word, he too is the life of vitality & the sight within vision; the calm of soul are liberated from these instruments and passing beyond this world become Immortals... There the eye goes not & speech cannot follow nor the mind; we know it not nor can we decide by reason how to teach of it; for verily it is other than the known & it is beyond the unknown; so have we heard from the men that went before us by whom to us this Brahman was declared. That which is not uttered by speech, but by which speech is expressed, know thou that to be the Soul of things and not this which men here pursue. That which thinketh not by the mind, but by which mind itself is realised, know thou that to be the Soul of things, not this which men here pursue. That which seeth not by sight, but by which one seeth things visible, know thou that to be the Soul of things and not this which men here pursue. That which heareth not by hearing but by which hearing becomes subject to knowledge through the ear, know thou that to be the Soul of things & not this which men here pursue. That which liveth not by the breathing, but by which the breath becometh means of vitality, know thou that to be the Soul of things & not this which men here pursue."

I

In order to understand the question with which the Upanishad opens its train of thought, it is necessary to remember the ideas of the Vedantic thinkers about the phenomena of sensation, life, mind and ideas which are the elements of all our activity in the body. It is noticeable that the body itself and matter, [the] principle of which the body is a manifestation, are not even mentioned in this Upanishad. The problem of matter the Seer supposes to have been so far solved for the inquirer that he no longer regards the physical state of consciousness as fundamental and no longer considers it as a reality separate from consciousness. All this world is only one conscious Being. Matter to the Vedantist is only one of several states — in reality, movements — of this conscious being, — a state in which this universal consciousness, having created forms within & out of itself as substance, absorbs & loses itself by concentration in the idea of being as substance of form. It is still conscious, but, as form, ceases to be self-conscious. The Purusha in matter, the Knower in the leaf, clod, stone, is involved in form, forgets himself in this movement of his Prakriti or Mode of Action and loses hold in outgoing knowledge of his self of conscious being & delight. He is not in possession of himself; He is not Atmavan. He has to get back what he has lost, to become Atmavan, and that simply means that He has to become gradually aware in matter of that which He has hidden from Himself in matter. He has to evolve what He has involved. This recovery in knowledge of our full and real self is the sole secret meaning & purpose of evolution. In reality it is no evolution, but a manifestation. We are already what we become. That which is still future in matter, is already present in Spirit. That which the mind in matter does not yet know, it is hiding from itself — that in us which is behind mind & informs it already knows — but it keeps its secret.

For that which we regard as matter, cannot be, if the Vedantic view is right, mere matter, mere inert existence, eternally bound by its own inertness. Even in a materialistic view of the world matter cannot be what it seems, but is only a form or movement of Force which the Indians call Prakriti. This Force, according to the Upanishads, is composed in its action & capable in its potentiality of several principles, of which matter, mind & life are those already manifestly active in this world, and where one of these principles is active, the others must also be there, involved in it; or, to put it in another way, Force acting as one of its own principles, one of its movements, is inherently capable even in that movement of all the others. If in the leaf, clod, stone & metal life and mind are not active, it is not because they are not present, but because they are not yet brought forward (prakrita) and organised for action. They are kept concealed, in the background of the consciousness-being which is the leaf, stone or clod; they are not yet vilu, as the Rigveda would say, but guha, not vyakta, but avyakta. It is a great error to hold that that which is not just now or in this or that place manifest or active, does not there & then exist. Concealment is not annihilation; non-action is not non-being nor does the combination of secrecy & inaction constitute non-existence.

If it is asked how we know that there is the Purusha or Knower in the leaf, clod or stone, — the Vedantin answers that, apart from the perceptions of the Seer & the subjective & objective experiences by which the validity of the perceptions is firmly established in the reason, the very fact that the Knower emerges in matter shows that He must have been there all the time. And if He was there in some form of matter He must be there generally & in all; for Nature is one & knows no essential division, but only differences of form, circumstance and manifestation. There are not many substances in this world, but one substance variously concentrated in many forms; not many lives, but one liver variously active in many bodies; not many minds, but one mind variously intelligent in many embodied vitalities.

It is, at first sight, a plausible theory that life & mind are only particular movements of matter itself under certain conditions & need not therefore be regarded as independent immaterial movements of consciousness involved in matter but only as latent material activities of which matter is capable. But this view can only be held so long as it appears that mind and life can only exist in this body & cease as soon as the body is broken up, can only know through the bodily instruments and can only operate in obedience to and as the result of certain material movements. The sages of the Upanishads had already proved by their own experience as Yogins that none of these limitations are inherent in the nature of life & mind. The mind & life which are in this body can depart from it, intact & still organised, and act more freely outside it; mind can know even material things without the help of the physical eye, touch or ear; life itself is not conditioned necessarily, and mind is not even conditioned usually, though it is usually affected, by the state of the body or its movements. It can always and does frequently in our experience transcend them. It can entirely master & determine the condition of the body. Therefore mind is capable of freedom from the matter in which it dwells here, — freedom in being, freedom in knowledge, freedom in power.

It is true that while working in matter, every movement of mind produces some effect & consequently some state or movement in the body, but this does not show that the mind is the material result of matter any more than steam is the mechanical result of the machine. This world in which mind is at present moving, in the system of phenomena to which we are now overtly related, is a world of matter, where, to start with, it is true to say Annam vai sarvam; All is matter. Mind and life awaken in it & seek to express themselves in it. Since & when they act in it, every movement they make, must have an effect upon it and produce a movement in it, just as the activity of steam must produce an effect in the machine in which its force is acting. Mind and life also use particular parts of the bodily machine for particular functions and, when these parts are injured, those workings of life & mind are correspondingly hampered, rendered difficult or for a time impossible — & even altogether impossible unless life & mind are given time, impulse & opportunity to readjust themselves to the new circumstances & either recreate or patch up the old means or adopt a new system of function. It is obvious that such a combination of time, impulse & opportunity cannot usually or even often occur, —

cannot occur at all unless men have the faith, the nistha — unless
that is to say, they know beforehand that it can be done & have
accustomed themselves to seek for the means. Bodies, drowned
& "lifeless", — nothing is really lifeless in the world, — can now
be brought back to life because men believe & know that it can
be done & have found a means to do it before the organised
mind & life have had time to detach themselves entirely from
the unorganised life which is present in all matter. So it is with
all powers & operations. They are only impossible so long as
we do not believe in their possibility & do not take the trouble
or have not the clarity of mind to find their right process.

Life & mind are sometimes believed to descend, — or the
hypothesis is advanced — into this world from another where
they are more at home. If by world is meant not another star or
system in this material universe, but some other systematisation
of universal consciousness, the Vedantin who follows the Vedas
& Upanishads, will not disagree. Life & mind in another star
or system of this visible universe might, it is conceivable, be
more free and, therefore, at home; but they would still be acting
in a world whose basis & true substance was matter. There
would therefore be no essential alteration in the circumstances
of their action nor would the problem of their origin here be at
all better solved. But it is reasonable to suppose that just as here
Force organises itself in matter as its fundamental continent &
movement, so there should be — the knowledge & experience of
the ancient thinkers showed them that there are — other systems
of consciousness where Force organises itself in life and in mind
as its fundamental continent & movement. — It is not necessary
to consider here what would be the relations in Time & Space
of such worlds with ours. Life & mind might descend, ready
organised, from such worlds and attach themselves to forms of
matter here; but not in the sense of occupying physically these
material forms & immediately using them, but in the sense of
rousing by the shock of their contact & awakening to activity the
latent life & mind in matter. That life & mind in matter would
then proceed, under the superior help & impulse, to organise a
nervous system for the use of life and a system of life-movements

in the nerves for the use of mind fit to express in matter the superior organisations who have descended here. It was indeed the belief of the ancients that — apart from the government of each living form by a single organised personality — such help from the worlds of life & mind was necessary to maintain & support all functionings of life & mind here below because of the difficulty otherwise of expressing & perfecting them in a world which did not properly belong to them but to quite other movements. This was the basis of the idea of Devas, Daityas, Asuras, Rakshasas, Pisachas, Gandharvas etc, with which the Veda, Upanishad & Itihasa have familiarised our minds. There is no reason to suppose that all worlds of this material system are the home of living things — on the contrary the very reverse is likely to be the truth. It is, probably, with difficulty & in select places that life & mind in matter are evolved.

If it were otherwise, if life & mind were to enter, organised or in full power, (such as they must be in worlds properly belonging to them) into material forms, those forms would immediately begin to function perfectly & without farther trouble. We should not see this long & laborious process of gradual manifestation, so laboured, so difficult, the result of so fierce a struggle, of such a gigantic toil of the secret Will in matter. Everywhere we see the necessity of a gradual organisation of forms. What is it that is being organised? A suitable system for the operations of life, a suitable system for the operations of mind. There are stirrings similar to those that constitute life in inanimate things, in metals — as Science has recently discovered, — vital response & failure to respond, but no system for the regular movement of vitality has been organised; therefore metals do not live. In the plant we have a vital system, one might almost say a nervous system, but although there is what might be called an unconscious mind in plants, although in some there are even vague movements of intelligence, the life system organised is suitable only for the flow of rasa, sap, sufficient for mere life, not for prana, nerve force, necessary for the operation in matter of mind. Apah is sufficient for life, vayu is necessary for life capable of mind. In the animal life is organised on a different plan and a nervous system capable of carrying currents of pranic force is developed as one rises in the scale of animal creation, until it becomes perfect in man. It is, therefore, life & mind awakening in matter & manifesting with difficulty that is the truth of this material world, not the introduction of a ready made life entirely foreign to it in its own potentiality.

If it be said that the life & mind attaching themselves to matter only enter it by degrees as the system becomes more fit, putting more & more of itself into the body which is being made ready for it, that also is possible & conceivable. We are indeed led to see, as we progress in self-knowledge, that there is a great mental activity belonging to us only part of which is imperfectly expressed in our waking thoughts & perceptions — a sub-conscious or super-conscious Self which stores everything, remembers everything, foresees everything, in a way knows everything knowable, has possession of all that is false & all that is true, but only allows the waking mind into a few of its secrets. Similarly our life in the body is only a partial expression of the immortal life of which we are the assured possessors. But this only proves that we ourselves are not in our totality or essentiality the life & mind in the body, but are using that principle for our purpose or our play in matter. It does not prove that there is no principle of life & mind in matter. On the contrary, there is reason to believe that matter is similarly involved in mind & life & that wherever there is movement of life & mind, it tends to develop for itself some form of body in which securely to individualise itself. By analogy we must suppose life & mind to be similarly involved & latent in matter & therefore evolvable in it & capable of manifestation.

We know then the theory of the early Vedantins with regard to the relations of life, mind and matter & we may now turn to the actual statements of the Upanishad with regard to the activities of life & mind and their relation to the soul of things, the Brahman.

II

Mind

If the Upanishads were no more than philosophical speculations, it would be enough in commenting upon them to state the general thought of a passage and develop its implications in modern language and its bearing upon the ideas we now hold. Or if they only expressed in their ancient language general conclusions of psychological experience, which are still easily accessible & familiar, nothing would be gained by any minute emphasis on the wording of our Vedantic texts. But these great writings are not the record of ideas; they are a record of experiences; and those experiences, psychological and spiritual, are as remote from the superficial psychology of ordinary men as are the experiments and conclusions of Science from the ordinary observation of the peasant driving his plough through a soil only superficially known or the sailor of old guiding his bark by the few stars important to his rudimentary investigation. Every word in the Upanishads arises out of a depth of psychological experience and observation we no longer possess and is a key to spiritual truths which we can no longer attain except by discipline of a painful difficulty. Therefore each word, as we proceed, must be given its due importance. We must consider its place in the thought and discover the ideas of which it was the spoken symbol.

The opening phrase of the Kena Upanishad, keneshitam patati preshitam manah, is an example of this constant necessity. The Sage is describing not the mind in its entirety, but that action of it which he has found the most characteristic and important, that which, besides, leads up directly to the question of the secret source of all mental action, its president and impelling power. The central and common experience of this action is expressed by the word patati, falls. Motion forward and settling upon an object are the very nature of mind when it acts.

Our modern conception of mind is different; while acknowledging its action of movement and forward attention, we are apt to regard its essential & common action to be rather receptivity of objects, than research of objects. The scientific explanation of mental activity helps to confirm this notion. Fixing its eye on the nervous system & the brain, the physical channels of thought, Physiology insists on the double action of the afferent and the efferent nerves as constituting the action of thought. An object falls on the sense-organ, — instead of mind falling on the object, — the afferent nerves carry the impact to the brain-cells, their matter undergoes modification, the brain-filaments respond to the shock, a message — the will of the cell-republic — returns through the efferent nerves and that action of perception, — whether of an object or the idea of an object or the idea of an idea, which is the essence of thinking — is accomplished. What else the mind does is merely the internal modification of the grey matter of the brain and the ceaseless activity of its filaments with the store of perceptions & ideas already amassed by these miraculous bits of organised matter. These movements of the bodily machine are all, according to Physiology. But it has been necessary to broach the theory of thought-waves or vibrations created by those animalcular amusements in order to account for the results of thought.

However widely & submissively this theory has been received by a hypnotised world, the Vedantist is bound to challenge it. His research has fixed not only on the physiological action, the movement of the bodily machine, but on the psychological action, the movement of the force that holds the machine, — not only on what the mind does, but on what it omits to do. His observation supported by that careful analysis & isolation in experiment of the separate mental constituents, has led him to a quite different conclusion. He upholds the wisdom of the sage in the phrase patati manas. An image falls on the eye, — admittedly, the mere falling of an image on the eye will not constitute mental perception — the mind has to give it attention; for it is not the eye that sees, it is the mind that sees through the eye as an instrument, just as it is not the telescope that sees an otherwise invisible sun, but the astronomer behind the telescope who sees. Therefore, physical reception of images is not sight; physical reception of sounds is not hearing. For how many sights & sounds besiege us, fall on our retina, touch the tympanum of the ear, yet are to our waking thought non-existent! If the body were really a self-sufficient machine, this could not happen. The impact must be admitted, the message must rush through the afferent nerve, the cells must receive the shock, the modification, the response must occur. A self-sufficient machine has no choice of action or non-action; unless it is out of order, it must do its work. But here we see there is a choice, a selection, an ample power of refusal; the practical researches of the Yogins have shown besides that the power of refusal can be absolute, that something in us has a sovereign & conscious faculty of selection or total prohibition of perception & thought & can even determine how, if at all, it shall respond, can even see without the eye & hear without the ear. Even European hypnotism points to similar phenomena. The matter cannot be settled by the rough & ready conclusions of impatient Physiology eager to take a shortcut to Truth & interpret the world in the light of its first astonished discoveries.

Where the image is not seen, the sound is not heard, it is because the mind does not settle on its object — na patati. But we must first go farther & inquire what it is that works in the afferent & efferent nerves & insures the attention of the nerves. It is not, we have seen, mere physical shock, a simple vibration of the bodily matter in the nerve. For, if it were, attention to every impact would be automatically & inevitably assured. The Vedantins say that the nerve system is an immensely intricate organised apparatus for the action of life in the body; what moves in them is prana, the life principle, materialised, aerial (vayavya) in its nature and therefore invisible to the eye, but sufficiently capable of self-adaptation both to the life of matter & the life of mind to form the meeting place or bridge of the two principles. But this action of life-principle is not sufficient in itself to create thought, for if it were mind could be organised in vegetable as readily as in animal life. It is only when prana has developed a sufficient intensity of movement to form a medium for the rapid activities of mind and mind, at last possessed of a physical instrument, has poured itself into the life-movement and taken possession of it that thought becomes possible. That which moves in the nerve system is the life-current penetrated & pervaded with the habitual movement of mind. When the movement of mind is involved in the life-movement, as it usually is in all forms, there is no response of mental knowledge to any contact or impression. For just as even in the metal there is life, so even in the metal there is mind; but it is latent, involved, its action secret, — unconscious, as we say, and confined to a passive reception into matter of the mind-forms created by these impacts. This will become clearer as we penetrate deeper into the mysteries of mind; we shall see that even though the clod, stone & tree do not think, they have in them the secret matrix of mind and in that matrix forms are stored which can be translated into mental symbols, into perception, idea and word. But it is only as the life-currents gain in intensity, rapidity & subtlety, making the body of things less durable but more capable of works, that mind-action becomes increasingly possible & once manifested more & more minutely & intricately effective. For body & life here are the pratistha, the basis of mind. A point, however, comes at which mind has got in life all that it needs for its higher development; and from that time it goes on enlarging itself & its activities out of all proportion to the farther organisation of its bodily & vital instruments or even without any such farther organisation in the lower man.

But even in the highest forms here in this material world, matter being the basis, life an intermediary and mind the third result, the normal rule is that matter & life (where life is expressed) shall always be active, mind only exceptionally active *in the body.* In other words, the ordinary action of mind is subconscious and receptive, as in the stone, clod & tree. The image that touches the eye, the sound that touches the ear is immediately taken in by the mind-informed life, the mind-informed & life-informed matter & becomes a part of the experience of Brahman in that system. Not only does it create a vibration in body, a stream of movement in life but also an impression in mind. This is inevitable, because mind, life & matter are one. Where one is, the others are, manifest or latent, involved or evolved, supraliminally active or subliminally active. The sword which has struck in the battle, retains in itself the mental impression of the stroke, the striker & the stricken and that ancient event can be read centuries afterwards by the Yogin who has trained himself to translate its mind-forms into the active language of mind. Thus everything that occurs around us leaves on us its secret stamp & impression. That this is so, the recent discoveries of European psychology have begun to prove & from the ordinary point of view, it is one of the most amazing & stupendous facts of existence; but from the Vedantist's it is the most simple, natural & inevitable. This survival of all experience in a mighty & lasting record, is not confined to such impressions as are conveyed to the brain through the senses, but extends to all that can in any way come to the mind, — to distant events, to past states of existence & old occurrences in which our present selves had no part, to the experiences garnered in dream & in dreamless sleep, to the activities that take place during the apparent unconsciousness or disturbed consciousness of slumber, delirium, anaesthesia & trance. Unconsciousness is an error; cessation of awareness is a delusion.

It is for this reason that the phenomenon on which the sage lays stress as the one thing important & effective in mental action here & in the waking state, is not its receptiveness, but its outgoing force — *patati*. In sense-activity we can distinguish three kinds of action — first, when the impact is received subconsciously & there is no message by the mind in the life current to the brain, — even if the life current itself carry the message — secondly, when the mind is aware of an impact, that is to say, falls on its object, but merely with the sensory part of itself & not with the understanding part; thirdly, when it falls on the object with both the sensory & understanding parts of itself. In the first case, there is no act of mental knowledge, no attention of eye or mind; as when we pass, absorbed in thought, through a scene of Nature, yet have seen nothing, been aware of nothing. In the second, there is an act of sensory knowledge, the mind in the eye attends & observes, however slightly; the thing is perceived but not conceived or only partly conceived, as when the maidservant going about her work, listens to the Hebrew of her master, hearing all, but distinguishing & understanding nothing, not really attending except through the ear alone. In the third, there is true mental perception & conception or the attempt at perception & conception, and only the last movement comes within the description given by the Sage — ishitam preshitam patati manas. But we must observe that in all these cases somebody is attending, something is both aware & understands. The man, unconscious under an anaesthetic drug in an operation, can in hypnosis when his deeper faculties are released, remember & relate accurately everything that occurred to him in his state of supposed unconsciousness. The maidservant thrown into an abnormal condition, can remember every word of her master's Hebrew discourse, & repeat in perfect order & without a single error long sentences in the language she did not understand. And, it may surely be predicted, one day we shall find that the thing our minds strove so hard to attend to and fathom, this passage in a new language, that new & unclassed phenomenon, was perfectly perceived, perfectly understood, automatically, infallibly, by something within us which either could not or did not convey its knowledge to the mind. We were only trying to make operative on the level of mind, a knowledge we already in some recess of our being perfectly possessed.

From this fact appears all the significance of the sage's sentence about the mind.

A Commentary
on the Kena Upanishad

Foreword

The Upanishads are an orchestral movement of knowledge, each of them one strain in a great choral harmony. The knowledge of the Brahman, which is the Universality of our existence, and the knowledge of the world, which is the multiplicity of our existence, but the world interpreted not in the terms of its appearances as in Science, but in the terms of its reality, is the one grand and general subject of the Upanishads. Within this cadre, this general framework each Upanishad has its smaller province; each takes its own standpoint of the knower and its resulting aspect of the known; to each there belongs a particular motive and a distinguishing ground-idea. The Isha Upanishad, for example, is occupied with the problem of spirituality and life, God and the world; its motive is the harmonising of these apparent opposites and the setting forth of their perfect relations in the light of Vedantic knowledge. The Kena is similarly occupied with the problem of the relations between God and the soul and its motive is to harmonise our personal activities of mental energy and human will with the movement of the infinite divine Energy and the supremacy of the universal Will. The Isha, therefore, has its eye more upon the outward Brahman and our action in and with regard to the world we see outside us; the Kena fixes rather on our psychological action and the movements within us. For on this internal relation with the Brahman must evidently depend, from it must evidently arise that attitude towards the external world, the attitude of oneness with all these multitudinous beings which the Isha gives to us as the secret of a perfect & liberated existence. For we are not here in the phenomenal world as independent existences; we appear as limited beings clashing with other limited beings, clashing with the forces of material Nature, clashing too with forces of immaterial Nature of which we are aware not with the physical senses but with the mind. We must become this multitudinous world, become it in our souls, obviously, not in our body & senses. The body & senses are intended to keep the multitudinousness, — they are there to prevent God's worldwide time-filling play from sinking back into the vague & inchoate. But in the soul there must be nothing but the sense & rapture of oneness in the various joy of multitude. How is that possible? It is possible because our relations with others are not in reality those of separate life-inspired bodies, but of the great universal movement of a single soul — ekah sanatanah, — broken up into separate waves by concentration in these many life-inspired bodies which we see appearing like temporary crests, ridges and bubbles in the divine ocean, apah. This soul in us is in relation to the outside world through the senses, through vitality, through mind. But it is entangled in the meshes of its instruments; it thinks they alone exist or is absorbed in their action with which it tends to identify itself preponderatingly or wholly; — it forgets itself in its activities. To recall the soul in man to self-knowledge, to lift it above the life of the senses [..] always refer its activities to that highest Self and Deity which [we] ultimately are, so that we may be free and great, may be pure and joyous, be fulfilled and immortal, — this is the governing aim of the Kena Upanishad. I propose in my commentary to follow with some minuteness & care the steps by which the Upanishad develops its aim, to bring out carefully the psychological ideas on which the ancient system was founded and to suggest rather than work out the philosophical positions which are presupposed in the ancient sage's treatment of his subject. To work them out in a volume of the present size and purpose would not be possible, nor, if possible, would it be convenient, since it would need a freer and ampler method delivered from the necessity of faithful subordination to the text. The first principle of a commentary must be to maintain the order of ideas and adhere to the purpose and connotation of the text which it takes as its authority.

Three Fragments of Commentary

The first two words of the Kena, like the first two words of the Isha, concentrate into a single phrase the subject of the Upanishad and settle its bounds & its spirit. By whom is our separate mental existence governed? Who is its Lord & ruler? Who sends forth the mind — kena preshitam, who guides it so that it falls in its ranging on a particular object and not another (kena patati)? The mind is our centre; in the mind our personal existence is enthroned. Manomayah pranasariraneta pratisthito 'nne, a mental guide and leader of the life & body has been established in matter, and we suppose & feel ourselves to be that mental being. But what guides the mind itself? Is it the mental ego as the unreflecting thinker usually & naturally supposes? As a matter of fact, it is perfectly within our knowledge and experience that the mental [ego] guides our actions only partially and imperfectly; it is governed by other forces, it is driven often by impulses that it cannot understand, it receives indications from a superconscious source; it is associated in the body with an immense amount of subconscious action of which it is ignorant or over which it has only a partial control. Guide & leader, perhaps, but certainly not the master. Who then is the master? Mind is not all we are. There is a vital force in us independent of mind. For although the two work together & act upon each other, they are still different movements. Our life goes on or ceases, rests or is active caring nothing, after all, about the mind & its notions. It serves it as a master whose interests it cannot afford to neglect, but does not always obey it & insists on the rights of its own separate existence. Who sent out this life force, who yoked it or applied it to these bodies & these actions, kena praiti yuktah Pranah prathamah — the epithet is used to indicate the essential life force as distinct from the particular life-functions called in Vedantic psycho-physics the five pranas.

*

The Kena Upanishad is remarkable for its omissions. It omits to tell us what in relation to the transcendent & immanent Brahman this mind, life, sense activity really are. It omits even to mention one tattwa which one would think as important as mind, life & sense-activity — there is no least reference to matter. These omissions are remarkable; they are also significant. The Sage of the Kena Upanishad has a distinct object in view; he has selected a particular province of knowledge. He is careful not to admit anything which does not bear upon that object or to overstep the strict limits of that province. Matter is beyond his immediate field, therefore he makes no reference to matter. Careless of comprehensiveness, he keeps to the exact matter of his revelation — the working relations between man's mental life and his supreme Existence. With the same scrupulous reserve he abstains from the discussion of the nature of these organs & their essential relation to the supreme Existence. For this knowledge we have to resort to other Scriptures.

*

The subject of the Talavakara Upanishad is indicated and precisely determined by its opening word, Kena, very much as we have seen the subject of the Isha Upanishad to be indicated and precisely determined by its opening words Isha Vasyam. To reveal the true Master of our mental life, the real Force of the Vitality which supports it and of the sense-activities which minister to it and of the mentality which fulfils it in this material existence, is the intention of the Upanishad.

Kena Upanishad

A Partial Translation with Notes

I

1. By whom willed falleth the Mind when it is sent on its mission? By whom yoked goeth forth the primal Breath? By whom controlled is this Speech that men utter? What God yokes the vision[1] and the hearing?

2. That which is the Hearing behind hearing, the Mind of mind, utters the Speech behind speech, — He too is the Life of the life-breath and the Vision behind seeing. The wise put these away and pass beyond; departing from this world they become immortal.

3. There Sight goes not, nor there Speech, nor the Mind arrives. We know it not, nor can we discern how one should teach of this. Other verily is That from the known and then it is beyond the unknown, — so do we hear[2] from those of old by whom That was expounded unto us.

4. That which remaineth unexpressed by Speech, by which Speech is expressed, know thou That Brahman and not this which men follow[3] after here.

---

[1] The words *chakshuh śrotram* do not refer to the physical eye & ear but to the sense activity that uses the organ. This is evident from the expressions in verses 6 & 7, *chakshúnshi pashyati* & *śrotram śrutam* — which cannot mean, "one sees the eyes" or "the ear is heard."

[2] *Púrve* is used here in the Vedic sense, the ancient sages before us and *śuśruma* means not the physical hearing but the reception by the Sruti, the inspired Word.

[3] *Upásate* is by some understood in the sense of adoration; but the force of the word is here the same as in the Isha Upanishad, *ye avidyám upásate*, which does not mean "those who adore Ignorance", but those who devote themselves to the state of Ignorance and make it the sole object of their consciousness.

5. That which thinketh[4] not with the Mind, by which, they say, Mind was made subject to mental perception, know thou that Brahman[5] and not this which men follow after here.

[4] Here and in the verses that follow my rendering differs from the received interpretation which runs, "That which one cannot think with the mind", "That which one cannot see with the eye", etc and in verse 8, "That which one cannot smell by the breath", *yat pránena na práṇiti. Prána* is undoubtedly used sometimes of the breath as the medium of the sense of smell & *práṇiti* to express the action of that sense. But in this Upanishad Prana has been used to indicate the nervous or vital force, the primal or principal Life-Energy, *práṇah prathamah*, and not a subordinate sense function; the expressions employed almost reconstitute the image of the Horse by which the Life-Energy is symbolised in the language of the Veda and in the opening of the Brihadaranyaka Upanishad. It is difficult to believe that one & the same word means the Life-Breath in the question proposed, verse 1, and the sense of smell in an integral part of the answer given, verse 8. But if Prana means the Life-Energy typified by its obvious physical function, the life-breath, verse 8 can only mean, "He who liveth (breatheth) not by the life-breath", & the other verses must follow suit. For a kindred idea we may compare Katha Upanishad II.2.5. "No mortal lives by the superior or the inferior life-energy, but by another thing men live in which both these have their foundation."

[5] The received interpretation runs "Know that to be the Brahman and not this which men follow after here," and by this text Shankara supports his metaphysical doctrine that the objective world is not Brahman and is therefore an illusion. The objections to the interpretation seem to me insuperable. The words are not Tadeva Brahmeti twam viddhi, but Tadeva Brahma twam viddhi, which we should naturally interpret "Seek to know that Brahman" ie, "seek to know Brahman in That Consciousness" and not in the form of this objective world to which most men are attached. Moreover, we ought to give their full value to the remarkable expressions "That by which the mind is thought, seeings seen, hearing heard." Such phrases can hardly refer to the pure Absolute remote from all relativity or to the pure Self of Shankara to whom the objective world is non-existent. They indicate another state of consciousness, intermediate, if you will, in which the universe exists not as an objective and external reality, but within the percipient consciousness and is no longer perceived only through the objective organs and their functions, but known directly to the power from which those organs & functions are derived. This idea is confirmed by the apologue in which Brahman appears as a Power governing the universe, the Ish or Lord of the Isha Upanishad, in whom and by whose existence the gods exist, but also by whose active might and its victories they conquer and reign. It is therefore a self-Existence which is active in its stability and conscious in the multiplicity of the universe as well as in its self-unity. The Upanishads, I think, nowhere deny but rather affirm that the objective world also is Brahman. The error of Ignorance is to accept it as represented by the mind & senses in their inadequate symbols and as if they were real in themselves, each in its own separate reality. The wise put from them the error of the mind and the senses and in the self-luminous & self-effective Consciousness beyond attain to that freedom, unity & immortality which we have seen set before humanity as its goal in the Isha Upanishad.

Section Five

Incomplete Translations
of Two Vedantic Texts

Circa 1900–1902

The Karikas of Gaudapada

The Karikas of Gaudapada are a body of authoritative verse maxims and reasonings setting forth in a brief and closely-argued manual the position of the extreme Monistic school of Vedanta philosophy. The monumental aphorisms of the Vedantasutra are meant rather for the master than the learner. Gaudapada's clear, brief and businesslike verses are of a wider utility; they presuppose only an elementary knowledge of philosophic terminology and the general trend of Monistic and Dualistic discussion. This preliminary knowledge granted they provide the student with an admirably lucid and pregnant nucleus of reasoning which enables him at once to follow the Monistic train of thought and to keep in memory its most notable positions. It has also had the advantage, due no doubt to its preeminent merit and the long possession of authority and general use, of a full and powerful commentary by the great Master himself and a farther exposition by the Master's disciple, the clearminded and often suggestive Anandagiri. To modern students there can be no better introduction to Vedanta philosophy — after some brooding over the sense of the Upanishads — than a study of Gaudapada's Karikas and Shankara's commentary with Deussen's System of the Vedanta in one hand and any brief & popular exposition of the Six Darshanas in the other. It is only after the Monistic School has been thoroughly understood that the Modified-Monistic and Dualistic-Monistic with their intermediary shades can be profitably studied. When the Vedantic theory has been mastered, the Sankhya, Yoga, Nyaya & Vaisheshika can in its light be easily mastered in succession with Vijnanabhikshu's work & the great synthesis of the Bhagavadgita to crown the whole structure. The philosophical basis will then be properly laid and the Upanishads can be studied with new interest, verifying or modifying as one goes one's original interpretation of the Sacred Books.

This will bring to a close the theoretical side of the Jnanakanda; its practical and more valuable side can only be mastered in the path of Yoga and under the guidance of a Sadguru.

Gaudapada begins his work by a short exposition in clear philosophic terms of the poetical and rhythmic phraseology of the Upanishad. He first defines precisely the essential character of the triune nature of the Self as manifested in the macrocosm & the microcosm, the Waker, the Dreamer & the Sleeper, who all meet and disappear in the Absolute.

बहिष्प्रज्ञो विभुर्विश्वो ह्यन्तःप्रज्ञस्तु तैजसः ।
घनप्रज्ञस्तथा प्राज्ञ एक एव त्रिधा स्मृतः ॥ १ ॥

1. Visva being the Lord who pervades and is conscious of the external, Taijasa he who is conscious of the internal, Prajna he in whom consciousness is (densified and) drawn into itself, the Self presents himself to the memory as One under three conditions.

Shankara: The position taken is this, as *the entity which cognizes* enters into three conditions one after another *and not simultaneously*, and is moreover *in all three* connected by the memory *which persists in feeling* "This is I" "This is I" "This is I", it is obvious that it is something beyond and above the three conditions, & therefore one, absolute and without attachment to its conditions. And this is supported by the illustrations like that of the large fish given in the Scripture.

दक्षिणाक्षिमुखे विश्वो मनस्यन्तस्तु तैजसः ।
आकाशे च हृदि प्राज्ञस्त्रिधा देहे व्यवस्थितः ॥ २ ॥

2. Visva in the gate of the right eye, Taijasa within in the mind, Prajna in the ether, the heart, this is its threefold station in the body.

Shankara: 1. The object of this verse is to show that these three, Visva, Taijasa & Prajna, are experienced even in the waking state. The right eye is the door, *the means*, through which especially Visva, the seer of gross objects, becomes subject to experience. The Sruti saith "Verily and of a truth Indha is he, even this Being as he standeth here in the right eye." Vaisvanor is Indha, because his essential principle is light and is at once the macrocosmic Self within the Sun and the seer in the eye.

2. "But" it will be objected "Hiranyagarbha is one and the cognizer of the material field, the guide and seer in the right eye is quite another, the master of the body." Not so; for in itself — *if we look into the real nature of our perceptions* — we do not realise any difference between them. And the Scripture saith "One God hidden in all creatures" and the Smriti also:

Know me, O son of Bharat, for the knower of the body in all bodies. I stand undivided in all creatures and only seem to be divided.

3. *Be it noted that* though Visva works indeed in all the organs of sense without distinction, yet because the perceptions of [the] right eye are noticed to be superior in acuteness and clearness it is for that reason only specifically mentioned as his abiding-place. After this Visva then dwelling in the right eye has seen a shape or appearance, he remembers it when he has closed his eyes and still sees within in the mind, as if in a dream, the same shape or appearance as manifested in the form of the idea or impression it has left. And it is just the same in a dream, *the impression or idea preserved by memory reproduces in sleep the same shape or appearance that was seen in waking.* It follows that this Taijasa who is within in the mind is no other than Visva himself.

4. Then by cessation of the process called memory Prajna in the ether or heart becomes unified or as it is said densified consciousness drawn into itself. And this happens because the processes of the mind are absent; for sight and memory are vibrations of the mind and in their absence the Self in the form of Prana takes its abode in the ether or heart without possibility of separation or distinction. For the Scripture saith "It is Prana that swalloweth up all these into itself." Taijasa is the same

as Hiranyagarbha because it has its abode in the mind, and the mind is the subtle part of the body, as is clear from the verse, "This *purusha* is all mind", and from other like sayings of Scripture.

5. It may be objected that Prana in the state of Sleep is really differenced and manifest & the senses become one with Prana, so how do you predicate of it absence of manifestation and differentia *by saying it becomes One*? But there is no real fault in the reasoning, since in the undifferenced the particularising conditions of space and time are absent *and the same is the case with Prana in the state of Sleep*. Although indeed the Prana is *in a sense* differenced because the idea of separate existence as Prana remains, yet the more special sense of separate existence as circumscribed by the body is brought to a stop in Prana and Prana is therefore undifferenced and unmanifest in the Sleep in relation *at least* to the possessors of this circumscribed egoism. And just as the Prana of those who have the circumscribed bodily egoism becomes undifferenced when it is absorbed *at the end of the world*, so it is with him who has the sense of existence as Prana only in the condition *of Sleep* which is *in reality* precisely the same *as that of the temporary disappearance of phenomena at the end of a world*; both states alike are void of differentia and manifestation and *both alike* are pregnant with the seeds of *future* birth. The *Self* governing either state is one & the same, it is *Self* in an undifferenced and unmanifest condition. It follows that the governing Self in each case and the experiencers of the circumscribed bodily egoism are one and the same; therefore the descriptions previously given *of Prajna* become One or become densified & self-concentrated consciousness etc are quite applicable; and the arguments already advanced support the same conclusion.

6. "But" you will say "why is the name, Prana, given to the Undifferenced?" On the ground of the Scripture "For, O fair son, the cord and fastening of the mind is Prana." "O but" you answer "there the words 'O fair son, Existence itself *is Prana*' show that it is Brahman Existent which being the subject of the verses must be intended by the word Prana." However, my

reasoning is not thereby vitiated, because we all understand the Existent to be pregnant with the seed *of future birth*. Although, then, it is Brahman Existent which is meant by Prana, all the same the name Prana is given to the Existent because the idea of pregnancy with the seed from which the Jiva or life-conditioned human spirit is to be born, has not been eliminated from it and *indeed* it is only when this idea is not eliminated from the idea of Brahman that he can be called Brahman Existent. For if it were the absolute seedless Brahman of which the Scripture had meant to speak, it would have used such expressions as "He is not this, nor that nor anything which we can call him"; "From whom words return baffled"; "He is other than the known and different from the Unknown." The Smriti also says "He (the Absolute) is called neither Existent nor non-Existent." Besides if the Existent be seedless, then there would be no ground for supposing that those who have coalesced with and become absorbed into the Existent in the state of Sleep or the destruction of a world can again awake *out of either of these conditions*. Or if they can, then we should immediately have the contingency of liberated souls again coming into phenomenal existence; for *on this hypothesis* the condition *of souls liberated into the Absolute and those absorbed into the Existent* would be alike, neither having seed *or cause of future phenomenal existence. And if to remove this objection you say that* it is the seed *of ignorance* which has to be burnt away in the fire of Knowledge *that is absent in the case of liberated souls and some other seed of things in the other case,* you are in danger of proving that Knowledge (*of the Eternal*) is without use or unnecessary *as a means of salvation*.

7. It is clear then that it is on the understanding that the Existent is pregnant with the seed of phenomenal life that in all the Scripture it is represented as Prana and the cause of things. Consequently it is by elimination of this idea of the seed that it is designated by such phrases as "He is the unborn in whom the objective & subjective are One", "From whom words return baffled", "He is not this nor that nor anything we can call him", and the rest. Our author will speak separately of this seedless condition of the Same Self which has been designated

by the term Prajna. This condition by its being the Fourth or Absolute is devoid of all relations such as body, *Prana* etc and is alone finally and transcendentally true. Now the condition of undifferenced seedfulness also is *like the two others* experienced in this body in the form of the idea of the awakened man which tells him *"For so long* I felt and knew nothing". Thus then the Self is said to have a threefold station in the body.

विश्वो हि स्थूलभुङ् नित्यं तैजसः प्रविविक्तभुक् ।
आनन्दभुक् तथा प्राज्ञस्त्रिधा भोगं निबोधत ॥ ३ ॥

3. Visva is the enjoyer of gross objects, Taijasa of subtle, and Prajna of pure (unrelated) pleasure, thus shall ye understand the threefold enjoyment *of the Self in the body.*

स्थूलं तर्पयते विश्वं प्रविविक्तं तु तैजसम् ।
आनन्दश्च तथा प्राज्ञं त्रिधा तृप्तिं निबोधत ॥ ४ ॥

4. The gross utterly satisfieth Visva, but the subtle Taijasa and pure pleasure satisfieth Prajna, thus shall ye understand the threefold satisfaction *of the Self in the body.*

Shankara: The meaning of these two verses has been explained.

त्रिषु धामसु यद् भोज्यं भोक्ता यश्च प्रकीर्तितः ।
वेदैतदुभयं यस्तु स भुञ्जानो न लिप्यते ॥ ५ ॥

5. That which is enjoyed in the three conditions and that which is the enjoyer, he who knoweth both these as one enjoyeth & receiveth no stain.

Shankara: That which is enjoyed under the names of gross objects, subtle objects and pure pleasure in the three conditions, waking, dream and sleep is one and the same thing although it has taken a threefold aspect. And that which enjoys under the names of Visva, Taijasa & Prajna, has been declared to be one because they are connected by the sense of oneness expressed in the continual feeling "This is I, This is I" and because the nature of cognition is one and without difference throughout. Whoever

knows both these to be one though split up into multiplicity by
the sense of being enjoyer or enjoyed, does not receive any stain
from enjoyment, because the subject of enjoyment is the One
universal and the enjoyer too is not different from the enjoyed.
For *note that* whoever be the enjoyer or whatever his object of
enjoyment, he does not increase with it or diminish with it, just
as in the case of fire when it has burnt up its object in the shape
of wood or other fuel; *it remains no less or greater than it was
before.*

प्रभवः सर्वभावानां सतामिति विनिश्चयः ।
सर्वं जनयति प्राणश्चेतोंशून् पुरुषः पृथक् ॥ ६ ॥

6. It is a certain conclusion that all existences which take birth
   are already in being; Prana brings the All into phenomenal
   being, it is this *Prana or* Purusha which *sends* its separate
   rays of consciousness abroad.

Shankara: All existences (divided as Visva, Taijasa & Prajna) are
already in being, that is, they existed before and it is only by their
own species & nature, an illusion of name and form created by
Ignorance, that they take birth or in other words [are] put forth
into phenomenal existence. As indeed the writer says later on
"A son from a barren woman is not born either in reality or
by illusion". For if birth of the nonexistent — *that is something
coming out of nothing* — were possible, then there would be
no means of grasping this world of usage and experience and
the Eternal itself would become an unreality. Moreover we have
seen that the snake in the rope and other appearances born of
the seed of illusion created by Ignorance do really exist as the self
of the rope *or other substratum in the case.* For the snake in the
rope, the mirage and other *hallucinations of the sort* are never
experienced by anybody unless there is some substratum. Just as
before the coming into phenomenal being of the snake it existed
already in the rope as the rope's self, so before the coming to
birth of all phenomenal existences, they already existed as the
self of the seed of things called Prana. And the Scripture also
saith, "This universe is the Eternal", "In the beginning all this

was the Spirit." The Prana gives birth to the All as separate rays of consciousness; — just as the rays of the Sun, so are these consciousness-rays of the Purusha who is Chid or conscious existence and they are clearly distinguished in different bodies of gods, animals, etc under three different lights as Visva, Taijasa & Prajna, in the same way as reflections of the sun are clearly seen in different pieces of water; they are thrown from the Purusha and though they differ according to the separate existences which are their field of action & enjoyment, yet they are all alike like sparks from a fire being all Jiva or conditioned Self. Thus the Prana or causal Self gives phenomenal birth to all other existences as the spider to his web. Compare the Scripture "As a fire sendeth forth sparks."

विभूतिं प्रसवं त्वन्ये मन्यन्ते सृष्टिचिन्तकाः ।
स्वप्नमायासरूपेति सृष्टिरन्यैर्विकल्पिता ॥ ७ ॥

7. Some who concern themselves with the *cause of* creation
   think that Almighty Power is the origin of things and by
   others creation is imagined as like to illusion or a dream.

Shankara: Those who concern themselves with creation think that creation is the pervading Power, the extension, so to speak, of God; but it is implied, those who concern themselves with final and transcendental truth do not care about speculations on creation. For when men see a conjurer throw a rope into the air and ascend it armed & accoutred and then after he has climbed out of sight fall hewn to pieces in battle and rise again *whole*, they do not care about inquiring into the illusion he has created with all its properties and origins. Just so this evolution of the Sleep, Dream and Waking conditions is just like the self-lengthening of the juggler's rope and the Prajna, Taijasa and Visva self abiding in the three conditions is like the conjurer climbing up the rope, but the real conjurer is other than the rope or its climber. Just as he stands on the ground invisible and hidden in illusion, so is it with the real and transcendental fact called the Fourth. Therefore it is for Him that the Aryan-minded care, those who follow after salvation, and they do not

care for speculations about creation which are of no importance
to them. Accordingly the writer implies that all these theories
are only imaginations of those who concern themselves with the
origin of creation and then goes on to say that by others creation
is imagined as like to an illusion or again as like to a dream.

इच्छामात्रं प्रभोः सृष्टिरिति सृष्टौ विनिश्चिताः ।
कालात्प्रसूतिं भूतानां मन्यन्ते कालचिन्तकाः ॥ ८ ॥

8. Those who have made up their minds on the subject of
   creation say it is merely the Will of the Lord; those who
   concern themselves about Time think that from Time is the
   birth of creatures.

Shankara: Creation is the Will of the Lord because the divine
ideas must be true facts — pots etc are ideas only and nothing
more than ideas. Some say that creation is the result of Time.

भोगार्थं सृष्टिरित्यन्ये क्रीडार्थमिति चापरे ।
देवस्यैष स्वभावोऽयमाप्तकामस्य का स्पृहा ॥ ९ ॥

9. Others say that creation is for the sake of enjoyment, yet
   others say it is for play. *Really*, this is the very nature of the
   Lord; *as for other theories, well*, He has all He can desire
   and why should He crave for anything?

Shankara: Others think creation *was made* for enjoyment or for
play. These two theories are criticised by the line "This is the
very nature of the Lord". Or, it may be, that the theory of Divine
Nature is resorted to in order to criticise all *other* theories *by the
argument*, He has all He can desire and why should He crave
for anything? For no cause can be alleged for the appearance
of the snake etc in the rope and other substrata except the very
nature of Ignorance.

निवृत्तेः सर्वदुःखानामीशानः प्रभुरव्ययः ।
अद्वैतः सर्वभावानां देवस्तुर्यो विभुः स्मृतः ॥ १० ॥

10. He who is called the Fourth is the Master of the cessation
of all ills, the Strong Lord and undecaying, the One without
second of all existences, the Shining One who pervadeth.

Shankara: The Fourth Self *or transcendental* is the master of the
cessation of all ills, which belong to the conditions of Prajna,
Taijasa & Visva. The expression Strong Lord is an explanation
of the word Master; it is implied that His strength & lordship
are in relation to the cessation of ills, because the cessation of
ills results from the knowledge of Him. Undecaying, because
He does not pass away, swerve or depart, ie, from His essential
nature. How is this? Because He is the One without a second
owing to the vanity of all phenomenal existences. He is also
called God, the Shining One, because of effulgence, the Fourth
and He who pervades, exists everywhere.

कार्यकारणबद्धौ ताविष्येते विश्वतैजसौ ।
प्राज्ञः कारणबद्धस्तु द्वौ तौ तुर्ये न सिध्यतः ॥ ११ ॥

11. Visva & Taijasa are acknowledged to be bound by cause &
effect, Prajna is bound by cause only; both of these are held
not to exist in the Fourth.

Shankara: The common and particular characteristics of Visva
& the two others are now determined in order that the real self
of the Fourth may become clear. Effect, that which is made or
done, is existence as result. Cause, that which makes or does,
is existence as seed. By inapprehension and misapprehension
of the Truth the aforesaid Visva & Taijasa are, it is agreed,
bound or imprisoned by existence as result and seed. But Prajna
is bound by existence as seed only. For the seed state which
lies in unawakening to the Truth alone *and not in misreading
of Him* is the reason of the state of Prajna. Therefore both of
these, existence as cause and existence as effect, inapprehension
and misapprehension of the Truth are held not to apply to the
Fourth, ie do not exist & cannot happen in Him.

नात्मानं न परांश्चैव न सत्यं नापि चानृतम् ।
प्राज्ञः किंचन संवेत्ति तुर्यं तत्सर्वदृक् सदा ॥ १२ ॥

12. Prajna cogniseth nought, neither self nor others, neither truth nor falsehood; the Fourth seeth all things for ever.

Shankara: But how then is Prajna bound by Cause, while in the Fourth the two kinds of bondage conditioned by inapprehension & misapprehension of the Truth are said to be impossible? Because Prajna does not cognize at all this duality of an outside universe born from Ignorance and conditioned as distinct from Self, so that like Visva & Taijasa he also is bound by inapprehension of the Truth, by that blind darkness which becomes the seed of misapprehension; and because the Fourth seeth all things for ever. That is to say, since nothing *really* exists except the Fourth, He is necessarily a seer of all that is, Omniscient & All-cognizant at all times & for ever; in Him therefore the seed state of which the conditioning feature is inapprehension of the Truth, cannot possibly exist. Absence of the misapprehension which arises out of inapprehension naturally follows. The Sun is for ever illuminative by its nature and non-illumination or misillumination as contrary to its nature cannot happen to it; *and the same train of reasoning applies to the Omniscience of the Turiya*. The Scripture also says "For of the Sight of the Seer there is no annihilation." Or indeed, since it is the Fourth that in the Waking and Dream State dwelling in all creatures is the light or reflection in them to which all objects *present themselves as* visible *ie cognizable objects*, it is *in this way too* the seer of all things for ever. The Scripture says "There is nought else than This that seeth."

Sadananda's Essence of Vedanta

INVOCATION

To the Absolute

अखण्डं सच्चिदानन्दमवाङ्मनसगोचरम् ।
आत्मानमखिलाधारमाश्रयेऽभीष्टसिद्धये ॥ १ ॥

1. I take refuge with Him who is *sheer* Existence, Intelligence
   and Bliss, impartible, beyond the purview of speech and
   mind, the Self in whom the whole Universe exists — may
   my desire & purpose attain fulfilment.

To the Masters

अर्थतोऽप्यद्वयानन्दानतीतद्वैतभानतः ।
गुरूनाराध्य वेदान्तसारं वक्ष्ये यथामति ॥ २ ॥

2. After homage to the Masters who in deed as well as word
   delight in the One without second and from whom the seemings of duality have passed away, I will declare the Essence
   of Vedanta according to my intellectual capacity.

PRELIMINARY STATEMENT

The Training of the Vedantin

वेदान्तो नामोपनिषत्प्रमाणं तदुपकारीणि शारीरकसूत्रादीनि च ॥ ३ ॥

3. By Vedanta is meant the Upanishads as authoritative basis
   of the philosophy and as useful supplementary inquiries the
   Aphoristic Books that treat of the Embodied Soul.

अस्य वेदान्तप्रकरणत्वात् तदीयैरेवानुबन्धैस्तद्वृत्तासिद्धेर्न ते पृथगा-
लोचनीयाः ॥ ४ ॥

4. Now since Vedanta is the subject of this work, its circum-
stantiae — the conclusions sought to be established being
similar in both, — are the same as those of the Vedanta and
need not be separately discussed.

तत्रानुबन्धो नामाधिकारिविषयसंबन्धप्रयोजनानि ॥ ५ ॥

5. In circumstantia we include four things, the fit hearer, the
subject, the logical relation, the object of the work.

अधिकारी तु विधिवदधीतवेदवेदाङ्गत्वेनापाततोऽधिगताखिलवेदार्थो
ऽस्मिन् जन्मनि जन्मान्तरे वा काम्यनिषिद्धवर्जनपुरःसरं नित्य-
नैमित्तिकप्रायश्चित्तोपासनानुष्ठानेन निर्गतनिखिलकल्मषतया नितान्त-
निर्मलस्वान्तः साधनचतुष्टयसंपन्नः प्रमाता ॥ ६ ॥

6. Now the fit hearer of Vedanta must be one who is compe-
tent to form a right judgment of it. He must therefore have
mastered [   ] by proper study of Veda and its accessory
sciences the entire meaning of Veda; he must in this life or
another have begun by abandoning forbidden actions and
actions prompted by desire and then by the performance
of daily observances, occasional observances, penance and
adoration freed himself from all sin and stain and attained
to perfect purity of the mind and heart; and he must be in
possession of the four Ways & Means.

काम्यानि स्वर्गादीष्टसाधनानि ज्योतिष्टोमादीनि ॥ ७ ॥

7. By actions of desire is understood all ways and means by
which we pursue various kinds of happiness from Paradise
downward — the Jyotisthom sacrifice for example.

निषिद्धानि नरकाद्यनिष्टसाधनानि ब्रह्महननादीनि ॥ ८ ॥

8. By forbidden actions is meant all ways & means by which
we compass all our ills from the torments of Hell downward,
— Brahminicide for example & other sins & disobediences.

नित्यान्यकरणे प्रत्यवायसाधनानि संध्यावन्दनादीनि ॥ ९ ॥

9. By regular observances is meant ceremonies like the evening prayer etc, the non-performance of which turns them into means of offence & stumbling blocks.

नैमित्तिकानि पुत्रजन्माद्यनुबन्धीनि जातेष्ट्यादीनि ॥ १० ॥

10. By occasional observances is understood ceremonies circumstantial to particular occasions, such as the Blessing of the New-born attendant on the birth of a son.

प्रायश्चित्तानि पापक्षयमात्रसाधनानि चान्द्रायणादीनि ॥ ११ ॥

11. By penances is understood vows & forms of self-discipline such as the Chandrayan vow which are means *only* towards the purging away of sin.

उपासनानि सगुणब्रह्मविषयकमानसव्यापाररूपाणि शाण्डिल्यविद्या-दीनि ॥ १२ ॥

12. By adoration is understood the various forms of mental working which have for their whole subject and purpose the Eternal in His aspect as a Personal Deity — Sandilya's Art of Divine Love, for example.

एतेषां नित्यादीनां बुद्धिशुद्धिः परं प्रयोजनमुपासनानां तु चित्तैका-ग्र्यम् । तमेतमात्मानं वेदानुवचनेन ब्राह्मणा विविदिषन्ति यज्ञेनेत्यादि-श्रुतेः तपसा कल्मषं हन्तीत्यादिस्मृतेश्च ॥ १३ ॥

13. The main object of the first three, observances regular and occasional and penance, is the purification of the Understanding; but the main object of adoration is singleness of heart & mind towards one object. This is proved by such passages as these from Revealed Scripture — "This is that Self of whom the Brahmins shall seek to know by exposition of Veda and by Sacrifice shall they seek to know Him" — and by other passages from the Unrevealed Scripture such as "By Tapasya (energism of will) one slayeth sin."

नित्यनैमित्तिकयोरुपासनानां चावान्तरफलं पितृलोकसत्यलोकप्राप्तिः ।
कर्मणा पितृलोको विद्यते देवलोक इत्यादिश्रुतेः ॥ १४ ॥

14. A secondary result of observances regular and occasional
and of adoration & worship is attainment to the world of
the fathers and to the world of the Living Truth. For so the
Scripture says "By action the World of the Fathers is found
and the World of the Gods also."

साधनानि   नित्यानित्यवस्तुविवेकेहामुत्रफलभोगविरागशमदमादिसं -
पत्तिमुमुक्षुत्वानि ॥ १५ ॥

15. By Ways & Means we understand, Discrimination of eternal
objects from the transient; Disattachment from enjoyment
in this world or another; Calm, Self-Conquest & the other
moral excellences; and Desire of Salvation.

नित्यानित्यवस्तुविवेकस्तावद् ब्रह्मैव   नित्यं   वस्तु   ततोऽन्यदखिल -
मनित्यमिति विवेचनम् ॥ १६ ॥

16. By Discrimination of eternal objects from the transient we
understand the discernment of Brahman as the one thing
eternal and of everything other than Brahman as transient
and perishable.

Part Three

Writings on Vedanta

These incomplete writings (c. 1902–1916) were not revised by Sri Aurobindo for publication. They have been transcribed from his manuscripts and arranged in chronological order.

Four Fragments

1

The answer to all philosophical problems hinges on the one question, What is myself? It is only by knowing man's real self that we can know God; for whatever we may think or know, the value of the thought and the knowledge must hinge upon the knower, the means of knowledge and

Vedanta's final & single answer to all the questions of philosophy is contained in a single mighty & ever-memorable phrase, So 'ham. I am He or more explicitly or to the question of the inquirer अहं ब्रह्मास्मि, I am Brahman. Cutting through all tremors & hesitations, scorning all doubt or reserve it announces with a hardy & daring incisiveness the complete identity of man & God. This is its gospel that the individual Self who seems so limited, thwarted, befouled, shamed & obscured with the bonds & shackles, the mud & stains of earthly life and the pure, perfect and illimitable Being who possesses & supports all existence, to Whom this vast and majestic Universe is but an inconsiderable corner of His mind and infinite Time cannot end and infinite Space cannot confine and the infinite net of cause and effect is powerless to trammel are equal, are of one nature, power, splendour, bliss, are One. It seems the very madness of megalomania, the very delirium of egoism. And yet if it be true?

And it is true. Reason can come to no other conclusion, Yoga ends in no less an experience, the voices of a hundred holy witnesses who have seen God face to face, bring to us no less wonderful a message. And since it is true, what eagerness should not fill us to

2

Ego or Self is an Ens which is not knowable by sight or any of the senses; it can only be grasped in the innate conception, "I am". This intuitive and inherent self-perception is called, subjective illumination; for there are two kinds of direct knowledge, one called subjective, the other objective illumination and the difference is that while objective illumination or as it is called the Supra-intelligence has for its object both the known & unknown, the object of subjective illumination is that which is perpetually & inevitably known, since even the supra-intelligence is illumined or revealed by the light of the Ego. For as it is said "The subtle self has consciousness for its

3

It has been said with a singularly subtle ineptitude that the existence of the One Formless Nameless Indivisible without Qualities & without desires may be admitted; and the existence of a multifold world of phenomena may be admitted; but that the one excludes the other. Since it is not possible that the Absolute should limit itself even illusorily; for any such limitation is an act and an act implies an object; but an Existence without desires can have no object to serve and cannot therefore act. Moreover the Infinite excludes the possibility of the Finite. This is a juggling with words. The Infinite instead of excluding the Finite supposes the Finite. When we think of the Infinite, it is not at first as a blind & limitless expanse but as the Finite Existence we know spreading on & on without beginning or limit. Having once formed the idea of the Infinite, we may then by an effort of the Mind blot out that vision of finite things informing it and imagine infinity as a blind & limitless expanse; but even so Infinity only exists to us on condition of the possibility of the Finite; it is there possible, latent, manifested in the past, to be yet manifested in the future. Destroy the possibility of the Finite and the Infinite becomes unimaginable. This is expressed in the Puranic philosophy of the Parabrahma absorbing all things into himself for a while only to put them forth again. Nor is the objection that an Act implies an object, in itself tenable; an act may be pure & objectless, ceasing indeed to be an action in the ordinary human sense of the word but not in the philosophic or scientific sense. The sun acts when it shines though it has no object in doing so (जडवत् समाचरेत्).

The Visishtadwait recognizing that the Infinite implies the Finite within it, bases its ontology on the fact; the Adwait points out however that the existence of the Finite is only a possibility and when it occurs implies no real change in the Infinite, nothing essential and permanent, but the objectless action of the Absolute, the working of a force which as it creates nothing real and lasting may well be called Maya or illusion. All turns on whether the Finite is a real ie an essential & permanent existence or a mere condition of thought. If the former, the Visishtadwaita view is correct, but if the latter the Adwaita must claim our adherence.

4

[.....] the next few centuries. This issue I prefer to call the issue between Science and Hinduism, not because there are not in the world other great embodiments of the old religious & moral spirit, but because Hinduism alone has shown an eternal & indestructible vitality and still more because Hinduism alone does not on the side of reason stand naked to the assaults of Science. And when I speak of Hinduism, I do not refer to the ignorant & customary Hinduism of today, which is largely a Buddhicised and vulgarised edition of the old faith, but the purer form which under the pressure of Science is now reasserting its empire over the Hindu mind.

The Spirit of Hinduism

God

OM *ityetad akṣaram idaṁ sarvam*; OM is the syllable, OM is the Universe; all that was, all that is, all that will be is OM. With this pregnant confession of faith Hinduism begins its interpretation of the Universe.

Metaphysical systems arise and metaphysical systems fall; Hegel disappears and Kant arrives; Pantheism, Theism, Atheism pursue their interminable round, and there is no finality. Then Science comes and declares the whole vanity, for all is physical and there is nothing metaphysical save in the brain of the dreamer; and yet tho' Science has spoken still there is no finality. For the soul of man refuses to be dissolved into a force or a procession of sensations or a composite effect created by the action of outward things on the neurons of the brain. It persists in saying "I am"; it persists in demanding an explanation of its existence, and will not be satisfied without an answer. But where is that answer to come from or how is it possible to arrive at any conclusion? The rock on which all metaphysics come to shipwreck is the same unsurpassable barrier before which Science itself becomes a baffled and impotent thing; it is that behind everything, beyond everything, when all knowledge has been acquired, when matter has been pursued into its subtlest unanalysable element, there is always an Inexplicable Something which remains. Metaphysics seeks to tell us What the Universe is and Why it is; in other words to explain the Inexplicable; but the end of this process is inevitably a juggling with words which must repel all clear-minded thinkers. At the end of all metaphysical systems we find an enthroned word which apparelled in the purple of finality professes to explain the Universe, and yet when we look into it, we find that it stands itself in need of explanation, that it is merely a Word which stands for the

Inexplicable. Science avoids the difficulty by professing that the ultimate results of its analysis are a sufficient description of the Universe, a sufficient answer to the What, and as to the Why it rests in the great fact of Evolution. Again we find that we have landed ourselves in unexplained words beyond which lies the same region of darkness involved in yet deeper darkness; the *tamas tamasā gūḍham* of the Scriptures; Evolution, Force, Kinesis, these are words in which we gather up our observation of certain phenomena; they are the sum of the workings of a nameless, unintelligible Thing, but what that Thing is and why It is, remains an unsolved mystery. Whether it is that the human mind is intrinsically unable to pierce beyond the veil or whether it has the power latent or potential but as yet unevolved, we may at least safely assert that so far man has not been able to understand Finality; he is constitutionally incapable of imagining a Final Cause which his reason when faithfully interrogated will not refuse to accept as Final, will not be forced by its own nature to subject to the query How & Why. There are only two ways of meeting the difficulty; one is to assert that the reason of man as at present constituted is imperfect and by reason of its imperfection unable to grasp Finality which for all that exists; the other is to assert that the reason of man is right and that Finality is inconceivable because it does not exist. The latter is the answer which Hinduism has selected; the human mind cannot arrive at anything final because there is nothing final, for all the universe is OM and OM is Infinite, without beginning and without end either in Time or in Space. It has indeed been advanced that the human mind can realise only the Finite and not the Infinite, — a sorry paradox, for it is truer to say that the only fact which the human mind can realise is Infinity; the Finite it grasps only as a phenomenon, the very conception of which depends on the wider conception of the Infinite. A finite thing, such as a house, we conceive as a limited phenomenon in relation to that which is not the house; limit is only imaginable in relation to something beyond the limit; a final limit to everything is unimaginable whether in Time or Space. Outside the house is the province and outside the limits of the province is the country and outside the limits of the country is the earth and outside the limits of the earth is the Universe and to the Universe we can only imagine limits if we imagine it as surrounded by other Universes, and so the mind of man goes travelling forward & ever forward without reaching an end. Having realised that there is no end the Mind refuses to proceed farther and returns on its traces into the world of phenomena. It is this refusal, this return which is meant when it is stated that the human mind cannot conceive Infinity. And yet what does the statement amount to? Simply to this that there is no end to the Infinite, in other words that the Infinite *is* infinite, that the boundless *has* no bound. The human mind works within limits, that is to say, within the Absolute apparently conditioned by phenomena because it is itself the Absolute apparently conditioned by phenomena. This fundamental idea of the Vedanta I shall have occasion to return upon in its proper place; here I follow out the argument so far in order to establish that the working of the human mind within limits does not militate against the undoubted experience that if rigidly interrogated it realises phenomena only as phenomena and the only fact to which it can give assent is the fact of infinity. If therefore we take reason or mental Experience as the final authority, the Hindu proposition demonstrates itself. The alternative proposition like the Roman Curia calls upon us to put reason out of Court and makes discussion of the question impossible. Although one cannot dogmatically declare it to be untrue, it is certainly contrary to all scientific probability; Hinduism does not deny, but rather asserts that the powers of the human mind can & will enlarge indefinitely, but it believes that this will be by the process of development, not by a radical alteration of its essential nature. To assert that man must believe in finality although he is constitutionally unable to grasp any finality, is to leave the terra firma on which all thought moves & reposes, the collective mental experience of the race affecting & affected by the mental experience of each individual and to launch into the void of dogmatic & irrational belief. Credo quia incredibile est, I believe because it is incomprehensible.

We come back therefore to the Hindu confession of faith, OM is the syllable, OM is the Universe; the past, the present and the future, — all that was, all that is, all that will be is OM. Likewise all that may exist beyond the bounds of Time, that too is OM.

Mark the determination to drive the idea of Infinity to its logical conclusion. *All that may exist beyond the bounds of Time, that too is OM.* Man can conceive nothing that is neither in the past, present nor future, but if there be such inconceivable thing, it does not by becoming beyond Time place itself beyond OM. That too is OM. In a similar spirit another verse of the Upanishad declares of God "He moves & He moveth not, He is near & He is far, He is within the Universe and He is outside the Universe." The Universe is all that exists, all that Man can know or conceive & there can be nothing outside it because it has no limits; but if there does exist such inconceivable thing as is beyond illimitable Space it does not by becoming beyond Space, put itself beyond OM. *He is within the Universe and He is outside the Universe.* All Hindu Scripture is precise upon this point, our God is not a gigantic polypus, not a term for infinite & Eternal Matter, not a stream of Tendency that makes for righteousness, or for the survival of the fittest, or for the goal of Evolution, whatever that may be. He is the Infinite and the Absolute, and what seems to be finite and conditioned, seems & is not; is phenomenon & not fact. God is the only fact, God is the only reality; God is the One than whom there is no other. He alone exists, all else appears. But of these things later. At present the conclusion which I wish to present is this that there is an Infinite who is the one fact; there is no Final Cause, because Final Cause implies an Effect different from itself & must therefore be finite, but the human mind cannot conceive of anything ultimate & finite; for there is no such thing; it cannot conceive of a beginning to all things because there was no beginning, or an end to all things because there is no end. There is only One Infinite who is without beginning and without End.

But if He is Infinite, He must be Unknowable, for knowledge implies limit & division. The human mind as has been said, works within limits; in order to know, we must define and analyse; but definition and analysis imply limits, imply conditions. The Infinite is conceivable to us, but not being measurable, it is also not knowable. This is the second great philosophical truth on which Hinduism insists. OM *tat sat* is its formula, OM, That is what Is. "That", the most non-committing expression discoverable in the language, is the one selected to express the idea of the Infinite One. "That is the one thing that is", but *what* That is and *why* That is, lies beyond the scope of our knowledge. Again and again the Scriptures asseverate our ultimate ignorance.[1]

---

[1] *The notes that follow were written by Sri Aurobindo at the top of the last page of this manuscript*:

Infinite, therefore Unknowable, Unknowable therefore Absolute. Prove the Existence of God. Known by Becoming.

The Philosophy of the Upanishads

Chapter I

Prefatory

The philosophy of the Upanishads is the basis of all Indian religion and morals and to a considerable extent of Hindu politics, legislation and society. Its practical importance to [our] race is therefore immense. But it has also profoundly [affected] the thought of the West in many of the most critical stages of [its] development; at first through Pythagoras and other Greek philosophers, then through Buddhism working into Essene, Gnostic and Roman Christianity and once again in our own times through German metaphysics, Theosophy, and a hundred strange and irregular channels. One can open few books now at all in the latest stream of thought without seeing the old Vedantism busy at its work of moulding and broadening the European mind, sometimes by direct and conscious impact as a force, more often by an unacknowledged and impalpable pressure as an atmosphere. This potent influence [in] modern times of a way of thinking many thousands of years old, is due to [a] singular parallelism between the fundamental positions arrived [at by] ancient Vedantism and modern Science. Science in its [researches] amid matter has stumbled on the basal fact of the [Unity] of all things; the Unity of all things is the rock on which the Upanishads have been built. Evolution has been discovered and [analyzed] by Science; Evolution of a kind is implied at every turn by the Vedanta. Vedantism like Science, [but] after its own fashion, [is] severely conscientious in its logical processes and rigorously experimental; [Vedantism] has mastered physical and psychical laws which Science [is] now beginning to handle.

But the parallelism is no more than a parallelism, [there is] no real point of contact; for the Hindu or Southern Asiatic mind differs fundamentally in its processes from either [the] Teutonic or the Mediterranean. The former is diffuse and comprehensive; the latter compact and precise. The Asiatic acquires a [deeper] and truer view of things in their totality, the European a more accurate and practically serviceable conception of their parts. [The] European seizes on an aspect and takes it for the whole; he is [a] fanatic of single ideas and the preacher of the finite: the Asiatic passes at once to the whole and slurs rapidly over the aspects; he [is] eclectic, inveterately flexible and large-minded, the priest of [the Infinite]. The European is an analytical reasoner proceeding from observations, the Asiatic a synthetic diviner, leaping to intuitions. Even [when] both analyze, the European prefers to dissect his observations, [the] Asiatic to distinguish his experiences: or when both [synthetize, the] European generalises and classifies what he has [observed,] the Asiatic masses into broad single truths what he [has seen] within. The one deals as a master with facts, but halts over [ideas and] having mastered an idea works round it in a circle; the other [masters ideas] unerringly [.........] but stumbles among facts and applications. The mind of the European is an Iliad or an Odyssey, fighting rudely but heroically forward, or, full of a rich curiosity, wandering as an accurate and vigorous observer in landlocked seas of thought; the mind of the Asiatic is a Ramayan or a Mahabharat, a gleaming infinity of splendid and inspiring imaginations and idealisms or else an universe of wide moral aspiration and ever varying and newly-grouped masses of thought. The mind of the Westerner is a Mediterranean full of small and fertile islands, studded with ports to which the owner, a private merchant, eagerly flees with his merchandise after a little dashing among the billows, and eagerly he disembarks and kisses his dear mother earth; the mind of the Eastern man is an Ocean, and its voyager an adventurer and discoverer, a Columbus sailing for months over an illimitable Ocean out of reach of land, and his ports of visit are few and far between, nor does he carry in his bottoms much merchandise you can traffick in; yet he opens for the trader new horizons, new worlds with new markets. By his intuitions and divinations he helps to widen the circles the European is always obstinately tracing. The European is essentially scientific, artistic and commercial; the Asiatic is essentially a moralist, pietist and philosopher. Of course the distinction is not rigid or absolute; there is much that is Asiatic in numbers of Europeans, and in particular races, notably the South Germans, the Celt and the Slav; there is much that is European in numbers of Asiatics, and in particular nations, notably the Arabs and the Japanese. But the fundamental divergence in speculative habits is very noticeable, for in the things of the mind the South imposes its law on the whole Continent.

We shall therefore expect to find, as we do find, that Vedantic Evolution and Monism are very different things from Evolution and Monism as European Science understands them. European thought seizes on Evolution as manifested in the outward facts of our little earth and follows it into its details with marvellous minuteness, accuracy and care. The Vedanta slurs over this part of the scheme with a brief acknowledgement, but divines the whole course of Evolution in the Universe and lays down with confident insight its larger aspects in the inward facts of the soul. In its Monism also Vedanta is far more profound and searching than the European scientific observer, for while the latter is aware only of this gross material world and resolves everything into the monism of gross Matter, the Vedanta, which is perfectly aware that gross matter can all be resolved into a single principle, does not pause at this discovery; it has pursued its investigations into two other worlds which surround & interpenetrate ours like two concentric but larger circles, the psychic or dream world of subtle Matter and the spiritual or sleep world of causal Matter, each with its own monistic unity; these three parallel monisms it resolves into a Supreme, Absolute and Transcendent Unity which is alone real and eternal. To the Indian consciousness at least these are no mere speculations; they are conclusions based on the actual experiences and observations of investigators who had themselves entered into these inner and yet wider worlds. The good faith of their observations cannot seriously be doubted and their accuracy can only be impugned when Science itself consents to explore the same fields of being whether by the methods hitherto practised in the East or by any other adequate means of its own invention.

We need not expect in the Upanishads a full statement of the facts on which its more grandiose statements of religious and philosophic truth are built, nor should we hope to find in them complete or reasoned treatises marshalling in a comprehensive and orderly manner the whole scheme of Vedantic philosophy. That is seldom the way in which the true Asiatic goes to work. He is a poet and a *divine* in the real sense of the word. His peculiar faculty is apparent in the very form of his philosophic books. The Aphorisms, that peculiarly Indian instrument of thought, by which our philosophers later on packed tons of speculation into an inch of space, give only the fundamental illuminations on which their philosophy depends. The Exegeses (*Karikas*) of Gaudapada and others are often a connected and logical array of concise and pregnant thoughts each carrying its burden of endless suggestion, each starting its own reverberating echo of wider and wider thought; but they are not comprehensive treatises. Nor can such a term be applied to the Commentaries (Bhashyas) of Shankara, Ramanuja and other powerful and original minds; they are, rather, forceful excursions into terse and strenuous logic, basing, strengthening, building up, adding a wing here and a story there to the cunning and multiform, yet harmonic structure of Indian thought. Nowhere will you find an exhaustive and systematic statement of a whole philosophy interpreting every part of the universe in the terms of a single line of thought. This habit of suggestiveness & reserve in thought leaves the old philosophies still as inspiring and full of intention and potential development as when the glowing divinations and massive spiritual experiences stored in the Upanishads were first annealed & hammered into philosophic form. It is the reason of the Vedanta's surprising vitality, of the extent to which it enters and the potency with which it governs Indian life, in a way that no European philosophy except recently the Evolutionary has entered into or governed the life of the West. The European metaphysician has something in him of the pedagogue, something indeed of the mechanic, at least of the geometrician;

his philosophies are masterpieces of consistent logic, admirable constructions of a rigid symmetry. But their very perfection militates against the vitality of the truth they set forth; for Life is not built on the lines of consistent logic, Nature does not proceed on the principle of a rigid symmetry: even where she seems most formal she loves to assert herself in even the slightest, just perceptible, perhaps hardly perceptible deflection from a strict correspondence. Nothing indeed can live permanently which has not in itself the potentiality of an unending Evolution; nothing — nothing finite at least — is completely true which is not incomplete. The moment a poem or work of art becomes incapable of fresh interpretation, or a philosophy of fruitful expansion or a species of change & variety, it ceases from that moment to be essential to existence and is therefore doomed, sooner or later, to extinction. The logical intellect may rebel against this law and insist passionately on finality in truth,[1] but it rebels vainly; for this *is* the law of all life and all truth.

This is the secret of the Upanishads and their undying fruitfulness. They are, to begin with, inspired poems, — not less so when they are couched in prose form than when they are poured into solemn and far-sounding verse, — grand and rhythmic intuitions where the speakers seem to be conveyors only of informing ideas cast out from a full and complete vision in the eternal guardian Mind of the race. The style in which they are couched is wonderfully grave, penetrating and mighty, suffused with strange light as if from another world, its rhythms unequalled for fathomless depth of sound and the rolling sea of solemn echoes they leave behind them. Here only in literature have philosophy and poetry at their highest met together and mingled their beings in the unison of a perfect love and understanding. For the Upanishads stand, as poetry, with the

---

[1] Observe for instance the phenomenon of Theosophy. The Western intellect seizes upon the profound researches of the East into the things behind the veil, the things of the soul & spirit — researches admirably firm in the outline of their results but incomplete in detail — and lo and behold! everything is arranged, classified, manualized, vulgarized, all gaps filled in, finality insisted on and the infinite future with its infinite possibilities and uncertainties audaciously barred out of its heritage.

greatest productions of creative force and harmonic beauty. As philosophy, they have borne the weight of three millenniums of thought and may well suffice for an equal period of future speculation. But exhaustive and balanced exposition is not to be expected; you must piece together their glowing jewels of thought if you would arrive at the forced symmetry of a system; and perhaps to the end of the world different minds will construct from them a different mosaic. To the systematic intellect this inevitably detracts from their philosophic value, but to the Indian mind, flexible, illimitable, unwilling to recognize any finality in philosophy or religion, it enhances their claim to reverence as Scriptures for the whole world and for all time to come.

Chapter II
Discovery of the Absolute Brahman

The idea of transcendental Unity, Oneness & Stability behind all the flux and variety of phenomenal life is the basal idea of the Upanishads: this is the pivot of all Indian metaphysics, the sum and goal of our spiritual experience. To the phenomenal world around us stability and singleness seem at first to be utterly alien; nothing but passes and changes, nothing but has its counterparts, contrasts, harmonised and dissident parts; and all are perpetually shifting and rearranging their relative positions and affections. Yet if one thing is certain, it is that the sum of all this change and motion is absolutely stable, fixed and unvarying; that all this heterogeneous multitude of animate & inanimate things are fundamentally homogeneous and one. Otherwise nothing could endure, nor could there be any certainty in existence. And this unity, stability, unvarying fixity which reason demands & ordinary experience points to, is being ascertained slowly but surely by the investigations of Science. We can no longer escape from the growing conviction that however the parts may change and shift and appear to perish, yet the sum and whole remains unchanged, undiminished and imperishable; however multitudinous, mutable and mutually irreconcilable forms and compounds may be, yet the grand substratum is one, simple and enduring; death itself is not a reality but a seeming, for what appears to be destruction, is merely transformation and a preparation for rebirth. Science may not have appreciated the full import of her own discoveries; she may shrink from an unflinching acceptance of the logical results to which they lead; and certainly she is as yet far from advancing towards the great converse truths which they for the present conceal, — for instance the wonderful fact that not only is death a seeming, but life itself is a seeming, and beyond life and death there lies a condition which is truer and therefore more permanent than either. But though Science dreams not as yet of her goal, her feet are on the road from which there is no turning back, — the road which Vedanta on a different plane has already trod before it.

Here then is a great fundamental fact which demands from philosophy an adequate explanation of itself; — that all variations resolve themselves into an unity; that within the flux of things and concealed by it is an indefinable, immutable Something, at once the substratum and sum of all, which Time cannot touch, motion perturb, nor variation increase or diminish; and that this substratum and sum has been from all eternity and will be for all eternity. A fundamental fact to which all Thought moves, and yet is it not, when narrowly considered, an acute paradox? For how can the sum of infinite variations be a sempiternally fixed amount which has never augmented or decreased and can never augment or decrease? How can that whole be fixed and eternal of which every smallest part is eternally varying and perishing? Given a bewildering whirl of motion, how does the result come to be not merely now or as a result, but from beginning to end a perfect fixity? Impossible, unless either there be a guiding Power, for which at first sight there seems to be no room in the sempiternal chain of causation; or unless that sum and substratum be the one reality, imperishable because not conditioned by Time, indivisible because not conditioned by Space, immutable because not conditioned by Causality, — in a word absolute & transcendent and *therefore* eternal, unalterable and undecaying. Motion and change and death and division would then be merely transitory phenomena, masks and seemings of the One and Absolute, the as yet undefined and perhaps indefinable It which alone *is*.

To such a conclusion Indian speculation had turned at a very early period of its conscious strivings — uncertainly at first and with many gropings and blunders. The existence of some Oneness which gives order and stability to the multitudinous stir of the visible world, the Aryan thinkers were from the first disposed to envisage and they sought painfully to arrive at the knowledge of that Oneness in its nature or its essentiality. The living Forces of the Cosmos which they had long worshipped, yet always with a floating but persistent perception of an Unity in their multitude, melted on closer analysis into a single concept, a single Force or Presence, one and universal. The question then arose, Was that Force or Presence intelligent or non-intelligent? God or Nature? "He alone" hazarded the Rigveda "knoweth, or perhaps He knoweth not." Or might it not be that the Oneness which ties together and governs phenomena and rolls out the evolution of the worlds, is really the thing we call *Time*, since of the three original conditions of phenomenal existence, Time, Space and Causality, Time is a necessary part of the conception of Causality and can hardly be abstracted from the conception of Space, but neither Space nor Causality seems necessary to the conception of Time? Or if it be not Time, might it not be *Swabhava*, the essential Nature of Things taking various conditions and forms? Or perhaps *Chance*, some blind principle working out an unity and law in things by infinite experiment, — this too might be possible. Or since from eternal uncertainty eternal certainty cannot come, might it not be *Fate*, a fixed and unalterable law in things in subjection to which this world evolves itself in a preordained procession of phenomena from which it cannot deviate? Or perhaps in the original atomic fountain of things certain *Elements* might be discovered which by perpetual and infinite combinations and permutations keep the universe to its workings? But if so, these elements must themselves proceed from something which imposes on them the law of their being, and what could that be but the *Womb*, the matrix of original and indestructible Matter, the plasm which moulds the universe and out of which it is moulded? And yet in whatever scheme of things the mind might ultimately rest, some room surely must be made for these conscious, thinking and knowing *Egos* of living beings, of whom knowledge and thought seem to be the essential selves and without whom this world of perceivable and knowable things could not be perceived and known; — and if not perceived and known, might it not be that without them it could not even exist?

Such were the gurges of endless speculation in which the old Aryan thinkers, tossed and perplexed, sought for some firm standing-ground, some definite clue which might save them from being beaten about like stumbling blind men led by a guide as blind. They sought at first to liberate themselves from the tyranny of appearances by the method which Kapila, the ancient prehistoric Master of Thought, had laid down for mankind, the method called Sankhya or the law of Enumeration. The method of Kapila consisted in guidance by pure discriminative reason and it took its name from one of its principal rules, the law of enumeration and generalisation. They enumerated first the immediate Truths-in-Things which they could distinguish or deduce from things obviously phenomenal, and from these by generalisation they arrived at a much smaller number of ulterior Truths-in-Things of which the immediate were merely aspects. And then having enumerated these ulterior Truths-in-Things, they were able by generalisation to reduce them to a very small number of ultimate Truths-in-Things, the Tattwas (literally Thenesses) of the developed Sankhya philosophy. And these Tattwas once enumerated with some approach to certainty, was it not possible to generalise yet one step farther? The Sankhya did so generalise and by this supreme and final generalisation arrived at the very last step on which, in its own unaided strength, it could take safe footing. This was the great principle of Prakriti, the single eternal indestructible principle and origin of Matter which by perpetual evolution rolls out through aeons and aeons the

unending panorama of things.[2] And for whose benefit? Surely
for those conscious knowing and perceiving Egos, the army of
witnesses, who, each in his private space of reasoning and perceiving Mind partitioned off by an enveloping medium of gross
matter, sit for ever as spectators in the theatre of the Universe!
For ever, thought the Sankhyas, since the Egos, though their
partitions are being continually broken down and built anew
and the spaces occupied never remain permanently identical, yet
seem themselves to be no less eternal and indestructible than
Prakriti.

This then was the wide fixed lake of ascertained philosophical knowledge into which the method of Sankhya, pure intellectual reasoning on definite principles, led in the mind of ancient
India. Branchings off, artificial canals from the reservoir were
not, indeed, wanting. Some by resolving that army of witnesses
into a single Witness, arrived at the dual conception of God and
Nature, Purusha & Prakriti, Spirit and Matter, Ego and Non-
ego. Others, more radical, perceived Prakriti as the creation,
shadow or aspect of Purusha, so that God alone remained, the
spiritual or ideal factor eliminating by inclusion the material
or real. Solutions were also attempted on the opposite side; for
some eliminated the conscious Egos themselves as mere seemings; not a few seem to have thought that each ego is only a series
of successive shocks of consciousness and the persistent sense of
identity no more than an illusion due to the unbroken continuity
of the shocks. If these shocks of consciousness are borne in on
the brain from the changes of Prakriti in the multitudinous stir
of evolution, then is consciousness one out of the many terms of
Prakriti itself, so that Prakriti alone remains as the one reality,
the material or real factor eliminating by inclusion the spiritual
or ideal. But if we deny, as many did, that Prakriti is an ultimate
reality apart from the perceptions of Purushas and yet apply the
theory of a false notion of identity created by successive waves of

---

[2] Note that Matter here not only includes gross matter with which Western Science is
mainly concerned, but subtle matter, the material in which thought & feeling work, and
causal matter in which the fundamental operations of the Will-to-live are conducted.

sensation, we arrive at the impossible & sophistic position of the old Indian Nihilists whose reason by a singular suicide landed itself in Nothingness as the cradle & bourne, nay, the very stuff and reality of all existence. And there was a third direction in which thought tended and which led it to the very threshold of Vedanta; for this also was a possible speculation that Prakriti & Purusha might both be quite real & yet not ultimately different aspects or sides of each other and so, after all, of a Oneness higher than either. But these speculations, plausible or imperfect, logical or sophistic, were yet mere speculations; they had no basis either in observed fact or in reliable experience. Two certainties seemed to have been arrived at, Prakriti was testified to by a close analysis of phenomenal existence; it was the basis of the phenomenal world which without a substratum of original matter could not be accounted for and without a fundamental oneness and indestructibility in that substratum could not be, what observation showed it to be, subject, namely, to fixed laws & evidently invariable in its sum and substance. On the other hand Purushas were testified to by the eternal persistence of the sense of individuality and identity whether during life or after death[3] and by the necessity of a perceiving cause for the activity of Prakriti; they were the receptive and contemplative Egos within the sphere of whose consciousness Prakriti, stirred to creative activity by their presence, performed her long drama of phenomenal Evolution.

But meanwhile the seers of ancient India had, in their experiments and efforts at spiritual training and the conquest of the body, perfected a discovery which in its importance to the future of human knowledge dwarfs the divinations of Newton and Galileo; even the discovery of the inductive and experimental method in Science was not more momentous; for they discovered down to its ultimate processes the method of Yoga and by the method of Yoga they rose to three crowning realisations. They

---

[3] Survival of the human personality after death has always been held in India to be a proved fact beyond all dispute; the Charvaka denial of it was contemned as mere irrational & wilful folly. Note however that survival after death does not necessarily to the Indian mind imply immortality, but only raises a presumption in its favour.

realised first as a fact the existence under the flux and multitudinousness of things of that supreme Unity and immutable Stability which had hitherto been posited only as a necessary theory,
an inevitable generalisation. They came to know that It is the one
reality and all phenomena merely its seemings and appearances,
that It is the true Self of all things and phenomena are merely
its clothes and trappings. They learned that It is absolute and
transcendent and, because absolute and transcendent, therefore
eternal, immutable, imminuable and indivisible. And looking
back on the past progress of speculation they perceived that this
also was the goal to which pure intellectual reasoning would
have led them. For that which is in Time must be born and perish;
but the Unity and Stability of things is eternal and must therefore
transcend Time. That which is in Space must increase & diminish, have parts & relations, but the Unity and Stability of things is
imminuable, not augmentable, independent of the changefulness
of its parts and untouched by the shifting of their relations, and
must therefore transcend Space; — and if it transcends Space,
cannot really have parts, since Space is the condition of material
divisibility; divisibility therefore must be, like death, a seeming
and not a reality. Finally that which is subject to Causality, is
necessarily subject to Change; but the Unity and Stability of
things is immutable, the same now as it was aeons ago and will
be aeons hereafter, and must therefore transcend Causality.

   This then was the first realisation through Yoga, NITYO
'NITYÂNÂM, the One Eternal in many transient.

   At the same time they realised one truth more, — a surprising truth; they found that the transcendent absolute Self of
things was also the Self of living beings, the Self too of man,
that highest of the beings living in the material plane on earth.
The Purusha or conscious Ego in man which had perplexed and
baffled the Sankhyas, turned out to be precisely the same in his
ultimate being as Prakriti the apparently non-conscious source
of things; the non-consciousness of Prakriti, like so much else,
was proved a seeming and no reality, since behind the inanimate
form a conscious Intelligence at work is to the eyes of the Yogin
luminously self-evident.

This then was the second realisation through Yoga, CHÉTA-NAṢ CHÉTANÂNÂM, the One Consciousness in many Consciousnesses.

Finally at the base of these two realisations was a third, the most important of all to our race, — that the Transcendent Self in individual man is as complete *because identically the same* as the Transcendent Self in the Universe; for the Transcendent is indivisible and the sense of separate individuality is only one of the fundamental seemings on which the manifestation of phenomenal existence perpetually depends. In this way the Absolute which would otherwise be beyond knowledge, becomes knowable; and the man who knows his whole Self knows the whole Universe. This stupendous truth is enshrined to us in the two famous formulae of Vedanta, SO 'HAM, He am I, and AHAM BRAHM' ÂSMI, I am Brahman the Eternal.

Based on these four grand truths, NITYO 'NITYÂNÂM, CHÉTANAṢ CHÉTANÂNÂM, SO 'HAM, AHAM BRAHM' ÂSMI, as upon four mighty pillars the lofty philosophy of the Upanishads raises its front among the distant stars.

Chapter III

Nature of the Absolute Brahman

Viewed in the light of these four great illuminations the utterances of the Upanishads arrange themselves and fall into a perfect harmony. European scholars like Max Muller have seen in these Scriptures a mass of heterogeneous ideas where the sublime jostles the childish, the grandiose walks arm-in-arm with the grotesque, the most petty trivialities feel at home with the rarest and most solemn philosophical intuitions, and they have accordingly declared them to be the babblings of a child humanity; inspired children, idiots endowed with genius, such to the Western view are the great Rishis of the Aranyaka. But the view is suspect from its very nature. It is not likely that men who handle the ultimate and most difficult intellectual problems with such mastery, precision and insight, would babble mere folly in matters which require the use of much lower faculties. Their utterances in this less exalted sphere may be true or they may be erroneous, but, it may fairly be assumed, they gave them forth with a perfectly clear idea of their bearing and signification. To an understanding totally unacquainted with the methods by which they are arrived at, many of the established conclusions of modern Science would seem unutterably grotesque and childish, — the babblings if not of a child humanity, at least of humanity in its dotage; yet only a little accurate knowledge is needed to show that these grotesque trivialities are well-ascertained and irrefragable truths.

In real truth the Upanishads are in all their parts, allowing for imaginative language and an occasional element of symbolism, quite rational, consistent and homogeneous. They are not concerned indeed to create an artificial impression of consistency by ignoring the various aspects of this manifold Universe and reducing all things to a single denomination; for they are not metaphysical treatises aiming at mathematical abstractness or geometrical precision and consistency. They are a great store of observations and spiritual experiences with conclusions and generalisations from those observations and experiences, set down without any thought of controversial caution or any anxiety to avoid logical contradictions. Yet they have the consistency of all truthful observation and honest experience; they arrange themselves naturally and without set purpose under one grand universal truth developed into a certain number of wide general laws within whose general agreement there is room for infinite particular variations and even anomalies. They have in other words a scientific rather than a logical consistency.

To the rigorous logician bound in his narrow prison of verbal reasoning, the Upanishads seem indeed to base themselves on an initial and fundamental inconsistency. There are a number of passages in these Scriptures which dwell with striking emphasis on the unknowableness of the Absolute Brahman. It is distinctly stated that neither mind nor senses can reach the Brahman and that words return baffled from the attempt to describe It; more, — that we do not discern the Absolute and Transcendent in Its reality, nor can we discriminate the right way or perhaps any way of teaching the reality of It to others; and it is even held, that It can only be properly characterised in negative language and that to every challenge for definition the only true answer is NÉTI NÉTI, *It is not this, It is not that*. Brahman is not definable, not describable, not intellectually knowable. And yet in spite of these passages the Upanishads constantly declare that Brahman is the one true object of knowledge and the whole Scripture is in fact an attempt not perhaps to define, but at least in some sort to characterise and present an idea, and even a detailed idea, of the Brahman.

The inconsistency is more apparent than real. The Brahman in Its ultimate reality is transcendent, absolute, infinite; but the senses and the intellect, which the senses supply with its material, are finite; speech also is limited by the deficiencies of the intellect; Brahman must therefore in Its very nature be unknowable to the intellect and beyond the power of speech to describe, — yet only in Its ultimate reality, not in Its aspects or manifestations. The Agnostic Scientist also believes that there must be some great ultimate Reality unknown and probably unknowable to man (ignoramus et ignorabimus) from which this Universe proceeds and on which all phenomena depend, but his admission of Unknowableness is confined to the ultimate Nature of this supreme Ens and not to its expression or manifestation in the Universe. The Upanishad, proceeding by a profounder method than material analysis, casts the net of knowledge wider than the modern Agnostic, yet in the end its attitude is much the same; it differs only in this important respect that it asserts even the ultimate Brahman to be although inexpressible in the terms of finite knowledge, yet realisable and attainable.

The first great step to the realisation of the Brahman is by the knowledge of Him as manifested in the phenomenal Universe; for if there is no reality but Brahman, the phenomenal Universe which is obviously a manifestation of *something* permanent and eternal, must be a manifestation of Brahman and of nothing else, and if we know it completely, we do to a certain extent and in a certain way, know Him, not as an Absolute Existence, but under the conditions of phenomenal manifestation. While, however, European Science seeks only to know the phenomena of gross matter, the Yogin goes farther. He asserts that he has discovered an universe of subtle matter penetrating and surrounding the gross; this universe to which the spirit withdraws partially and for a brief time in sleep but more entirely and for a longer time through the gates of death, is the source whence all psychic processes draw their origin; and the link which connects this universe with the gross material world is to be found in the phenomena of life and mind. His assertion is perfectly positive and the Upanishad proceeds on it as on an ascertained and indisputable fact quite beyond the limits of mere guesswork, inference or speculation. But he goes yet farther and declares that there is yet a third universe of causal matter penetrating and surrounding both the subtle and the gross, and that this universe to which the spirit withdraws in the deepest and most abysmal states of sleep and trance and also in a remote condition beyond the state of man after death, is the source whence all phenomena take their rise. If we are to understand the Upanishads we must accept these to us astounding statements, temporarily at least; for on them the whole scheme of Vedanta is built. Now Brahman manifests Himself in each of these Universes, in the Universe of Causal Matter as the Cause, Self and Inspirer, poetically styled Prajna the Wise One; in the universe of subtle matter as the Creator, Self and Container, styled Hiranyagarbha the Golden Embryo of life and form, and in the universe of gross matter as the Ruler, Guide, Self and Helper, styled Virat the Shining and Mighty One. And in each of these manifestations He can be known and realised by the spirit of Man.

Granted the truth of these remarkable assertions, what then is the relation between the Supreme Self and man? The position has already been quite definitely taken that the transcendent Self in man is identically the same as the transcendent Self in the Universe and that this identity is the one great key to the knowledge of the Absolute Brahman. Does not this position rule out of court any such differences between the Absolute and the human Self as is implied in the character of the triple manifestation of Brahman? On the one hand completest identity of the Supreme Self and the human is asserted as an ascertained & experienced fact, on the other hand widest difference is asserted as an equally well-ascertained and experienced fact; there can be no reconciliation between these incompatible statements. Yet are they both facts, answers Vedanta; identity *is* a fact in the reality of things; difference *is* a fact in the appearance of things, the world of phenomena; for phenomena are in their essence nothing but seemings and the difference between the individual Self and the Universal Self is the fundamental seeming which makes all the rest possible. This difference grows as the manifestation of Brahman proceeds. In the world of gross matter, it is complete; the difference is so acute, that it is impossible for the material sensual being to conceive of the Supreme Soul as having any point of contact with his own soul and it is only by a long process of evolution that he arrives at the illumination in which some kind of identity becomes to him conceivable. The basal conception for Mind as conditioned by gross matter is Dualistic; the knower here must be different from the Known and his whole intellectual development consists in the discovery, development and perfected use of ever new media and methods of knowledge. Undoubtedly the ultimate knowledge he arrives at brings him to the fundamental truth of identity between himself and the Supreme Self, but in the sphere of gross phenomena this identity can never be more than an intellectual conception, it can never be verified by personal realisation. On the other hand it can be *felt* by the supreme sympathy of love and faith, either through love of humanity and of all other fellow-beings or directly through love of God. This feeling of identity is very strong in religions based largely on the sentiment of Love and Faith. I and my Father are One, cried the Founder of Christianity; I and my brother man & my brother beast are One, says Buddhism; St Francis spoke of Air as his brother and Water as his sister; and the Hindu devotee when he sees a bullock lashed falls down in pain with the mark of the whip on his own body. But the feeling of Oneness remaining only a feeling does not extend into knowledge and therefore these religions while emotionally pervaded with the sense of identity, tend in the sphere of intellect to a militant Dualism or to any other but always unMonistic standpoint. Dualism is therefore no mere delusion; it is a truth, but a phenomenal truth and not the ultimate reality of things.

As it proceeds in the work of discovering and perfecting methods of knowledge, the individual self finds an entry into the universe of subtle phenomena. Here the difference that divides it from the Supreme Self is less acute; for the bonds of matter are lightened and the great agents of division and disparity, Time and Space, diminish in the insistency of their pressure. The individual here comes to realise a certain unity with the great Whole; he is enlarged and aggrandized into a part of the Universal Self, but the sense of identity is not complete and cannot be complete. The basal conception for Mind in this subtle Universe is Dualo-Monistic; the knower is not quite different from the known; he is like and of the same substance but inferior, smaller and dependent; his sense of oneness may amount to similarity and consubstantiality but not to coincidence and perfect identity.

From the subtle Universe the individual self rises in its evolution until it is able to enter the universe of Causal matter, where it stands near to the fountain-head. In this universe media and methods of knowledge begin to disappear, Mind comes into almost direct relations with its source and the difference between the individual and the Supreme Self is greatly attenuated. Nevertheless there is here too a wall of difference, even though it wears eventually thin as the thinnest paper. The knower is aware that he is coeval and coexistent with the Supreme Self, he is aware in a sense of omnipresence, for wherever the Supreme Self is, there also he is; he is, moreover, on the other side of phenomena and can see the Universe at will without him or within him; but he has still not necessarily realised the Supreme as utterly himself, although the perfect realisation is now for the first time in his grasp. The basal perception for Mind in this Universe is Monism with a difference, but the crowning perception of Monism becomes here possible.

And when it is no longer only possible but grasped? Then the individual Self entering into full realisation, ceases in any sense to be the individual Self, but merges into & becomes again the eternal and absolute Brahman, without parts, unbeginning, undecaying, unchanging. He has passed beyond causality and phenomena and is no longer under the bondage of that which is only by seeming. This is the *laya* or utter absorption of Hinduism, the highest *nirvana* or extinction from phenomena of the Upanishads and of Buddhist metaphysics. It is obviously a state which words fail to describe, since words which are created to express relations and have no meaning except when they express relations, cannot deal successfully with a state which is perfectly pure, absolute and unrelated; nor is it a condition which the bounded & finite intellect of man on this plane can for a moment envisage. This unintelligibility of the supreme state is naturally a great stumblingblock to the undisciplined imagination of our present-day humanity which, being sensuous, emotional and intellectual, inevitably recoils from a bliss in which neither the senses, emotions nor intellect have any place. Surely, we cry, the extinction or quietude of all these sources & means of sensation and pleasure implies not supreme bliss but absolute nothingness, blank annihilation. "An error", answers the Vedanta, "a pitiful, grovelling error! Why is it that the senses cease in that supreme condition? Because the senses were evolved in order to sense external being and where externality ceases, they having no action cease to exist. The emotions too are directed outwards and need another for their joy, they can only survive so long as we are incomplete. The intellect similarly is and works only so long as there is something external to it and ungrasped. But to the Most High there is nothing ungrasped, the Most High depends on none for His joy. He has therefore neither emotions nor intellect, nor can he either who merges in and becomes the Most High, possess them for a moment after that high consummation. The deprivation of the limited senses in His boundlessness is not a loss or an extinction, but must be a fulfilment, a development into Being which rejoices in its own infinity. The disappearance of our broken & transient emotions in His completeness must bring us not into a cold void but rather into illimitable bliss. The culmination of knowledge by the supersession of our divided

& fallible intellect must lead not to utter darkness and blank vacuity but to the luminous ecstasy of an infinite Consciousness. Not the annihilation of Being, but utter fullness of Being is our Nirvana." And when this ecstatic language is brought to the touchstone of reason, it must surely be declared just and even unanswerable. For the final absolution of the intellect can only be at a point where the Knower, Knowledge and the Known become one, Knowledge being there infinite, direct and without media. And where there is this infinite and flawless knowledge, there must be, one thinks, infinite and flawless existence and bliss. But by the very conditions of this state, we can only say of it that it is, we cannot define it in words, precisely because we cannot realize it with the intellect. The Self can be realized only with the Self; there is no other instrument of realization.

Granted, it may be said, that such a state is conceivably possible, — as certainly it is, starting from your premises, the only and inevitable conclusion, — but what proof have we that it exists as a reality? what proof can even your Yoga bring to us that it exists? For when the individual Self becomes identified with the Supreme, its evolution is over and it does not return into phenomena to tell its experiences. The question is a difficult one to handle, partly because language, if it attempts to deal with it at all precisely, must become so abstract and delicate as to be unintelligible, partly because the experiences it involves are so far off from our present general evolution and attained so rarely that dogmatism or even definite statement appears almost unpardonable. Nevertheless with the use of metaphorical language, or, in St Paul's words, speaking as a fool, one may venture to outline what there is at all to be said on the subject. The truth then seems to be that there are even in this last or fourth state of the Self, stages and degrees, as to the number of which experience varies; but for practical purposes we may speak of three, the first when we stand at the entrance of the porch and look within; the second when we stand at the inner extremity of the porch and are really face to face with the Eternal; the third when we enter into the Holy of Holies. Be it remembered that the language I am using is the language of metaphor and must not be pressed with a savage literalness. Well then, the first stage is well within the possible experience of man and from it man returns to be a Jivanmukta, one who lives & is yet released in his inner self from the bondage of phenomenal existence; the second stage once reached, man does not ordinarily return, unless he is a supreme Buddha, — or perhaps as a world Avatar; from the third stage none returns nor is it attainable in the body. Brahman as realised by the Jivanmukta, seen from the entrance of the porch, is that which we usually term Parabrahman, the Supreme Eternal and the subject of the most exalted descriptions of the Vedanta. There are therefore five conditions of Brahman. Brahman Virat, Master of the Waking Universe; Brahman Hiranyagarbha, of the Dream Universe; Brahman Prajna or Avyakta of the Trance Universe of Unmanifestation; Parabrahman, the Highest; and that which is higher than the highest, the Unknowable. Now of the Unknowable it is not profitable to speak, but something of Parabrahman can be made intelligible to the human understanding because — always if the liberal use of loose metaphors is not denied, — it can be partially brought within the domain of speech.

Chapter IV
Parabrahman

So far the great Transcendent Reality has been viewed from the standpoint of the human spirit as it travels on the upward curve of evolution to culminate in the Supreme. It will now be more convenient to view the Absolute from the other end of the cycle of manifestation where, in a sense, evolution begins and the great Cause of phenomena stands with His face towards the Universe He will soon create. At first of course there is the Absolute, unconditioned, unmanifested, unimaginable, of Whom nothing can be predicated except negatives. But as the first step towards manifestation the Absolute — produces, shall we say? let the word serve for want of a better! — produces in Itself a luminous Shadow of Its infinite inconceivable Being, — the image is trivial and absurd, but one can find none adequate, — which is Parabrahman or if we like so to call Him, God, the Eternal, the Supreme Spirit, the Seer, Witness, Wisdom, Source, Creator, Ancient of Days. Of Him Vedanta itself can only speak in two great trilogies, subjective and objective, Sacchidanandam, Existence, Consciousness, Bliss; Satyam Jnanam Anantam, Truth, Knowledge, Infinity.

SACCHIDANANDAM. The Supreme is Pure Being, Absolute Existence, SAT. He is Existence because He alone *Is*, there being nothing else which has any ultimate reality or any being independent of His self-manifestation. And He is *Absolute* Existence because since He alone is and nothing else exists in reality, He must necessarily exist by Himself, in Himself and to Himself. There can be no cause for His existence, nor object to His existence; nor can there be any increase or diminution in Him, since increase can only come by addition from something external and diminution by loss to something external, and there is nothing external to Brahman. He cannot change in any way, for then He would be subject to Time and Causality; nor have parts, for then He would be subject to the law of Space. He is beyond the conceptions of Space, Time and Causality which He creates phenomenally as the conditions of manifestation but which cannot condition their Source. Parabrahman, then, is Absolute Existence.

The Supreme is also Pure Awareness, Absolute Consciousness, CHIT. We must be on our guard against confusing the ultimate consciousness of Brahman with our own modes of thought and knowledge, or calling Him in any but avowedly metaphorical language the Universal Omniscient Mind and by such other terminology; Mind, Thought, Knowledge, Omniscience, Partial Science, Nescience are merely modes in which Consciousness figures under various conditions and in various receptacles. But the Pure Consciousness of the Brahman is a conception which transcends our modes of thinking. Philosophy has done well to point out that consciousness is in its essence purely subjective. We are not conscious of external objects; we are only conscious of certain perceptions and impressions in our brains which by the separate or concurrent operation of our senses we are able to externalise into name and form; and in the very nature of things and to the end of Time we cannot be conscious of anything except these impressions & perceptions. The fact is indubitable, though Materialism and Idealism explain it in diametrically opposite directions. We shall eventually know that this condition is imperative precisely because consciousness *is* the fundamental thing from which all phenomenal existence proceeds, so much so that all phenomena have been called by a bold metaphor distortions or corruptions (*vikaras*) of the absolute consciousness. Monistic philosophers tell us however that the true explanation is not corruption but illation (*adhyaropa*), first of the idea of not-self into the Self, and of externality into the internal, and then of fresh and ever more complex forms by the method of Evolution. These metaphysical explanations it is necessary indeed to grasp, but even when we have mastered their delicate distinctions, refined upon refinement and brought ourselves to the verge of infinite ideas, there at least we must pause; we are moored to our brains and cannot in this body cut the rope in order to spread our sails over the illimitable ocean. It is enough if we satisfy ourselves with some dim realisation of the fact that all sentience is ultimately self-sentience.

The Upanishads tell us that Brahman is not a blind universal Force working by its very nature mechanically, nor even an unconscious Cause of Force; He is conscious or rather is Himself Consciousness, CHIT, as well as SAT. It necessarily follows that SAT and CHIT are really the same; Existence is Consciousness and cannot be separated from Consciousness. Phenomenally we may choose to regard existence as proceeding from sentience or culminating in it or being in and by it; but culmination is only a return to a concealed source, an efflorescence already concealed in the seed, so that from all these three standpoints sentience is eventually the condition of existence; they are only three different aspects of the mental necessity which forbids us to imagine the great Is as essentially unaware that He Is. We may of course choose to believe that things are the other way about, that existence proceeds from insentience through sentience back again to insentience. Sentience is then merely a form of insentience, a delusion or temporary corruption (*vikara*) of the eternal and insentient. In this case Sentience, Intelligence, Mind, Thought and Knowledge, all are Maya and either insentient Matter or Nothingness the only eternal reality. But the Nihilist's negation of existence is a mere reductio ad absurdum of all thought and reason, a metaphysical *harakiri* by which Philosophy rips up her own bowels with her own weapons. The Materialist's conclusion of eternal insentient Matter seems to stand on firmer ground; for we have certainly the observed fact that evolution seems to start from inanimate Matter, and consciousness presents itself in Matter as a thing that appears for a short time only to disappear, a phenomenon or temporary seeming. To this argument also Vedanta can marshal a battalion of replies. The assertion of eternally insentient Matter (*Prakriti*) without any permanently sentient reality (*Purusha*) is, to begin with, a paradox far more startling than the Monistic paradox of Maya and lands us in a conclusion mentally inconceivable. Nor is the materialistic conclusion indisputably proved by observed facts; rather facts seem to lead us to a quite different conclusion, since the existence of anything really insentient behind which there is no concealed Sentience is an assumption (for we cannot even positively say that inanimate things are absolutely inanimate,) and the one fact we surely and indisputably know is our own sentience and animation. In the workings of inanimate Matter we everywhere see the operations of Intelligence operating by means and adapting means to an end and the intelligent use of means by an unconscious entity is a thing paradoxical in itself and unsupported by an atom of proof; indeed the wider knowledge of the Universe attainable to Yoga actually does reveal such a Universal Intelligence everywhere at work.

Brahman, then, is Consciousness, and this once conceded, it follows that He must be in His transcendental reality Absolute Consciousness. His Consciousness is from itself and of itself like His existence, because there is nothing separate and other than Him; not only so but it does not consist in the knowledge of one part of Himself by another, or of His parts by His whole, since

His transcendental existence is one and simple, without parts. His consciousness therefore does not proceed by the same laws as our consciousness, does not proceed by differentiating subject from object, knower from known, but simply *is*, by its own right of pure and unqualified existence, eternally and illimitably, in a way impure and qualified existences cannot conceive.

The Supreme is, finally, Pure Ecstasy, Absolute Bliss, ÂNANDA. Now just as SAT and CHIT are the same, so are SAT and CHIT not different from ÂNANDA; just as Existence is Consciousness and cannot be separated from Consciousness, so Conscious Existence is Bliss and cannot be separated from Bliss. I think we feel this even in the very finite existence and cramped consciousness of life on the material plane. Conscious existence at least cannot endure without pleasure; even in the most miserable sentient being there must be pleasure in existence though it appear small as a grain of mustard seed; blank absolute misery entails suicide and annihilation as its necessary and immediate consequence. The will to live, — the desire of conscious existence and the instinct of self-preservation, — is no mere teleological arrangement of Nature with a particular end before it, but is fundamental and independent of end or object; it is merely a body and form to that pleasure of existence which is essential and eternal; and it cannot be forced to give way to anything but that will to live *more* fully and widely which is the source on one side of all personal ambition and aspiration, on the other of all love, self-sacrifice and self-conquest. Even suicide is merely a frenzied revolt against limitation, a revolt not the less significant because it is without knowledge. The pleasure of existence can consent to merge only in the greater pleasure of a widened existence, and religion, the aspiration towards God, is simply the fulfilment of this eternal elemental force, its desire to merge its separate & limited joy in the sheer bliss of infinite existence. The Will to live individually embodies the pleasure of individual existence which is the outer phenomenal self of all creatures; but the will to live infinitely can only proceed straight from the transcendent, ultimate Spirit in us which is our real Self; and it is this that availeth towards immortality. Brahman, then,

being infinity of conscious existence, is also infinite bliss. And the
bliss of Brahman is necessarily absolute both in its nature and as
to its object. Any mixture or coexistence with pain would imply
a cause of pain either the same or other than the cause of bliss,
with the immediate admission of division, struggle, opposition,
of something inharmonious and self-annulling in Brahman; but
division and opposition which depend upon relation cannot exist in the unrelated Absolute. Pain is, properly considered, the
result of limitation. When the desires and impulses are limited
in their satisfaction or the matter, physical or mental, on which
they act is checked, pressed inward, divided or pulled apart by
something alien to itself, then only can pain arise. Where there
is no limitation, there can be no pain. The Bliss of Brahman is
therefore absolute in its nature.

It is no less absolute with regard to its object; for the subject
and object are the same. It is inherent in His own existence
and consciousness and cannot possibly have any cause within
or without Him who alone Is and Is without parts or division.
Some would have us believe that a self-existent bliss is impossible; bliss, like pain, needs an object or cause different from
the subject and therefore depends on limitation. Yet even in this
material or waking world any considerable and deep experience
will show us that there is a pleasure which is independent of
surroundings and does not rely for its sustenance on temporary
or external objects. The pleasure that depends on others is tur-
bid, precarious and marred by the certainty of diminution and
loss; it is only as one withdraws deeper and deeper into oneself
that one comes nearer and nearer to the peace that passeth
understanding. An equally significant fact is to be found in the
phenomena of satiety; of which this is the governing law that
the less limited and the more subjective the field of pleasure, the
farther is it removed from the reach of satiety and disgust. The
body is rapidly sated with pleasure; the emotions, less limited
and more subjective, can take in a much deeper draught of
joy; the mind, still wider and more capable of internality, has
a yet profounder gulp and untiring faculty of assimilation; the
pleasures of the intellect and higher understanding, where we

move in a very rare and wide atmosphere, seldom pall and, even then, soon repair themselves; while the infinite spirit, the acme of our subjectiveness, knows not any disgust of spiritual ecstasy and will be content with nothing short of infinity in its bliss. The logical culmination of this ascending series is the transcendent and absolute Parabrahman whose bliss is endless, self-existent and pure.

This then is the Trinity of the Upanishads, Absolute Existence; which is *therefore* Absolute Consciousness; which is therefore Absolute Bliss.

And then the second Trinity SATYAM JNANAM ANANTAM. This Trinity is not different from the first but merely its objective expression. Brahman is *Satyam*, Truth or Reality because Truth or Reality is merely the subjective idea of existence viewed objectively. Only that which fundamentally exists is real and true, and Brahman being absolute existence is also absolute truth and reality. All other things are only relatively real, not indeed false in every sense since they are appearances of a Reality, but impermanent and therefore not in themselves ultimately true.

Brahman is also JNÂNAM, Knowledge; for Knowledge is merely the subjective idea of consciousness viewed objectively. The word *Jnâna* as a philosophic term has an especial connotation. It is distinguished from *samjnâna* which is awareness by contact; from *âjnâna* which is perception by receptive and central Will and implies a command from the brain; from *prajnâna* which is Wisdom, teleological will or knowledge with a purpose; and from *vijnâna* or knowledge by discrimination. *Jnâna* is knowledge direct and without the use of a medium. Brahman is absolute *Jnâna*, direct & self-existent, without beginning, middle or end, in which the Knower is also the Knowledge and the Known.

Finally, Brahman is ANANTAM, Endlessness, including all kinds of Infinity. His Infinity is of course involved in His absolute existence and consciousness, but it arises directly from His absolute bliss, since bliss, as we have seen, consists objectively in the absence of limitation. Infinity therefore is merely the subjective idea of bliss viewed objectively. It may be otherwise expressed by the word Freedom or by the word Immortality. All phenomenal things are bound by laws and limitations imposed by the triple idea of Time, Space and Causality; in Brahman alone there is absolute Freedom; for He has no beginning, middle or end in Time or Space nor, being immutable, in Causality. Regarded from the point of view of Time, Brahman is Eternity or Immortality, regarded from the point of view of Space He is Infinity or Universality, regarded from the point of view of Causality He is absolute Freedom. In one word He is ANANTAM, Endlessness, Absence of Limitation.

Chapter V

Maya: the Principle of Phenomenal Existence

Brahman then, let us suppose, has projected in Itself this luminous Shadow of Itself and has in the act (speaking always in the language of finite beings with its perpetual taint of Time, Space & Causality) begun to envisage Itself and consider Its essentialities in the light of attributes. He who is Existence, Consciousness, Bliss envisages Himself as existent, conscious, blissful. From that moment phenomenal manifestation becomes inevitable; the Unqualified chooses to regard Himself as qualified. Once this fundamental condition is granted, everything else follows by the rigorous logic of evolution; it is the one postulate which Vedanta demands. For this postulate once granted, we can see how the Absolute when it projects in itself this luminous Shadow called the Parabrahman, prepares the way for and as it were necessitates the evolution of this manifest world, — by bringing into play the great fundamental principle of Maya or Illusion. Under the play of that one principle translating itself into motion, the great transformation spoken of by the Upanishad becomes possible, — the One becomes the Many.

(But this one fundamental postulate is not easily conceded. The question which will at once spring up armed and gigantic in the European mind is the teleological objection, Why? All action implies a purpose; with what purpose did Brahman regard Himself as qualified? All Evolution is prompted by a desire, implies development, moves to an intelligible goal. What did Brahman who, being Absolute, is self-sufficing, desire, of what development did He stand in need or to what goal does He move? This is, from the teleological standpoint, the great crux of any theory of the Universe which tries to start from an essential and original Unity; a gulf is left which the intellect finds it impossible to bridge. Certain philosophies do indeed attempt to bridge it by a teleological explanation. The Absolute One, it is argued, passes through the cycle of manifestation, because He then returns to His original unity *enriched* with a new store of experiences and impressions, richer in love, richer in knowledge, richer in deed. It is truly amazing that any minds should be found which can seriously flatter themselves with the serene illusion that this is philosophy. Anything more unphilosophical, more vicious in reasoning cannot be imagined. When the Veda, speaking not of the Absolute but of Brahman Hiranyagarbha, says that He was alone and grew afraid of His loneliness, it passes, as a daring poetical fancy; and this too might pass as a poetical fancy, but not as serious reasoning. It is no more than an unreasoning recoil from the European idea of absolute, impersonal Unity as a blank and empty Negation. To avoid this appalling conclusion, an Unity is imagined which can be at the same time, not phenomenally but in its ultimate reality, manifold, teeming with myriad memories. It is difficult to understand the precise argumentation of the idea, whether the One when He has reentered His unity, preserves His experiences in detail or in the mass, say, as a pulp or essence. But at any rate several radical incoherences are in its conception. The Absolute is imaged as a thing incomplete and awaking to a sense of Its incompleteness which It proceeds in a business-like way to remedy; subject therefore to Desire and subject also to Time in which It is now contained! As to the source whence these new impressions are derived which complete the incompleteness of Brahman, that is a still greater mystery. If it was out of Himself, then it was latent in Him, already existing unknown to Himself.

One therefore presumes He produced in Himself, since there was no other place to produce them from, things which had no existence previously but now are; that which was not, became; out of nothing, something arose. This is not philosophy but theology; not reasoning, but faith. As faith it might pass; that God is omnipotent and can therefore literally create something out of nothing, is a dogma which one is at liberty to believe or reject, but it is outside the sphere of reasoning.)

There seems at first to be a fatal objection to the concession of this postulate; it seems really to evade the fundamental question of the problem of Existence or merely carry the beginning of the problem two steps farther back. For the great crux of the Universe is precisely the difficulty of understanding How and Why the One became Many, and we do not get rid of the difficulty by saying that it proceeds from the Unqualified willing to regard Himself as qualified. Even if the question How were satisfactorily met by the theory of Maya, the Why of the whole process remains. The goal of Evolution may have been determined, — it is, let us concede, the return of the Infinite upon Itself through the cycle of manifestation; but the beginning of Evolution is not accounted for, its utility is not made manifest. Why did the Absolute turn His face towards Evolution? There seems to be no possible answer to this inquiry; it is impossible to suggest any teleological reason why the Unqualified should will to look on Himself as qualified and so set the wheel of Evolution rolling, — at any rate any reason which would not be hopelessly at variance with the essential meaning of Absoluteness; and it is only an unphilosophic or imperfectly philosophic mind which can imagine that it has succeeded in the attempt. But the impossibility does not vitiate the theory of Maya; for the Vedantist parries this question of the Why with an unanswerable retort. The question itself, he says, as directed to the Brahman, is inadmissible and an impertinence. He, being Absolute, is in His very nature beyond Causality on which all ideas of need, utility, purpose depend, and to suppose purpose in Him is to question His transcendent and absolute nature: That which is beyond causality, has no need to act on a purpose. To catechise the Mighty Infinite as to why It chose to veil Its infinity in Maya, or to insist that the Universe shall choose between being utilitarian or not being at all, is absurd; it betrays a want of perfect intellectual lucidity. The question Why simply cannot arise.

But even when the question of utility is set aside, the intelligibility of the process is not established. The Unqualified willing to regard Himself as qualified is, you say, His Maya. But what is the nature of the process, intellectual or volitional, and how can an intellectual or volitional process be consistently attributed to the Absolute? — on this head at least one expects intellectual satisfaction. But the Vedantist strenuously denies the legitimacy of the expectation. If the "Will to regard" were put forward as a literal statement of a definable fact and its terms as philosophically precise, then the expectation would be justifiable. But the terms are avowedly poetical and therefore logically inadequate; they were merely intended to present the fact of Maya to the intellect in the imperfect and totally inadequate manner which is alone possible to finite speech and thought in dealing with the infinite. No intellectual or volitional process as we conceive will and intellect has really taken place. What then has happened? What is Maya? How came it into existence?

The Vedanta answers this question with its usual uncompromising candour and imperturbable clearness of thought; — we cannot tell, it says, for we do not and cannot know; at least we cannot intelligibly define; and this for the simple reason that the birth of Maya, if it had any birth, took place on the other side of phenomena, before the origin of Time, Space and Causality; and is therefore not cognizable by the intellect which can only think in terms of Time, Space and Causality. A little reflection will show that the existence of Maya is necessarily involved even in the casting of the luminous shadow called Parabrahman. A thing so far removed in the dark backward and abysm before Time, a state, force or process (call it what we will) operating directly in the Absolute Who is but cannot be thought of, may be perceived as a fact, but cannot be explained or defined. We say therefore that Maya is a thing *anirdeshyam*, impossible to define, of which we cannot say that it is, — for it is Illusion, —

and we cannot say that it is not, — for it is the Mother of the Universe; we can only infer that it is a something inherent in the being of Brahman and must therefore be not born but eternal, not in Time, but out of Time. So much arises from our premises; more it would be dishonest to pretend to know.

Still Maya is no mere assumption or its existence unprovable! Vedanta is prepared to prove that Maya is; prepared to show *what* it is, not ultimately but as involved in Parabrahman and manifested in the Universe; prepared to describe *how* it set about the work of Evolution, prepared to present Maya in terms of the intellect as a perfectly possible explanation of the entire order of the Universe; prepared even to contend that it is the only explanation perfectly consistent with the nature of being and the recognized bases of scientific and philosophical truth. It is only not prepared to represent the ultimate infinite nature and origin of Maya in precise terms comprehensible to finite mind; for to attempt philosophical impossibilities constitutes an intellectual pastime in which the Vedantist is too much attached to clear thinking to indulge.

What then is Maya? It is, intellectually envisaged, a subjective necessity involved in the very nature of Parabrahman. We have seen that Parabrahman is visible to us in the form of three subjective conceptions with three corresponding objective conceptions, which are the essentialities of His being. But Parabrahman is the Brahman as envisaged by the individual self in the act of returning to its source; Brahman externalized by His own will in the form of Maya is looking at Himself with the curtains of Maya half-lifted but not yet quite thrown back. The forms of Maya have disappeared, but the essentiality stands behind the returning Self at the entrance of the porch, and it is only when he reaches the inner end of the porch that he passes utterly out of the control of Maya. And the essentiality of Maya is to resolve Existence, Consciousness and Bliss which are really one, into three, the Unity appearing as a Trinity and the single Essentiality immediately breaking up into manifold properties or attributes. The Absolute Brahman at the inner entrance is the bright triune Parabrahman, absolute also, but cognizable; at the threshold of the porch He is Parabrahman envisaging Maya, and the next step carries Him into Maya, where Duality begins, Purusha differentiates from Prakriti, Spirit from Matter, Force from Energy, Ego from Non-Ego; and as the descent into phenomena deepens, single Purusha differentiates itself into multitudinous receptacles, single Prakriti into innumerable forms. This is the law of Maya.

But the first step, speaking in the terms of pure intellect, is the envisaging of the Essentiality as possessing Its three subjective and three objective properties, — Existence; Consciousness; Bliss: Truth; Knowledge; Infinity. The moment this happens, by inevitable necessity, the opposite attributes, Nothingness, Non-Sentience, Pain, present themselves as inseparable shadows of the three substances, and with them come the objective triad, Falsehood, Ignorance, Limitation; Limitation necessitates Divisibility, Divisibility necessitates Time and Space; Time and Space necessitate Causality; Causality, the source from which definite phenomena arise, necessitates Change. All the fundamental laws of Duality have sprung into being, necessitated in a moment by the appearance of Saguna Brahman, the Unqualified Infinite become Qualified. They do not really or ultimately exist, because they are inconsistent with the absolute nature of Parabrahman, for even in the sphere of phenomena we can rise to the truth that annihilation is an illusion and only form is destroyed; nothingness is an impossibility, and the Eternal cannot perish; nor can He become non-sentient in whose being sentience and non-sentience are one; nor can He feel pain who is infinite and without limitation. Yet these things, which we know cannot exist, must be conceived and therefore have phenomenally an existence and a reality in impermanence. For this is the paradox of Maya and her works that we cannot say they exist, because they are in reality impossible, and we cannot say they do not exist, because we must conceive them subjectively and, knowledge being now turned outward, envisage them objectively.

Surely this is to land ourselves in a metaphysical morass! But the key of the tangle is always in our hands; — it is to remember that Parabrahman is Himself only the aspect of the indefinable Absolute who is beyond Science and Nescience, Existence and Non-existence, Limitation and Infinity, and His sixfold attributes are not really six but one, not really attributes of Brahman, but in their unity Brahman Himself. It is only when we conceive of them as attributes that we are driven to regard Annihilation, Non-sentience and Limitation and their correspondings subjective or objective, as realities. But we are driven so to conceive them by something datelessly inherent in the infinite Will to live, in Brahman Himself. To leave for a moment the difficult language of metaphysics which on this dizzy verge of infinity, eludes and bewilders our giddy understanding and to use the trenchant symbolic style of the Upanishads, Parabrahman is the luminous shadow of the Absolute projected in Itself by Itself, and Maya is similarly the dark shadow projected by the Absolute in Parabrahman; both are real because eternal, but sheer reality is neither the light nor the darkness but the Thing-in-itself which they not merely like phenomena represent, but which in an inexplicable way they are. This, then, is Maya in its subjective relation to Parabrahman.

In phenomena Maya becomes objectivised in a hundred elusive forms, amid whose complex variety we long strive vainly to find the one supreme clue. The old thinkers long followed various of the main threads, but none led them to the mysterious starting point of her motions. "Then" says the Svetasvatara "they followed after concentration of Yoga and saw the Might of the Spirit of the Lord hidden deep in the modes of working of its own nature;" *Devatmashakti*, the Energy of the Divine Self, Parabrahman, is Maya; and it is in another passage stated to have two sides, obverse & reverse, Vidya and Avidya, Science and Nescience. Nescience eternally tends to envelop Science, Science eternally tends to displace Nescience. Avidya or Nescience is Parabrahman's power of creating illusions or images, things which seem but are not in themselves; Vidya or Science is His power of shaking off His own imaginations and returning upon His real and eternal Self. The action and reaction of these two great Energies doing work upon each other is the secret of Universal activity. The power of Nescience is evident on every plane of existence; for the whole Universe is a series of images. The sun rises up in the morning, mounts into the cusp of the blue Heavens and descends at evening trailing behind it clouds of glory as it disappears. Who could doubt this irrefragable, overwhelmingly evidenced fact? Every day, through myriads of years, the eyes of millions of men all over the world have borne concurrent and unvarying testimony to the truth of these splendid voyagings. Than such universal ocular testimony, what evidence can be more conclusive? Yet it all turns out to be an image created by Nescience in the field of vision. Science comes & undeterred by prison & the stake tells us that the sun never voyages through our heavens, is indeed millions of miles from our heavens, and it is we who move round the Sun, not the Sun round us. Nay those Heavens themselves, the blue firmament into which poetry and religion have read so much beauty and wonder, is itself only an *image*, in which Nescience represents our atmosphere to us in the field of vision. The light too which streams upon us from our Sun and seems to us to fill Space turns out to be no more than an image. Science now freely permitted to multiply her amazing paradoxes, forces us at last to believe that it is only motion of matter affecting us at a certain pitch of vibration with that particular impression on the brain. And so she goes on resolving all things into mere images of the great cosmic ether which alone is. Of such unsubstantialities is this marvellous fabric of visible things created! Nay, it would even appear that the more unsubstantial a thing seems, the nearer it is to ultimate reality. This, which Science proves, says the Vedantist, is precisely what is meant by Maya.

Never dream, however, that Science will end here and that we have come to the last of her unveilings. She will yet go on and tell us that the cosmic ether itself is only an image, that this universe of sensible things and things inferable from sense is only a selection of translations from a far vaster universe of forms built out of subtler matter than our senses can either show or imply to us. And when she has entered into that subtler world with fit instruments of observation and analysis, that too she will relentlessly resolve into mere images of the subtler ether out of which it is born. Behind that subtler universe also there looms a profounder and vaster, but simpler state of existence where there is only the undetermined universality of things as yet involved in their causes. Here Science must come to her latest dealings with matter and show us that this indeterminate universality of things is after all only an image of something in our own self. Meanwhile with that very self she is busy, continually and potently trying to persuade us that all which we believe to be ourselves, all in which our Nescience would have us contentedly dwell, is mere imagery and form. The animal in us insists that this body is the real Self and the satisfaction of its needs our primal duty; but Science (of whom Prof. Haeckel's Riddle of the Universe is not the concluding utterance) bids us beware of identifying our Self with a mere mass of primitive animal forms associated together by an aggregating nucleus of vital impulses; this surely is not the reality of Shakespeare & Newton, Buddha & St Francis! Then in those vital impulses we seek the bedrock of our being. But these too Science resolves into a delusion or image created by Nescience; for in reality these vital impulses have no existence by themselves but are merely the link established between that material aggregation of animal forms and something within us which we call Mind. Mind too she will not permit us long to mistake for anything more than an image created by the interaction of sensations and response to sensations between the material aggregation of the body and something that governs and informs the material system. This governing power in its action upon mind reveals itself in the discriminating, selecting, ordering and purposeful entity called by Vedanta the Buddhi, of which reason is only one aspect, intellect only one image. Buddhi also turns out eventually to be no entity, only an image, and Science must end by showing us that body, vitality, mind, buddhi are all images of what Philosophy calls Ananda, the pleasure of existence or Will to live; and she reveals to us at last that although this Will divides itself into innumerable forms which represent themselves as individual selves, yet all these are images of one great Cosmic Will to live, just as all material forms are merely images of one great undifferentiated Universality of cosmic matter, causal ether, if we so choose to describe it. That Will is Purusha, that Universality is Prakriti; and both are but images of Parabrahman.

So, very briefly and inadequately stated in some of its main principles, runs the Vedantic theory of Maya, for which analytic Science is, without quite knowing it, multiplying a stupendous mass of evidence. Every fresh certainty which this Science adds, swells the mass, and it is only where she is incomplete and therefore should be agnostic, that Vedanta finds no assistance from her analysis. The completion of Science means the final conquest over Nescience and the unveiling of Maya.

Chapter VI

Maya; the Energy of the Absolute

Maya then is the fundamental fact in the Universe, her dualistic system of balanced pairs of opposites is a necessity of intellectual conception; but the possibility of her existence as an inherent energy in the Absolute, outside phenomena, has yet to be established. So long as Science is incomplete and Yoga a secret discipline for the few, the insistent questions of the metaphysician can never be ignored, nor his method grow obsolete. The confident and even arrogant attempt of experimental Science to monopolise the kingdom of Mind, to the exclusion of the metaphysical and all other methods, was a rash and premature aggression, — rash because premature; successful at first its victorious usurping onrush is beginning to stagger and fail, even to lose hold on positions once thought to be permanently secured. The slow resurgence of metaphysics has already begun. Certainly, no metaphysic can be admissible which does not take count of the standards and undoubted results of Science; but until experimental analysis has solved the whole mystery of the Universe, not by speculation through logic (a method stolen from metaphysics with which Science has no business) but by experimental proof and hypotheses checked & confirmed by experimental proof, leaving no phenomenon unaccounted for and no fact ignored, — until then metaphysics must reign where analytic experiment leaves a void. Vedanta, though it bases itself chiefly on the subjective experimental methods of Yoga and admits no metaphysical hypothesis as valid which is not in agreement with its results, is yet willing to submit its own conclusions to the tests of metaphysical logic. The Vedantic Yogin shrinks at present, because of certain moral scruples, from divulging his arcana to the crowd, but he recognises that so long as he refuses, he has no right to evade the inquisition of the metaphysical logician. Atharvan & Svetasvatara having spoken, Shankara and Ramanuja must be allowed their arena of verbal discussion.

The metaphysical question involved turns upon the nature of Avidya, Nescience, and its possibility in Parabrahman who is, after all, absolute, — Absolute Consciousness and therefore Absolute Knowledge. It is not sound to say that Parabrahman envisaging Maya, *becomes* capable of Avidya; for envisagement of Maya is simply a metaphorical expression for Avidya itself. Neither can the Vedantist take refuge in the theologian's evasion of reason by an appeal to lawless Omnipotence, to the Credo quia Impossibile. The Eternal is undoubtedly in His own nature free and unlimited, but, as undoubtedly, He has deliberately bound Himself in His relation to phenomena by certain fundamental principles; He has willed that certain things shall not and cannot be, and to use a human parallel He is like a King who having promulgated a certain code is as much bound by his own laws as the meanest subject, or like a poet whose imaginations in themselves free, are limited by laws the moment they begin to take shape. We may say, theoretically, that God being Omnipotent can create something out of nothing, but so long as no single clear instance can be given of a something created out of nothing, the rule of ex nihilo nihil fit remains an universal and fundamental law and to suppose that God has based the Universe on a violation of a fundamental law of the Universe, is to kick Reason out of the house and slam the door against her return. Similarly, if the coexistence of Avidya with Vidya in the same field and as it were interpenetrating each other, is against the Law, it does by that very fact become impossible and the theory of Maya will then be proved an error; no appeal to Omnipotence will save it.

The objection to Avidya may be stated thus that Absolute Knowledge cannot at the same time not know, cannot imagine a thing to be real which is not real; for such imagination involves an element of self-deception, and self-deception is not possible in the Absolute. But is it really a law of consciousness — for there lies the point — that things can in no sense be at the same time real and unreal, that you cannot by any possibility imagine things to be real which *at the same time* you know perfectly well to be unreal? The dualist objector may contend that this impossibility is a law of consciousness. The Vedantin replies at once, Negatur, your statement is refuted by a host of examples; it is inconsistent with universal experience. The most utter and avowed unrealities can be and are firmly imagined as realities, seen as realities, sensed as realities, conceived as realities without the mind for a moment admitting that they are indeed real. The mirage of the desert we know after a time to be unreal, but even then we see & firmly image it as a reality, admire the green beauty of those trees and pant for the cool shining delight of those waters. We see dreams and dreams are unrealities, and yet some of them at least are at the same time not positive unrealities, for they image, and sometimes very exactly, events which have happened, are happening or will happen in the future. We see the juggler throw a rope in the air, climb up it, kill the boy who has preceded him and throw down his bleeding limbs piecemeal on the earth; every detail and circumstance of the unreal event corresponding to the event as it would have been, were it real; we do not imagine it to be unreal while it lasts, and we cannot so imagine it; for the visualisation is too clear & consistent, the feelings it awakes in us are too vivid, and yet all the time we perfectly well know that no such thing is happening. Instances of this sort are not easily numbered.

But these are distant, unimmediate things, and for some of them the evidence may not be considered ample. Let us come nearer to our daily life. We see a stone and we note its properties of solidity and immobility, nor can we by any persuasion be induced to imagine it as anything else but solid and immobile; and we are right, for it is both: and yet we know that its immobility and solidity are not real, that it is, and to a vision sensible of the infinitesimal would appear, a world of the most active motion, of myriads of atoms *with spaces between them*. Again, if there is one thing that is real to me, it is this, that I am vertical and upright, whatever the people at the Antipodes may be and that I walk in all directions horizontally along the earth; and yet alas! I know that I am in reality not vertical but nearer the horizontal, walking often vertically up and down the earth, like a fly on the wall. I know it perfectly, yet if I were constantly to translate my knowledge into imagination, a padded room in Bedlam would soon be the only place for me. This is indeed the singular and amazing law of our consciousness that it is perfectly capable of holding two contradictory conceptions at the same time and with equal strength. We accept the knowledge which Science places at our disposal, but we perpetually act upon the images which Nescience creates. I know that the sun does not rise or set, does not move round the earth, does not sail through the heavens marking the time of day as it proceeds, but in my daily life I act precisely on the supposition that this unreality really happens; I hourly and momently conceive it and firmly image it as real and sometimes regulate on it my every movement. The eternal belligerents, Science and Nescience, have come in this matter of the sun's motion, as in so many others, to a working compromise. To me as an untrammelled Will to live who by the subtle intellectual part of me, can wander through Eternity and place myself as a spectator in the centre of the sun or even outside the material Universe the better to observe its motions, the phenomenon of the earth's movement round the sun is the reality, and even Nescience consents that I shall work on it as an acknowledged fact in the operations of pure intellect; but to me as a trammelled body unable to leave the earth and bound down in my daily life to the ministry of my senses, the phenomenon of the sun's movement round the earth is the reality and to translate my intellectual knowledge into the stuff of my daily imaginations would be intolerably inconvenient; it would take my secure resting-place, the earth, from under my feet and make havoc of my life in sensation; even Science therefore consents that I shall work on the evidence of my senses as an acknowledged fact in my material life of earth-bounded existence. In this duplicity of standpoint we see as in a glass darkly some image of the manner in which the Absolute wills to be phenomenally conditioned; at once knows perfectly what is, yet chooses to image what is not, having infinite Science, yet makes room for self-limiting Nescience. It is not necessary to labour the point, or to range through all scientific knowledge for instances; in the light of modern knowledge the objection to the coexistence of Vidya & Avidya cannot stand; it is a perpetual fact in the daily economy of Consciousness.

Yes, it may be argued, but this does not establish it as anything more than a possibility in regard to the Absolute. A state of things true throughout the range of phenomenal existence, may cease to operate at the point where phenomena themselves cease. The possibility, however, once granted, Vedanta is entitled to put forward Maya as the one successful explanation yet advanced of this manifold existence; first, because Maya does explain the whole of existence metaphysically and is at the same time an universal, scientifically observable fact ranging through the whole Universe and fundamentally present in every operation of Consciousness; secondly, because it does transcend phenomena as well as inform them, it has its absolute as well as its conditioned state and is therefore not only possible in the Absolute but must be the Absolute Himself in manifestation; and thirdly, because no other possible explanation can logically contain *both* the truth of sheer transcendent Absoluteness of the Brahman and the palpable, imperative existence of the phenomenal Universe.[4] Illogical theories, theories which part company with reason, theories which, instead of basing themselves in observed laws,

---

[4] Of course I am not prepared, in these limits, to develop the final argument; that would imply a detailed examination of all metaphysical systems, which would be in itself the labour of a lifetime.

take their stand in the void, may be had in plenty. Maya is no theory but a fact; no mere result of logic or speculation, but of careful observation, and yet unassailable by logic and unsurpassable by speculation.

One of the most remarkable manifestations of Avidya in human consciousness, presenting in its nature and laws of working a close analogy to its parent is the power of imagination, — the power of bodying forth images which may either be reabsorbed into the individual consciousness which gave them forth or outlast it. Of the latter kind poetical creation is a salient example. At a certain time in a certain country one named Shakespeare created a new world by the force of his Avidya, his faculty of imagining what is not. That world is as real and unreal today as it was when Shakespeare created it or in more accurate Vedantic language *asrijata*, loosed it forth from the causal world within him. Within the limits of that world Iago is real to Othello, Othello to Desdemona, and all are real to any and every consciousness which can for a time abstract itself from this world [of] its self-created surroundings and enter the world of Shakespeare. We are aware of them, observe them, grow in knowledge about them, see them act, hear them speak, feel for their griefs and sorrows; and even when we return to our own world, they do not always leave us, but sometimes come with us and influence our actions. The astonishing power of poetical creation towards moulding life and history, has not yet been sufficiently observed; yet it was after all Achilles, the swift-footed son of Peleus, who thundered through Asia at the head of his legions, dragged Batis at his chariot-wheels and hurled the Iranian to his fall, — Achilles, the son of Peleus, who never lived except as an image, — nay, does not omniscient learning tell us, that even his creator never lived, or was only a haphazard assortment of poets who somehow got themselves collectively nicknamed Homer! Yet these images, which we envisage as real and confess by our words, thoughts, feelings, and sometimes even by our actions to be real, are, all the time and we know them perfectly well to be as mythical as the dream, the mirage and the juggler on his rope. There is no Othello, no Iago, no Desdemona but all these are merely varieties

of name & form, not of Shakespeare, but in which Shakespeare
is immanent and which still exist merely because Shakespeare is
immanent in them. Nevertheless he who best succeeds in imaging
forth these children of illusion, this strange harmonic Maya, is
ever adjudged by us to be the best poet, Creator or Maker,
even though others may link words more sweetly together or
dovetail incidents more deftly. The parallel between this work
of imagination and the creation of phenomena and no less between the relation of the author to his creatures and the relation
of the Conditioned Brahman to His creatures is astonishingly
close in most of their details no less than in their general nature.
Observe for instance that in all that multitude of figures vicious
& virtuous, wise and foolish, he their creator who gave them
forth, their Self and reality without whom they cannot exist, is
unaffected by their crimes and virtues, irresponsible and free.
The Lord [*sentence left incomplete*]

What then? Is this analogy anything more than poetic fancy,
or is not after all, the whole idea of Brahman and Maya itself
a mere poetic fancy? Perhaps, but not more fanciful or unreal,
in that case, than the Universe itself and its motions; for the
principle & working of the two are identical.

Let us ask ourselves, what it is that has happened when a
great work of creation takes place and how it is that Shakespeare's creatures are still living to us, now that Shakespeare
himself is dead and turned to clay. Singular indeed that Shakespeare's creations should be immortal and Shakespeare himself a
mere shortlived conglomeration of protoplasmic cells! We notice
first that Shakespeare's dramatic creatures are only a selection
or anthology from among the teeming images which peopled
that wonderful mind; there were thousands of pictures in that
gallery which were never produced for the admiration of the
ages. This is a truth to which every creator whether he use stone
or colour or words for his thought-symbols will bear emphatic
testimony. There was therefore a subtler and vaster world in
Shakespeare than the world we know him to have bodied forth
into tangible material of literature. Secondly we note that all
these imaginations already existed in Shakespeare unmanifested

and unformed before they took shape and body; for certainly they did not come from outside. Shakespeare took his materials from this legend or that play, this chronicle or that history? His framework possibly, but not his creations; Hamlet did not come from the legend or the play, nor Cassius or King Henry from the history or the chronicle. No, Shakespeare contained in himself all his creatures, and therefore transcended & exceeded them; he was and is more than they or even than their sum and total; for they are merely limited manifestations of him under the conditions of time & space, and he would have been the same Shakespeare, even if we had not a scene or a line of him to know him by; only the world of imagination would have remained latent in him instead of manifest, *avyakta* instead of *vyakta*. Once manifest, his creatures are preserved immortally, not by print or manuscript, for the Veda has survived thousands of years without print or manuscript, — but, by words, shall we say? no, for words or sounds are only the physical substance, the atoms out of which their shapes are built, and can be entirely rearranged, — by translation, for example — without our losing Othello and Desdemona, just as the indwelling soul can take a new body without being necessarily changed by the transmigration. Othello and Desdemona are embodied in sounds or words, but thought is their finer and immortal substance. It is the subtler world of thought in Shakespeare from which they have been selected and bodied forth in sounds, and into the world of thought they originally proceeded from a reservoir of life deeper than thought itself, from an ocean of being which our analysis has not yet fathomed.

Now, let us translate these facts into the conceptions of Vedanta. Parabrahman self-limited in the name and form of Shakespeare, dwells deepest in him invisible to consciousness, as the unmanifest world of that something more elemental than thought (may it not be causal, elemental Will?), in which Shakespeare's imaginations lie as yet unformed and undifferentiated; then he comes to a surface of consciousness visible to Shakespeare as the inwardly manifest world of subtle matter or thought in which those imaginations take subtle thought-shapes

& throng; finally, he rises to a surface of consciousness visible to others besides Shakespeare as the outwardly manifest world, manifest in sound, in which a select number of these imaginations are revealed to universal view. These mighty images live immortally in our minds because Parabrahman in Shakespeare is the same as Parabrahman in ourselves; and because Shakespeare's thought is, therefore, water of the same etheric ocean as that which flows through our brains. Thought, in fact, is one, although to be revealed to us, it has to be bodied forth and take separate shapes in sound forms which we are accustomed to perceive and understand. Brahman-Brahma as Thought Creative in Shakespeare brings them forth, Brahman-Vishnu as Thought Preservative in us maintains them, Brahman-Rudra as Thought Destructive or Oblivion will one day destroy them; but in all these operations Brahman is one, Thought is one, even as all the Oceans are one. Shakespeare's world is in every way a parable of ours. There is, however, a distinction — Shakespeare could not body forth his images into forms palpable in gross matter either because, as other religions believe, that power is denied to man, [or] because, as Vedantism suggests, mankind has not risen as yet to that pitch of creative force.

There is one class of phenomena however in which this defect of identity between individual Imagination and universal Avidya seems to be filled up. The mind can create under certain circumstances images surviving its own dissolution or departure, which do take some kind of form in gross matter or at least matter palpable to the gross senses. For the phenomena of apparition there is an accumulating mass of evidence. Orthodox Science prefers to ignore the evidence, declines to believe that a prima facie case has been made out for investigation and shuts the gate on farther knowledge with a triple polysyllabic key, mysticism, coincidence, hallucination. Nevertheless, investigated or not, the phenomena persist in occurring! Hauntings, for example, for which there are only scattered indications in Europe, are in India, owing to the more strenuous psychical force and more subtle psychical sensitiveness of our physical organisation, fairly common. In these hauntings we have a signal instance of the triumph of imagination. In the majority of cases they are images created by dying or doomed men in their agony which survive the creator, some of them visible, some audible, some both visible and audible, and in rare cases in an unearthly, insufficient, but by no means inefficient manner, palpable. The process of their creation is in essence the same as attends the creation of poetry or the creation of the world; it is *tapas* or *tapasya*, — not penance as English scholars will strangely insist on translating it, but HEAT, a tremendous concentration of will, which sets the whole being in a flame, masses all the faculties in closed ranks and hurls them furiously on a single objective. By *tapas* the world was created; by *tapas*, says the Moondaca, creative Brahman is piled up, *chiyate*, gathered & intensified; by *tapas* the rush of inspiration is effected. This *tapas* may be on the material plane associated with purpose or entirely dissociated from purpose. In the case of intense horror or grief, fierce agony or terrible excitement on the verge of death it is totally dissociated from any material purpose, it is what would be ordinarily called involuntary, but it receives from its origin an intensity so unparalleled as to create living images of itself which remain & act long after the source has been dissolved or stilled by death. Such is the ultimate power of imagination, though at present it cannot be fully used on the material plane except in a random, fortuitous and totally unpurposed manner.

In the manner of its working, then, Imagination is a carefully executed replica of Avidya; and if other marks of her essential identity with Avidya are needed, they can be found. Both are, for instance, preponderatingly purposeless. The workings of imagination are often totally dissociated, on the material plane at least, from any intelligible purpose and though it is quite possible that the latent part of our consciousness which works below the surface, may have sometimes a purpose of which the superficial part is not aware, yet in the most ordinary workings of Imagination, an absolute purposelessness is surely evident. Certainly, if not purposelessness there is colossal waste. A few hundreds of images were selected from Shakespeare's mind for a definite artistic purpose, but the thousands that never found verbal expression, many of them with as splendid potentialities as those which did materialize in Hamlet and Macbeth seem to have risen & perished without any useful purpose. The same wastefulness is shown by Nature in her works; how many millions of lives does she not shower forth that a few may be selected for the purposes of evolution! Yet when she chooses to work economically and with set purpose, she like Imagination can become a scrupulous miser of effort and show herself possessed of a magical swiftness and sureness in shaping the means to the end. Neither Nature nor Imagination, therefore, can be supposed to be blind, random energies proceeding from an ungoverned force and teleological only by accident. Their operations are obviously guided by an Intelligence as perfectly capable, when it so wills, of purposing, planning, fitting its means to its ends, economising its materials and labour as any intelligent and careful workman in these days of science and method. We need therefore some explanation why this great universal Intelligence should not be, as a careful workman, always, not occasionally, economical of its materials and labour. Is not the truth this that Nature is not universally and in all her works teleological, that purpose is only one minor part of existence more concentrated than most and therefore more intense and triumphant, while for the greater part of her universal operation we must find another explanation than the teleological? or rather [one that] will at once contain and exceed the teleological? If it had only been Shakespeare, Michelangelo, Edison, Beethoven, Napoleon, Schopenhauer, the creators in poetry, art, science, music, life or thought, who possessed imagination, we might then have found an use for their unused imaginations in the greater preparatory richness they gave to the soil from which a few exquisite flowers were to spring. The explanation might not be a good one, little more indeed than a poetical fancy, but it could have passed for want of a better. But every human being possesses the divine faculty, more or less developed; every mind is a teeming world of imaginations; and indeed, imagination for imagination the opium-smoker's is more vivid, fertile and gorgeous than Shakespeare's. Yet hardly in one case out of a thousand are these imaginations of use to the world or anything but a practical hindrance or at best a purposeless pastime to the dreamer. Imagination is a fundamental energy of consciousness, and this marvellous, indomitable energy works on without caring whether she is put to use or misuse or no use at all; she exists merely for the sake of delight in her own existence. Here I think we touch bottom. Imagination is outside purpose, sometimes above, sometimes below it, sometimes united with it, because she is an inherent energy not of some great teleological Master-Workman, but of Ananda, the Bliss of existence or Will to live, and beyond this delight in existence she has no reason for being. In the same way Maya, the infinite creative energy which peoples the phenomenal Universe, is really some force inherent in the infinite Will to be; and it is for this reason that her operations seem so wasteful from the standpoint of utilitarian economy; for she cares nothing about utilitarianism or economy and is only obeying her fundamental impulse towards phenomenal existence, consciousness, and the pleasure of conscious existence. So far as she has a purpose, it is this, and all the teleologic element in Nature has simply this end, to find more perfect surroundings or more exquisite means or wider opportunities or a grander gust and scope for the pleasure of conscious phenomenal existence. Yet the deepest bliss is after all that which she left and to which she will return, not the broken and pain-bounded bliss of finite life, but the perfect and infinite Bliss of transcendent undivided and illimitable consciousness. She seeks for a while to find perfect bliss by finite means and in finite things, the heaven of the socialist or anarchist, the heaven of the artist, the heaven of knowledge, the heaven of thought, or a heaven in some other world; but one day she realises that great truth, "The Kingdom of Heaven is within you," and to that after all she returns. *This* is Maya.

One metaphysical test remains to be satisfied before we can be sure that Avidya and Vidya, the outcurve and incurve of Maya, go back to something eternally existent in the Absolute and are not created by phenomenal causes. If inherent in the Absolute, Maya must culminate in conceptions that are themselves absolute, infinite and unconditioned. Vidya tapers off into infinity in the conceptions, SAT or Pure Existence, CHIT or Pure Consciousness, ANANDA or Pure Bliss; Avidya rises at her apex into ASAT, Nothingness, ACHETANAM, Non-sentience, NIRANAN-DAM, Blisslessness or Misery. Nothingness & Non-sentience are certainly absolute conceptions, infinite and unconditioned; but the third term of the negative Trinity gives us pause. Absolute pain, blank infinite unconditioned and unrelieved Misery is a conception which Reason shies at and Consciousness refuses, violently refuses to admit as a possibility. A cypher if you like to make metaphysical calculations with, but by itself sheer nought, nowhere discoverable as existing or capable of existence. Yet if infinite misery could be, it would in the very act of being merge into Nothingness, it would lose its name in the very moment of becoming absolute. As a metaphysical conception we may then admit Absolute Blisslessness as a valid third term of the negative Trinity, not as a real or possible state, for no one of the three is a real or possible state. The unreality comes home to us most in the third term, just as reality comes home to us most in the third term of the positive Trinity, because Bliss and its negative blisslessness appeal to us on the material plane vividly and sensibly; the others touch us more indirectly, on the psychic & causal planes. Yet the Nothingness of nothingness is taught us by Science, and the unreality of non-sentience will become clear when the nature of sentience is better understood.

It will be said that the escape from pleasure as well as pain is after all the common goal of Buddhism & Vedanta. True, escape from limited pleasure which involves pain, escape from pain which is nothing but the limitation of pleasure. Both really seek absolute absence of limitation which is not a negative condition, but a positive, infinity and its unspeakable, unmixed bliss; their escape from individuality does not lead them into nothingness, but into infinite existence, their escape from sensation does not purpose the annihilation of sentience but pure absolute consciousness as its goal. Not ASAD ACHETANAM NIRANANDAM, but SACCHIDANANDAM is the great Reality to which Jivatman rises to envisage, the TAT or sole Thing-in-itself to whom by the force of Vidya he tends ever to return.

Chapter VII

The Triple Brahman

Parabrahman is now on the way to phenomenal manifestation; the Absolute Shakespeare of Existence, the infinite *Kavi*, Thinker & Poet, is, by the mere existence of the eternal creative force Maya, about to shadow forth a world of living realities out of Himself which have yet no independent existence. He becomes phenomenally a Creator & Container of the Universe, though really He is what He ever was, absolute and unchanged. To understand why and how the Universe appears what it is, we have deliberately to abandon our scientific standpoint of transcendental knowledge and speaking the language of Nescience, represent the Absolute as limiting Itself, the One becoming the Many, the pure ultra-Spiritual unrefining Itself into the mental and material. We are like the modern astrologer who, knowing perfectly well that the earth moves round the sun, must yet persist in speaking of the Sun as moving and standing in this part of the heavens or that other, because he has to do with the relative *positions* of the Sun and planets with regard to men living in the earth and not with the ultimate astronomical realities.

From this point of view we have to begin with a dualism of the thing and its shadow, Purusha & Prakriti, commonly called spirit and matter. Properly speaking, the distinction is illusory, since there is nothing which is exclusively spirit or exclusively matter, nor can the Universe be strictly parcelled out between these; from the point of view of Reality spirit and matter are not different but the same. We may say, if we like, that the entire Universe is matter and spirit does not exist; we may say, if we like, that the entire Universe is spirit and matter does not exist. In either case we are merely multiplying words without counsel, ignoring the patent fact visible throughout the Universe that both spirit and matter exist and are indissolubly welded, precisely because they are simply one thing viewed from two sides. The distinction between them is one of the primary dualisms and a first result of the great Ignorance. Maya works out in name and form as material; Maya works out in the conceiver of name and form as spiritual. Purusha is the great principle or force whose presence is necessary to awake creative energy and send it out working into and on shapes of matter. For this reason Purusha is the name usually applied to the Conditioned Brahman in His manifestations; but it is always well to remember that the Primal Existence turned towards manifestation has a double aspect, Male and Female, positive and negative; He is the origin of the birth of things and He is the receptacle of the birth and it is to the Male aspect of Himself that the word Purusha predominatingly applies. The image often applied to these relations is that of the man casting his seed into the woman; his duty is merely to originate the seed and deposit it, but it is the woman's duty to cherish the seed, develop it, bring it forth and start it on its career of manifested life. The seed, says the Upanishad, is the self of the Male, it is spirit, and being cast into the Female, Prakriti, it becomes one with her and therefore does her no hurt; spirit takes the shaping appearance of matter and does not break up the appearances of matter, but develops under their law. The Man and the Woman, universal Adam and Eve, are really one and each is incomplete without the other, barren without the other, inactive without the other. Purusha the Male, God, is that side of the One which gives the impulse towards phenomenal existence; Prakriti the Female, Nature, is that side which is and evolves the material of phenomenal existence; both of them are therefore unborn & eternal. The Male is Purusha, he who lurks in the Wide; the Female is Prakriti, the working of the Male, and sometimes called Rayi, the universal movement emanating from the quiescent Male. Purusha is therefore imaged as the Enjoyer, Prakriti as the enjoyed; Purusha as the Witness, Prakriti as the phenomena he witnesses; Purusha as the *getter* or father of things, Prakriti as their *bearer* or mother. And there are many other images the Upanishad employs, Purusha, for instance, symbolising Himself in the Sun, the father of life, and Prakriti in the Earth, the bearer of life. It is necessary thus clearly to define Purusha from the first in order to avoid confusion in endeavouring to grasp the development of Maya as the Upanishads describe it.

Parabrahman in the course of evolving phenomena enters into three states or conditions which are called in one passage his three habitations and, by a still more suggestive figure, his three states of dream. The first condition is called *avyakta*, the state previous to manifestation, in which all things are involved, but in which nothing is expressed or imaged, the state of ideality, undifferentiated but pregnant of differentiation, just as the seed is pregnant of the bark, sap, pith, fibre, leaf, fruit and flower and all else that unites to make the conception of a tree; just as the protoplasm is pregnant of all the extraordinary variations of animal life. It is, in its objective aspect, the seed-state of things. The objective possibility, and indeed necessity of such a condition of the whole Universe, cannot be denied; for this is the invariable method of development which the operations of Nature show to us. Evolution does not mean that out of protoplasm as a material so many organisms have been created or added by an outside power, but that they have been developed out of the protoplasm; and if developed, they were already there existent, and have been manifested by some power dwelling and working in the protoplasm itself. But open up the protoplasm, as you will, you will not find in it the rudiments of the organs and organisms it will hereafter develop. So also though the protoplasm and everything else is evolved out of ether, yet no symptom of them would yield themselves up to an analytical research into ether. The organs and organisms are in the protoplasm, the leaf, flower, fruit in the seed and all forms in the ether from which they evolve, in an undifferentiated condition and therefore defy the method of analysis which is confined to the discovery of differences. This is the state called involution. So also ether itself, gross or subtle, and all that evolves from ether is involved in Avyakta; they are present but they can never be discovered there because there [they] are undifferentiated. Plato's world of ideas is a confused attempt to arrive at this condition of things, confused because it unites two incompatible things, the conditions of Avyakta and those of the next state presided over by Hiranyagarbha.

The question then arises, what is the subjective aspect of

Parabrahman in the state of Avyakta? The organs and organisms are evolved out of protoplasm and forms out of ether by a power which resides and works in them, and that power must be intelligent consciousness unmanifested; *must*, because it is obviously a power that can plan, arrange and suit means to ends; *must* because otherwise the law of subtler involving grosser cannot obtain. If matter is all, then from the point of view of matter, the gross is more real because more palpable than the subtle and unreality cannot develop reality; it is intelligent consciousness and nothing else we know of that not only has the power of containing at one and the same time the gross & the subtle, but does consistently proceed in its method of creation or evolution from vagueness to precision, from no-form to form and from simple form to complex form. If the discoveries of Science mean anything and are not a chaos, an illusion or a chimaera, they can only mean the existence of an intelligent consciousness present and working in all things. Parabrahman therefore is present subjectively even in the condition of Avyakta no less than in the other conditions as intelligent consciousness and therefore as bliss.

For the rest, we are driven to the use of metaphors, and since metaphors must be used, one will do as well as another, for none can be entirely applicable. Let us then image Avyakta as an egg, the golden egg of the Puranas, full of the waters of undifferentiated existence and divided into two halves, the upper or luminous half filled with the upper waters of subjective ideation, the lower or tenebrous half with the lower waters of objective ideation. In the upper half Purusha is concealed as the final cause of things; it is there that is formed the idea of undifferentiated, eternal, infinite, universal Spirit. In the lower half he is concealed as Prakriti, the material cause of things; it is there that is formed the idea of undifferentiated, eternal, infinite, universal matter, with the implications Time, Space and Causality involved in its infinity. It is represented mythologically by Vishnu on the causal Ocean sitting on the hood of Ananta, the infinite snake whose endless folds are Time, and are also Space and are also Causality, these three being fundamentally one, — a Trinity. In the upper half Parabrahman is still utterly Himself, but with a Janus face, one side contemplating the Absolute Reality which He *is*, the other envisaging Maya, looking on the endless procession of her works not yet as a reality, but as a phantasmagoria. In the lower half, if we may use a daring metaphor, Parabrahman forgets Himself. He is subjectively in the state corresponding to utter sleep or trance from which when a man awakes he can only realise that he was and that he was in a state of bliss resulting from the complete absence of limitation; that he was conscious in that state, follows from his realisation of blissful existence, but the consciousness is not a part of his realisation. This concealment of Consciousness is a characteristic of the seed-state of things and it is what is meant by saying that when Parabrahman enters into matter as Prakriti, He forgets Himself.

Of such a condition, the realisations of consciousness do not return to us, we can have no particular information. The Yogin passes through it on his way to the Eternal, but he hastens to this goal and does not linger in it; not only so, but absorption in this stage is greatly dreaded except as a temporary necessity; for if the soul finally leaves the body in that condition, it must recommence the cycle of evolution all over again; for it has identified itself with the seed state of things and must follow the nature of Avyakta which is to start on the motions of Evolution by the regular order of universal manifestation. This absorption is called the Prakriti laya or absorption in Prakriti. The Yogin can enter into this state of complete Nescience or Avidya and remain there for centuries, but if by any chance his body is preserved and he returns to it, he brings nothing back to the store of our knowledge on this side of Avyakta.

Parabrahman in the state of Avyakta Purusha is known as Prâjna, the Master of Prajnâ, Eternal Wisdom or Providence, for it is here that He orders and marshals before Himself like a great poet planning a wonderful masterpiece in his mind, the eternal laws of existence and the unending procession of the worlds. Vidya and Avidya are here perfectly balanced, the former still and quiescent though comprehensive, the latter not yet at active work, waiting for the command, Let there be darkness. And then the veil of darkness, Vidya seems to be in abeyance, and from the disturbance of the balance results inequality; then out of the darkness Eternal Wisdom streams forth to its task of creation and Hiranyagarbha, the Golden Child, is born.

An Incomplete Work of Vedantic Exegesis

Book II

The Nature of God

Chapter I

The view of cosmic evolution which has been set forth in the first book of this exegesis,[1] may seem deficient to the ordinary religious consciousness which is limited & enslaved by its creeds and to which its particular way of worship is a master and not a servant, because it leaves no room for a "Personal" God. The idea of a Personal God is, however, a contradiction in terms. God is Universal, he is Omnipresent, Infinite, not subject to limits. This all religions confess, but the next moment they nullify their confession by assuming in Him a Personality. The Universal cannot be personal, the Omnipresent cannot be excluded from any thing or creature in the world He universally pervades and possesses. The moment we attribute certain qualities to God, we limit Him and create a double principle in the world. Yet no religion[2]

Brahman, we have seen, is the Universal Consciousness which Is and delights in Being; impersonal, infinite, eternal, omnipresent, sole-existing, the One than whom there is no other, and all things and creatures have only a phenomenal existence [in] Brahman and by Brahman.

In the Vedantic theory of this Universe and its view of the nature of the Brahman and Its relations to the phenomena that make up this Universe, there is one initial paradox from which the

---

[1] *This first book was not written or has not survived. — Ed.*
[2] *After this incomplete sentence, the rest of the notebook page was left blank. — Ed.*

whole Vedantic philosophy, religion and ethics take their start. We have seen that in existence as we see it there is Something that is eternal, immutable and one, to which we give the name of Brahman, amidst an infinite deal that is transient, mutable and multifold. Brahman as the eternal, immutable and one, is not manifest but latent; It supports, contains and pervades the changing & unstable Universe and gives it eternity as a whole in spite [of the] transience of its parts, unity as a whole in spite of the multiplicity of its parts, immutability as a whole in spite of the mutability of its parts. Without It the persistence of the Universe would be inexplicable, but itself is not visible, nameable or definable except as Sacchidanandam, absolute and therefore unnameable and indefinable self-existence, self-awareness, self-bliss. But when we ask what is it then which is mutable, transient, multiple, and whether this is something other than and different from Brahman, we get the reply that this also is Brahman and that there can be nothing other than Brahman, because Brahman is the One without a second, ekamevadwitiyam. This one, eternal, immutable became the many who are transient and mutable, but this becoming is not real, only phenomenal. Just as all objects & substances are phenomena of and in the single, eternal & unchanging ether, so are all existences animate or inanimate, corporeal, psychical or spiritual phenomena of and in Brahman. This phenomenal change of the One into the Many, the Eternal into the perishable, the Immutable into the everchanging, is a supreme paradox but a paradox which all scientific investigation shows to be the one fundamental fact of the Universe. Science considers the One eternal & permanent reality to be eternal Matter, Vedanta for reasons already stated holds it to be eternal Consciousness of which Spirit-Matter are in phenomena the positive-negative aspects. This Brahman, this Sacchidanandam, this eternal Consciousness unknowable, unnameable and indefinable, which reason cannot analyse, nor imagination put into any shape, nor the mind and senses draw within their jurisdiction, is the Transcendent Reality which alone truly exists. The sole existence of this Turiya Brahman or Transcendent Eternal Consciousness is the basis of the Adwaita philosophy.

But where in all this is there any room for religion, for the spirit of man, for any idea of God? Who is the Lord, Isha, Maheshwar, Vishnu, Rudra, Indra, the Lord of the Illusion, the Ruler, the Mighty One of which all the Upanishads speak? Who is this triple Prajna-Hiranyagarbha-Virat? Who is this twofold Purusha-Prakriti, God & Nature, without which the existence of the phenomenal world and consciousness in matter would not be intelligible or conceivable? To whom does the Bhakti of the Bhakta, to whom do the works of the Karmayogin direct themselves? Why and Whom do men worship? What is it to which the human self rises in Yoga? The answer is that this also is Brahman, — Brahman not in His absolute Self but in relation to the infinite play of multiplicity, mobility, mortality which He has phenomenally created for His own delight on the surface of His really eternal immutable & single existence. Above is the eternal surge, the innumerable laughters of the million-crested, multitudinous, ever-marching, ever-shifting wilderness of waves; below is the silent, motionless, unchanging rest of the Ocean's immeasurable and unvisited depths. The rest and immobility is the Sea, and the mutable stir and motion of the waves is also the Sea, and as the Sea is to its waves, so is Brahman to His creation. What is the relation of the Sea of Brahman to its waves? Brahman is the One Self and all the rest, innumerable souls of creatures and innumerable forms of things are His Maya, illusions which cannot be eternal and therefore cannot be true, because there is only One Eternal; the One Self is real, all else is unreal and ends. This is Adwaita. But even though Brahman be the One Self, He has become Many by His own Iccha or Will and the exercise of His Will is not for a moment or limited by time & space or subject to fatigue, but for ever. He is eternal and therefore His Iccha is eternal and the Many Selves which live in Him by His Iccha are eternal and do not perish, for they also being really Brahman the Self are indistinguishable from Him in nature and though their bodies, mind-forms and all else may perish, cannot themselves perish. He may draw them into Himself in utter communion, but He can also release them again into separate communion, and this is actually what happens. All else is transient and changes & passes, but the Self that is One and the Self that is Many are both of them real and eternal; and still they are One Self. This is Visishtadwaita. This eternity of the One Self and eternity of the Many-Selves shows that both are real without beginning and without end and the difference between them is therefore without beginning and end. The One is true and the Many are true, and the One is not and cannot be the Many, though the Many live in and for the One. This is Dwaita.

The only tests to which we can subject these three interpretations of the relation between the One and the Many, all of which are equally logical and therefore equally valid to the reason, are the statements of the Upanishads and the Gita and the experiences of Yoga when the Jivatman or individual Self is in direct communion with the Paramatman or Supreme Universal Self and aware therefore of its real relations to Him. The supreme experience of Yoga is undoubtedly the state of complete identification in Sacchidananda in which the Jivatman becomes purely self-existent, self-aware and self-joyous and phenomenal existence no longer is. Adwaita, therefore, is true according to the experience of Yoga. On the other hand the Jivatman can come out of this state and return into phenomenal existence, and there is also another Yogic state in which it is doubly conscious of its reality apart from the world and its reality in the world or can see the Universe at will in itself or outside itself possessing and enjoying it as an omniscient, omnipotent, all-seeing, all-hearing, all-conscious Being; Visishtadwaita therefore is also true. Finally, there is the state in which the Jivatman is entirely aware only of itself and the Paramatman and lives in a state of exalted love and adoration of the Eternal Being; and without this state[3]

To put the individual Self in intimate relation with the Eternal is the aim of Hindu life, its religion, its polity, its ethics. Morality is not for its own sake, nor for the pleasures of virtue, nor for any reward here or in another life, nor for the sake of society; these

---

[3] *This sentence was not completed; the rest of this notebook page and the next were left blank. — Ed.*

are false aims and false sanctions. Its true aim is a preparation and purification of the soul to fit it for the presence of God. The sense-obscured, limited and desire-driven individual self must raise itself out of the dark pit of sense-obsession into the clear air of the spirit, must disembarrass itself of servile bondage to bodily, emotional & intellectual selfishness and assume the freedom & royalty of universal love and beneficence, must expand itself from the narrow, petty, inefficient ego till it becomes commensurate with the infinite, all-powerful, omnipresent Self of All; then is its aim of existence attained, then is its pilgrimage ended. This may be done by realising the Eternal in oneself by knowledge, by realising oneself in Him by Love as God the Beloved, or by realising Him as the Lord of all in His universe and all its creatures by works. This realisation is the true crown of any ethical system. For whether we hold the aim of morality to be the placing of oneself in harmony with eternal laws, or the fulfilment of man's nature, or the natural evolution of man in the direction of his highest faculties, Hinduism will not object but it insists that the Law with which man must put himself into relation is the Eternal in the universe, that in this permanent and stable Truth man's nature fulfils itself out of the transient seemings of his daily existence and that to this goal his evolution moves. This consummation may be reached by ethical means through a certain manner of action and a certain spirit in action which is the essence of Karmamarga, the Way of Works, one of the three ways by which the spirit of man may see, embrace & become God. The first law of Karmamarga is to give up the natural desire for the fruits of our works and surrender all we do, think, feel and are into the keeping of the Eternal, and the second is to identify ourself with all creatures in the Universe both individually and collectively, realising our larger Self in others. These two laws of action together make what is called Karmayoga or the putting of ourselves into relation with that which is Eternal by means of and in our works. Before, then, we can understand what Karmayoga is, we must understand entirely and utterly what is this Eternal Being with whom we must put ourselves in relation and what are His relations with our self, with the phenomena of the Universe and with the creatures that people it. The Vedantic knowledge of Brahman, the Vedantic Cosmogony, the Vedantic explanation of the coexistence of Brahman with the Universe, the Eternal with the Transient, the Transcendent with the Phenomenal, the One with the Many, are what we have first to study.

Chapter II

The Brahman in His Universe

Three verses of the Isha Upanishad describe directly the Brahman & His relations with the Universe, the [fourth] and [fifth:]

*Anejad ekaṁ manaso javīyo nainad devā āpnuvan pūrvam
                                                                arṣat
Tad dhāvato 'nyān atyeti tiṣṭhat tasminn apo mātariśvā
                                                                dadhāti.
Tad ejati tannaijati tad dūre tadvantike
Tad antar asya sarvasya tad u sarvasyāsya bāhyataḥ.*

and the [eighth:]

*Sa paryagācchukram akāyam avraṇam asnāviraṁ
                                        śuddham apāpaviddham
Kavir manīṣī paribhūḥ svayambhūr yāthātathyato 'rthān
                            vyadadhācchāśvatībhyaḥ samābhyaḥ.*

We may for the present postpone the minuter consideration of the last verse and proceed on the basis of the earlier two alone.

The first conclusion of Vedanta is that the Brahman in this shifting, multifold, mutable Universe is One, stable & unmoving, therefore permanent and unchanging.

*   *   *

The second conclusion of Vedanta is that Brahman pervades this Universe & possesses it.

*   *   *

The third conclusion of Vedanta is that Brahman which pervades, possesses, causes and governs the world is the same as the Absolute Transcendental Existence of which metaphysics speaks. Of this Transcendental Existence Vedanta always speaks in the neuter as Tat, that or it; of the Eternal Will which pervades & governs the Universe it speaks in the masculine as स, He. But in the [fourth] verse we find that to Tat are attributed that universal action and pervasiveness which is properly only attributable to स, the Eternal & Universal Will; the identification of the two could not be more complete. It is yet more strikingly brought out in the [eighth] verse where the description of the cosmical action of Brahman begins with स but the negative attributes of this masculine subject immediately following are in the neuter as appropriate only to the Conditionless Brahman and those that follow later on & apply to the Universal Will revert to the masculine, — all without any break in the sentence.

*   *   *

The fourth conclusion of the Vedanta is that Brahman [is] not only the Absolute Transcendental Self, not only the One, Stable Immutable Reality in the phenomenal Universe, not only pervades, possesses, causes and governs it as an Eternal Universal Will, but contains and in a figurative sense is it as its condition, continent, material cause and informing force. *Tasminnapo mātariśvā dadhāti.* It is in this infinitely motionless etc.

Book III
Brahman in the individual Self

Chapter I

We have now ascertained in some detail the nature of the Vedantic Cosmogony and have some idea of the relations of Brahman to His universe; but to us human beings, the crown and last glorious evolution of conscious phenomenal existence in psychophysical matter, the real question of interest is not a knowledge of the nature of the Universe for its own sake, but a knowledge of our selves. γνῶθι σεαυτόν, Know thyself, is still and always the supreme command for humanity, and if we seek to know the universe, it is because that knowledge is necessary to the more important knowledge of ourselves. Science has adopted a different view; looking only at man as a separate bodily organism it fairly enough regards the Universe as more important than man and seeks to study its laws for their own sake. But still it remains true that humanity persists in its claim and that only those discoveries of the physicist, the zoologist and the chemist have been really fruitful which have helped man practically to master physical nature or to understand the laws of his own life and progress. Whatever moralist or philosopher may say, Yajnavalkya's great dictum remains true that whatever man thinks or feels or does he thinks, feels & does not for any other purpose or creature but for the sake of his Self. The supreme question therefore yet remains imperfectly answered, "So much then for Brahman and the Universe; but what of the things we have cherished so long, what of religion, what of God, what of the human soul?" To some extent the answer to this question has been foreshadowed, but before we get our foundations right for the structure of a higher ethical conception of life and conduct, we must probe to the core in comparison with the current and longstanding ideas on the subject the nature of the Supreme Being as set forth by the Vedanta and His relations to the individual self in man which are the chief preoccupation of religion. We may postpone till later the question whether ethics can or cannot be satisfactorily based on a materialistic interpretation of the world and nonreligious sanctions and aims.

A question of the first importance arises at once, how far does the Vedanta sanction the ordinary ideas of God as a Personal Active Being with definite qualities which is all the average religionist understands by the Divine Idea? Whether we regard him with the Jews as a God of Power and Might & Wrath and Justice, or with the Moslems as God the Judge and Governor and Manager of the world or with the early Christians as a God of Love, yet all agree in regarding Him as a Person, definable, imaginable, limited in His Nature by certain qualities though not limited in His Powers, omniscient, omnipotent, omnipresent & yet by a mysterious paradox quite separate from His creatures and His world. He creates, judges, punishes, rewards, favours, condemns, loves, hates, is pleased, is angry, for all the world like a man of unlimited powers, and is indeed a Superior Man, a shadow of man's soul thrown out on the huge background of the Universe. The intellectual and moral difficulties of this conception are well-known. An Omnipotent God of Love, in spite of all glosses, remains inconsistent with the anguish and misery, the red slaughter and colossal sum of torture and multitudinous suffering which pervades this world and is the condition of its continuance; an Omnipotent God of Justice who created & caused sin, yet punishes man for falling into the traps He has Himself set, is an infinite & huge inconsistency, an insane contradiction in terms; a God of wrath, a jealous God, who favours & punishes according to His caprice, fumes over insults and preens Himself at the sound of praise is much lower than the better sort of men and, as an inferior, unworthy of the adoration of the saints. An omnipresent God cannot be separate from His world, an infinite God cannot be limited in Time or Space or qualities. Intellectually the whole concept becomes incredible. Science, Philosophy, the great creeds which have set Knowledge as the means of salvation, have always been charged with atheism because they deny these conceptions of the Divine Nature. Science and Philosophy & Knowledge take their revenge by undermining the faith of the believers in the ordinary religions through an exposure of the crude and semi-savage nature of the ideas which religion has woven together into a bizarre texture of clumsy paradoxes and dignified with the name of God. They show triumphantly that the ordinary conceptions of God when analysed are incredible to the intellect, unsatisfactory and sometimes revolting to the moral sense and, if they succeed in one or two cases in satisfying the heart, succeed only by magnificently ignoring the claims of the reason. They find it an easy task to show that the attempts of theologians to reconcile the difficulties they have created are childish to the trained reason and can find no acceptance with any honest and candid intellect. Theology in vain denies the right of reason to speak in matters of spiritual truth, and demands that the incredible should be believed. Reason is too high a faculty to be with impunity denied its rights. In thus destroying the unsatisfactory intellectual conceptions with which it has been sought to bring the Eternal Being into the province of the reasoning powers, the core & essence of popular religion which is true and necessary to humanity is discredited along with its imperfect coverings; materialism establishes itself for a while as the human creed and the intellect of man holds despotic empire for a while at the expense of his heart and his ethical instincts, until Nature revenges itself and saves the perishing soul of mankind by flooding the world with a religious belief which seeks to satisfy the heart and the ethical instincts only and mocks at and tramples upon the claims of the intellect. In this unnatural duel between faculties which should work harmoniously for our development, the internal peace and progress of the human self is marred & stunted. Much that has been gained is repeatedly being lost and has to be recovered with great difficulty and not always in its entirety.

If reason unaided could solve the enigma of the world, it would be a different matter. But the reason is able only to form at the best an intellectually possible or logically consistent conception of the Eternal in the Universe; it is not able to bring Him home to the human consciousness and relate the human soul to Him as it should be related if He exists. For nothing is more certain than this that if a universal & eternal Consciousness exists, the life and development of the human soul must be towards It and governed by the law of Its nature; and a philosophy which cannot determine these relations so as to bring light and help to humanity in its long road is merely an intellectual plaything and might just as well have been kept as a private amusement when minds of a ratiocinative turn meet in the lecture-room or the study. Philosophy can see clearly that the Universe can be explicable only in the terms of the Eternal Consciousness by which it exists. Either God is the material universe in which case the name is a mere convenient abstraction like the materialist's "Nature", or He is the Self within the Universe. If the Self, then He is either transcendent and beyond phenomena and the phenomenal Universe can only be Maya, an imagination in the Universal Mind, or else He is involved in phenomena, Consciousness His soul, the Universe His form, Consciousness the witnessing and inspiring Force, the Universe the work or Energy of the Consciousness. But whichever of these possibilities be the truth, Knowledge is not complete if it stops with this single conception and does not proceed to the practical consequences of the conception. If the universe is Maya, what of the human soul? Is that also Maya, a phenomenon like the rest which disappears with the dissolution of the body or is it permanent and identical with the Eternal Consciousness? If permanent, why then has it confused itself with phenomena and how does it escape from the bondage of this confusion? On the other hand if He is involved in phenomena, what is the relation of the human consciousness to the Eternal? Are our souls parts of Him or manifestations or emanations? And if so do they return into Him at the dissolution of the body or do they persist? And if they persist, what is their ultimate goal? Do they remain by individuality separated from Him for ever even after the end of phenomena or are both the Universe and the individual soul eternal? Or is the individual soul only phenomenally different from the eternal, and the phenomenal difference terminable at the pleasure of the Eternal or by the will of the individual Ego?

What are the present relations of the self to the Eternal? What are sin & virtue? pleasure & pain? What are we to do with our emotions, desires, imaginations? Has the Eternal Consciousness any direct action on the phenomenal Universe and, if so, how is He different from the popular conception of God?

These are the questions which Philosophy has to answer, and in answering them the great difficulty it has to meet is its inability to find any better sanction for its conclusions than the play of speculative logic or to evolve anything better than a speculative system of metaphysics which may satisfy the argumentative faculty of the mind but cannot satisfy the reason of the heart or find its way to a mastery of that inner self in man which controls his life. Religion, however imperfect, has the secret of that mastery; religion can conquer the natural instincts and desires of man, metaphysics can only convince him logically that they ought to be conquered — an immense difference. For this reason philosophy has never been able to satisfy any except the intellectual few and was even for a time relegated to oblivion by the imperious contempt of Science which thought that it had discovered a complete solution of the Universe, a truth and a law of life independent of religion and yet able to supersede religion in its peculiar province of reaching & regulating the sources of conduct and leading mankind in its evolution. But it has now become increasingly clear that Science has failed to substantiate its claims, and that a belief in evolution or the supremacy of physical laws or the subjection of the ephemeral individual to the interests of the slightly less ephemeral race is no substitute for a belief in Christ or Buddha, for the law of Divine Love or the trust in Divine Power & Providence. If Philosophy failed to be an ethical control or a spiritual force, Science has failed still more completely, and for a very simple reason — the intellect does not control the conduct. There is quite another mental force which controls it and which turns into motives of action only those intellectual conceptions of which it can be got to approve. We arrive therefore at this dilemma that Philosophy & Science can satisfy the reason but cannot satisfy the heart or get mastery of the source of conduct; while Religion which satisfies the heart and controls conduct, cannot in its average conceptions permanently satisfy the reason and thus exposes itself to gradual loss of empire over the mind.

A religion therefore which claims to be eternal, must not be content with satisfying the heart and imagination, it must answer to the satisfaction of the intellect the questions with which philosophy is preoccupied. A philosophy which professes to explain the world-problem once for all, must not be satisfied with logical consistency and comprehensiveness; it must like Science base its conclusions not merely on speculative logic, but on actual observation and its truths must always be capable of verification by experiment so that they may be not merely conceivable truth but ascertained truth; it must like religion seize on the heart & imagination and without sacrificing intellectual convincingness, comprehensiveness & accuracy impregnate with itself the springs of human activity; and it must have the power of bringing the human self into direct touch with the Eternal. The Vedantic religion claims to be the eternal religion because it satisfies all these demands. It is intellectually comprehensive in its explanation of all the problems that perplex the human mind; it brings the contradictions of the world into harmony by a single luminous law of being; it has developed in Yoga a process of spiritual experience by which its assertions can be tested and confirmed; the law of being it has discovered seizes not only on the intellect but on the deepest emotions of man and calls into activity his highest ethical instincts; and its whole aim and end is to bring the individual self into a perfect and intimate union with the Eternal.

Chapter II

[*This chapter was not written.*]

The Religion of Vedanta

If it were asked by anyone what is this multitudinous, shifting, expanding, apparently amorphous or at all events multimorphous sea of religious thought, feeling, philosophy, spiritual experience we call Hinduism, what it is characteristically and essentially, we might answer in one word, the religion of Vedanta. And if it were asked what are the Hindus with their unique and persistent difference from all other races, we might again answer, the children of Vedanta. For at the root of all that we Hindus have done, thought and said through these thousands of years of our race-history, behind all we are and seek to be, there lies concealed, the fount of our philosophies, the bedrock of our religions, the kernel of our thought, the explanation of our ethics and society, the summary of our civilisation, the rivet of our nationality, this one marvellous inheritance of ours, the Vedanta. Nor is it only to Hindu streams that this great source has given of its life-giving waters. Buddhism, the teacher of one third of humanity, drank from its inspiration. Christianity, the offspring of Buddhism, derived its ethics and esoteric teaching at second-hand from the same source. Through Persia Vedanta put its stamp on Judaism, through Judaism, Christianity and Sufism on Islam, through Buddha on Confucianism, through Christ and mediaeval mysticism and Catholic ceremonial, through Greek and German philosophy, through Sanscrit learning and [*sentence left incomplete*]

Evolution in the Vedantic View

We must not however pass from this idea,[1] as it is easy to pass, into another which is only a popular error, — that evolution is the object of existence. Evolution is not an universal law, it is a particular process, nor as a process has it any very wide applicability. Some would affirm that every particle of matter in the universe is bound to evolve life, mind, an individualised soul, a finally triumphant spirit. The idea is exhilarating, but impossible. There is no such rigid law, no such self-driven & unintelligent destiny in things. In the conceptions of the Upanishads Brahman in the world is not only Prajna, but Ishwara. He is not subject to law, but uses process. It is only the individual soul in a state of ignorance on which process seems to impose itself as law. Brahman on the other hand has an omnipotent power of selection and limitation. He is not bound to develop self-conscious individuality in every particle of matter, nor has He any object in such a colossal and monotonous application of one particular movement of things. He has nothing to gain by evolving, nothing to lose by not evolving. For to Him all being is only a play of His universal self-consciousness, the will so to exist the only reason of this existence and its own pleasurability its only object in existence. In that play He takes an equal delight in all, He is sama in ananda — an equal delight in the evolved state, the unevolved & the evolving. He is equal also in Being; when He has evolved Himself in the perfect man, He is no more than He already was in the leaf & clod. To suppose that all existence has one compelling purpose of growth, of progress, of consummation is to be guilty of the Western error and misunderstand the nature of being. Existence is already consummate, all change

---

[1] *It is not known what "idea" Sri Aurobindo is referring to here, or whether the writing in which he discussed it has survived. — Ed.*

& variety in it is for delight, not for a gain or a development. The Vedantist cannot admit that anything is really developed in the sense of something new emerging into existence by whatever combination or accident which had no previous being. Nasato vidyate bhavah. That which was not cannot come into existence. The play of Brahman is not in its real nature an evolution, but a manifestation, it is not an adding of something that was wanting or a developing of something that was non-existent, but merely a manifesting of something that was hidden. We are already what we shall become. That which is still future in matter, is present in spirit.

We say, then, in the Vedanta that if the human form appears on earth or the tree grows out of the seed, it is because the human form already exists in the seed that is cast into the womb and the form and nature of the tree already exists in the seed that is cast into the earth. If there were not this preexistence as idea or implied form in the seed, there would be no reason why any seed should bring forth according to its kind. The form does not indeed exist sensibly in the form of consciousness which we see as matter, but in the consciousness itself it is there, and therefore there is a predisposition in the matter to produce that form & no other, which is much more than tendency, which amounts to a necessity. But how came this preconception into unintelligent matter? The question itself is erroneous in form; for matter is not unintelligent, but itself a movement of conceiving Spirit. This conceiving Spirit which in man conceives the idea of human form, being one in the mind of the man, in his life principle, in every particle of his body, stamps that conception on the life principle so that it becomes very grain of it, stamps it on the material part so that it becomes very grain of it, so that when the seed is cast into the woman, it enters full of the conception, impregnated with it in the whole totality of its being. We can see how this works in man; we know how the mental conceptions of the father & mother work powerfully to shape body, life & temperament of the son. But we do not perceive how this works in the tree, because we are accustomed to dissociate from the tree all idea of mind & even of life. We therefore talk vaguely of the law of Nature that the tree shall produce according to its kind without understanding why such a law should exist. Vedanta tells us that the process in the tree is the same as in man, except that mind not being active & self-conscious cannot produce those variations of delicate possibility which are possible in the human being. The supramental conceiving Spirit stamps, through unconscious mind, on the life principle in the tree and on all matter in the tree the conception of its nature & kind so that the seed falls into earth with every atom of its being full of that secret conception and every moment of the tree's growth is presided over by the same fixed idea. Not only in thinking man & living tree but in substances in which life & mind are inactive, this conceiving Spirit presides & determines its law & form. So 'rthan vyadadhach chhaswatibhyah samabhyah.

We must not for a moment imagine that Brahman of the Upanishads is either an extracosmic God entering into a cosmos external to Him or that last refuge of the dualising intellect, an immanent God. When Brahman the conceiving Spirit is said to be in life & mind and matter, it is only as the poet is said to be in his own thought and creations; as a man muses in his mind, as the river pours forward in swirls & currents. It would be easy, by quoting isolated texts from the Upanishads, to establish on them any system whatever; for the sages of the Upanishads have made it their business to see Brahman in many aspects, from many standpoints, to record all the most important fundamental experiences which the soul has when it comes into contact with the All, the Eternal. This they did with the greater freedom because they knew that in the fundamental truth of this All & Eternal, the most varied & even contradictory experiences found their harmony & their relative truth and necessity to each other. The Upanishads are Pantheistic, because they consider the whole universe to be Brahman, yet not Pantheistic because they regard Brahman as transcendental, exceeding the universe & in his final truth other than phenomena. They are Theistic because they consider Brahman as God & Lord of His universe, immanent in it, containing it, governing & arranging it; yet not Theistic because they regard the world also as God, containing

Himself & dwelling in Himself. They are polytheistic because they acknowledge the existence, power & adorability of Surya-Agni, Indra and a host of other deities; yet not polytheistic, because they regard them as only powers and names & personalities of the one Brahman. Thus it is possible for the Isha Upanishad to open with the idea of the indwelling God, Isha vasyam jagat, to continue with the idea of the containing Brahman, Tasminn apo Matariswa dadhati, and at the same time to assert the world, the jagat, also as Brahman, Tad ejati, sa paryagat. That this catholicity was not born of incoherence of thinking is evident from the deliberate & precise nicety [of] statement both in the Gita & the Upanishad. The Gita continually dwells on God in all things, yet it says Naham teshu te mayi, "I am not in them, they are in me"; and again it says God is Bhutabhrit not bhutastha, and yet na cha matsthani bhutani pashya me yogam aishwaram. "I bear up creatures in myself, I do not dwell in them; they exist in me, & yet they do not exist in me; behold my divine Yoga." The Upanishads similarly dwell on the coexistence of contradictory attributes in Brahman, nirguno guni, anejad ekam manaso javiyo, tadejati tannaijati. All this is perfectly intelligible & reconcilable, provided we never lose sight of the key word, the master thought of the Upanishads, that Brahman is not a Being with fixed attributes, but absolute Being beyond attributes yet, being absolute, capable of all, and the world a phenomenal arrangement of attributes in Intelligent Being, arranged not logically & on a principle of mutual exclusion, but harmoniously on a principle of mutual balancing & reconciliation. God's immanence & God's extramanence, God's identity with things & God's transcendence of things, God's personality & God's impersonality, God's mercy & God's cruelty & so on through all possible pairs of opposites, all possible multiplicity of aspects, are but the two sides of the same coin, are but different views of the same scene & incompatible or inharmonious to our ideas only so long as we do not see the entire entity, whole vision.

In Himself therefore God has arranged all objects according to their nature from years sempiternal. He has fixed from the beginning the relations of his movements in matter, mind and life. The principle of diversity in unity governs all of them. The world is not comprised of many substances combining variously into many forms, — like the elements of the chemist, which now turn out not to be elements, — nor yet of many substances composing by fusion one substance, — as hydrogen & oxygen seem to compose water, — but is always & eternally one substance variously concentrated into many elements, innumerable atoms, multitudinous forms. There are not many lives composing by their union & fusion or by any other sort of combination one composite life, as pluralistic theories tend to suppose, but always & eternally one Life variously active in multitudinous substantial bodies. There are not many minds acting upon each other, mutually penetrative and tending to or consciously seeking unity, as romantic theories of being suppose, but always & eternally one mind variously intelligent in innumerable embodied vitalities. It is because of this unity that there is the possibility of contact, interchange, interpenetration and recovery of unity by & between substance & substance, life & life, mind and mind. The contact & union is the result of oneness; the oneness is not the result of contact & union. This world is not in its reality a sum of things but one unalterable transcendental integer showing itself to us phenomenally as many apparent fractions of itself, — fractional appearances simultaneous in manifestation, related in experience. The mind & sense deal with the fractions, proceed from the experience of fractions to the whole; necessarily, therefore, they arrive at the idea of an eternal sum of things; but this totality of sum is merely a mental symbol, necessary to the mind's computations of existence. When we rise higher, we find ourselves confronted with a unity which is transcendental, an indivisible and incomputable totality. That is Parabrahman, the Absolute. All our thoughts, perceptions, experiences are merely symbols by which the Absolute is phenomenally represented to the movements of its own Awareness conditioned as matter, life, mind or supermind.

Just as each of these tattwas, principles of being, movements of Chit, conditions of Ananda which we call life, matter, mind, are eternally one in themselves embracing a diversity of mere transient forms & individual activities which emerge from, abide in & one day return into their totality, material form into the substance of the pancha bhutas, individual life into the oceanic surge of the world-pervading life principle, individual mind, whenever that is dissolved, into the secret sukshmatattwa or sea of subtle mind-existence, so also these three tattwas & all others that may exist are a diversity embraced in an eternal unity — the unity of Brahman. It is Brahman who moves densely as the stability of matter, forcefully as the energy of life, elastically in the subtlety of mind. Just as different vibrations in ether produce the appearances to sense which we call light & sound, so different vibrations in Chit produce the various appearances to Chit which we call matter, life & mind. It is all merely the extension of the same principle through stair & higher stair of apparent existence until, overcoming all appearances, we come to the still & unvibrating Brahman who, as we say in our gross material language, contains it all. The Sankhya called this essential vibration the kshobha, disturbance in Prakriti, cosmic ripple in Nature. The Vedanta continually speaks of the world as a movement. The Isha speaks of things as jagatyam jagat, particular movement in the general movement of conscious Being steadily *viewed* by that Being in His own self-knowledge, atmani atmanam atmana, self by self in self. This is the motion & nature of the Universe.

This then is Matter, a particular movement of the Brahman, one stream, one ocean of His consciousness fixed in itself as the substance of form. This is life, mind; other movements, other such streams or oceans active as material of thought & vitality. But if they are separate, though one, how is it that they do not flow separately — for obviously in some way they meet, they intermingle, they have relations. Life here evolves in body; mind here evolves in vitalised substance. It is not enough to say, as we have said, that the conception of Brahman is stamped in grain of mind, through mind in grain of life, through life in grain of matter & so produces particular form. For what we actually start with seems to be not life moulding matter, but life evolving out of matter or at least in matter. Afterwards, no doubt, its needs & circumstances react on matter & help to mould it. Even if we suppose the first moulding to be only latent life and mind, the primacy of matter has to be explained.

The Means of Realisation

Vedanta is merely an intellectual assent, without Yoga. The verbal revelation of the true relations between the One and the Many, the intellectual acceptance of the revelation and the dogmatic acknowledgement of the relations do not lead us beyond metaphysics, and there is no human pursuit more barren and frivolous than metaphysics practised merely as an intellectual pastime, a play with words & thoughts, when there is no intention of fulfilling thought in life or of moulding our inner state and outer activity by the knowledge which we have intellectually accepted. It is only by Yoga that the fulfilment and moulding of our life and being in the type of the true relations between God and the soul can become possible. Therefore every Upanishad has in it an element of Yoga as well as an element of Sankhya, the scientific psychology on which Yoga is founded. Vedanta, the perception of the relations between God in Himself and God in the world, Sankhya, the scientific, philosophical and psychological analysis of those relations and Yoga, called also by the Rishis Yajna, their practical application in social life, religious worship and individual discipline & self-perfection, is and has always been the whole substance of the Hindu religion. Whatever we know of God, that we ought in every way to be and live, is almost the only common dogma of all Hindu sects and schools of every description.

If then we know this of God and ourselves that we and He are one, So 'ham asmi, but divided by a movement of self-awareness which differentiates our forward active movement of waking life from the great life behind that knows and embraces all, then to recover that oneness in our waking state becomes the supreme aim and meaning of every individual existence. Nothing connected only with the movement of division can be of any moment to us, neither our bodily life and health, nor our family welfare, nor our communal wellbeing compared with this immense self-fulfilment; they can only be of importance as means or movements in the self-fulfilment. If, farther, we know that by recovering our secret oneness with God we shall also be at one with the world and that hatred, grief, fear, limitation, sickness, mortality, the creations of the divided movement, will no longer be able to exercise their yoke upon us, then the abandonment of all else, if necessary, for the one thing needful, becomes not only the supreme aim and meaning of human life, but our only true interest. Even if, as is quite probable, we cannot in one birth attain to the fullness of this grand result yet it is clear that even a little progress towards it must mean an immense change in our life & inner experience and be well worth the sacrifice and the labour. As the Gita says with force, "A little of this rule of life saves man out of his great fear." If farther a man knows that all mankind is intended to attain this consummation, he being one life with that divine movement called humanity, it must also be part of his self-fulfilment to pour whatever fullness of being, knowledge, power or bliss he may attain, out on his fellow beings. It is his interest also, for humanity being one piece, it is difficult for the individual to attain fullness of life here when the race creates for him an atmosphere of darkness, unrest and base preoccupation with the cares of a half-intellectualised animal existence. So strong has this atmosphere become in the Iron Age, that it is the rule for the individual who seeks his own salvation to sever himself from life and society and content himself with only the inner realisation. Modern Hinduism has become, therefore, in all but its strongest spirits, absorbed in the idea of an individual salvation. But our Vedic forefathers were of a different stuff. They had always their eye on the individual in the race. Nothing is more remarkable in the Veda than the absolute indifference & even confusion with which the singular and plural are used by the Singer, as if "I" & "we" were identical in meaning, and the persistence with which the Rishi regards himself as a representative soul, as it were, of the *vishám devayatínám*, the peoples in their seeking after the Godhead. We find the same transition in the Isha from the singular "pashyami" of the successful representative soul realising his oneness with God to the plural asman when he turns to pray for the equal purification and felicity of his fellows. Our ideal, therefore, is fixed, — to become one with God and lead individually the divine life, but also to help others to the divine realisation and prepare, by any means, humanity for the kingdom of God on earth, — satyadharma, satyayuga.

Our means is Yoga. Yoga is not, as the popular mind too often conceives, shutting oneself in a room or isolating oneself in a monastery or cave and going through certain fixed mental and bodily practices. These are merely particular and specialised types of Yogic practice. The mental and bodily practices of Rajayoga and Hathayoga are exercises of great force and utility, but they are not indispensable. Even solitude is not indispensable, and absolute solitude limits our means and scope of self-fulfilment. Yoga is the application, by whatever means, of Vedanta to life so as to put oneself in some kind of touch with the high, one, universal and transcendent Existence in us & without us in our progress towards a final unity. All religious worship, sincerely done, all emotional, intellectual and spiritual realisation of that which is higher than ourselves, all steadily practised increase of essential power, purity, love or knowledge, all sacrifice and self-transcending amounts to some form of Yoga. But Yoga can be done with knowledge or without knowledge, with a higher immediate object or with a lower immediate object, for a partial higher result or for the fullest divine perfection and bliss. Yoga without knowledge can never have the force of Yoga with knowledge, Yoga with the lower object the force of Yoga with the higher object, Yoga for a partial result the force of Yoga for the full & perfect result. But even in its lowest, most ignorant or narrowest forms, it is still a step towards God.

A Fragmentary Chapter for a
Work on Vedanta

[.....] Each of the great authoritative Upanishads has its own peculiar character and determined province as well as the common starting point of thought and supreme truth in the light of which all their knowledge has to be understood. The unity of universal existence in the transcendental Being who alone is manifested here or elsewhere forms their common possession & standpoint.

All thought & experience here rest upon this great enigma of a multiplicity that when questioned resolves itself to a unity of sum, of nature & of being, of a unity that when observed seems to be a mere sum or convention for a collection of multiples. The mind when it starts its business of experience in sensation and thought, finds itself stumbling about in a forest of details of each of which it becomes aware individually by knocking up against it, like a wayfarer in a thick and midnight forest stumbling & dashing himself against the trees, — by the shock & the touch only he knows of them. Mind cannot discriminate & put these details into their place except, imperfectly, by the aid of memory — the habit of the [mind] of sensations. Like the women imprisoned in the magic forests of the old Tantra the mind is a prisoner in the circle of its own sensations wandering round & round in that narrow area and always returning to the original source of its bondage, — its inability to go beyond its data, the compulsion under which it lies of returning to the object it meets merely the image of that object as mirrored through the senses & in the mind. It is reason, the faculty that can discriminate as objects, that first attempts to deliver mind from its bondage by standing apart from the object and its mental reflection and judging them in its own terms & by its own measurements and not in the terms & measurements of the senses. The knowledge which the mind gives is sanjna, awareness not passing beyond contact with and response to the thing known, the knowledge which reason gives

is prajna, awareness placing the object in front of it and studying it as a thing affecting but yet apart from and unconnected
with the feelings & needs of that which experiences. Therefore
it is, according to our philosophy, in buddhi & not in manas
that ahankara, the discriminative ego-sense is born. Mind like
matter has an inert unity of all things in experience born of non-
discrimination; the perception of an object outside & a sensation
within it stand on the same footing to sanjna. We must discriminate and reflect, in order to be aware of separate multiplicity
as distinguished from a multitude [of] sensations in the unity
of our consciousness. Afterwards when we rise through reason
but above it, to Veda, we recover, however rudimentarily, the
original unity, but discriminating, knowing the tattwa of things,
perceiving them to be circumstances not of an individual &
sense bound [but] of universal & sense delivered consciousness.
This consummation of knowledge & the ordering of life on
that knowledge is man's summit of evolution, the business for
which he is here upon the earth. To climb to it from the animal
mentality [*sentence left incomplete*]

   The first thing that this discriminating reason effects is to put
each detail in its place & then to arrange the details in groups.
It travels from the individual to the group, from the group to
the class, from the class to the kind, from the kind to the mass.
And there until help arrives it has to pause. It has done much. It
has distinguished each individual tree in the magical forest from
its neighbour; it has arranged them in groves and thickets; it has
distinguished & numbered the various species of trees and fixed
their genus. It has mapped them out collectively & known the
whole mass as the forest. But it is not yet free. It has not escaped
from the ensorcelled gyre of the Almighty Magician. It knows
every detail of its prison, nothing more. It has discovered the
vyashti & the samashti; it has arrived only at a collective & not
at a real unity. It has discovered the relations of unit to unit, the
units to the smaller group and the smaller group to the larger
group & the whole to the mass. It has its laws of life fixed upon
that knowledge, its duties of individual to individual, of man
to the family, of the man & family to the class, of [all] three

to the nation, of the nation & its constituents to humanity. It has ordered excellently our life in the prison house. But it still travels in the magic circle, it is still a prisoner & a [......] It has even discovered one pregnant truth that the farther we travel from the many, the nearer we draw to the one, the less is the transience, the greater the permanence. The family outlasts the individual, the class endures when the single family has perished, the kind survives the disappearance of the class, the collective whole endures & outlives all the revolutions of its component parts. Therefore a final law and morality is found, the sacrifice & consummation of the less in the greater, of the few for the many, — an evolutionary utility, a consummate altruism. And when all is said and done, we are still in the prison house. For even the most permanent is here transient, the world perishes as inevitably as the midge & the ant & to our ranging vision seems hardly mightier in its ultimate reality or the importance of its fate. For who has made individual follow individual & nation follow nation & world follow world through the brilliant mirage of life into the incomprehensible mystery of death; and when all is ended, what profit has a man had of all his labour that he has done under the sun?

Reason cannot deliver us. The day of our freedom dawns when we transcend reason, not by imagination, which is itself only an intellectual faculty, not [by] the intuition even, but by illumination. The intuitive reason can do much for us, can indicate to us the higher truth. The intellectual reason can only arrive, as we have seen, at a collective unity; it is still bound by its data. The intuitive reason first suggests to us a unity which is not collective but essential, the Brahman of the Veda [....................] It is intuitive reason that [.............] infinity. We [.........................] its non-existence to the observing intellect. [None] has ever [travelled] beyond the uttermost limit of the stars and assured [himself that] there is always a beyond, or lived from all time before the stars shone out in the heavens so that he can say, Time never began. The imagination can indeed add tract to tract of Space and millennium to millennium of Time and, returning tired &

appalled, say "I at least find no end and infinity is possible." But still we have no proof — there are no data on which we can stand. Infinity remains to the intellect a surmise, a hypothesis, a powerful inference. Reason is essentially a measuring & arranging faculty & can only deal with the finite. It is ensorcelled within the limits of the forest. Yet we have an intuitive perception of the truth of infinity, not collectively, not as a never ending sum of miles or moments but as a thing in itself not dependent on that which it contains. We have, if we examine ourselves, other such intuitive perceptions, of immortality although we cannot look beyond the black wall of death, of freedom although the facts of the world seem to load us with chains.

Are we yet free by the force of this intuitive reason? We cannot say so, — for this reason that it gives us suggestions, but not realisations. It is in its nature what the old psychologists would have called smriti, a memory of truth, rather than a perception. There is a suggestion to us in ourselves of infinity, of immortality, of freedom and knowledge in us replies, Yes, I know that to be true, though I do not see it, there is something in me that has always known it, it is in me like some divine memory. The reason of this movement is that the intuitive reason works in the intellect. It is the memory of freedom coming to the woman in the forest which tells her that there is something outside this green & leafy, but yet to her dark, fatal & dismal forest of imprisonment, some world of wide & boundless skies where a man can move freely doing what he wills, *kamachari*. And because it works in the intellect, its movement can be imitated by the other inhabitants of the intellect, by the brilliancy of imagination, by the fond thought that is only the image of our wish. The rationalist is right in distrusting intuition although it gave him Newton's theory of gravitation and most of the brilliant beginnings of Science & Free Thought, — right, yet not right; right from the standpoint of a scepticism that asks for intellectual certainty, wrong from the standpoint of ultimate truth & the imperative needs of humanity. Faith rests upon the validity of this faculty of intuitive reason, and faith has been the great helper and consoler of humanity in its progress, the indispensable staff on which he supports his thought & his action. But because the divine smriti is aped by the voices of desire & fancy, faith has also been the parent & perpetuator of many errors.

It is knowledge that loosens our bonds, that snaps asunder the toils of sense & dispels the force of the world-enchantment. In order to be free, we must pass from intuition to illumination. We must get the direct perception of the knowledge of which intuitive reason is the memory. For within us there are unawakened folds in folds of conscious experience which we have yet to set in action in order to fulfil our nature's possibilities. In these inner realms we are sushupta, asleep; but the whole movement of humanity is towards the awakening of these centres. Science is in error when it imagines that man is from all time & to all time a rational animal & the reason the end & summit of his evolution. Man did not begin with reason, neither will he end with it. There are faculties within us which transcend reason and are asleep to our waking consciousness, just as life is asleep in the metal, consciousness in the tree, reason in the animal. Our evolution is not over, we have not completed even half of the great journey. And if now we are striving to purify the intellect & to carry reason to its utmost capacities, it is in order that we may discourage the lower movements of passion and desire, self-interest and prejudice and dogmatic intolerance which stand in the way of the illumination. When the intellectual buddhi is pure by vichara & abhyasa of these things, then it becomes ready to rise up out of the mind into the higher levels of consciousness and there lose itself in a much mightier movement which because of its greatness & perfection is called in the Rigveda mahas and in the Vedanta vijnana. This is what [is] meant in the Veda by Saraswati awakening the great ocean. Pavaka nah saraswati maho arnash chetayati. This is the justification of the demand in our own Yoga that desire shall be expelled, the mind stilled, the very play of reason & imagination silenced before a man shall attain to knowledge, — as the Gita puts it, na kinchid api chintayet.

The illumination of the vijnana, when it is complete, shows us not a collective material unity, a sum of physical units, but a real unity. It reveals to us Space, Time and the chain of apparent circumstance to be merely conventions & symbols seen in His own being by One Seer and dependent purely on a greater transcendental existence of which they are not separate realities & divisions but the manifold expressions of its single Truth. It is this knowledge that gives us freedom. We escape from the enchanted forest, we know once more the world outside this petty world, see the boundless heavens above & breast the wide & circumambient air of our infinite existence. The first necessity is to know the One, to be in possession of the divine Existence; afterwards we can have all the knowledge, joy & power for action that is intended for our souls, — for He being known all is known, tasmin vijnate sarvam vijnatam, not at once by any miraculous revelation, but by a progressive illumination or rather an application of the single necessary illumination to God's multiplicity in manifestation, by the movement of the mahat & the bhuma, not working from petty details to the whole, but from the knowledge of the one to the knowledge of relation & circumstance, by a process of knowledge that is sovereign & free, not painful, struggling & bound. This is the central truth of Veda & Upanishad & the process by which they have been revealed to men.

This free & great movement of illumination descending from above to us below and not like our thought here which climbs painfully up the mountain peaks of thought only to find at the summit that it is yet far removed from the skies to which it aspires, this winged & mighty descent of Truth is what we call Sruti or revelation. There are three words which are used of illumined thought, drishti, sruti & smriti, sight, hearing and remembrance. The direct vision or experience of a truth or the thought-substance of a truth is called drishti, and because they had that direct vision or experience, that pratyaksha not of the senses, but of the liberated soul, the Rishis are called drashtas. But besides the truth and its artha or thought-substance in which it is represented to the mind, there is the vak or sound symbol, the inevitable word in which the truth is naturally enshrined & revealed & not as in ordinary speech half concealed or only suggested. The revelation of the vak is sruti. The revealed word is also revelatory and whoever has taken it into his soul, though the mind may not understand it, has the Truth ready prepared in the higher or sushupta reaches of his being from whence it must inevitably descend at a future date or in another life to his lower & darkened consciousness in order to liberate & illumine. It is this psychological truth which is the foundation of the Hindu's trust in the Name of God, the vibrations of the mantra and the sound of the Veda. For the vak carries, in the right state of the soul, an illumination with it of the truth which it holds, an inspiration of its force of satyam which is less than drishti but must in the end lead to drishti. A still more indirect action of the vijnana is smriti; when the truth is presented to the soul and its truth immediately & directly recognised by a movement resembling memory — a perception that this was always true and already known to the higher consciousness. It is smriti that is nearest to intellect action and forms the link between vijnanam & prajnanam, ideal thought & intellectual thought, by leading to the higher forms of intellectual activity, such as intuitive reason, inspiration, insight & prophetic revelation, the equipment of the man of genius.

But what proof have we that this illumination exists? how can we say that this illuminated sight, this revelatory hearing, this confirming remembrance of eternal knowledge is not a self-delusion or a peculiarly brilliant working of imagination and of rapid intellectuality? To those who have the illumination, the question does not arise. The prisoner released from his fetters does not doubt the reality of the file that undid their rivets; the woman escaped from the forest does not ask herself whether this amazing sunlight & wide-vaulted blue sky is not a dream and a delusion. The scientist himself would not be patient with one who began the study of science by questioning the reality of the revealing power of microscope and telescope and suggesting that the objects as seen underneath were so presented merely by an optical illusion. Those who have experienced & seen, know [.....................................] sceptic. "Learn how to use the instruments [.........] yourself, study all these wonders invisible to the ordinary eye, examine their constancy, coherency, fidelity to fixed wide & general laws, and then judge; do not vitiate inquiry from the beginning by denying on a priori grounds its utility or the right to inquire." It is only by faith in the instruments of our knowledge that we can acquire knowledge, — by faith in the evidence of the senses that we can think at all, by faith in the validity of reason that we can deduce, infer and argue. So also it is only by faith in illumination that we can see truth from above & come face to [face with God.] It is true that all faith must have its limits. The faith in the senses must be transcended & checked by the faith in our reason. The faith in the reason itself is checked by agnosticism [and] will one day be transcended & checked by the faith in the vijnana. The faith in the vijnana must be checked & harmonised by a faith in a still higher form of knowledge, — knowledge by identity. But within its own province each instrument is supreme and must be trusted. In relying, therefore, upon the vijnana, in asserting and demanding a preliminary faith in it, the Yogin is making no mystic, irrational or obscurantist claim. He is not departing from the universal process of knowledge. He claims to exceed reason, just as the scientist claims to exceed the evidence of the senses. When he asserts that things are not what they seem, that there are invisible forces and agencies at work about us and that the whole of our apparent existence and environment is only phenomenal, he is no more departing from rationality or advancing anything wild or absurd than the scientist when he asserts that the earth moves round the sun and the sun is relatively still, affirms the existence of invisible gases or invisible bacilli, or finds in matter only a form of energy. Nor are faith in the Guru & faith in the Sruti irrational demands, any more than the scientist is irrational in saying to his pupil "Trust my expert knowledge, trust my method of experiment & the books that are authoritative and when you have made the experiments, you can use your intellect to confirm, refute, amend or enlarge whatever scientific knowledge is presented to you in book or lecture or personal instruction," — or than the man of the Indian village who has been to London is irrational in expecting his fellow villagers to accept his statement of the existence, sights, scenes and characteristics of London or in supporting [it] by any book that may have been written with authority on the subject. If the Indian Teacher similarly demands faith in himself as an expert, faith in the Sruti as the evidence of ancient experts, drishti as revealed truth coming direct to them by vijnanam from the divine Knowledge, he is following the common, the necessary rule. He has the right to say, Trust these, follow these, afterwards you will yourself look on the unveiled face of Truth & see God. In each case there is a means of confirmation, — the evidence of the observation & deduction has to be confirmed by observation & deduction; the evidence of the senses by the senses, the evidence of the vijnanam by the vijnanam. One cannot exceed one's instrument.

There is also the evidence of common experience — there is this eternal witness to the truth of the vijnana, that men who have used it, in whatever clime & whatever age, however they may differ in their intellectual statement or the conclusions of the reason about what they have seen, are at one in the substance of their experience & vision. Whoever follows in these days the paths indicated, makes the experiments prescribed, goes through the training needed, cannot go beyond, in the substance of his knowledge, or depart from what the ancients observed. He may not go beyond [*sentence left incomplete*]

God and Immortality

Chapter I

The Upanishad

The Upanishads stand out from the dim background of Vedic antiquity like stupendous rock cathedrals of thought hewn out of the ancient hills by a race of giant builders the secret of whose inspiration and strength has passed away with them into the Supreme. They are at once Scripture, philosophy and seer-poetry; for even those of them that dispense with the metrical form, are prose poems of a rhythmically mystic thought. But whether as Scripture, philosophical theosophy or literature, there is nothing like them in ancient, mediaeval or modern, in Occidental or Oriental, in Egyptian, Chaldean, Semitic or Mongolian creation; they are unique in style, structure and motive, entirely *sui generis*. After them there were philosophic poems, aphorisms, verse and prose treatises in great number, Sutras, Karikas, Gitas, their intellectual children; but these are a human progeny very different in type from their immortal ancestors. Pseudo-Upanishads there have been in plenty, a hundred or more of them; some have arrived at a passable aping of the more external features of the type, but always betray themselves by the pseudo-style, the artificial falsetto, the rasping creak of the machine; others are pastiches; others are fakes. The great Upanishads stand out always serene, grand, inimitable with their puissant and living breath, with that phrase which goes rolling out a thousand echoes, with that faultless spontaneous sureness of the inevitable expression, with that packed yet easy compression of wide and rich wisdom into a few revelatory syllables by which they justify their claim to be the divine word. Neither this inspiration nor this technique has been renewed or repeated in later human achievement.

And if we look for their secret, we shall find it best expressed in the old expression of them as the impersonal *shabda-brahman*. They are that is to say, the accents of the divine Gnosis, —a revelatory word direct and impersonal from the very heart of a divine and almost superconscious self-vision. All supreme utterance which is the inspired word and not merely speech of the mind, does thus come from a source beyond the human person through whom it is uttered; still it comes except in rare moments through the personal thought, coloured by it, a little altered in the transit, to some extent coloured by the intellect or the temperament. But these seers seem to have possessed the secret of the rapt passivity in which is heard faultlessly the supreme word; they speak the language of the sons of Immortality. Its truth is entirely revelatory, entirely intuitive; its speech altogether a living breath of inspiration; its art sovereignly a spontaneous and unwilled discerning of perfection.

The plan and structure of their thought corresponds; it has a perfection of supra-intellectual cohesion in its effortless welling of sound and thought, a system of natural and unsystematic correspondences. There is no such logical development, explicitly or implicitly satisfying the demands of the intellect, such as we find in other philosophical thought or the best architectonic poetry; but there is at the same time a supreme logic, only it is the logic of existence expressing itself self-luminously rather than of thought carefully finding out its own truth. It is the logic of the Himalayas or of a causeway of giants, not the painful and meticulous construction effected with labour by our later intellectual humanity. There is in the whole a unity of vision; the Upanishad itself rather than a human mind sees with a single glance, hears the word that is the natural body of the truth it has seen, perceives and listens again, and still again, till all has been seen and heard: this is not the unity of the intellect carefully weaving together its connections of thought, choosing, rejecting, pruning to get terseness, developing to get fullness. And yet there is a perfect coherence; for every successive movement takes up the echoes of the old and throws out new echoes which are taken up in their turn. A wave of seeing rises and ends to rise into another wave and so on till the final fall and natural ceasing of the whole sea of thought on its shore. Perhaps the development of a great and profound strain of music is the nearest thing we have to this ancient poetry of pure intuitive thought. This at least is the method of the metrical Upanishads; and even the others approximate to it, though more pliant in their make.

Note on the Texts

Note on the Texts

KENA AND OTHER UPANISHADS comprises Sri Aurobindo's translations of and commentaries on Upanishads other than the Isha Upanishad, as well as translations of later Vedantic texts, and writings on the
Upanishads and Vedanta philosophy in general. Translations of and
commentaries on the Isha Upanishad are published in *Isha Upanishad*,
volume 17 of THE COMPLETE WORKS OF SRI AUROBINDO.

Sri Aurobindo's work on the Upanishads occupied more than
twenty years, from around 1900 until the early 1920s. (One translation was revised some twenty-five years after that.) Between 1914
and 1920, he published translations of the Isha, the Kena and the
Mundaka Upanishads, along with commentaries on the Isha and the
Kena, in the monthly review *Arya*. These, along with the translation of
the Katha Upanishad, which was published in 1909 and subsequently
revised, may be said to represent his Upanishadic interpretation in its
most definitive form. His other translations and commentaries were
not published during his lifetime. Most of them belong to an earlier
period and only a few are complete. Some were used in producing the
final translations and commentaries published in Part One. They are
of interest as steps in the development of his thought, as well as for
their own inherent value.

In the present volume, the editors have placed material published
during Sri Aurobindo's lifetime in Part One, and material found among
his manuscripts in Parts Two and Three. The Sanskrit texts have been
included for the convenience of Sanskrit-knowing readers.

PART ONE: TRANSLATIONS AND COMMENTARIES
PUBLISHED BY SRI AUROBINDO

This part contains the final versions of Sri Aurobindo's translations of
three Upanishads, the Kena, Katha and Mundaka, and commentaries
on the Kena and parts of the Taittiriya.

The Kena Upanishad. Sri Aurobindo first translated the Kena Upanishad in Baroda around 1900. (This translation forms part of a typewritten manuscript, hereafter referred to as TMS, which Sri Aurobindo entitled "The Upanishads rendered into simple and rhythmic English".) The TMS translation of the Kena was lightly revised and published in the weekly review *Karmayogin* in June 1909. In 1920 the *Karmayogin* translation was reproduced in *The Seven Upanishads*, published by Ashtekar & Co., Poona. (Only three of the seven translations in this book were by Sri Aurobindo: Isha, Kena and Mundaka.)

Between 1912 and 1914, Sri Aurobindo began three commentaries on and one annotated translation of the Kena. All of these pieces were left incomplete. They are published in Part Two, Section Four.

Between June 1915 and July 1916, Sri Aurobindo published a new translation of the Kena Upanishad and a fifteen-chapter commentary on it in the *Arya*. He wrote each of the instalments immediately before its publication. Sometime between 1916 and 1920, he lightly revised the *Arya* translation and commentary. Their publication in book-form was planned, and production was actually begun in the summer of 1920; but the proposed book was never issued. Questioned about the possibility of publishing *Kena Upanishad* in December 1927, Sri Aurobindo wrote: "My present intention is not to publish it as it stands. This must be postponed for the present." He never found time to return to this work.

When the publication of Sri Aurobindo's Upanishadic translations and commentaries was undertaken after his passing, the existence of the revised versions of his translation of and commentary on the Kena Upanishad was not known. The unrevised *Arya* versions were published by the Sri Aurobindo Ashram as *Kena Upanishad* in 1952, and included in the same publisher's *Eight Upanishads* in 1953. The revised translation (but unrevised commentary) first appeared in the second edition of *Kena Upanishad* in 1970. The same texts were reproduced in *The Upanishads: Texts, Translations and Commentaries*, volume 12 of the Sri Aurobindo Birth Centenary Library, in 1971. The revised commentary first appeared in *The Upanishads: Part One*, published by the Sri Aurobindo Ashram in 1981.

The *Arya* text of the commentary had no chapter-titles. While revising the work, Sri Aurobindo gave titles to all the chapters except

8, 9 and 12. In the present edition, the editors have provided titles for these three chapters.

The Katha Upanishad of the Black Yajurveda. Sri Aurobindo first translated this Upanishad in Baroda around 1900; it forms part of TMS. He later said that he had tried "to convey the literary merit of the original". The translation, slightly revised, was published in the *Karmayogin* in July and August 1909. The *Karmayogin* translation was published as *The Katha Upanishad* by Ashtekar & Co., Poona, in 1919. Sometime during the early part of his stay in Pondicherry (1910–20), Sri Aurobindo began a more extensive revision of TMS, but reached only the end of the First Cycle. When it was proposed to bring out the translation in a book during the late 1920s, he replied that he did not have the time to make the necessary revisions. A new edition of *Katha Upanishad* was published by the Sri Aurobindo Ashram in 1952. In that edition, in *Eight Upanishads* (1953), and in *The Upanishads* (1971), the partially revised TMS version was used as text, with some editorial modernisation of the language. The *Karmayogin* version, containing the last revision of the Second Cycle, was disregarded. In the present volume, the revised TMS is followed for the First Cycle, and the *Karmayogin* text for the Second.

Mundaka Upanishad. Sri Aurobindo first translated this Upanishad in Baroda around 1900; it forms part of TMS. A revised version of the translation was published in the *Karmayogin* in February 1910. (This revised translation was included in *The Seven Upanishads*.) A further revised translation was published in the *Arya* in the issue of November/December 1920. Sri Aurobindo thoroughly revised the *Arya* translation during the late 1940s. This version was used when the translation was published in *Eight Upanishads* in 1953 and in *The Upanishads* in 1971.

Readings in the Taittiriya Upanishad. Sri Aurobindo translated the Taittiriya Upanishad in Baroda around 1902 (see below), but never revised it for publication. He wrote "The Knowledge of Brahman: Readings in the Taittiriya Upanishad" in 1918 for publication in the *Arya*. It appeared in the November 1918 issue of the review. "Truth, Knowledge, Infinity" was apparently intended for a later issue, but it was never completed and not published during Sri Aurobindo's lifetime. Its first appearance in a book was in the 1981 edition of *The Upanishads*.

PART TWO: TRANSLATIONS AND COMMENTARIES
FROM MANUSCRIPTS

The texts in this part were not published during Sri Aurobindo's lifetime. Several of the translations and all the commentaries are incomplete. They have been arranged in five sections, the first comprising an introductory essay.

Section One. Introduction

On Translating the Upanishads. Editorial title. Sri Aurobindo wrote this text in Baroda around 1900–1902 under the heading "OM TAT SAT". He evidently intended it to be the introduction to a collection of his translations, probably "The Upanishads rendered into simple and rhythmic English". It was first published in a book as the introduction to *Eight Upanishads* in 1953, and was included in *The Upanishads* in 1971 and subsequently.

Section Two. Complete Translations (circa 1900–1902)

"The Upanishads rendered into simple and rhythmic English". This is the title page of the typewritten manuscript (TMS), which dates from around the turn of the century. Two of the six translations in the manuscript—those of the Prashna ("Prusna") and Mandukya ("Mandoukya") Upanishads—were never revised or published by Sri Aurobindo. These two are published here in their original form.

The Prusna Upanishad of the Athurvaveda. Circa 1900. From TMS. The translation was published in *Eight Upanishads* in 1953 and was included in *The Upanishads* in 1971.

The Mandoukya Upanishad. Circa 1900. From TMS. The translation was first published in *Eight Upanishads* in 1953 and was included in *The Upanishads* in 1971.

The Aitereya Upanishad. Sri Aurobindo translated this Upanishad in Baroda around 1902. (It does not form part of TMS.) The translation was never revised and is published here in its original form. It was first published in *Eight Upanishads* in 1953 and was included in *The Upanishads* in 1971.

Taittiriya Upanishad. Sri Aurobindo translated this Upanishad in Baroda around 1902. (It does not form part of TMS.) It was never revised and is published here in its original form. It was first published in *Eight Upanishads* in 1953 and was included in *The Upanishads* in 1971.

Section Three. Incomplete Translations and Commentaries
(circa 1902–1912)

Svetasvatara Upanishad. Sri Aurobindo translated the fourth to sixth chapters of this Upanishad sometime during the first decade of the century. (It is not known whether he ever translated the first three chapters.) Judging by the notebook and handwriting, it would appear that he did the translation during the period of his stay in Baroda; yet he is recorded as saying, "I translated the Shwetashwatara Upanishad while I was in Bengal." It is possible that he did the translation in Bengal during one of his vacations from Baroda College between 1902 and 1906. He retranslated the fourth chapter in Pondicherry several years later. The early translation of chapters 4 to 6 was first published in the 1971 edition of *The Upanishads*. The revised version of the fourth chapter first appeared in the 1981 edition.

Chhandogya Upanishad. Around 1902 Sri Aurobindo translated the first two sections and part of the third section of the first chapter of this Upanishad in the margins of his copy of *The Chhándogya Upanishad* (Madras, 1899). He later recopied and revised the first two sections in the notebook he used for his translations of the Aitareya and Taittiriya. The editors have reproduced the recopied translation for sections 1–2, and fallen back on the marginal translation for section 3, verses 1–7. The translation of the first two sections was first published in *The Upanishads* in 1971; the translation of the opening of section 3 first appeared in 1986 in the second impression of the second edition of that book.

Notes on the Chhandogya Upanishad. Circa 1912. Sri Aurobindo wrote these two passages of commentary separately in Pondicherry. The first is entitled in the manuscript "Notes on the Chhandogya Upanishad/ First Adhyaya" (but only the first sentence is treated). Part of the first page was included in *The Upanishads* in 1971; the full text was published in the 1981 edition. The second commentary, also incomplete, is entitled in the manuscript "Vedic Interpretations/Satyakama Jabala". In most editions of the Chhandogya Upanishad, the story of Satyakama Jabala occupies sections 4–9 of the fourth chapter, not sections 3–8 as in the edition Sri Aurobindo used. The commentary was first published in the 1981 edition of *The Upanishads.*

The Brihad Aranyak Upanishad. Around 1912 Sri Aurobindo translated the first two sections and part of the third section of the first chapter of this Upanishad in the margins of his copy of the text (Poona: Ananda Ashram, 1902). This marginal translation was first reproduced in the 1981 edition of *The Upanishads.*

The Great Aranyaka. Circa 1912. Shortly after writing the above translation, Sri Aurobindo began a commentary on the Brihadaranyaka Upanishad that he entitled "The Great Aranyaka/A Commentary on the Brihad Aranyak Upanishad". This was not completed even to the extent of what had been translated. The commentary was included in *The Upanishads* in 1971.

The Kaivalya Upanishad. Sri Aurobindo wrote this translation and commentary, which cover only the first verse of the Upanishad, in Pondicherry around 1912. It was first published in *The Upanishads* in 1971. The commentary in English is followed by a commentary in Sanskrit, which is published in *Writings in Bengali and Sanskrit*, volume 9 of THE COMPLETE WORKS OF SRI AUROBINDO.

Nila Rudra Upanishad. Sri Aurobindo translated the first of the three parts of this Upanishad, with a commentary on the first five verses, in Pondicherry around 1912. It was first published in *The Upanishads* in 1971.

Section Four. Incomplete Commentaries on the Kena Upanishad
(circa 1912–1914)

Kena Upanishad: An Incomplete Commentary. Circa 1912. Editorial subtitle. Sri Aurobindo wrote only the "foreword" and portions of one "part" of this planned commentary before abandoning it. It was first published in *The Upanishads* in 1971.

A Commentary on the Kena Upanishad: Foreword. Circa 1912. This fragmentary work appears to be a rewriting of the foreword of the preceding incomplete commentary. The manuscript has been damaged and one entire line is missing. This piece is being published here for the first time in a book.

Three Fragments of Commentary. Circa 1912–13. Sri Aurobindo wrote these three untitled fragments on sheets used otherwise for linguistic notes, undated entries for the *Record of Yoga* and the essay "The Origin of Genius". They are being published here for the first time in a book.

Kena Upanishad: A Partial Translation with Notes. Editorial subtitle. Sri Aurobindo wrote this on 23 May 1914. The *Record of Yoga* for that day states: "Kena Upanishad I Kh [Khanda] translated with notes". It is being published here for the first time.

Section Five. Incomplete Translations of Two Vedantic Texts (circa 1900–1902)

The Karikas of Gaudapada. Editorial title. Circa 1900. This classic Vedantic text was written by Gaudapada in or around the eighth century. Sri Aurobindo translated only the first twelve verses, along with Shankaracharya's commentary on them. The words italicised in his translation were supplied by him to make the meaning of the Sanskrit more clear. It was first published in *The Upanishads* in 1971.

Sadananda's Essence of Vedanta. Circa 1902. The *Vedāntasāra* or "Essence of Vedanta" was written by Sadananda in the fifteenth century. Sri Aurobindo translated only the first sixteen of the work's 227 aphorisms. The incomplete translation was first published in *The Upanishads* in 1971.

PART THREE: WRITINGS ON VEDANTA

These pieces found among Sri Aurobindo's manuscripts were not completed or published by him. Written at various times from around 1902 to 1916, they have been arranged chronologically from earlier to later.

With the exception of *The Philosophy of the Upanishads*, the writings in this part are being published here for the first time in a book. Most of them previously appeared in the journal *Sri Aurobindo: Archives and Research* between 1978 and 1984.

Four Fragments. Circa 1902–4. These jottings are among Sri Auro-bindo's earliest independent philosophical writings. Before revision, the last sentence of the final fragment ended: ". . . the purer form in which Vedanta, Sankhya & Yoga are harmonised". This final fragment is being published here for the first time, the other three for the first time in a book.

The Spirit of Hinduism: God. Circa 1903–4. This piece opens with the first words of the Mandukya Upanishad.

The Philosophy of the Upanishads. Circa 1904–6. Sri Aurobindo wrote this piece during the latter part of his stay in Baroda. (He seems to have left the manuscript in western India when he came to Bengal in February 1906.) After completing six chapters and part of a seventh, he broke off work and never took it up again. The second to the seventh chapters of this work were included in *The Upanishads* in 1971, where they were numbered from one to six. The full text was published as a book in 1994.

The present text has been checked carefully against the manu-script, which unfortunately lacks its first two pages. For those pages the editors have relied on a typewritten transcript that was made before the pages were lost. The transcript contains several blanks, which occur in such a way as to suggest that the outer edge of the missing leaf of the manuscript was broken off. Making use of the indications found in the transcript, the editors have filled in the blanks with conjectural reconstructions; these have been printed within square brackets if they admitted of any doubt.

An Incomplete Work of Vedantic Exegesis. Circa 1906–8. Editorial title. This piece seems to have been written during the same period as "The Karmayogin: A Commentary on the Isha Upanishad", an extensive work published in *Isha Upanishad*, volume 17 of THE COM-PLETE WORKS. It is quite incomplete. Not all the projected chapters were finished, and some of the completed chapters contain unfinished passages. Sri Aurobindo wrote the following outline at the end of the notebook:

II. God
    Turiya Brahman. Swayambhu.
    Prajna. Kavih.

Sacchidananda.

The Sakshi.

Isha in contemplation. Maheshwara.

Ananda. The Seed State. Sleep.

Hiranyagarbha. Manishi

The Will in Buddhi

God Manifold. The Saguna Brahman.

The Qualities of God. The Dream State.

Virat. Paribhu

The Almighty. Mahat.

The Self in creatures. God in Man (Avatars.)

The Self in Nature.

Images

God as Fate

God as Providence

Worship (Prayer & Praise)

Purusha & Prakritih.

III. Vidya & Avidya

Salvation. Escape from Avidya.

Knowledge, Love & Works. Nirguna & Saguna
Brahman.

Self-realisation in Virat.

States of moksha (Hir[anyagarbha]). Laya (Prajna).

Yoga.

IV. I The Law of Karma. Sin & Virtue. Heaven & Hell.

Salvation by Works

V. Ethics of Vedanta.

The Religion of Vedanta. 1906–8. An earlier draft of this fragment is published in the Reference Volume, volume 35 of THE COMPLETE WORKS. That draft continues slightly beyond the point where this version stops. After work on the present draft was broken off, Sri Aurobindo wrote the following, apparently a chapter-outline for a planned work:

1. Vedantic Cosmos   4.5
2. God in the Vedanta   1.8
3. Salvation by Works   1.2.3

4. The Ethics of Vedanta   6.7
5. The Twofold Will   9.10.11.12.13.14.15.16
6. Works and Immortality   17.18
7. The Great Release.

It would appear that the proposed work was to be based on the Isha Upanishad, which has eighteen verses.

Evolution in the Vedantic View. Circa 1912. Editorial title. It is evident from the first sentence that the piece was written as part of a larger work, which either was not completed or has not survived.

The Means of Realisation. Circa 1912. The actual heading in the manuscript is "Chapter XI/ The Means of Realisation". The ten chapters that presumably preceded this one have not been found or identified.

A Fragmentary Chapter for a Work on Vedanta. Circa 1912–13. Editorial title. The manuscript of this piece is badly damaged in places. The opening lines are lost, as are a number of words and parts of sentences written near the edges and especially at the tops and bottoms of the pages.

God and Immortality. Circa 1916. This incomplete chapter is all that was written of a proposed book.

PUBLISHING HISTORY

Sri Aurobindo published translations of the Kena, Katha and Mundaka Upanishads in the *Karmayogin*, a weekly journal of political opinion, during the years 1909 and 1910. Between 1914 and 1920 he published revised or new translations of the Kena and Mundaka, and commentaries on all of the Kena and parts of the Taittiriya in the *Arya*, a monthly review of philosophy. He revised most of these works with a view to publishing them in books, but never did so. The unrevised *Karmayogin* translation of the Katha Upanishad was reprinted by Ashtekar & Co., Poona, in 1919; the unrevised *Karmayogin* translations of the Isha, Kena and Mundaka were included in the same publisher's *Seven Upanishads* in 1920. It is uncertain whether or not Sri Aurobindo authorised these publications.

The pieces published in Parts Two and Three of the present volume were found among Sri Aurobindo's manuscripts after his passing in 1950. Many of them were first published in journals connected with the Sri Aurobindo Ashram. In 1953 Sri Aurobindo's published translations of the Isha, Kena, Katha and Mundaka Upanishads and his unpublished translations of the Prashna, Mandukya, Aitareya and Taittiriya were brought out by the Sri Aurobindo Ashram as *Eight Upanishads*. In 1971 all these translations, the *Arya* commentaries on the Isha and Kena, the first of the "Readings in the Taittiriya Upanishad", and a number of pieces from the author's notebooks, were published in *The Upanishads*, volume 12 of the Sri Aurobindo Birth Centenary Library. This book was reprinted several times. In 1981 most of the contents of the volume were rearranged and republished under the title *The Upanishads: Part One*. Several pieces that had appeared in the 1971 edition were removed from the 1981 edition with the intention of including them, along with other, recently discovered pieces, in a proposed second volume; but this was never brought out. The 1981 edition was reprinted in 1986 (when the translation of Chapter One, Section 3 of the Chhandogya Upanishad was included) and subsequently.

The present edition is the first to appear under the title *Kena and Other Upanishads*. In it, two pieces are published for the first time: "Kena Upanishad: A Partial Translation with Notes" and the last of the "Four Fragments" in Part Three. Several other pieces in Parts Two and Three have previously appeared only in the journal *Sri Aurobindo: Archives and Research* and are included here for the first time in a book.